NUMBER 4
BOBBY ORR!

A Chronicle of the Boston Bruins' Greatest Decade
Led by Their Legendary Superstar
1966–1976

KEVIN VAUTOUR AND KERRY KEENE

PAGE PUBLISHING, INC.
New York, NY

First originally published by Page Publishing, Inc. 2019

Cover image credit: Jerry Buckley from S&B archives

ISBN 978-1-64424-597-2 (Paperback)
ISBN 978-1-64424-598-9 (Digital)

Printed in the United States of America

THIS BOOK IS DEDICATED TO Zachary Keene and Ron Vautour Jr., who both passed away unexpectedly, and to New York City firefighter Gerry Dewan, who died at the World Trade Center on September 11, 2001.

This effort also honors the fans of Bobby Orr of which there are legions and the happy memories that he provided to so many over his outstanding career. We may never see another like him again.

Contents

Introduction...7

Chapter 1:   1966–1967: The Rookie Season 15
Chapter 2:   1967–1968: A New Beginning...55
Chapter 3:   1968–1969: The Final Stumbling Block............................85
Chapter 4:   1969–1970: Mission Accomplished 111
Chapter 5:   1970–1971: The Dynasty Ends.......................................143
Chapter 6:   1971–1972: Redemption 171
Chapter 7:   1972–1973: The Long Drought Commences...................199
Chapter 8:   1973–1974: One Last Crack at the Cup...........................225
Chapter 9:   1974–1975: The Bleeding Accelerates 247
Chapter 10: 1975–1976: Over So Fast..267

Epilogue: The Aftermath 281
Appendices: A Season-by-Season Review 291
Bibliography...387

Introduction

IN THE ANNALS OF PROFESSIONAL sports, it is a time-honored tradition to analyze the skills, abilities, and achievements of athletes in order to identify those who qualify as among the greatest. Seemingly once in a lifetime, a player comes along who rises head and shoulders above an accepted standard of greatness. In these isolated cases, the player performs in such a manner that they change, perhaps even revolutionize their sport.

Baseball's Babe Ruth, as iconic an athlete as there has been, exemplified the concept. He excelled in two diverse aspects of his sport, establishing himself as an outstanding pitcher in his first few seasons, then transitioned into a home run–hitting slugger the likes of which the game had not seen. His slugging prowess spawned an army of hitters swinging for the fences, and a new era was born.

By the mid-1960s, the sport of hockey was witnessing the development of a prodigy in the Canadian junior hockey circuit that was prompting longtime observers of the sport to take notice. Veteran coaches and hockey pundits throughout Ontario were bestowing superlatives on young Bobby Orr's ability and potential as a professional that had scarcely been heard or seen before in nearly a half century of NHL play. By his midteens, Orr was being hailed as the coming savior of a Boston Bruins team that had been mired at the bottom of the league for several seasons. By the opening of his first training camp in September of 1966, Boston fans were hopeful and anxious to see if he could live up to the hype.

While he didn't alter the team's place in the standings that first season, his remarkable natural skill was obvious to all. As Orr made his first appearances in each city throughout the league, opposing players, coaches, and hockey writers gave high praise, citing his ability to control the puck and the pace of the game, his anticipatory skills, and ability to see the whole ice as if he had eyes in the back of his head. Like baseball's Ruth, he was recognized early on as an extremely rare type of player who could excel at the highest level in two completely different aspects of their game. It was clear from Orr's first season of his NHL career that he would likely monopolize the Norris Trophy for best defenseman for the foreseeable future. At the same time, he was displaying skills in the offensive zone—scoring, passing, and setting up plays that would have authored a Hall of Fame type of career had he spent his entire time as a forward.

Beginning young Orr's second season, team management began to surround him with better players, including future superstar Phil Esposito, and they finally made their return to Stanley Cup Playoff action after a eight-year absence. Led by Orr, the team steadily improved and ultimately reached the top of the mountain for the first time in twenty-nine years in the spring of 1970, his fourth season. Orr's Stanley Cup–clinching goal has provided the hockey world with its most famous photograph.

On the strength of that championship victory and the popularity they had been building over the previous few years, Bobby Orr and the Bruins virtually owned the hearts and minds of countless sports fans in the greater Boston area. Once merely a loyal hockey town, Boston was now positively hockey mad. Dozens and dozens of ice hockey rinks began popping up in the region, and youth hockey programs flourished. For those who didn't skate, street hockey also became popular to the point where iceless rinks designed to accommodate the sneaker-clad player began appearing in many Boston-area neighborhoods. Thousands of young players were skating or running around pretending to be Bobby Orr.

As outstanding as Orr's 1969–70 season was, the twenty-two-year-old had yet to reach his greatest heights as an offensive force. Three more times in his early-to-mid twenties, he eclipsed that season's point total (120), coming just three points shy a fourth year. He was amassing goals and assists in many of his seasons that would have surpassed the totals of many of the most productive forwards in any number of seasons previously. Directly due to Orr's influence, defensemen becoming offensive threats was now commonplace. As the decade of the 1970s progressed, Orr was cementing his standing as one of the very greatest to have ever laced up a pair of hockey skates.

But all the greatness he possessed could not overcome that Achilles' heel—in this case, Orr's left knee. A series of injuries and subsequent surgical procedures had taken their toll, and by the end of 1975, he was unable to be the force he had always been on any consistent basis. Orr gamely wanted to bounce back, but when it came time to negotiate a new contract with the Bruins in the summer of 1976, his relationship with the team took an unexpected turn. Though it would not be revealed for many years, bad advice from an unscrupulous agent prompted Orr to leave Boston for an ill-fated stint with the Chicago Blackhawks. Strictly in hockey terms, it is a near tragedy that Bobby Orr played his final game in the NHL at the age of thirty.

It took little time for career achievement accolades to come his way. His trademark number 4 was hoisted to the Boston Garden rafters, and he took his rightful place in the Hockey Hall of Fame along with the game's greatest. At least two impressive statues of his likeness would be chiseled in his honor.

Within the realm of the hockey world, the only thing Orr did not achieve was the type of longevity that would have put his career statistics far out of reach for any other defenseman. But while some have and may continue to eclipse his numbers, it may well be a very long time before anyone approaches the sheer greatness he displayed at his very best.

Left to right: Tim Horton, Dave Keon, Jim Dorey, and Norm Ullman of Toronto surround Orr in this 1968 photo.

Chasing redux 1971, *left to right*: Terry Harper, J. C. Tremblay, Peter Mahovlich, and Rejean Houle of Montreal are seen all chasing Orr.

Oshawa Tops Flyers at Garden

Future Bruin Star Orr Excels in Rough Clash

December 27, 1965, at Boston Garden
Attendance: 5,773
Oshawa (6), Niagara Falls (3)
Referee: Hugh McLean
Linesmen: Bill Cleary, Bob Cleary

Niagara Falls Flyers	Oshawa Generals
Ring	Young
Ley	Orr
Arbour	Cadieux
Paiment	Babcock
Pronovost	Heindl
Marcotte	Dussiamme
Allen	Beverly
Woodley	Wilkins
Gray	Roberts
Snell	O'Shea

Debrody	Morenz
Haggerty	Hayes
Sanderson	Nevin
Webster	Black
Lajeunnese	Cashman
Lorentz	Dionne
Webley	White
Wilson	

First Period

Penalty	(NF)	Arbour (hooking) 0:20
Penalty	(NF)	Snell (holding) 1:53
Penalty	(OSH)	Roberts (slashing) 5:40
Goal	(OSH)	Babcock (Orr, Heindl) 8:01
Penalty	(OSH)	Nevin (hooking) 8:33
Penalty	(OSH)	Orr (elbowing and fighting) 9:38
Penalty	(NF)	Sanderson (high sticking and fighting) 9:38
Penalty	(NF)	Arbour (charging) 9:38
Penalty	(OSH)	Beverly (charging) 9:50
Goal	(NF)	Snell (Ley) 10:35
Penalty	(OSH)	Gladieux (slashing) 11:31
Penalty	(NF)	Allen (butt ending) 11:31
Goal	(OSH)	O'Shea (Orr, Beverly) 13:48
Goal	(NF)	Paiment (Ley, Sanderson) 15:13
Goal	(OSH)	Orr (Cadieux, Nevin) 16:49
Penalty	(OSH)	Cashman, Cadieux, (fighting) 20:00
Penalty	(NF)	Arbour, Pronovost (fighting) 20:00

Second Period

Penalty	(OSH)	O'Shea (tripping) 1:00
Penalty	(OSH)	Nevin (tripping) 18:53

Third Period

Goal	(OSH)	Heindl (Wilkins) 2:37

Penalty	(OSH)	Roberts (holding) 6:50
Penalty	(OSH)	Wilkins (holding) 13:57
Goal	(NF)	Arbour (Sanderson, Pronovost) 14:38
Goal	(OSH)	O'Shea (Hayes, Cadieux) 18:00
Penalty	(OSH)	White (tripping) 18:57
Penalty	(NF)	Sanderson (slashing) 18:57

Saves by period		1	3	**Total**
Young	(OSH)	11	13	38
Ring	(NF)	15		23
Wilson	(NF)		4	

The above game summary does not record the sixth Oshawa goal.

Flyers Triumph; Orr Scores One

The Niagara Falls Flyers are the defending Memorial Cup Champions, symbolic of the Junior Amateur titlists in Canada, but it wasn't until Sunday night at the Garden that they were able to prove it to local hockey fans.

A crowd of 6644 fans saw the Flyers score four third period goals for a 5-2 victory over the other Bruins' junior affiliate, the Oshwa Generals. It was the first triumph for the Flyers in three games here against the Generals and one a year ago against the Montreal junior Canadiens.

The Flyers, who stand second in the junior OHA, a point behind the leading Peterborough Petes and two ahead of Oshwa, trailed 2-to-1 going into the final period, mainly due to the goal tending of Scottish born Ian Young, the latter living up to his Scottish heritage was very stingy in allowing but one goal.

But in the final frame the Flyers came on strong pouring 25 shots at Young and young Kelly Orr, his replacement late in the period.

Oshwa which played at home Saturday night, faded under the pressure.

Left winger Don Marcotte rapped in Jean Pronovost's pass out from the back boards to tie it up 20 seconds after the period began. Captain Dave Woodly knocked in his own rebound to break the tie at 9:16. Young made the stop on the blistering shot, but didn't know where the puck dropped and Woodly swooped in to hit it into the open corner.

Against Orr, a cousin of the Generals star Bobby, Derek Sanderson and Guy Allen iced the verdict in the final minutes.

The Flyers scored first on a power play at 16:33 of the opening period. Bud DeBrody tipped in Pronovost's shot from the point, but 55 seconds later Pete Nevin tied it up, converting Bill Little's pass in front of the net against Wakefield's Bobby Ring.

Bobby Orr, the 17-year-old junior star and top Bruins prospect gave the Generals a 2-1 advantage in the second period. He snapped a 30-foot shot to the far corner.

Ring, former Wakefield high All-Scholastic goalie, played the first half of the game. Then Dunk Wilson, who started the season with Oshwa, blanked his former mates the rest of the way.

In the preliminary game, Waterville scored three times in the second period and once in the third period to top the Greater Boston Peewees, 4-1. Jim McKeon scored the lone Boston tally in the final period.

NIAGARA FALLS — Goal, Ring; Defense, Ley, Woodley; Center, Sanderson; Right Wing, Webster; Left Wing, Palement.
OSHAWA — Goal, Young; Defense, Orr, Beverly; Center, Morenz; Right Wing, Black; Left Wing, Sandford.
NIAGARA FALLS SPARES —Arbour, Atkinson, Snell, Marcotte, Pronovost, Debrody, LaJeunesse, Weberly, Wilson.
OSHAWA SPARES — Roberts, Wilkins, O'Shea, Heindl, Hayes, Little, White, Dussiaume, Nevin, Dickson.

FIRST PERIOD
Scoring — Debrody (Pronovost, Sanderson) 16:33; Nevin (Little) 17:18; Penalties — Sanderson (Hooking) 6:45; Nevin (Holding) 2:15; Roberts (Interference) 7:10; Ley (Charging) 11:31; Hayes (Board Check) 18:16.

SECOND PERIOD
Scoring—Orr (Heindl, Dussiaume) 3:42. Penalties—Atkinson (elbow check) 2:05; White (tripping) 2:32; Atkinson (tripping) 7:03, White (forecheck) 8:39; Allen (slashing) 12:18. Shots—Oshawa 10, Niagara 14, 10.

THIRD PERIOD
Scoring—Marcotte (Provono. Sanderson) 0:20; Woodly (Atkinson) 9:16; Sanderson (Pronovo) 17:07; Allen (unassisted) 10:23, Penalties—Atkinson (elbow check) 11:20. Shots—Oshawa 9, Niagara 21, total Oshawa 24, Niagara 45.

CHAPTER 1

1966–1967: The Rookie Season

We have too many high-sounding words, and too
few actions that correspond with them.
—Abigail Adams, letter to future American
president John Adams, 1774

I don't think this applies to Bobby Orr.

—Anonymous

THE PICTURE HISTORY OF THE *Boston Bruins* by Harry Sinden and Dick Grace was published in 1976 and featured a chapter titled "The Quiet Fifties." The Bruins had advanced to the Finals in 1953, 1957, and 1958. Three Stanley Cup final appearances in a six-season span would seem to contradict Sinden's assessment of the decade. All the series were lost to the mighty Montreal Canadiens. In 1959, the B's came within one win of a third consecutive trip to the finals only to lose *game 7* 3–2 in the semifinal round to the Toronto Maple Leafs. Boston had been rightfully regarded as one of the league's elite teams, but that would change dramatically with the onset of the 1959–1960 season. Finishing in fifth place, the Bruins missed the playoffs for only the third time in the previous quarter century.

Beginning in October of 1959, Boston was embarking on an eight-season span in which they would fail to qualify for the playoffs. Of the 560 regular season they would play in that period (this was the seventy-game schedule era), the Bruins would win only 149 games. Their ineptness earned them seven last place, and one fifth-place finish.

As the decade of the 1960s was dawning, the Boston Bruins franchise was entering what remains its darkest, least-productive extended period. However, the discovery of a twelve-year-old phenom in a small Ontario town would provide a light at the end of a long dreary tunnel.

As the league gathered in Montreal for the NHL's June 1966 meetings, former Bruins' general manager Lynn Patrick, who helped discover Orr, had this to say about him: "This is a dedicated player. Defensively, he can be great if the Bruins tell him to concentrate on defense. To me, he is in the same class as Gordie Howe as a player and as a fellow, and that's the highest tribute you can pay any hockey player. Twenty years from now, you will rate Orr in Howe's class, not as scorer, but as an all-around player."

Jim Cherry, coach of the 1963–64 Oshawa Generals, observed this: "Orr reminds me of Red Kelly when Red was in his last year at St. Mike's. He plays thirty-five to forty minutes a game and he's the team leader. He can't miss. He'd make the NHL at any position." Oshawa's General Manager Wren Blair commented that "he's a combination of Doug Harvey and Eddie Shore."

September 1966

The Bruins and Orr came to a contract agreement on board Bruins' General Manager Hap Emms's boat, the *Barbara Lynch*, on September 2, 1966. Terms of the agreement were not disclosed although rumors had it that Orr, having never played a single NHL game, was the highest-paid player in the league.

With the September 2 signing now in the rearview mirror, Bobby Orr would finish preparations for his first NHL season. Prognosticators around the circuit saw the Bruins inching closer to a playoff spot, a position that they had not been in for seven consecutive seasons.

Training camp opened on Saturday, September 10, at the Treasure Island Gardens in London, Ontario. Thirty-eight players were invited to training camp as part of the process of winnowing out the squad that would open the season on October 19 in Boston.

During the early days of training camp, Orr was quoted as saying, "I spent the summer wondering where I'd report, here in London or in St. Thomas." St. Thomas was the training site of the Bruins' minor league team, the Oklahoma City Blazers. Orr, noticeably shy and humble, seemed to have doubts about his ability to make the Bruins. A touch of homesickness was also present as he explained that mother Arva cried a lot about him leaving the nest in Parry Sound. "I've been away before playing junior hockey, but I guess this was different, like going away to college or something."

At training camp, Orr would be greeted by new Bruins' coach, Harry Sinden. He had replaced Milt Schmidt, who moved up to the Assistant General Manager's position with the B's. Orr was assigned uniform number 27. In the era before expansion, numbers above 25 were not seen often on Boston players. In the year prior to

Orr's arrival, 1965–66, the number 27 had been passed around on a limited basis and had been worn by John Arbour, Wayne Maxner, Jean Paul Parise, and Derek Sanderson. During the Canadian portion of the exhibition season, the number 27 would grace the back of Orr's jersey.

1966–67 Exhibition Games

Friday	September 23	vs. Toronto at London (tie, 1–1)
Saturday	September 24	vs. Oklahoma City (CPHL) at Oshawa (win, 6–4)
Thursday	September 29	vs. Detroit at Hamilton (win, 4–2)
Friday	September 30	vs. New York at London (lose, 3–0)
Saturday	October 1	vs. New York at Kingston (lose, 3–0)
Sunday	October 2	vs. Toronto at Peterborough (win, 3–1)
Friday	October 7	vs. Detroit at London (lose, 3–1)
Saturday	October 8	vs. Rochester (AHL) at Rochester (win, 5–2)
Tuesday	October 11	vs. New York at Boston (lose, 3–1)
Sunday	October 16	vs. Montreal at Boston (win, 3–0)

Left to right: Dick Cherry, Ross Lonsberry, and Orr at 1966 training camp in Boston Garden.

Bobby Orr, number 27, begins a rush up ice against the New York Rangers.
Defense partner Gilles Marotte looms in the background while New
York's Reg Fleming, number 9, and Red Berenson (white helmet) pursue.
Action took place in September during the 1966 exhibition season.

The exhibition season finally arrived on Friday night, September 23. The Bruins hosted the Toronto Maple Leafs in London, Ontario. The game ended in a 1–1 draw. Pit Martin scored the goal for Boston with Orr getting the assist. Gerry Cheevers started in goal for the Bruins but had to be replaced by Bernie Parent after being struck in the head by a puck in the first period.

As the exhibition season wore on, Orr found himself paired regularly with second-year pro and General Manager Hap Emms's favorite Gilles Marotte. Marotte was a graduate of Emms's Niagara Falls Flyers. Both Bobby and Gilles were left-handed shots, but Orr manned the right defense position. Emms thought that having two left shots on the points was fine since both players usually had their sticks out in front of them. Emms also was excited about Orr's skating and his ability to get back on defense after an offensive thrust. "Marotte's all fired up to stop them, and Orr is all geared up to bring it back out," enthused Emms.

October 1966

The exhibition games became more intense in early October as the Bruins were scheduled to play four games in four nights. The Bruins took on the Toronto Maple Leafs at their Peterborough, Ontario, camp on October 2. While the Bruins defeated the Leafs 3–1, it was also learned that Orr had suffered a shoulder injury in a game played the previous evening in Kingston against the New York Rangers. X-rays of Orr's shoulder indicated a slight muscle tear.

The Bruins wrapped up four weeks of training camp in London, Ontario, on October 7. After a stop-off in Rochester, the next evening to play the American Hockey League's Rochester Americans in an exhibition game, the team headed to Boston to play the final two preseason games before the start of the regular season. The B's hosted the Rangers on October 11 and the Canadiens on the 16th to close out training camp. Due to his shoulder problem and as a precaution to prevent more injury, Orr was kept out both games.

During the exhibition season, defenseman Al "Junior" Langlois continued to play for the Bruins wearing his number 4 sweater. Langlois had toiled for the B's playing 65 games during the 1965–66 season. After the October 16 exhibition game against Montreal, Langlois was sold to the Los Angeles Blades of the Western Hockey League. Three days later, the Bruins opened the 1966–1967 season against the Detroit Red Wings with Bobby Orr wearing the famous number 4.

To put things in perspective, numbers in the high twenties were not common during the early-to-mid 1960s in the NHL. Perusing rosters from the 1965–66 season, numbers 28 and 29 were not worn by any NHL player. Only one National Hockey League performer wore number 27, Toronto Maple Leafs' superstar Frank Mahovlich. Montreal's Jim Roberts' number 26 and the Blackhawks' number 21, worn by Stan Mikita, were the high numbers for those clubs. New York and Detroit's highest number was 22. Don Marshall carried that number with the Rangers and Ab McDonald wore the digits with the Red Wings.

During the 1964–65 season, the NHL legislated that teams must dress back up goaltenders. Prior to that, the home team had to provide a "house" goalie to replace an injured goaltender who could not continue in the game. On December 29, 1957, Bruins' goaltender Don Simmons suffered a dislocated shoulder in a game at Detroit. Ross "Lefty" Wilson, the Red Wings trainer, played the last two periods of the game for Boston. Normally, goaltenders would wear either number 1 or number 30, although there would be exceptions. The Bruins' Jack Norris sported number 17 during his twenty-three-game stint in Boston during the 1964–65 season. Forwards and defensemen did not delve into numbers north of 29.

With regards to Orr's number 4, it was theorized that the Bruins wanted him to wear a low number usually accorded stars like Gordie Howe and Rocket Richard, who both carried the number 9 on their backs. At the time of Orr's debut, the jerseys number 2 (Eddie Shore), number 3 (Lionel Hitchman), number 5 (Dit Clapper), and number 15 (Milt Schmidt) were all retired by Boston. Single-number jerseys already in use by the Bruins included number 6 (Ted Green), number 7 (Pit Martin), number 8 (Bob Woytowich), and number 9 (John Bucyk). Therefore, the only single number available was 4. That number was worn around the league by such luminaries as Jean Beliveau in Montreal, Bill Gadsby in Detroit, and Red Kelly in Toronto, so the number possessed a bit of cache. The president of the Bruins, Weston Adams, chimed in about his wishing Orr to wear the number, and miraculously, by opening night, 27 morphed into 4.

Boston Garden public address announcer Frank Fallon's "Boston goal scored by number 4, Orr" had a nice alliteration to it and may have been subliminally thought out by club management. Fallon served as the public address announcer for the Bruins from 1957 until 1973. He also broadcast the first major league night baseball game played in Boston on May 11, 1946. The game was played at Braves Field between the Boston Braves and the New York Giants.

Frank Fallon

(Four before Orr)

Orr would be the last Bruin to wear number 4. The list of the eighteen players that had previously worn number 4 follows:

Bob Armstrong
Herb Cain
Pat Egan
Fernie Flaman
Harry Frost
Ted Graham
Jimmy Herberts
Myles Lane

Al "Junior" Langlois (the last player to wear number 4 before Orr)

Bob McCord
Bert McInenly
George Owen
Eric Pettinger
Walter "Babe" Pratt
Max Quackenbush
Charlie Sands
Alex Smith
Pat Stapleton

In anticipation of Orr's NHL debut, Tom Fitzgerald of the *Boston Globe* got to speak by phone with Orr's mother, Arva, who said, "I think it's wonderful, but I can't help being a little anxious. I guess I'll be the same as always, biting my nails until it is over and we hear how the game comes out on the late news. I'm always interested, but I can't help having this other feeling. You know, I'm always afraid he will get hurt." Arva went on, "When the games got rough and Bobby was out there, I couldn't watch at all." Bobby's father, Doug Orr, planned on attending Orr's first road game on Saturday night in Montreal. Arva continued, "He had been away from home, of course, but somehow, this time it seemed he was going far away, and it was kind of final, packing his big trunk as well as bags. I guess his sister Pat and I cried a little, and he seemed lonesome too."

1966–67 Boston Bruins Press and Radio Guide

As the Bruins readied for their October 19 opening, the team issued the 1966–67 press guide featuring the B's forward Murray Oliver and Chicago's Pierre Pilote on the cover.

Ted Hodgson was listed, with his photo on page 14 of the Bruins' guide. Ted had the satisfaction of playing on the winning Memorial Cup team with Edmonton as they beat Oshawa for the title. New teammate Bobby Orr was a member of the losing Oshawa Generals.

Moving on to page 22 of the guide, Orr's bio read thusly:

> Bobby Orr is the most highly regarded junior amateur player to enter the NHL in years. Even the great Bobby Hull never had the pre-pro buildup that Orr received. For four years, starting at the age of 14, Orr played in Junior A competition. He not only held his own with the older boys, he became an all-star. The first three years with the Oshawa, Ontario Generals, in the junior OHA, the fastest league of its kind in the world, Bobby set records for goal scoring by defensemen. The first year with the Generals, he rang up 30 goals, beat this mark by four goals the second year, and then last season, wound up with 38 goals and 56 assists for 94 points in 47 games. Despite all the notoriety he has received, Bobby remains the same unaffected man. He has always been a team man and has always insisted that his teammates be included in everything that he does. Orr has always been a defenseman. But because he does

everything, skating, shooting, passing, so well many hockey men feel he might be better up front as a forward. Present Bruins plans call for him to stay on defense, but if an emergency arises, there is no telling where he might be used—even in goal.

Boston, Massachusetts, October 19, 1966 (10:00 a.m.)

The temperature was in the low fifties on a drizzly Wednesday morning in downtown Boston. The area around the Boston Garden was dank and always seemed rather depressing due to the shadows of the elevated railway overhead on Causeway Street. Steve Adamson, a textbook salesman, was heading to a local school and passed one of the locked entrances to the Garden. In about nine hours, this area would be teeming with fans anticipating the beginning of a new Boston Bruins' season.

As he approached the Garden, he noticed a young man nervously pacing back and forth in front of the grimy old building. When he realized the young man was wearing an Oshawa Generals warm-up jacket, he recognized that it was Bobby Orr. As a loyal Bruins' follower at the time, he was well aware of the coming of the young phenom.

Adamson said, "I always wished that I had stopped to offer some encouragement and good luck, but I am pleased that I got to witness his career right from the beginning."

Adamson, a Brookline, Massachusetts, native, began following the Bruins as a young teen in the late 1940s.

At last, Orr, now eighteen years and seven months, was ready for his NHL debut. The game was set for Wednesday evening, October 19, 1966, at the Boston Garden. The opponent would be Gordie Howe and the Detroit Red Wings. Howe would begin his twenty-first season in the league on this evening, breaking the record of twenty years held by Bruins' Hall of Famer Aubrey "Dit" Clapper and former Ranger, Blackhawk, and Red Wing Bill Gadsby.

The National Hockey League, founded in 1917, celebrated the beginning of its fiftieth season on this evening. In addition to the Boston-Detroit encounter, the New York Rangers hosted the Chicago Blackhawks at Madison Square Garden.

Hockey fever in Boston was at a seemingly all-time high. The ticket windows closed down at 6:45 p.m., a full one hour and fifteen minutes prior to the opening face-off. There was not a ducat to be had.

At 8:00 p.m., organist John Kiley serenaded the Bruins with the strains of "Paree" as they clomped onto the Garden ice at the center ice red line on the north side of the building. The Bruins were dressed in their white sweaters with gold-and-black trim. One note of significance regarding their opponent the Detroit Red Wings, who were clad in their blood red jerseys. The name of each Wings' player appeared above the rear number on their uniforms. This was the first time in NHL history that players' names would be on their livery. Within a few years, nameplates became mandatory for all teams, but on this date, it was a sartorial first.

Although a bottom feeder for the last eight seasons, attendance at Bruins' games held up remarkably well. Sellout crowds were commonplace, and the Bruins seemed to have found a niche in the working-class communities surrounding Boston. Longshoremen, factory workers, police officers, firefighters, and bus drivers found a place to relieve the tensions of their workdays by screaming at their beloved hockey team whether losing, which was often, or winning. However, on this evening, the 13,909 in attendance came to see Orr, and he didn't disappoint. The NHL score sheet on this night recorded that Bobby Orr earned his first point during a second-period power play. As Orr explains, "I actually fanned on the shot from the point. I really meant to slap it, but I just didn't get a hold of it. I'm glad it got through there." Standing in front of Detroit goaltender Roger Crozier was Boston's Wayne Connelly, who tipped the shot past the goalkeeper at 5:44 of the second frame.

Almost an afterthought was that the Bruins defeated Detroit 6–2. Bruins' fans were so giddy after the contest that dreams of the Stanley Cup floated through their ever-faithful minds.

Anticipation seemed to be the common thread when assessing Orr's first game by the players and coach of the Wings.

"He'll do for sure," uttered Detroit's Howe in describing Orr's efforts after the Bruins thumped the Wings, 6–2. Howe continued, "The kid's all right. He anticipates well, he makes good passes, and I guess he does just about what you would expect of a good defenseman. If they don't want him, we'll be willing to take him off your hands." Detroit coach Sid Abel bellowed, "A good one, no question about it. He has great anticipation."

Orr's First Game, Wednesday, October 19 (8:00 p.m.)

Boston Bruins Lineup	Detroit Red Wings Lineup
Ed Johnston	Roger Crozier
Bernie Parent	Hank Bassen
Bobby Orr	Bert Marshall
Gilles Marotte	Leo Boivin
Ted Green	Gary Bergman
Dallas Smith	Bob Wall
Bob Woytowich	Bart Crashley
Joe Watson	Murray Hall
Murray Oliver	Bruce MacGregor
John McKenzie	Paul Henderson

Johnny Bucyk	Norm Ullman
Pit Martin	Gordie Howe
Ron Stewart	Dean Prentice
Ross Lonsberry	Alex Delvecchio
Ron Schock	Floyd Smith
Wayne Connelly	Peter Mahovlich
Ed Westfall	Brian Watson
Bob Dillabough	Andy Bathgate
Ron Murphy	
Ted Hodgson	

Referee: Art Skov
Linesmen: Matt Pavlich, Pat Shetler
Attendance: 13,909 (sellout)

First Period

Boston	Oliver (McKenzie, Bucyk)	9:36
Penalties:	Detroit: Bergman	2:48
	Detroit: MacGregor	11:12
	Detroit: Smith	19:10

Second Period

Boston	Connelly (Orr, Oliver)	5:44 (power play)
Boston	McKenzie (Westfall)	6:32
Boston	Martin (Lonsberry, Stewart)	17:08
Detroit	Hall (Boivin)	18:12
Boston	Schock (Murphy, Connelly)	19:00
Penalties:	Detroit: Crashley	4:27
	Detroit: Smith	10:20

Third Period

Detroit	Bathgate (Hall, Howe)	12:55
Boston	McKenzie (Bucyk, Oliver)	19:16 (power play)
Penalties:	Detroit: Hall	9:56
	Detroit: Watson	18:47

Shots on Goal

Boston	36	
Detroit	25	

Saves

Boston:	Johnston	23 saves on 25 shots
Detroit	Crozier	30 saves on 36 shots

A harsher test was upcoming as a common "original six" scheduling quirk; the home-and-home series would kick in on the weekend. Their opponents would be the 1966 Stanley Cup winning Montreal Canadiens. Saturday night would be featured on *Hockey Night in Canada* with the return match twenty-four hours later in Boston.

After a two-day respite, the Bruins headed to Montreal for the Canadiens' home opener and Orr's first road game. In a tight checking contest, the Habs edged the Bruins on goals by Ted Harris, a future Orr antagonist, Bobby Rousseau, who was believed to have just signed a five-year contract, and Leon Rochefort. At 7:43 of the second period, Orr earned his first minor penalty. The resultant Montreal power play produced the goal by Rousseau and gave the Canadiens a 2–0 lead in a game won by Montreal 3–1. It was now home to Boston for the return matchup.

Game 3 of the season had the Bruins wearing their gold jerseys with the black shoulder yokes. The visiting Canadiens wore their traditional "home" red uniforms trimmed in blue and white. Sunday night game times during this season were played at 7:30 p.m. Two errors in the defensive zone ruined what would have been a memorable night as the Bruins fell to the Canadiens by a score of 3–2. The most glaring mistake occurred on a Boston power play late in the third period. With the scores tied 2–2 and Montreal's Jimmy Roberts off for tripping, Murray Oliver's pass was picked off by Montreal defenseman, J. C. Tremblay, who quickly reversed directions and went in on Boston goalie Eddie Johnston and ripped a slapper into the net for the game winner.

The good news on the evening was provided by the prized Boston rookie early in the third stanza. With Orr manning the right point, he eluded the Montreal defenders and fired a slap shot so hard, Habs goalie Gump Worsley didn't even react to the missile fired at him from some sixty feet out. The tally at 4:13 caused a long and sustained eruption from the 13,909 in attendance.

Montreal goaltender Lorne "Gump" Worsley had this to say about Orr: "I wouldn't want to be in his shoes. The fans will jump him the first time he makes a mistake. He'll have to be awfully tough to take it."

And so a scant three games into his rookie season, Bobby Orr was being touted as the most highly publicized rookie to play in Boston since the arrival of twenty-year-old Ted Williams in 1939. Harold Kaese of the *Boston Globe* on October 30, 1966, compared Orr thusly. "Williams is loudly confidant of meeting the big league challenge. Orr awaits his season with quiet assurance and considerable curiosity. He does not match Williams's exuberance but probably has a much determination, natural talent and physical equipment. The pressure will be fierce, but Orr's attitude was this: 'If my teammates accept me, everything will be fine.'"

Kaese went on, "Orr has always been sensitive about being set above his teammates. When a *Sports Illustrated* photographer asked him to go onto the ice for pictures before practice, Orr refused. He would not take the picture without his mates. When the Oshawa Generals were in Boston last year and Orr was asked to do radio and television, he always brought two or three teammates along with him."

Finally, Kaese expressed that "playing before a large critical gallery of fans, Orr faces as hard a test as any rookie in any sport." With this comparison, Bobby Orr ended his first week with the Boston Bruins.

Due to an early season scheduling quirk, the Bruins would wait five days before their next game in Toronto, which was part of a three-game road trip, which included visits to Detroit and Chicago. "Cowboy" Johnny McKenzie became Orr's road roommate for the sojourn to all three cities.

As the Bruins prepared to take on the Maple Leafs in Toronto, it should be noted that this would be Orr's first game at Maple Leaf Gardens as a member of the Bruins. Orr had played a number of games at the Gardens with both the Oshawa Generals and as a member of the Toronto Marlboros in a December 1965 game against the Russian National Team. In this contest, Boston came back from a 3–1 deficit and tied the Leafs on two third-period goals by Eddie Westfall and Ron Murphy. Orr's second period minor penalty did not result in any scoring for Toronto.

In Orr's former junior home of Oshawa, television sets were installed in the arena so that fans of the Generals could observe Orr playing against the nearby Leafs.

The next evening, the Bruins headed to Detroit and Orr's first game at the Olympia. A Sunday night crowd of 13,545 fans watched the Wings thrash the Bruins 8–1. After Pit Martin of the Bruins opened the scoring, the Red Wings fired home eight unanswered goals. Eddie Johnston still managed thirty-eight saves in the losing effort. Orr picked up a second period minor penalty but Detroit did not score during the man advantage.

October 1966					Orr's Stats				
	Game			Season					
Date	Venue	Versus	W-L-T	Score	G	A	G	A	PTS
19	Boston	Detroit	W	6–2	0	1	0	1	1
22	Montreal	Canadiens	L	3–1	0	0	0	1	1
23	Boston	Montreal	L	3–2	1	0	1	1	2
29	Toronto	Maple Leafs	T	3–3	0	0	1	1	2
30	Detroit	Red Wings	L	8–1	0	0	1	1	2

November 1966

With the team winless in four games, the Bruins moved into hostile Chicago Stadium for Orr's first game in the Windy City. While young Bernie Parent was making thirty saves, the Bruins beat Chicago by a score of 3–2. Orr picked up two minor penalties, one each in the first and third periods that were successfully killed.

Two nights later, the Bruins returned to Boston to meet the New York Rangers for the first time this season. A nonsellout crowd of 12,720 witnessed a humiliating 7–1 pasting at the hands of the Rangers. Future Norris Trophy winning defenseman Harry Howell scored two goals for the Broadway Blueshirts. Ex-Bruin Orland Kurtenbach scored a second-period shorthanded goal for the visitors. Two of the Rangers goals, including the Kurtenbach strike, were the results of plays in which Orr lost the puck due to tight checking. Orr also received a minor for elbowing at 12:58 of the second stanza. The New Yorkers did not score on the ensuing power play.

After two days off, the Bruins had a rematch with the Blackhawks, the team they had beaten earlier in the week in Chicago. This time, the results would be reversed with the Hawks coming back from a 2–1 deficit and scoring three unanswered goals in a 4–2 Chicago victory. Orr scored the first Boston goal on a slapper at 9:03 of the first period tying the game at 1. However, his first period minor penalty resulted in a goal by the Hawks' Wally Boyer just as the Orr penalty was expiring. Orr had also received a double minor for slashing and roughing with Boyer at 10:27 of the second period.

Two injuries of significance occurred in the game as Orr's defense partner Gilles Marotte suffered a knee injury and goaltender Eddie Johnston an eye injury. Johnston's injury occurred at 14:06 of the first period, and he had to be taken to the Massachusetts Eye and Ear infirmary. He was replaced by backup goaltender Bernie Parent. Gerry Cheevers was called up from Oklahoma City as Johnston was expected to miss a week to ten days of action.

Chicago's chief scout Bob Wilson, who discovered Bobby Hull said that Bobby Orr had better puck sense than Hull at the same age.

Now that the season had moved into its third week, the Bruins traveled to New York for their first game of the season at Madison Square Garden and Orr's first ever game in Manhattan. Orr was kept off the score sheet as the Bruins and Rangers played to a 3–3 tie. After the game, the Bruins headed back to Boston and a meeting with the Maple Leafs on the following evening. Since Toronto had played in Montreal the previous night, neither team had an apparent edge heading into the game. With Gerry Cheevers turning in his first NHL shutout, the Bruins toppled the Leafs by a 4–0 score. Orr assisted on Wayne Connelly's third-period goal. A couple of days of rest followed, and next up would be the Montreal Canadiens on Sunday.

Before another jam-packed crowd (fifth sellout in six games) at the Garden, the Bruins defeated the Canadiens 2–1 on Sunday night. Cheevers was back in goal to earn his second consecutive victory. Prior to the game, coach Toe Blake of the

Canadiens was commenting that "this kid Orr is certain to be one of the league's great stars. Not just a good player—a star. If he isn't, I'm going to be just another one of a lot of people who are very wrong." Although he did not appear on the score sheet, Orr played a sound defensive game, especially when the Bruins were short-handed. He did manage to earn a minor penalty in the second period, but there was no damage on the Montreal power play. The victory moved the Bruins into fourth place and dropped Montreal into the cellar.

For the second time, an early season quirk in the schedule had the Bruins off for five more days, this time coming from the 14th to the 18th of November. The next game on Saturday at Boston Garden featured the Bruins and New York Rangers. A late third-period goal by Johnny Bucyk helped the Bruins to a 3-all tie against the New Yorkers. The Rangers had leads of 1–0, 2–1, and 3–2 before Bucyk's late game heroics. The game also featured Bobby Orr's first NHL major for fighting. The fight started after Orr charged Vic Hadfield of the Rangers, which initially earned him a two-minute minor penalty. When Hadfield showed his displeasure at Orr, a fight ensued with Orr holding his own against the Rangers' tough winger. Boston's first goal was a shorthanded effort by Johnny McKenzie. The Bruins unbeaten streak had now reached four games.

The next evening, the Detroit Red Wings made their second visit of the season to the Garden. With Cheevers again in goal, the B's easily handled the Wings by a score of 5–2. The Bruins played before the seventh sellout in eight games as fans continued to flock to Boston Garden to see the seemingly improved Boston sextet. Both Orr and defense partner Gilles Marotte beat Detroit goaltender Roger Crozier. Orr's goal was the first shorthanded tally of his career. He was also whistled off for two minor penalties, elbowing in the first period and charging in the second stanza. Neither penalty proved harmful to the B's as the penalty killers successfully nixed any scoring chances during the Detroit power plays.

Wednesday night was a traditional *Hockey Night* in Manhattan as the B's visited the Big Apple on November 23. In a losing effort to the Rangers, Orr enjoyed the first two-goal game of his career, which included his first career power play goal at 14:27 of the third period. The final score was 5–4 in favor of New York. Orr's power play goal was scored against goaltender Eddie Giacomin of the Rangers.

After the game, the Bruins headed back to Boston for a Thursday evening game with the Detroit Red Wings, their second visit to Boston in four days. The game was switched from an 8:00 p.m. start to 7:30 p.m. due to the Thanksgiving holiday. The Bruins moved out to a 4–0 first-period lead and never looked back as they crushed the Wings by a score of 8–3. Orr recorded two assists in the contest, but most of the attention centered on a hit that Detroit great Gordie Howe leveled on Orr in the third period. The hit stunned Orr, and he was treated on the ice, although he continued in the game. Later in the period, Orr reciprocated with a crunching hit on

Howe, which delighted the 13,909 in attendance on the "turkey holiday." Next up would be the Maple Leafs in Toronto on Saturday night.

Orr netted his sixth goal of the season, but the Maple Leafs, on goals by Ron Ellis, Frank Mahovlich, Peter Stemkowski, and Larry Jeffrey, skated past the Bruins by a 4–2 count. Orr had tallied an assist on the first Boston goal scored by Gilles Marotte in the opening period. After the game, Orr was picked as the First Star of the Game.

Unfortunately for Bruins' fans and the NHL as a whole, Orr suffered the first of seemingly endless knee injuries in this contest. The injury was severe enough to have him sit out the next night's game back in Boston against Chicago. The team physician said he had a sprained ligament in the left knee and designated that the injury was a mild one. The injury might have originally occurred during the past Wednesday's practice. Although he had played on Thanksgiving night, the knee gave him some problems that were certainly aggravated during the game at Maple Leaf Gardens on Saturday. The early prognostication was that Orr would be out for three weeks. He was also ordered on crutches immediately.

In the Sunday evening game played without Orr, Chicago's slick center Stan Mikita scored the eighth "hat trick" of his career as the Blackhawks upended the Bruins. The Hawks had raced out to a 5–1 lead early into the third period, but Boston came on strong and pumped in three consecutive goals, which were not enough as Chicago won the game by a 5–4 count. The crowd, though disappointed by the absence of Orr, helped swell the attendance as it became the ninth sellout in ten home games.

November 1966					Orr's Stats				
					Game		Season		
Date	Venue	Versus	W-L-T	Score	G	A	G	A	PTS
1	Chicago	Blackhawks	W	3–2	0	0	1	1	2
3	Boston	New York	L	7–1	0	0	1	1	2
6	Boston	Chicago	L	4–2	1	0	2	1	3
9	New York	Rangers	T	3–3	0	0	2	1	3
10	Boston	Toronto	W	4–0	0	1	2	2	4
13	Boston	Montreal	W	2–1	0	0	2	2	4
19	Boston	New York	T	3–3	0	1	2	3	5
20	Boston	Detroit	W	5–2	1	0	3	3	6
23	New York	Rangers	L	5–4	2	0	5	3	8
24	Boston	Detroit	W	8–3	0	2	5	5	10
26	Toronto	Maple Leafs	L	4–2	1	1	6	6	12
27	Boston	Chicago	L	5–4	DNP		6	6	12

December 1966

Orr returned to action on Thursday night, the 1st, as the Bruins traveled to the Olympia in Detroit for a game with the struggling Red Wings who had lost six straight. Gordie Howe's first-period goal propelled the Red Wings to a 4–1 victory and handed the Bruins their third straight defeat. The B's returned to Boston for a Saturday night meeting with the New York Rangers and a Sunday night game against Toronto.

In the Rangers' game, the Bruins rolled out to a second period 2–0 lead only to have the Broadway Blues come back on goals by Donnie Marshall and Arnie Brown to secure a 2–2 tie. Orr assisted on the first-period goal by Ron Stewart as the Bruins were now winless in four straight games.

Things went from bad to worse the next evening as the Bruins were stuffed by the Toronto Maple Leafs 8–3. Playing to the eleventh sellout in twelve games, the B's reverted to prior years' form and played an awful game. To make matters worse, Orr suffered a sprained ligament to his left knee. The injury occurred when Orr tried to sneak by Toronto defender Marcel Pronovost near the Boston bench. Orr did not play the rest of the contest. After the game, the team physician estimated that Orr would be sidelined at least three weeks. Orr was given a pair of crutches to aid in his walking. The winless streak now extended to five games. Slick Toronto center Dave Keon scored two goals for the victorious Leafs.

Toronto Assistant General Manager King Clancy, commenting on the hit, said the following: "It was an unfortunate accident, but for the life of me, I don't know what possessed the boy to try to get through that way. He's a left-handed shot, and he couldn't have made a play coming down that side. That's a tough break for the Bruins. He's a great prospect."

Postgame, Coach Harry Sinden was quite honest about his assessment of the team's chances without Orr in the lineup. "We might as well be realistic. With Orr out, we'll be missing a lot of ability. That doesn't mean we should lose anything in spirit. This team's trouble is a lack of scoring, and right now, I just don't know what we can do about that."

The Bruins headed to New York for a Wednesday night game against the Rangers. The Broadway Blues extended the B's winless streak to six games with a 4–2 victory over the Bruins. The Bruins had jumped out to a 2–0 lead in the first period, but the New Yorkers fired home four straight markers for the going away victory.

In the latest update on Orr's left knee, team officials, trainers, and doctors ordered him off his leg for at least ten days. With that, he was admitted into the Newton-Wellesley Hospital, where it was decided that complete rest was the best course of action. The team was on the road, and the training staff of Dan Canney and John Forristall would be unavailable to provide treatment while roommate Joe Watson, also travelling with the team, would be unable to assist him at their home in Nahant.

The next night, Bobby Hull's Chicago Blackhawks visited the Boston Garden. With the Hawks scoring a touchdown and field goal, Chicago walked away with a 10–2 victory. Former Bruin Doug "Diesel" Mohns notched a hat trick against beleaguered goaltender Eddie Johnston. Mohns's third goal was scored at 19:59 of the third period and was originally disallowed by Referee Vern Buffey. His ruling was eventually overruled by the NHL's Brian O'Neill, and the goal was awarded to Mohns. It was the second straight game Chicago had played in Boston where a Hawk player had scored a hat trick. Stan Mikita netted three in the November 27 victory over the Bruins. The winless streak was extended to seven games.

With the next two days off, the Bruins headed to the Windy City and a Sunday night encounter with the same Blackhawks. After spotting Chicago a two-goal lead, the Bruins came back on goals by Gilles Marotte and Ron Murphy to earn a 2–2 tie before 16,666 fans in the Chicago Stadium.

The good news from Boston was that Orr was released from the hospital and would start training on a bicycle and receive whirlpool treatments to strengthen his left knee.

When the Bruins lost at Toronto on December 14, it extended their winless streak to nine games. The final score was 2–1 in favor of the Leafs. The next night, the winless skein reached ten as the Bruins were whitewashed at the Olympia in Detroit by a score of 4–0. Roger Crozier earned the shutout while veteran Andy Bathgate notched two goals for the winners.

After a two-day layoff, the Bruins returned to the friendly confines of Boston Garden and a meeting with the Montreal Canadiens. Third-period goals by John McKenzie and Ron Schock helped the Bruins break their ten-game winless streak with a 3–1 win over the Habs.

Although the win over Montreal provided temporary relief from the winless column, it would not last long. During practice the next day, Orr returned to the ice and declared himself ready to play. However, he did not accompany the team to Madison Square Garden for the Wednesday night game. The Bruins were upended by the Rangers 5–1. For the living room crowd, this would be a historic evening as the Bruins make their debut on WKBG-TV56.

In the pre-expansion era, NHL games were traditionally played on both Christmas night and, quite often, Christmas Eve. This year, the B's were scheduled to be in Toronto on Christmas Eve in the first of a home-and-home match up with the Leafs. George Armstrong, Peter Stemkowski, and John Brennerman were the goal scorers; and veteran Johnny Bower provided the stoppers as the Leafs blanked the Bruins 3–0.

While Santa was making his rounds, the teams headed back to Boston for a Christmas night rematch. The game would feature the return of Boston's prized rookie to the lineup. Surprisingly, a less-than-full house of 13,188 was present for the holiday contest. Orr returned to the line-up in a gradual manner. At first, he manned the point on the power play. Next, Orr lined up at center in an effort to produce more offense. Lastly, he returned to his normal position of right defense. As for the game itself, the Bruins were again downed by the Leafs, this time 4–2.

On December 27, the Red Wings moved into Boston for what was at the time a rare Tuesday night game. Pit Martin's two goals helped the Bruins earn a 4–4 tie. Orr assisted on goals by Ron Stewart and Eddie Westfall. These were his first points since December 1, and in an effort to generate more scoring, Coach Sinden started him at center between Eddie Westfall and Ron Stewart.

A sad note occurred after the game as a Buddliner train that left North Station below the Garden was involved in a collision with an oil truck at a crossing in nearby Everett. Twenty-five passengers were aboard the train when it struck the truck. The ensuing fire killed twelve people. Many of the deceased had attended the Bruins' game and had waited for the train that was heading for Boston's North Shore.

The Bruins immediately headed for Montreal and a clash with the Canadiens the next evening. Behind twenty-two saves by goaltender Gerry Cheevers, the Bruins managed to tie the Canadiens at 1–1.

The Bruins closed out the 1966 portion of the schedule in Detroit and a meeting with the Red Wings. Despite an unassisted goal by Orr, his first since November 26, the Bruins fell to the Wings by a 3–1 score.

The Bruins had a disappointing 1-10-4 record for the month of December. They reached the midpoint of the season in a familiar position, last in the standings, eleven points behind fourth place Montreal. Surprisingly, the New York Rangers sat on top of the league.

December 1966					Orr's Stats				
					Game		Season		
Date	Venue	Versus	W-L-T	Score	G	A	G	A	PTS
1	Detroit	Red Wings	L	4–1	0	0	6	6	12
3	Boston	New York	T	2–2	0	1	6	7	13
4	Boston	Toronto	L	8–3	0	0	6	7	13
7	New York	Rangers	L	4–2	DNP		6	7	13
8	Boston	Chicago	L	10–2	DNP		6	7	13
11	Chicago	Blackhawks	T	2–2	DNP		6	7	13
14	Toronto	Maple Leafs	L	2–1	DNP		6	7	13
15	Detroit	Red Wings	L	4–0	DNP		6	7	13
18	Boston	Montreal	W	3–1	DNP		6	7	13
21	New York	Rangers	L	5–1	DNP		6	7	13

24	Toronto	Maple Leafs	L	3–0	DNP		6	7	13
25	Boston	Toronto	L	4–2	0	0	6	7	13
27	Boston	Detroit	T	4–4	0	2	6	9	15
28	Montreal	Canadiens	T	1–1	0	0	6	9	15
31	Detroit	Red Wings	L	3–1	1	0	7	9	16

January 1967

The Bruins moved into the city of Chicago for a New Year's night game with the Hawks. Chicago carried a 3–0 lead into the early portion of the third period before Boston finally got on the board, striking for two goals in sixty-five seconds. J. P. Parise and John McKenzie scored the goals for Boston, but it was not enough as they were downed by the Blackhawks 3–2 in their first game of 1967.

The Bruins now enjoyed five consecutive nights off before travelling to Toronto to meet the Maple Leafs in a *Hockey Night in Canada* telecast. Five different Leafs scored as Toronto cruised past the B's by a score of 5–2. Orr added an assist to his scoring totals on Pit Martin's first-period goal. The Bruins, winless in eight games, headed back to Chicago for the second consecutive Sunday evening game against the Hawks.

Kenny Wharram netted an early marker for Chicago, but the B's came back with three unanswered goals and broke their eight-game winless streak with a 3–1 decision over the Hawks. Orr assisted on Bob Dillabough's first-period goal. With the Ice Capades wrapping up their annual stay in the Garden, the Bruins headed back east for some home cooking as four of the next five games would be played on Causeway Street.

Home hospitality didn't help the Bruins as they were shut out by the New York Rangers 3–0 behind the solid goaltending of Eddie Giacomin, who stopped twenty-one Boston shots. On Friday afternoon, the Bruins headed for the Sheraton Mount Royal Hotel in Montreal to prepare for their Saturday night game with the Canadiens.

After the Habs took a 4–2 lead into the third period, the Bruins pulled off an unusual comeback, scoring three unanswered goals to defeat Montreal, 5–4. Orr had an assist on the game-tying goal by Pit Martin at 12:01 of the third frame. "Home and home" being the flavor of the weekend, it was back to Boston to meet the same Haughty Habs on Sunday evening.

In a surprise move, the Canadiens inserted Gary Bauman in net for the game. Making thirty-two saves against the Boston attack, Montreal managed to defeat the Bruins by a 3–1 score. After the loss, the Bruins decided to make some personnel changes.

The next day, the Bruins sent Gerry Cheevers and Dallas Smith back to Oklahoma City and recalled goaltender Bernie Parent and defenseman Gary Doak.

Also brought back to the big club was forward Wayne Rivers, who had been toiling with the Hershey Bears of the American Hockey League.

The NHL All-Star Game was played in midseason for the first time. The previous year's Stanley Cup champions, the Montreal Canadiens, hosted the game at the Forum. Only one Bruin, Murray Oliver, participated in the game, which was won by the Canadiens, 3–0. General Manager Hap Emms was somewhat peeved at the exclusion of Orr from the game.

With the brief All-Star Game break over, it was back to regular season action. The Chicago Blackhawks provided the opposition for the Thursday night game at the Garden. A rather smallish crowd of 11,029 watched former Bruin Doug Mohns notch his second "hat trick" on successive visits to Boston as Chicago topped the B's 4–2. On the medical front, Bobby Orr received a twelve-stitch cut in the mouth early in the first period but returned to action in the second.

A story in the *Boston Globe* noted a report out of Toronto in which members of the Bruins met with attorney Alan Eagleson in Montreal. Eagleson was involved in representing the American Hockey League's Springfield Indians in their dispute with owner Eddie Shore. The Boston players told Eagleson that they were behind the Springfield players 100 percent. Collectively, the Bruins players iterated through Eagleson that they were for anything that benefits the players.

In an afternoon tilt on the 21st, the Bruins were locked up with rival New York. Eight previous contests against the Rangers only produced three tie games. Eddie Westfall, with two goals and two assists helped propel the Bruins to a relatively easy 6–2 win.

The next evening, the Toronto Maple Leafs visited Beantown for a Sunday night tilt. Orr assisted Ron Stewart for the game's first goal as the Bruins defeated the Maple Leafs, 3–1. A third-period fight involving Orr and Toronto's Larry Jeffrey earned him a five-minute major and his first career ten-minute misconduct. Referee John Ashley handed out the penalties to both Orr and Jeffrey. For only the second time this year, the Bruins cobbled together two wins in a row.

Bobby Orr was named to the midyear, second All-Star team. In the voting, Orr trailed Harry Howell of the Rangers, Pierre Pilote of the Blackhawks, and Tim Horton of the Maple Leafs.

The Bruins headed to New York for a midweek clash against the Rangers. Before a sellout crowd at Madison Square Garden, the teams played two scoreless periods. In the third stanza, Phil Goyette and Bob Nevin of the Rangers sandwiched goals around one by Johnny Bucyk as the Rangers downed the Bruins 2–1. After the game, it was on to Montreal for a rare Thursday night encounter at the Forum.

After Dick Duff opened the scoring for the Canadiens, the Bruins scored four straight markers and defeated Montreal, 4–1. Orr assisted on Ron Stewart's second-period goal. Three nights later, the same teams were to meet again in Boston.

To close out January, the Bruins had seemingly managed to gain a stranglehold on the N.H.L. cellar spot. With only twelve wins in the first forty-four games, the team was heading for their eighth straight "do not qualify" for the playoffs. At the Garden on the 31st, the Canadiens rolled out to a 3–0 lead until the Bruins gained their skating legs and scored the final two goals of the game. Unfortunately, the two goals were not enough as the Bruins went down to defeat, 3–2. Orr did assist on John Bucyk's second-period goal.

January 1967					Orr's Stats				
					Game		Season		
Date	Venue	Versus	W-L-T	Score	G	A	G	A	PTS
1	Chicago	Blackhawks	L	3–2	0	0	7	9	16
7	Toronto	Maple Leafs	L	5–2	0	1	7	10	17
8	Chicago	Blackhawks	W	3–1	0	1	7	11	18
12	Boston	New York	L	3–0	0	0	7	11	18
14	Montreal	Canadiens	W	5–4	0	1	7	12	19
15	Boston	Montreal	L	3–1	0	0	7	12	19
19	Boston	Chicago	L	4–2	0	0	7	12	19
21	Boston	New York	W	6–2	0	0	7	12	19
22	Boston	Toronto	W	3–1	0	1	7	13	20
25	New York	Rangers	L	2–1	0	0	7	13	20
26	Montreal	Canadiens	W	4–1	0	1	7	14	21
29	Boston	Montreal	L	3–2	0	1	7	15	22

Orr fends off Arnie Brown of the New York Rangers
in this 1966–67 game at Boston Garden.

February 1967

Commenting on being voted the top rookie for the first half of the 1966–67 season, Orr opined that "I didn't expect anything like this. I thought I had a chance, but I guess everyone in his first year thinks that. It certainly is a thrill."

February opened with the Bruins on a short midweek Midwest road trip to Chicago and Detroit. The trip would produce two losses, a thrashing at Chicago by a score of 6–1, and a close loss to the Red Wings by a 4–3 margin. Orr assisted on the only Boston goal, scored by Pit Martin, midway through the first stanza in the game at Chicago.

In the game at Detroit, the Bruins attempted a late game comeback but fell short. Orr assisted Ted Green on his third-period goal. Two weekend tilts were scheduled for the Boston Garden.

On Saturday, the Bruins fell to the second place Rangers by a score of 4–3. Orr's eighth goal of the season was assisted by goaltender Eddie Johnston. Orr also assisted on Ron Schock's second-period goal. The Bruins held a two-goal lead midway through the second period before the Rangers came back with three unanswered goals.

The following headline from the *Boston Globe* said it all: "BLACK HAWKS RIP BRUINS, 5–0: ORR BRILLIANT, TEAMMATES INEPT."

Although the game attracted the sixteenth sellout in twenty-four home games, the theme of the game was reflected by a fan who bellowed, "Why don't you trade that kid? He makes the rest of the team look so bad." Doug Mohns had one of the goals for Chicago, giving him seven goals in his last three visits to Boston. The Bruins losing streak reached five consecutive games.

In a Wednesday night game in New York, the Bruins defeated the Rangers, 2–1. The end of the game was delayed due the fans' displeasure of the officials, John Ashley, John D'Amico, and Walt Atanas.

Normally, Montreal and Toronto were awarded Saturday evening home games by the NHL schedule maker. In an unusual twist, the Canadiens were in Boston for this Saturday soiree. The Bruins 2–0 lead was accentuated by a first-period brawl featuring Jean Guy Talbot of Montreal against Ted Green and Habs defenseman Ted Harris taking on Orr. Although the B's had leads of 2–0 and 3–2, they managed to lose to the Canadiens by a final score of 4–3.

The next evening, the Maple Leafs came to town where goals by Red Kelly and Peter Stemkowski help the Leafs nip the B's, 2–1. Toronto's victory ended an eleven-game winless streak for Toronto.

Valentine's night would be the last home game for two weeks as the Ice Follies invaded the Boston Garden. All the league cities, save New York, were on the Bruins' schedule for this trip with two visits to Montreal on the itinerary. The Bruins faced the Detroit hockey club in the game on the 14th at the Boston Garden. Ron Murphy scored two goals to lead the Bruins to a 6–3 victory with Orr assisting on Ron Schock's third-period tally.

On the first game of the five-game trip at Montreal, the Bruins beat the Habs, 5–1. Tommy Williams notched two tallies for the B's with Orr assisting on Bob Dillabough's first-period score.

Hockey Night in Canada featured the Bruins and Maple Leafs with Toronto coming out on top by a 5–3 count. Orr scored his ninth goal of the season in the second period.

For the second time in a week, the Bruins were at the Montreal Forum to face the Canadiens. Johnny Bucyk scored two goals for the Bruins, including a short-handed goal as the Bruins and Canadiens fought to a 2–2 tie. Orr was voted the first star of the game despite being held off the score sheet. His stellar play warranted the accolades of the voters. It was now off to Chicago and Detroit for weekend contests against the Hawks and Wings.

Saturday's game in Chicago was televised on WKBG Channel 56 with Fred Cusick at the microphone. The Bruins lost to the Hawks, 6–3, but Bruins' rookie Skip Krake scored two goals in a losing effort.

The following afternoon, the Bruins were featured on the NHL's Game of the Week while visiting Detroit. The B's trailed the Wings 3–2 late in the game when Ron Stewart hit a bouncing puck past Goalie Roger Crozier in the Detroit net to tie the game at three all. The goal was scored at 19:51 of the final frame with the Bruins' goaltender pulled for the extra attacker.

February 1967					Orr's Stats				
					Game		Season		
Date	Venue	Versus	W-L-T	Score	G	A	G	A	PTS
1	Chicago	Blackhawks	L	6–1	0	1	7	16	23
2	Detroit	Red Wings	L	4–3	0	1	7	17	24
4	Boston	New York	L	4–3	1	1	8	18	26
5	Boston	Chicago	L	5–0	0	0	8	18	26
8	New York	Rangers	W	2–1	0	0	8	18	26
11	Boston	Montreal	L	4–3	0	0	8	18	26
12	Boston	Toronto	L	2–1	0	0	8	18	26
14	Boston	Detroit	W	6–3	0	1	8	19	27
16	Montreal	Canadiens	W	5–1	0	1	8	20	28
18	Toronto	Maple Leafs	L	5–3	1	0	9	20	29
23	Montreal	Canadiens	T	2–2	0	0	9	20	29
25	Chicago	Blackhawks	L	6–3	0	0	9	20	29
26	Detroit	Red Wings	T	3–3	1	0	10	20	30

March 1967

The Bruins announced a major shakeup in the hierarchy of the front office. Leighton "Hap" Emms would be replaced by current Assistant General Manager Milt Schmidt. The change would take effect after the summer expansion draft.

For their first home game in over two weeks, the Bruins hosted the Chicago Blackhawks, the team running away with the NHL regular season title. The Bruins provided little resistance as the Chihawks defeated the B's by a score of 5–2. Bobby Orr garnered one assist on Wayne Connelly's third-period goal.

In the Saturday night clash with the New York Rangers, Orr's goal with three seconds left on the clock enabled the Bruins to tie the Rangers, 4–4. Orr's goal was a forty-five-foot shot from just inside the blue line that went between goaltender Eddie Giacomin's legs. The game attracted the eighteenth sellout in twenty-nine games.

For the next two Sunday nights, the Detroit Red Wings would provide the opposition for the Bruins at the Garden. The first game on March 5 went to the team from the Motor City as the Wings defeated the B's by a score of 5–3. Orr collected two points in the game on a goal and an assist.

Moving to Chicago for a Wednesday night game at the Stadium, the Blackhawks bested the Bruins by a 3–1 score. Skip Krake opened the scoring in the first period, and the B's held a lead for just under five minutes when the Hawks went to work and fired home three straight goals to win going away.

As the season began to wind down and the Bruins were looking at another cellar finish, they would act as spoilers the rest of the way. One of the teams on the outside of the playoff structure, the Detroit Red Wings, would be in Boston for the second consecutive Sunday night. After Gordie Howe opened the scoring at 1:22 of the first period, Orr fired home the game-tying goal seven minutes later. On this goal, Orr's thirteenth of the season, he moved past Harry Howell of the Rangers and led in the goal scoring department among the league's defensemen. The Bruins scored a 7–3 victory over the Wings. The seven goals was the Bruins' second-highest total of the season. Speedster Bob Dillabough netted two goals in the game. Dillabough had recently been fitted with contact lenses and wore them for the first time in this contest. With four games left in the season, the Bruins had already played before four hundred thousand fans in what was a once promising season.

On Wednesday night, the Bruins moved into Montreal. John McKenzie opened the scoring at 1:37 of the first period. By the time McKenzie's linemate Johnny Bucyk scored at 6:39 of the third, the Canadiens had scored seven goals. John Ferguson and Bobby Rousseau had notched two goals apiece during the onslaught. Four more goals by the Canadiens late in the third period iced the game for the Habs, 11–2. The eleven Montreal goals against the Bruins proved to be the worst drubbing against Boston on the season.

After licking their wounds, the Bruins moved into Detroit for a Saturday afternoon clash. Coach and General Manager Sid Abel of the Red Wings turned over the coaching reins to thirty-nine-year-old Gordie Howe. The Red Wings were also headed to a nonplayoff season, so this gave Abel the opportunity to evaluate his team from Detroit owner Bruce Norris's private box.

The Bruins had five different goal scorers—McKenzie, Bucyk, Murray Oliver, Pit Martin, and Bill Goldsworthy. Orr assisted on Bucyk's second-period goal as the B's slipped by Detroit 5–3. The victory would prove to be the last Boston win of the 1966–67 season. After the game, the Bruins headed out for New York City and a Sunday night contest against the Rangers. Boston could only muster one third-period goal as they were defeated in New York by a score of 3–1.

While they were being rubbed out in New York, back in Boston, the Bruins' Old Timers were entertaining the Montreal Old Timers in an exhibition game that benefitted the Jimmy Fund, which is devoted to cancer research in children. The game attracted a sellout crowd of 13,909. Former Bruins in the lineup included Milt Schmidt, Woody Dumart, Eddie Shore, John Peirson, Ed Sanford, Dit Clapper, Paul Ronty, Pat Egan, Bill Quackenbush, Cal Gardner, Eddie Wiseman, and Bill Cowley. The following day, Orr celebrated his nineteenth birthday.

With a scant five games remaining, the Bruins faced Toronto on Thursday night at the Garden. Peter Stemkowski scored three goals for the Leafs while McKenzie fired home two markers for the Bruins as the Leafs down the B's, 5–3. Both teams moved on to Toronto for a Saturday evening tilt on *Hockey Night in Canada*.

The Leafs, jockeying with Montreal and New York for a playoff position behind Chicago, defeated the Bruins by a score of 4–3. George Armstrong scored the winning goal at 18:44 of the third session. Terry Sawchuk was outstanding in goal as he made thirty-nine saves. Orr assisted on Murray Oliver's second-period score. This was the last road game for this season's Bruins, who were set to finish off the slate with home games against Montreal, Chicago, and Toronto.

After scoring the first two goals of Sunday afternoon's encounter with Montreal, the Canadiens peppered the Bruins with six straight goals of their own as the Habs coasted to a 6–3 victory. The game was televised as part of the NHL's Game of the Week and was blacked out in Boston. Local residents never saw the debacle in which Montreal scored five goals in a matter of 5:44 of the third period.

The Bruins closed out the March portion of the schedule against the Chicago Blackhawks. In a surprisingly tight game, the Hawks defeated the B's by a score of 3–1. Tommy Williams, with an assist from Orr and Eddie Westfall, opened the scoring. This was the last Boston goal of the night. Although 52-goal scorer Bobby Hull did not play, his brother Dennis more than adequately replaced him by scoring the winning goal at 12:33 of the third period. Phil Esposito assisted on Hull's goal. Unbeknownst to anybody at the time, Esposito's next appearance at Boston Garden would be as a member of the Boston Bruins.

Now barely nineteen years old, the honors associated with being the league's most outstanding rookie started to come to fruition.

The Gallery Gods, patrons who populated the second balcony at all Boston home games and who were considered to be the most loyal of Bruins' fans, bestowed their Eddie Shore Trophy, given to the player deemed most valuable player at home games award to Orr. Next, he won the Elizabeth C. Dufresne Trophy. This trophy is awarded to the Bruin deemed most outstanding at home games. The award was voted on by the Boston sportswriters and broadcasters.

Orr was developing a reputation as being completely unassuming and humble as the day is long. This story buttressed those credentials. When Orr was told that the writers in voting for the Dufresne Trophy had simply listed the name Bobby on many of the ballots, Orr said, "How do you know they were voting for me? They might have meant Bobby Dillabough or Bobby Woytowich. You should give the trophy to one of them as well."

March 1967					Orr's Stats				
					Game		Season		
Date	Venue	Versus	W-L-T	Score	G	A	G	A	PTS
2	Boston	Chicago	L	5–2	0	1	10	21	31

4	Boston	New York	T	4–4	1	1	11	22	33
5	Boston	Detroit	L	5–3	1	1	12	23	35
8	Chicago	Blackhawks	L	3–1	0	0	12	23	35
12	Boston	Detroit	W	7–3	1	0	13	23	36
15	Montreal	Canadiens	L	11–2	0	1	13	24	37
18	Detroit	Red Wings	W	5–3	0	1	13	25	38
19	New York	Rangers	L	3–1	0	0	13	25	38
23	Boston	Toronto	L	5–3	0	0	13	25	38
25	Toronto	Maple Leafs	L	4–3	0	1	13	26	39
26	Boston	Montreal	L	6–3	0	1	13	27	40
30	Boston	Chicago	L	3–1	0	1	13	28	41

April 1967

The Bruins wound up the regular season with a tilt against the Toronto Maple Leafs. The Leafs raced out to a 3–0 lead and Bob Pulford's two goals cemented a 5–2 Toronto win to close out the 1966–67 regular season.

April 1967					Orr's Stats				
	Game		Season						
Date	Venue	Versus	W-L-T	Score	G	A	G	A	PTS
2	Boston	Toronto	L	5–2	0	0	13	28	41

1966–1967 Final Standings

	W	L	T	PTS	GF	GA
Chicago	41	17	12	94	264	170
Montreal	32	25	13	77	202	188
Toronto	32	27	11	76	204	211
New York	30	28	12	72	188	189
Detroit	27	39	4	58	212	241
Boston	17	43	10	44	182	253

The 1966–67 awards were handed out during the Stanley Cup finals. In the Hart Trophy (most valuable player) race, Orr finished sixth behind eventual winner Stan Mikita, Ed Giacomin, Bobby Hull, Henri Richard, and Harry Howell.

A scant twelve years later, Richard, Howell, and Orr were inducted together in the Hockey Hall of Fame.

The Norris Trophy (best defenseman) was given to Harry Howell of the New York Rangers. Pierre Pilote of Chicago was runner-up with Bobby Orr holding up the third spot in the voting. Howell was later quoted as saying, "I'm glad I won the trophy this year because Bobby Orr will win it for the next ten years."

Lastly, the Calder Trophy (best rookie) was won overwhelmingly by Orr, who finished with 168 points in the balloting. Orr was followed by Chicago's Ed Van Impe with 86 points, Toronto's Brian Conacher with 47 points, and Orr's roommate Joe Watson with 10 points. Orr became the first Boston player to win a trophy since Don McKenney won the Lady Byng Trophy in the 1959–60 season. In addition to winning the Calder Trophy, Orr was selected to the second All-Star team.

Teammate Eddie Westfall joked about Orr's rookie season in this manner: "I often told this story at functions, especially if Orr was there. We struggled through the early 1960s, and finally, in the 1965–66 season, we moved ahead of the Rangers and finished in fifth place in the standings. And of course, we had been hearing and learning about this messiah, this Moses who was going to lead the Bruins out of the wilderness, this wunderkind, Bobby Orr. And the first year he gets here, we go from fifth back to sixth place."

Detroit's Gordie Howe had this to say about Bobby: "When the other players start watching a kid like Bobby, he must have something. They used to watch me because I could use my stick with either hand, but Orr can do this, and I hardly can see when he changes hands."

Teammate Joe Watson noticed this about Orr: "He held them high on his hands as well. He held them high on the stick and could pass and stickhandle or shoot without sliding them down the shaft. You knew Bobby Hull's slapshot was coming because he dropped his hands low, but with Orr, you could never tell what he was going to do next." Orr later served as the best man at Joe Watson's wedding.

Bobby Orr himself had these season-ending thoughts:

> If I had to pick the hardest man to stop, it would be Stan Mikita of Chicago. He is a heck of a hockey player. Mikita is in complete control of the puck and the game when he is on the ice. The way he sets up his line mates, I don't think they touch the puck until it's on the way to the net.
>
> Gordie Howe is a great player, and so is Bobby Hull. I thought Harry Howell had a heck of a year on defense, and defenseman Tim Horton is pretty good.
>
> Howe is the strongest player, and Hull has a great slap shot. I had a chance to meet both players off the ice. I was very impressed with Bobby Hull. He is a real gentleman. Hull told me if I ever needed advice to give him a call. He is a heck of a guy.

"Orr wasn't good this rookie season, he was sensational" were the words of Kevin Walsh of the *Boston Globe* in his postseason analysis where he got Orr's impressions and hopes on his first NHL campaign. "Nothing that happened on the ice really surprised me," said Orr.

> There are so many good players in this league, you expect them to do the things and play the way they do. I received so much pre-season publicity there was added pressure. It's something a young fellow can do without. I know I can.
>
> There is so much to learn in the N.H.L. I guess I improved over the year. I know I learned a lot. The biggest thing I had to learn as a defenseman was to force the play at the blue line.

Coach Harry Sinden worked with me all year. If you don't make the play at the blue line, you screen the goalie. In this league, if you make a mistake, it results in a goal. It was different in junior hockey. When you made a mistake you could recover and still prevent a goal. This is one of the big differences.

I just have to keep on working. Playing hockey is just like any other job. The more you work at it, the better you get. There are so many good players I don't know who is best.

This is a different life for me. Playing junior hockey, I spent the day going to school. I had to adjust to just playing hockey. I have a lot of spare time now. I read, go to movies, get together with some of the other guys, and take trips to see Boston. All the guys on the Bruins have been good to me. I guess Eddie Johnston has helped me most. He sees everything that is going on in the game and knows more about the players than most of us.

Early in the season, some fans thought players were running at me. I don't think they were doing it because I was a rookie. The guys that did run at everybody. It's part of the game. I never really fight. I don't think I had a fight in junior hockey. This season, I fought in self-defense. If the other players see that you can't defend yourself, they are after you more often.

It has been a good season. Only one thing bothered me playing in Boston—the people in the stands that heckle the team. I didn't hear it that much, but it did bother me to hear the Boston fans heckle some of the guys. Everybody makes mistakes.

On the experiment of playing center: "I was glad the experiment at center lasted only one game. I would have played there if they wanted but I prefer to be a defenseman."

On the improvement of the Bruins: "The team will improve. We will be better next year. The team lost a lot of games by one goal [12]. I know we will make the Stanley Cup Playoffs next season."

On his off-season plans: "I expect to be very busy. I have been asked to do some television work during Stanley Cup play. I am not sure if I can fit the dates into my schedule. I sell cars at an auto dealership back home, and I plan to help my brother who just opened a big sporting goods store. I expect to travel a great deal. I have several banquets to attend. I am involved in a hockey school that will take me to Manitoba and British Columbia."

As the off-season begins for the Bruins, Milt Schmidt is readying himself to take over as General Manager. Hap Emms will be relinquishing the General Manager's post after the NHL expansion draft. With that in mind, an excited Milt had this to say about Orr's worth to the Bruins: "Orr is worth $2,000,000 to us because we are a last place club which can build around him for fifteen to twenty years and don't think we don't intend to do just that." Bruins' ownership and the five other teams' managements were likely not thrilled at Milt's comment.

Changes would be coming to the NHL in a fast and furious manner upon the completion of the league's fiftieth season. Prior to the June meetings and the expansion draft to stock the six new entries into the circuit, the Bruins pulled off a major trade. Near the midnight hour of May 15 when rosters would be frozen for the expansion draft, the Bruins traded promising young defenseman Gilles Marotte, center Pit Martin, both fan favorites, and minor league goaltender Jack Norris to the Chicago Blackhawks. Coming back to Boston were Phil Esposito, Ken Hodge, and Fred Stanfield. Shortly after, center Murray Oliver was shipped off to the Toronto Maple Leafs for rambunctious forward Eddie Shack. The trades would completely change the direction and complexion of the Bruins.

In spite of the ramifications of these trades, the publicity that should have been generated became an undercurrent as the activity of Boston's local baseball team, also longtime patsies, was also changing their direction and complexion, but that's another "Impossible Dream" story to be read in the baseball annals.

It isn't hard to describe the importance of the arrival of Bobby Orr to the Bruins and what it meant to the hockey fans in all of New England. The team had been renting the bottom flats of the National Hockey League standings for eight consecutive seasons. Although the fans still came in large numbers, the murmuring among the faithful was that a prodigy was on the way, be patient. The Garden was filling to 90 percent capacity for each game to see the wunderkind. Despite the hype, Orr exceeded the expectations. If only a few complementary players could be obtained, the Bruins could soon vacate the league's basement.

With the close of the 1966–67 Stanley Cup finals, the "original six" was no longer. It was an era of great memories, intense rivalries, dynasties (see Montreal, Toronto, Detroit), and extended failures (see Boston, New York, Chicago). As these generations of fans fade away, let it be known that being able to remember whole rosters, faces without helmets, goalies without masks, home-and-home series played on consecutive nights, and stars seemingly so bright (think Richard, Beliveau, Howe, Sawchuk, Schmidt, Hull, Hall, Mahovlich, Bower, Bathgate, Worsley), the brightest of them all was an eighteen-year-old, hearty but humble, poised to battle with men whose job it was to extinguish his flame and who, more often than not, could not. Bobby Orr was about to venture into the hearts of grandfathers and grandmothers, dads and moms, brothers and sisters. They had seen no other like him before and probably never like him again.

Excerpts from an Interview with Jim Laing

Jim Laing from the broadcast booth at the Boston Garden, 1966–67 season

During Orr's first season in Boston, television coverage was scant. Video clips would appear on the nightly news at eleven o'clock and the morning news the following day. If you were not at the Garden or you wanted to hear how the Bruins were faring in New York, Montreal, Toronto, Detroit, and Chicago, you depended on the Bruins' radio network with the broadcast originating on WHDH radio, 850 on the AM dial.

Jim Laing broadcasted Bruins' games for one season, 1966–67. It was a historic year for the Bruins and Laing as he described the emergence of Bobby Orr during his first season, which included Orr's first game on October 19 and his first goal on October 23.

The Bruins' great announcer Fred Cusick described Laing's play-by-play as a "dead ringer in voice and inflection for Foster Hewitt, the great announcer of the Toronto Maple Leafs." Laing had been the radio voice of both the Estevan Bruins and the Weyburn Red Wings. The final choice for broadcaster was made by Weston Adams, the President of the Boston Bruins who was impressed with Laing's impartial calling of the game.

Since the Bruins were not on local television at the start of the season, coverage of Orr's first season was almost exclusively broadcasted by Jim Laing.

Q. Did you cover training camp at London, Ontario in the fall of 1966?

A. Yes, WHDH asked me to go to London to do the play-by-play of an exhibition game with Bruins and I think the Rangers. They had a local station engineer there to put my broadcast on reel to reel and sent it to WHDH. I went back to Weyburn to await word as to whether I was going to get the job or not. It depended a lot, I assume, on how happy they were with the tape.

Q. When did you first meet Orr?

A. I was also the play-by-play guy for the Estevan Bruins of the Saskatchewan Junior Hockey League from 1963–1966. In those days, the NHL had direct sponsorship with junior teams in Canada, and Boston Bruins sponsored the Estevan Bruins. Some of the Estevan guys were at the Boston camp when I was there. Joe Watson, Ross Lonsberry, Ted Hodgson, Skip Krake were some of them. These guys ended up staying with Orr in a big house on North Shore, and that's when I met Bobby. Actually, I stayed there a few nights. One night, Alan Eagleson was there with Bobby's dad. The Eagle was playing the piano. Because of the direct relationship between Estevan and Boston, I had met Weston Adams on a couple of occasions on his visits to Estevan, and I know that the only reason I got the Boston job was because of Mr. Adams. After the first week or two, I arranged an interview with the Estevan guys and Bobby. We had to go to the WHDH studios to do it. Bob was pretty shy but cooperative. WHDH would not give me a portable tape machine that I could keep to do player interviews, which would have made our broadcasts more interesting. I would have to drag everyone back to WHDH to do interviews. I did not have a car, so I gave up on the idea.

Q. Orr has been described as a shy teenager. It's hard to believe that you knew him at eighteen and a half? Was he typical teenager, worried about clothes, girls, and a social life?

A. I was only a few years older than Bobby. I don't think he was very worried about girls. I remember one night we returned to the house on the North Shore and there must have been 15–20 cars sitting outside the house on the street with the motors running—full of girls hoping to be invited in.

Q. When you were broadcasting Bruins' games, did you realize that you were describing a historic beginning to a Hall of Fame career?

A. You didn't have to be too brilliant to realize that Orr was that "special" athlete that comes along once in your lifetime. His skating ability and speed was what put him in another class of hockey player. The simple proof of his impact in 1966–67 was evident. Bruins got off to a great start as you describe so well. I think it happened something like this: We were in second place in mid-December. We were at home. Orr was attempting to go between Marcel Pronovost and the boards at Toronto's blue line and Marcel threw one of his famous and punishing hip checks into Orr, and down he went and went off on a stretcher. He was out for six weeks, and we went from second to last place and never got out of the cellar. Coach Harry Sinden said, "If the future of this franchise rests on the shoulders of an eighteen-year-old kid we are in deep trouble," Thus the famous trade with Chicago, which I have always said was the smartest and dumbest trade in the history of hockey. It provided Boston with the Stanley Cup. I recall talking to Fred Cusick prior to the 1967–1968 expansion, and we wondered how the Bruins would be hurt by expansion. We didn't have many good players to lose. We were in last place—and then the magic of the Chicago trade. In those, days it was widely known that those Wirtz folks were very wealthy but not that bright—that trade proved it.

Q. I know you attended a few affairs with Orr. How often did this occur, and does any event stick out in your mind?

A. I emceed a few banquet-type events with Bob and some of the other guys. I have a newspaper clipping of one in North Reading on March 31, 1967, with Bobby, Joe Watson, and John McKenzie. Tickets were $2.50 per person! He was not a "speaker" in those days, so I don't remember anything special. I don't think he was very comfortable in that format. He was an eighteen-year-old shy kid.

Q. Was there any special feeling to opening night at Boston Garden on October 19, 1966?

A. Just the most exciting night of my life, that's all! The odds of a twenty-three-year-old kid from Weyburn, Saskatchewan getting a broadcast job in a six-team NHL would be many millions to one! I was staying at the Somerset Hotel until my wife came to Boston (Ted Williams stayed there), and Bob Wilson phoned me and asked if I wanted to join him and a couple of guys from WHDH for dinner before the game. We ate at the Union Oyster House. Being from the prairies, I had a steak! Later I got up some courage and learned to eat oysters and ate there often. I was nervous, but like the players, once the puck is dropped, it was just like doing any other game but one hell of a lot faster. I knew all the players. There wasn't much to know in those days, and it all went well. It was pretty exciting to see Gordie Howe in the flesh, and of course, Bobby Orr in his first regular season N.H.L. game. A guy from Regina, Saskatchewan, seventy miles from my home town, was living in Boston and was sitting behind our broadcast post and called my name. I turned around, and he took my picture—my first N.H.L broadcast. I still have it hanging on the wall. So glad he was there.

Q. Four nights later, Orr scored his first career goal. Do you remember the call?

A. Honestly I don't. I just remember Orr as the best player in the N.H.L., and how very fortunate I was to be able to see him play in person whenever he was healthy. After that Pronovost event, I was always worried for him, concerned he would get hurt as he played at top speed, wide open and unprotected. He always seemed to me to be very vulnerable. You remember Ted Green's comment: "Orr has fourteen different speeds of fast."

Top Hockey Stories from 1967

Stanley Cup Champions	Toronto Maple Leafs
Art Ross Trophy	Stan Mikita, Chicago Blackhawks
Hart Trophy	Stan Mikita
Lady Byng Trophy	Stan Mikita
Vezina Trophy	Glenn Hall and Denis DeJordy, Chicago Blackhawks
Calder Trophy	Bobby Orr, Boston Bruins
Smythe Trophy	Dave Keon, Toronto Maple Leafs
Norris Trophy	Harry Howell, New York Rangers
Calder Cup Champions	Pittsburgh Hornets
Memorial Cup Champions	Toronto Marlboros
NCAA Hockey Champions	Cornell

The Lester Patrick Trophy was presented to the N.H.L. by the New York Rangers to be awarded annually for outstanding service to hockey in the United States. The first winner was Jack Adams, a member of the Hockey Hall of Fame and longtime executive with the Detroit Red Wings.

Top Sports Stories

World Series Champions	St. Louis Cardinals
Super Bowl II Champions	Green Bay Packers (game played on 1/14/1968 at Orange Bowl, Miami, Florida)
NBA Champions	Philadelphia 76ers
Kentucky Derby Winner	Proud Clarion
NCAA Football Champions	USC
NCAA Basketball Champions	UCLA

Phil Goyette of the Rangers chases Orr in rookie season photo.

1966-'67 BOSTON BRUINS

Front row: Bernie Parent, Weston Adams, Harry Sinden, Johnny Bucyk, Hap Emms, Milt Schmidt, Eddie Johnston. *Middle:* Dan Canney, Ron Murphy, Dallas Smith, Tommy Williams, Eddie Westfall, Ron Stewart, Bobby Orr, Bob Woytowich, Ted Green, Frosty Forristall. *Back:* Ted Hodgson, John McKenzie, Murray Oliver, Bob Dillabough, Wayne Connelly, Joe Watson, Ross Lonsberry, Ron Schock, Gilles Marotte, Gary Doak, Pit Martin.

CHAPTER 2

1967–1968: A New Beginning

W ITH THE SMOKE BEGINNING TO clear from the May 15 trades with Chicago and Toronto, it was time to prepare for the annual league meetings in Montreal in early June. An important milestone occurred during these meetings, as the NHL Players' Association was finally recognized by the league. The association was represented at the gathering by Alan Eagleson, known as the hockey players' lawyer. Orr was and would remain Eagleson's most famous client throughout his playing career.

This year's confab had the additional task of stocking the six new teams that would comprise the Western Division of the National Hockey League. The new teams were spread out geographically from east to central to west on the map of the United States. Ironically, no teams from Canada made the first expansion cut. Games would be played in cities that had not seen the NHL since the 1920s and '30s, Philadelphia, Pittsburgh, and St. Louis. It would also move into new havens like Minneapolis, Oakland and Los Angeles.

The 1967 expansion draft was held in Montreal on June 6, 1967. Each of the six established teams was allowed to protect eleven skaters and one goaltender. The first two rounds focused on the goalies. Once a team lost a goaltender, they were permitted to protect another.

On the bright side, the Bruins did not have to protect Bobby Orr since he still had junior eligibility left. In mid-August, Orr participated in an exhibition game in Winnipeg. During the contest, his right knee sustained damage, and he would need an operation. According to Milt Schmidt, Orr did not have permission to play in the game and had been told to cease all outside activities until the start of training camp, which was scheduled to open on September 7 in London, Ontario. The prognosis on Orr's knee, operated on by Dr. John Palmer, was that it was a sprain of a minor ligament and that Orr would require a cast for three weeks. This would keep him out of the exhibition games until at least late September.

The game was played between a team called the Pro All-Stars and Canada's national team. The match was for the benefit of the Manitoba Hockey Players Benevolent Association. Most of the players were from Manitoba, including Peter Stemkowski of the Toronto Maple Leafs, Joe Daley of the Pittsburgh Penguins, and Bruin teammate Bobby Leiter. Although Ted Green, a Manitoba native, did not play in the game, Leiter did. While General Manager Milt Schmidt was upset about Orr playing in the game, there was no mention of Schmidt being upset that Leiter played in the game. Though clearly miffed at first by the incident, Schmidt calmed down and said, "I'd probably have done the same thing at his age."

As the summer began to wane, the Bruins announced their exhibition slate of games for the coming season. Boston's training site was the Treasure Island Gardens in London, Ontario.

September 15   vs. Toronto at London, Ontario (lose, 6–4)
September 17   vs. New York at Kitchener, Ontario (lose, 7–0)
September 19   vs. New York at London, Ontario (win, 9–3)
September 22   vs. Toronto at Peterboro, Ontario (lose, 4–2)
September 24   vs. Detroit at Hamilton, Ontario (lose, 3–2)
September 26   vs. Detroit at London, Ontario (win, 3–1)
September 29   vs. Chicago at London, Ontario (lose, 3–2)
October 3   vs. New York at Boston Garden (win, 2–1)
October 6   vs. Montreal at Boston Garden (win, 2–1)
October 7   vs. Hershey Bears (AHL) at Hershey to benefit goaltender Claude Dufour, whose career was ended by an eye injury (win 7–3)

One noticeable feature of this Boston team was that they were bigger than any of their predecessors. It certainly could be attributed to the trades made on May 15 when the Bruins bulked up with forwards Phil Esposito, Ken Hodge, and Eddie Shack, all six-footers.

Orr wearing the newly designed uniforms for the 1967–68 Boston Bruins
October 1967

Bobby Orr made his first exhibition game appearance in the Bruins lineup in the 2–1 squeaker against New York on October 3. In the final exhibition game on October 6 against the Montreal Canadiens, a total of 34 penalties for 122 minutes were called as the Bruins nipped the Habs 2–1. Orr received two majors (fights against Ted Harris and Bryan Watson) and a ten-minute misconduct. Orr also injured his hand in the fight with Watson.

The Bruins and visiting teams traditionally used the center ice entrance at Boston Garden to enter the playing surface for games. Starting this season, the Bruins entered the rink, where the Zamboni entered at the east end of the building. The locker rooms, both home and road, were refurnished.

The Bruins also introduced new uniforms for the season with a black home jersey and a white road jersey. The basic uniform and logo would remain the same during Orr's career although the shoulder yokes would be removed after the 1973-1974 season.

Bobby Orr Featured on the Cover of 1967–68 Boston Bruins Official Guide

Bobby Orr's bio appeared on page 21 of the 1967–68 *Bruins' Guide*.

This teenager came into the National Hockey League with one of the greatest build ups ever preceding a rookie, and he lived up to every one of the nice things said about him, on and off the ice. From the first moment he stepped onto the ice at Bruins' training camp, there was never any question but that he was ready to take a regular turn. This was a youngster who had played Junior A amateur hockey for four years since he was 14 and had turned pro at the age of 18. As a junior with Oshawa, he set scoring records for defensemen in each of his last two seasons. Then in his rookie year in the NHL, he had 13 goals and 28 assists for 41 points. No other NHL defensemen scored as many goals as he did. He was the unanimous choice in both halves and overall for the Calder Memorial Trophy as the rookie of the year. He also was named to the second All-Star team and finished up high in

the balloting for the Norris Memorial Trophy, as the league's outstanding defenseman. Through all the publicity and fuss about
him, Bobby never lost his humility. Although he had signed a
whopping two-year contract with a bonus, when he reported to
the Bruins' London, Ontario, training camp, he called veteran
players Mr. Bucyk and Mr. Johnston. When the 1966–67 season
was over, he thanked each of the Boston writers individually for
what they had done for him during the year. The past summer,
Orr travelled from coast to coast, making public appearances and
teaching at hockey schools. An enterprising young man, he is
in the sporting goods business with his brother in Parry Sound,
Ontario with an eye to the future.

For the second season in a row, the Bruins opened at home against the Detroit
Red Wings. Orr registered two assists in the 4–4 tie against the Wings. In the season's
second game, the Bruins, behind four goals by newly acquired Esposito, thrashed the
Canadiens at the Boston Garden by a score of 6–2.

In the first road game of the season, the Bruins traveled to Chicago to meet the
Blackhawks. Chicago, in recent seasons, had routinely handled the Bruins, but this
night, it was a little different. With Phil Esposito, Ken Hodge, and Fred Stanfield
returning to the Windy City for the first time since the May trade to Boston, the
Bruins swept the Blackhawks by a 7–1 score. Orr scored his first goal of the season
at 7:06 of the second period. Fred Stanfield powered home two goals for the B's. The
game was a painful reminder to Blackhawk fans that the Bruins had swindled the
Hawks out of three (Esposito, Hodge, Stanfield) useful players.

The Bruins moved on to meet the Red Wings in Detroit the next evening. For
the third game in a row, Boston scored at least six goals. Orr assisted on Eddie Shack's
third-period goal as the Bruins doubled up on the Wings by a score of 6–3. Stanfield
scored two markers in twenty-seven seconds of each other midway through the third
period. Two nights later, it was the bright lights of *Hockey Night in Canada* and a
Saturday match against the Canadiens in Montreal.

Orr opened the scoring with an unassisted first-period goal, but the Montreal
sextet responded with four straight in a 4–2 Habs victory over the Bruins.

Next up on the docket at Boston Garden would be the inaugural game against a
West Division rival, this being the purple and gold of Jack Kent Cooke's Los Angeles
Kings. The Bruins peppered 40 shots on Kings' goalie Wayne Rutledge on route to
a 2–0 victory.

The Pittsburgh Penguins made their first ever trip into Boston on Sunday,
October 29. Before a sellout crowd, the Bruins edged the Penguins by a 4–2 score.
Orr tallied an assist on Esposito's first-period goal, while Eddie Shack scored two for

the Bruins. As a precaution, Coach Sinden sat out Orr in the third period, as he had been suffering from a strained back muscle.

With the first month of the schedule now history, Bruins' fans were already comparing the team to the just completed Red Sox "Impossible Dream" squad. The chant of "It's the Bruins turn" was being heard all over the region. Even Celtics' coach Bill Russell said, "We can't afford to lose a game in the same town with the Red Sox and Bruins."

The Bruins ended October in third place behind Detroit and Montreal in the new East Division. In another note on this successful October, Boston had its first winning opening month since the 1958–1959 season when they went 4-3-3. The 1958–1959 season was also the last time the Bruins qualified for the playoffs.

October 1967					Orr's Stats				
					Game		Season		
Date	Venue	Versus	W-L-T	Score	G	A	G	A	PTS
11	Boston	Detroit	T	4–4	0	2	0	2	2
15	Boston	Montreal	W	6–2	0	0	0	2	2
18	Chicago	Blackhawks	W	7–1	1	0	1	2	3
19	Detroit	Red Wings	W	6–3	0	1	1	3	4
21	Montreal	Canadiens	L	4–2	1	0	2	3	5
26	Boston	Los Angeles	W	2–0	0	0	2	3	5
29	Boston	Pittsburgh	W	4–2	0	1	2	4	6

November 1967

Ex-Bruins figure prominently in the Bruins first road game against the West Division as they traveled to St. Louis on November 1. Ron Stewart scored the first two goals of the game for the Blues while Wayne Rivers netted the third Blues' goal as St. Louis coasted to a 5–1 win over Boston. Orr's back problems kept him out of the game.

The Bruins were involved in a bench-clearing brawl during the November 5 game against Toronto in Boston Garden. Brian Conacher's high stick to Bobby Orr's face precipitated the brawl in a game that ended in a 2–2 deadlock. Orr had scored the first goal of the game for the Bruins. Bob Pulford of Toronto was unsuccessful in a penalty shot attempt against Gerry Cheevers in the Boston net.

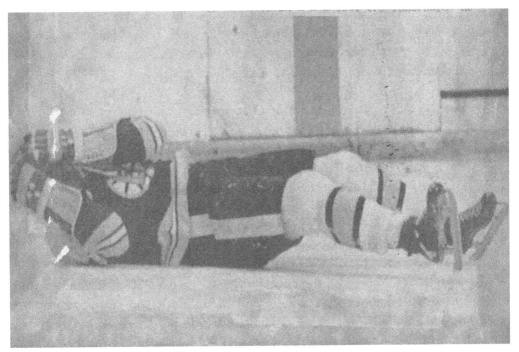

November 5, 1967, Boston Garden. Bobby Orr covers his face
after being hit in the nose by Toronto's Brian Conacher.

As far as the brawl was concerned, Orr received three stitches on the bridge of his now-broken nose. He also sprained his thumb in the ensuing melee. With the Bruins on a power play, Conacher was moving out of the Leafs' zone. Orr made a move at him just inside the blue line when Conacher's stick came up and struck Orr on the bridge of his nose. As Orr was down holding his bleeding proboscis, little Johnny McKenzie chased after Conacher, caught him, and tackled him. After Orr had received first aid from the trainer, he also went after Conacher. When Orr started to pummel him, blood from his nose splattered all over Conacher's white Toronto jersey.

The game summary reports that Captain George Armstrong of the Leafs led the charge off the bench to aid Conacher. As the Leafs followed onto the ice, the Bruins' bench quickly emptied, and the donnybrook was on. After Orr and Conacher were separated, Ken Hodge chased down Conacher for another battle. When things finally calmed down, Orr and Conacher had received major penalties.

From the Boston perspective, the incident was deemed deliberate. Coach Harry Sinden said, "There is no doubt in my mind that it was deliberate. I'm not saying it was premeditated, but it happened right in front of our bench, and from where I was standing, it was a two-handed swing."

From the Maple Leafs' point of view, Conacher had this to say: "I have no comment. I was playing the game of hockey, and you saw what happened." Assistant

General Manager King Clancy said of Conacher, "As clean a player as ever came into this league. It's a damn shame Orr jumped on him when he was being held by two of the Bruins." Orr only played one more shift for the rest of the game. Every player leaving the bench received a twenty-five-dollar fine.

Poem on a Proboscis

Who broke the nose of Bobby Orr,
And bathed our star in his own gore,
To start the brawl we must deplore?
Young Brian, of the Clan Conacher.

(Harold Kaese, *Boston Globe*, November 8, 1967)

Later, Orr commented on the episode with Conacher: "I was in the best position to know what happened. The fellow lifted my stick and swung at my face. That's not easy to take." Although Orr had trouble sleeping and was nursing a sore thumb from the pounding he handed Conacher, he was still scheduled to play on Wednesday night in New York.

Brian Conacher had this to say about the incident: "I wasn't mad at Orr before or after the play, but I can understand Orr being mad. How do you fight fifteen guys? I had no reason to fight. My eyes were burning, and I was more concerned with it than taking on the whole Bruins' team."

A few days after the incident, Kevin Walsh of the *Boston Globe* penned an open letter to Orr titled "Chasing Conacher Error—Hurts B's" a letter very critical of Orr's behavior. After seventeen critical paragraphs, Walsh closed with this advice to Orr: "At nineteen, you are on the threshold of being a superstar. Don't let a low boiling point overshadow your ability."

The damage to Orr's nose was seen on the cover of the December 11 issue of *Sports Illustrated* titled "Hockey's Wildest Season." The magazine had been reporting about the expanded N.H.L. and the rise of the Boston Bruins. This would be the first of five *Sports Illustrated* covers on which Orr would appear.

The Bruins next game was Wednesday evening, the 8th, in New York. For an early season contest, it would give a good indication on the status of the Bruins since the Rangers also had an improved club.

Rookie Derek Sanderson scored two goals to lead the Bruins past the Rangers at Madison Square Garden by a score of 6–3. Orr scored a third-period power play goal.

The Bruins hosted new West Division teams—the Oakland Seals and Philadelphia Flyers—on the weekend of November 11 and 12. The B's defeated the Seals 2–1 in a squeaker on Saturday but lost to the Philadelphia Flyers by a score of

4–2 on Sunday. In the Oakland contest, Orr had his nose broken for the second time in a week when he was hit by Billy Hicke of the Seals. Ex-Bruin goaltender Bernie Parent stopped thirty-seven of thirty-nine shots in the loss to the Flyers. The Bruins, looking slightly out of sorts, got the next day off. It was the team's first off day since training camp began in September.

Mike Walton of the Leafs fired the three-goal hat trick in Toronto's 4–2 victory over the Bruins at Maple Leaf Gardens on November 15. Two of Walton's scores were against Gerry Cheevers while the other goal was against Eddie Johnston. Coach Sinden thought that Cheevers was not sharp and changed goaltenders. Orr assisted on Derek Sanderson's third-period tally.

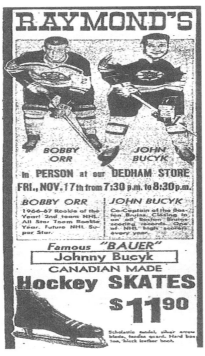

This ad for Raymond's Department Store appeared in the
local Boston papers during the 1967–68 season.

After spotting the Rangers a one-goal lead, the Bruins came back and scored three unanswered goals in a 3–1 win over New York at the Boston Garden. Orr assisted Bucyk on his late third-period score in a game played on November 18.

The next evening, the B's hosted the Toronto Maple Leafs. With former Leaf Eddie Shack leading the way with two goals, the Bruins romped over Toronto, 6–2. Orr assisted on goals by Phil Esposito and Glen Sather. Boston outshot the Leafs 56 to 23. When Leafs' coach Punch Imlach took out goaltender Johhny Bower late in the second period, he received a long and thunderous ovation from the sellout crowd of 13,909. After the game, the alleged forty-three-year-old Bower claimed he was touched by the tribute of the Boston fans. A fan favorite, Bower had a history of prevaricating his age.

A late Tuesday afternoon flight to Pittsburgh helped prepare the Bruins for their first game in the Steel City since February 12, 1930. The Pittsburgh entry in the N.H.L. at the time was known as the Pirates. In the present-day encounter on November 22, the Penguins rolled past the Bruins, 4–1. With little time to lick their wounds, the team headed back to Boston for an encounter with the Rangers on the next evening. When the Bruins bested the New York Rangers 4–2, they moved into a first place tie with the Toronto Maple Leafs. Johnny Bucyk scored twice to pace the Boston win.

Hockey Night in Canada featured the legendary B's-Habs rivalry. After Montreal scored the first goal of the game, the Bruins bounced back with three straight scores and defeated Les Habs, 3–1. Orr assisted on Ken Hodge's game-winning goal in the third frame.

Back in Boston the next evening, Johnny McKenzie's three goals sparked the Bruins to a 7–5 win over Detroit at Boston Garden. Bobby Orr scored a second period power play goal on a setup by Phil Esposito.

November 1967					Orr's Stats				
					Game		Season		
Date	Venue	Versus	W-L-T	Score	G	A	G	A	PTS
1	St. Louis	Blues	L	5–1	DNP		2	4	6
5	Boston	Toronto	T	2–2	1	0	3	4	7
8	New York	Rangers	W	6–3	1	0	4	4	8
11	Boston	Oakland	W	2–1	0	0	4	4	8
12	Boston	Philadelphia	L	4–2	0	0	4	4	8
15	Toronto	Maple Leafs	L	4–2	0	1	4	5	9
18	Boston	New York	W	3–1	0	1	4	6	10
19	Boston	Toronto	W	6–2	0	2	4	8	12
22	Pittsburgh	Penguins	L	4–1	0	0	4	8	12
23	Boston	New York	W	4–2	0	0	4	8	12
25	Montreal	Canadiens	W	3–1	0	1	4	9	13
26	Boston	Detroit	W	7–5	1	0	5	9	14
29	Boston	Minnesota	W	5–1	0	0	5	9	14

The Minnesota North Stars made their first ever appearance at Boston Garden on November 29. The Bruins defeated the Stars, 5–1. Johnny Bucyk's two goals, his eleventh and twelfth of the season, put him number one on the all-time Bruins' goal scoring list, tying Milt Schmidt with 229 goals scored.

The Bruins ended November on top of the East Division, two points over second place Detroit.

December 1967

At the winter baseball meeting in Mexico City, it was reported that Red Sox manager Dick Williams had sublet his North Shore Gardens apartment in Peabody to Orr. He shared the apartment with Gary Doak, Eddie Johnston, and trainer John Forristall.

The Bruins opened the month of December on top of the East Division. On the first Saturday night of December, the Blackhawks moved into the Boston Garden. John Bucyk scored two goals, but Chico Maki's third-period goal gave the Hawks a 4–4 tie. Orr received an assist on a first-period goal by John McKenzie. Bucyk's two goals lofted him into the number one spot on the Bruins' all-time-goal scoring list.

The next evening, the Montreal Canadiens were in town, and the Bruins vaulted into first place again. Before another Sunday-night sellout crowd of 13,909, the Bruins literally outbrawled the Canadiens, 5–3. In the scoring department, McKenzie fired home two goals while Bobby Orr scored an unassisted goal and had an assist on Johnny Bucyk's second-period marker.

Fisticuffs played a major role in the game. Eleven major penalties, three game misconducts, and two misconducts were doled out by referee Art Skov. The main event of the first period started when Montreal's Ralph Backstrom was high-sticked in the Boston crease. Longtime hockey writer Stan Fischler described it thusly: "The action of the Bruins against Backstom so piqued defenseman Terry Harper that he led the charge off the Montreal bench. It was a noble crusade but less than smart from a tactical viewpoint because he skated in a straight line for Ted Green. Teddy's arm withdrew into sock formation, and Harper went down in a straight line." The bench-clearing brawl, the second involving the Bruins in less than a month, delayed the game for twenty-five minutes. In all, $1,625 in fines was assessed against both teams.

After three days off, the Bruins returned to action with a Thursday night game at the Garden with the visiting New York Rangers. Orr scored his seventh goal of the season as the Bruins edged the New Yorkers, 3–1.

On Saturday night at Maple Leaf Gardens, the Bruins and Leafs played to a 3–3 draw before the second largest crowd (16,157) in the thirty-six-year history of Maple Leaf Gardens. The Bruins had led the game by a 3–0 score on two goals by Fred Stanfield but allowed Toronto back in the game with Leafs' Captain George Armstrong scoring the tying goal with three seconds left on the clock. More importantly, the Bruins suffered two serious injuries in the contest. Big Leafs' winger Frank

Mahovlich was involved in both injuries. One of Frank's slappers badly bruised Ted Green's right knee. Another Mahovlich rocket broke Orr's collar bone. Initial indications were that Orr would be out for a month.

Back in Boston, the next evening, the B's lost to the expansion Los Angeles Kings by a score of 3–1. On the 13th, they faced Montreal, where they also went down to defeat, this time by a 6–2 score. Both games were played without Orr.

The Bruins headed for California, and their first ever encounters on the West Coast. In the Friday tilt in Oakland, the Bruins were beaten by a score of 4–1 before 6,095 fans in the Oakland Coliseum. The next evening, Stanfield's two goals paced the Bruins to a 5–2 victory in a game played at the Los Angeles Sports Arena. This marks the only game in Bruins' history played at the South Figueora Street site since the Kings would be moving into the new Fabulous Forum in a few days.

After the West Coast swing, it was on to Chicago Stadium and a midweek game with the Hawks. Bobby and Dennis Hull each scored two goals to lift the Chihawks over the B's by a 6–3 margin. Derek Sanderson potted two for the losers before 16,666 roaring fans.

The four-game road trip ended in New York as rookie goaltender Andre Gill called up from Hershey of the American Hockey League, recorded the 4–0 shutout. The victory, Boston's seventeenth of the season, matched the win total for the entire 1966–67 campaign.

In an interview with Tom Fitzgerald of the *Boston Globe*, Orr expressed frustration with his injury and his plan to return to game action. "I've done a little cooking for myself, and I try to keep busy, but I get restless. It's just as well that I'm single. It would be a nuisance for anybody to have me around the house at a time like this. The shoulder is not sore now, and I've skated at the Lynn Arena. It really won't take me long to get ready once I get permission to play." Orr expressed displeasure at some fans during the recent three-game losing streak. "You'd think it was the end of something. I just can't understand people. The guys showed in Los Angeles that this team can come back." Bobby believed the effect of his own absence was somewhat magnified by those wavering believers who originated the slogan, "Without Orr, we're number 4."

While Orr was convalescing from his injury, he delighted in an unusual assignment. Bobby would be an honorary godfather at the christening of Patricia Boyle, infant daughter of Don and Peg Boyle of Lynn, Massachusetts. Don and Peg were among the first friends Orr made in the Boston area the previous spring.

During Orr's absence, the team garnered a record of two wins and four losses. For the third time in two months, the Bruins were involved in a bench clearing brawl. The event occurred on, of all nights, Christmas night at the Boston Garden. The opponent for the contest was the Oakland Seals. The brawl was precipitated when the Bruins Ken Hodge and the Seals Charlie Burns got into a row along the boards. When Seals' goaltender Gary Smith left his crease and intervened, players from both benches reported for combat. Seals' coach, Bert Olmstead, also left the bench, wielding a hockey stick while going after a fan sitting rink side. In all, fines of $1,450 were assessed to both teams. As for the game, Bobby Orr returned to action after missing six games due to his collarbone injury. The Bruins doubled up on the Seals by a score of 6–3. Rookie Derek Sanderson fired home two goals for the winners.

Two nights later, the Bruins faced the Chicago Blackhawks at the Garden. The Hawks scored the first and last goals of the game, but unfortunately for Chicago, they were sandwiched around seven Boston scores. Former Hawk Phil Esposito had the "hat trick," and Eddie Shack scored two goals in the seven-goal onslaught. Orr garnered two assists for the B's. The win moved the Bruins into a first place tie with Chicago. The Bruins now headed out on a six-game road trip featuring their first visits to Minneapolis–St. Paul and Philadelphia.

Will McDonough of the *Boston Globe* reported that Orr's recent collarbone injury, which was reported, was also accompanied by a shoulder separation, which was not reported.

In the Bruins first ever visit to Minnesota, the North Stars squeaked past the B's by a 5–4 score. Bill Masterton, who would later pass away after a head injury, scored a goal for the Stars. Orr had an assist on Johnny Bucyk's first-period goal. After the game, the Bruins headed for Detroit and a New Year's Eve game with the Red Wings.

In the Detroit game, Bruce MacGregor and Norm Ullman scored two goals each as the Bruins were downed by the Wings, 6–4. Orr assisted on the first goal of the game by John McKenzie.

As 1967 ended, the Bruins were in a first place tie with the Chicago Blackhawks. The Bruins, by way of playing three less games, stood over the Hawks although both teams had 42 points.

December 1967					Orr's Stats				
					Game		Season		
Date	Venue	Versus	W-L-T	Score	G	A	G	A	PTS
2	Boston	Chicago	T	4–4	0	1	5	10	15
3	Boston	Montreal	W	5–3	1	1	6	11	17
7	Boston	New York	W	3–1	1	0	7	11	18
10	Boston	Los Angeles	L	3–1	DNP		7	11	18
13	Boston	Montreal	L	6–2	DNP		7	11	18
15	Oakland	Seals	L	4–1	DNP		7	11	18
16	Los Angeles	Kings	W	5–2	DNP		7	11	18
20	Chicago	Blackhawks	L	6–3	DNP		7	11	18
23	New York	Rangers	W	4–0	DNP		7	11	18

25	Boston	Oakland	W	6–3	0	0	7	11	18
27	Boston	Chicago	W	7–2	0	2	7	13	20
30	Minnesota	North Stars	L	5–4	0	1	7	14	21
31	Detroit	Red Wings	L	6–4	0	1	7	15	22

January 1968

The Bruins opened the 1968 portion of the schedule on January 3 at Madison Square Garden in New York. In spite of holding 3–1 and 5–3 leads over the Rangers, New York came back with two goals in the third period to tie the Bruins 5–5.

The next evening, the Bruins made their first trip to Philadelphia since February 24, 1931, when they defeated the now defunct Philadelphia Quakers by a score of 5–1. On this occasion, the score was a bit closer, but the Bruins prevailed by a 3–2 count. With the win, the Bruins moved back into a first place tie with Chicago. Esposito scored two goals in the third period to ice the victory for Boston.

After the game, former teammate Joe Watson had this to say about Orr: "That Orr is the greatest defenseman I've ever seen. I learned a lot by playing with him. When he is playing his regular game, there is no finer defenseman anywhere." Orr would later serve as the best man in Watson's wedding.

On Friday morning, the Bruins gathered for the flight to Toronto and a Saturday night engagement with the Maple Leafs. The contest ended in a 3–3 draw, and with the tie, the B's fell out of first place in the East Division standings. Orr scored his eighth goal of the season, which turned out to be the game-tying goal late in the second period. After the game, the Bruins headed to Chicago for a first-place showdown the next evening.

While playing their fourth game in five nights, the Bruins ran out of gas. Being at the tail end of a long road trip, the B's were expecting to look rather tired. Instead, they played one of their strongest games in recent weeks. However, Bobby Hull netted his four hundredth career goal, and Chicago defeated the Bruins by a 4–2 margin.

In the loss, Hull was awarded a goal after being interfered at the Boston bench. The Bruins were playing with the extra man on the ice while trying to erase a 3–2 Hawk lead late in the game. As Hull broke out heading to the empty Bruins' goal, he passed the Bruins' bench, where goaltender Gerry Cheevers had retreated for the extra man. When Hull passed by, Cheevers reached over the boards with his stick and checked the puck off his stick. Hull recovered the puck and scored on the empty net, although Referee Vern Buffey would have allowed the goal due to interference from the bench.

With the next three days off, the Bruins got much needed rest before their next game against the Detroit Red Wings. In the meantime, Toe Blake, coach of the Montreal Canadiens named Orr and Johnny Bucyk to the All-Star team that would face the Stanley Cup Champion Maple Leafs on January 18.

After a fourteen-day hiatus, the Bruins returned to the Garden on January 11. Esposito scored two goals, and Orr assisted on Sanderson's game winner as the Bruins took out the Red Wings by a 5–4 margin. At one point in the game, the Bruins held a 3–0 lead but had to stave off the charging Wings before securing the victory.

Two nights later, the Bruins were back in Montreal to meet the Habs. The Canadiens coasted to an easy 5–1 win paced by John Ferguson's two goals. Near the conclusion of the game, Orr and Montreal's Yvan Cournoyer became involved in a fight resulting in each player receiving two minors and one major penalty.

A restless mood enveloped the Boston Garden the next night as the Bruins were scheduled to meet the Minnesota North Stars in a 7:30 p.m. Sunday contest. The Stars were hung up by a snowstorm in the Midwest and did not arrive until just before the original game time. The contest was delayed an hour. Once the game started, the Bruins easily handed the North Stars winning by a score of 9–2. Esposito and Stanfield each deposited two goals while Orr notched his ninth of the season.

On a very somber note, the NHL experienced the first fatal on-ice casualty in history. On the previous evening in Minnesota, Bill Masterton of the North Stars was checked heavily by two Oakland defensemen, flipped backward, and crashed headfirst to the ice. Masterton was kept alive for thirty hours by use of a respirator before he finally succumbed to his injuries.

The Bill Masterton trophy has been awarded since 1968 by the Professional Hockey Writers' Association to the National Hockey League player who best exemplifies the qualities of perseverance, sportsmanship, and dedication to hockey.

The Minnesota North Stars appeared at the Boston Garden on January 14, 1968. Bill Masterton was scheduled to play in this contest but suffered a life ending injury the previous evening. Masterton passed away on January 15, 1968, and is the only player in league history to die as a direct result of injuries suffered during a contest.

The NHL All-Star Game was played on January 16 in Toronto. Orr and Bucyk represented the Bruins' in the game. Orr assisted on Maple Leaf Norm Ullman's goal at 8:23 of the third period. Orr was voted the number 3 star of the game. First star of the game went to Toronto goaltender Bruce Gamble, while the second star was awarded to Chicago's Stan Mikita.

During the game, Orr was injured when he was hit by Leafs' winger Peter Stemkowski. He suffered a muscle injury to the right shoulder. It was the fourth time in his young career that he had been injured in games involving the Maple Leafs. "I just thought it was a bruise. It didn't hurt at the time. I didn't think much of it," said the exasperated Orr. General Manager Milt Schmidt, who attended the game, added, "I saw Bobby coming off the ice. He was favoring his right arm. He didn't say anything to anyone. The first I heard of it was in the morning. He called me in my room and said he couldn't raise his right arm."

Two nights later back in Boston, the Bruins hosted the Leafs in the first of three straight home games. Despite holding leads of 1–0 and 2–1, the Leafs slipped past the Orr-less Bruins by a score of 4–2. "I certainly didn't miss Orr," said Leafs' coach Punch Imlach after the game. "But I guess the Bruins missed him."

In the nationally televised Saturday afternoon game against the Philadelphia Flyers at the Boston Garden, the Bruins, paced on goals by Bucyk, Green, Williams, and Hodge, defeated the Flyers by a score of 4–2. Orr sat out for the second straight game. The next evening, Stan Mikita, Bobby Hull, and the Chicago Blackhawks visited the Garden to complete the Boston three-game home stand.

Six different Bruins scored goals as the Bruins throttled the Hawks by a score of 6–0. Gerry Cheevers made thirty-three saves in the win. The goals scorers for Boston were Westfall, Esposito, Shack, Stanfield, Sanderson, and Glen Sather. With the win, the Bruins moved into first place in the East Division. The game also featured a stick-swinging dual by ex-teammates Ted Green of the Bruins and Doug Mohns of the Hawks. Both players were assessed match penalties and tossed from the game.

The Bruins would now embark on their longest winless streak of the season, a total of six games that included four losses and two ties. In the first game of the streak, the B's traveled to Madison Square Garden to take on the Rangers. The team fell short by a 2–1 margin. The following evening, they hosted the Montreal Canadiens at the Garden in the first of back to back games with the Montrealers.

The loss to the Habs by a score of 2–0 was the first time that season the Bruins had been shut out. Goaltender Rogatien Vachon, who managed 21 saves in the game, pitched the shutout for Montreal. It was also the first time in the last sixty-eight games, extending into the previous season that the B's had been blanked. Orr returned for the game and got a standing ovation when he took the ice for the first time.

On Saturday night in Montreal, the B's suffered their third straight loss, 5–2, though Orr did manage two assists in the losing effort.

The next evening, the Bruins were back in the friendly confines of the Boston Garden, but Pittsburgh goaltender Les Binkley spoiled the visit by blanking the Bruins, 1–0. Binkley was outstanding, making 33 saves, and eventually received a standing ovation from the sold-out Garden. George Konik scored the lone goal for the Penguins when he shot it off the skate of a Bruin defender.

Orr, Stan Mikita, and Bobby Hull of the Blackhawks were all selected as unanimous choices for the NHL's midseason All-Star team.

As the month of January folded, the Bruins fell out of the top spot in the East Division and tumbled to third place behind Montreal and Toronto.

January 1968					Orr's Stats				
					Game		Season		
Date	Venue	Versus	W-L-T	Score	G	A	G	A	PTS
3	New York	Rangers	T	5–5	0	0	7	15	22
4	Philadelphia	Flyers	W	3–2	0	0	7	15	22
6	Toronto	Maple Leafs	T	3–3	1	0	8	15	23
7	Chicago	Blackhawks	L	4–2	0	1	8	16	24
11	Boston	Detroit	W	5–4	0	1	8	17	25
13	Montreal	Canadiens	L	5–1	0	0	8	17	25
14	Boston	Minnesota	W	9–2	1	0	9	17	26
18	Boston	Toronto	L	4–2	DNP		9	17	26
20	Boston	Philadelphia	W	4–2	DNP		9	17	26
21	Boston	Chicago	W	6–0	DNP		9	17	26
24	New York	Rangers	L	2–1	DNP		9	17	26
25	Boston	Montreal	L	2–0	0	0	9	17	26
27	Montreal	Canadiens	L	5–2	0	2	9	19	28
28	Boston	Pittsburgh	L	1–0	0	0	9	19	28

February 1968

The Bruins opened February with a contest against the Chicago Blackhawks at the Garden. Behind Orr's goal and assist, the Bruins managed to stop their four-game losing streak but had to settle for a 4–4 finish with the Chihawks. Orr's goal at 18:01, a spectacular rush that had him end up in the net with the puck, sent the sellout crowd into a frenzy. However, two goals by Dennis Hull, the latter at the 19:00 mark of the third period, helped the Hawks avoid defeat.

On Saturday night, the Bruins entertained the Rangers at the North End rail station. With the fifth-place Rangers nipping at their heels, the Bruins needed some points to widen the gap between the two teams as the playoff push was now on. Going into the third period, the Bruins were up 3–2, but a goal by ex-Bruin Ron Stewart helped the Rangers to a 3–3 draw with the B's.

The next evening, the Bruins hosted the Detroit Red Wings back at the Garden. On a solo rush with a rare assist from Gerry Cheevers, Orr led off the scoring at 1:13 of the opening frame. Gordie Howe tied it up some seven minutes later, but McKenzie fired home three goals as the B's defeated Detroit by a final of 5–4. This was McKenzie's second hat trick of the season, the first coming last November 26 against these same Red Wings. The win ended the Bruins' six-game winless streak.

The team now moved on to a brief Midwest swing through St. Louis and Detroit. For the second consecutive game, a Bruin enjoyed a hat trick. This time it was Eddie Westfall who did the honors as the Bruins bested the Blues by a 6–4 score. Orr played only one shift in the last two periods as his right knee continued to bother him. Coach Harry Sinden said Orr remained on the bench because of difficulty with the knee "that has been troubling him for a couple of weeks."

The victory in St. Louis was marred by a disputed goal scored by McKenzie. After he shot on goal, the puck reverted in the other direction, where Al Arbour fired on Eddie Johnston to score the game tying goal. However, the goal was disallowed when Linesman Brent Casselman convinced Referee Bob Sloan that the puck McKenzie had originally shot on goal had entered the St. Louis net. The goal judge, Rich Schweigler, did not see the puck enter the cage.

Orr Lost 4-5 Weeks, Faces Surgery

In a nationally televised game, the Bruins and Red Wings played to a 1–1 draw at the Olympia. Orr did not play but was examined by the Detroit doctors. The diagnosis on Orr's left knee was that the cartilage was damaged, and it would take an operation to fix it. "It locks up on him, and it is getting worse. When he lifts the leg up and tries to skate, the joint sticks and won't come down easily," declared the B's general manager Milt Schmidt.

Back in Boston, Orr would be examined by team physicians to determine the exact extent of the injury. On Sunday evening, the Bruins hosted the St. Louis Blues and played to a 3–3 tie without Orr in lineup.

On Monday, February 12, Orr went under the knife at the Newton-Wellesley Hospital. "The operation was completely successful and badly needed," said Dr. Ronald Adams, who performed the procedure. "There is no reason to assume Bobby can't skate in five weeks," the doctor continued. Barry Gibbs was recalled from Oklahoma City to replace Orr in the lineup.

While Orr was recovering from his latest operation, the Boston newshounds began speculation on his contract status. The original document was a two-year deal, which would conclude at the end of this season. Orr's superior talents had been on display since he first suited up the previous season. The Bruins were drawing consistent sellouts, making the top brass extremely happy but also aware that Orr's value as a player was skyrocketing.

Toronto attorney Alan Eagleson would be handling the contract talks as Orr's agent, coming face-to-face with Bruins' attorney Charles Mulcahy. Eagleson opined that "there would be a good many meetings, but I'm sure we'll reach a satisfactory agreement before next season. If Bobby isn't a millionaire by the time he is forty, we'll have done something wrong. Barring injury or any untoward development, he could make that by the time he is thirty."

The Bruins now embarked on a seven-game road trip beginning Valentine's Day in Chicago. Bobby Hull scored a goal for Chicago as the second place Hawks edged the fourth-place Bruins, 2–1. The second West Coast swing of the season was now upon the team. First up would be the Seals in Oakland.

For the second consecutive game, the offense was anemic and the Bruins went down to defeat by a score of 3–1. After the game, the team chartered to Los Angeles for a contest the next evening. It would be the team's first visit to Jack Kent Cooke's Fabulous Forum. On top of the looming game, they were now enveloped in a four-game winless streak.

The winless skein ended in Los Angeles as the B's nudged out the Kings, 6–5. The Bruins moved on to Minnesota, where they would face the North Stars in a Wednesday night encounter. After Skip Krake's early first period tally, the North Stars scored four straight goals on the way to a 5–3 win. Former Bruin Wayne Connelly scored two goals for the winners as the Bruins were now 1–3 on their annual February foray away from the Garden.

The next night, the Bruins were in Detroit for a game against the Red Wings. Phil Esposito's third-period score, twenty-seven seconds after Gordie Howe had tied the game for Detroit proved to be the game winner as the B's defeated the Wings, 3–2.

A full house of 16,149 partisan fans was on hand at Maple Leaf Gardens where the B's and Leafs prepared to do a Saturday night battle. The Leafs squeaked by the Bruins, 1–0, as Toronto rookie defenseman Jim McKenney scored the lone goal of the game at 4:33 of the third stanza. Gerry Cheevers stopped 43 of 44 shots while Bruce Gamble, in goal for the Leafs, swept aside all thirty-four Boston chances.

The road trip finally concluded with a visit to the Igloo in Pittsburgh. Before a small crowd of 6,546 fans, the Bruins took a 5–3 win over the Penguins. Skip Krake's first period shorthanded goal, and Ken Hodge's two markers paced the Bruins to the victory.

The Bruins dropped another notch in the standings at the end of February, now taking up residence in fourth place of the East Division behind Montreal, Chicago, and New York.

After the seven-game road swing, the Bruins returned to Boston Garden for a Leap Day game with the Toronto Maple Leafs. Derek Sanderson scored twice, and Gerry Cheevers stopped thirty shots as the Bruins moved past the Leafs by a 4–1 score. On Sunday evening, the Bruins hosted the St. Louis Blues at the Garden.

February 1968					Orr's Stats				
					Game		Season		
Date	Venue	Versus	W-L-T	Score	G	A	G	A	PTS
1	Boston	Chicago	T	4–4	1	1	10	20	30
3	Boston	New York	T	3–3	0	0	10	20	30
4	Boston	Detroit	W	5–4	1	0	11	20	31
7	St. Louis	Blues	W	6–4	0	0	11	20	31
10	Detroit	Red Wings	T	1–1	0	0	11	20	31
11	Boston	St. Louis	T	3–3	DNP		11	20	31
14	Chicago	Blackhawks	L	3–1	DNP		11	20	31
17	Oakland	Seals	L	3–1	DNP		11	20	31
18	Los Angeles	Kings	W	6–5	DNP		11	20	31
21	Minnesota	North Stars	L	5–3	DNP		11	20	31
22	Detroit	Red Wings	W	3–2	DNP		11	20	31
24	Toronto	Maple Leafs	L	1–0	DNP		11	20	31
27	Pittsburgh	Penguins	W	5–3	DNP		11	20	31
29	Boston	Toronto	W	4–1	DNP		11	20	31

March 1968

Eddie Shack scored the first hat trick of his career in a 9–3 rout of the St. Louis Blues in Boston on March 3. Bucyk also scored two goals for the B's. It was onto Chicago for a midweek game against the Blackhawks at the Stadium. When Kenny Wharram of the Hawks scored his second goal to make it 3–0, the Hawks appeared ready to rout the Bruins. Instead, Boston countered with goals by Hodge, Sather, McKenzie, Esposito, and Bucyk to roll past Chicago by a 5–3 margin before a packed house of 16,666 fans. The next evening, the Bruins were scheduled to play the Flyers in Philadelphia; however, a major problem prevented the game from being played there.

A late winter storm in Philadelphia caused the roof of the Spectrum to blow off. The March 7 game against the Flyers was moved to Maple Leaf Gardens in Toronto. Ken Hodge and Gary Doak scored for the Bruins, and Gerry Cheevers made thirty-nine saves in the 2–1 Boston victory over the Flyers before 10,452 fans.

Sometimes, a hockey game can turn ugly, and this game was solid proof when a vicious stick swinging duel erupted between Larry Zeidel of the Flyers and Eddie Shack of the Bruins. Zeidel received a four-game suspension for being the aggressor in the incident while Shack received a three-game suspension for retaliating. Both players received match penalties at 9:33 of the first period. Zeidel claimed that the Bruins were making derogatory remarks toward him. He also claimed that the Bruins chirped that "they would put him on a slab and send him to the gas chamber." One of the players that Zeidel fingered, forward Tommy Williams, was not dressed for the game. Coach Harry Sinden did not hear any remarks although he did say that he did not doubt that someone may have called Zeidel "Jew boy" since Zeidel was calling Esposito "wop."

NHL President Clarence Campbell and Flyers Chairman of the Board Ed Snider said the incident was blown way out of proportion in the press but anti-defamation groups in both the United States and Canada sought thorough investigations.

After two days off, the Bruins hosted Detroit on Sunday night. For the second night in a row, the Red Wings were involved in a 7–5 game. On Saturday night in Toronto, the Leafs topped Detroit 7–5. In the Sunday game, the Red Wings ran off to a 5–0 lead by midway through the second period. Finally, at 11:29, Ted Green potted one for Boston. Goals followed quickly at 14:32 by McKenzie, at 16:22 by Tommy Williams, at 16:47 by Hodge, and finally at 19:23 by Glen Sather to complete the comeback. Understandably, the crowd was in a frenzy as the siren for the second period ended. Detroit did manage to score the winner and an empty net goal in the third period to blunt the B's comeback, but it still had to be classified as the "almost comeback game of the year."

The B's loss also stopped a five-game winning streak. Playoff hopes seemed brighter as they were now putting some distance between themselves and fifth-place Toronto. Speculation was also rampant that Bobby Orr would start skating and could be ready if the B's qualify for the postseason. Although he wouldn't say when, Harry Sinden had quietly set a return date for Orr.

The next day, March 11, Orr donned his skates for the first time since his operation. "I was anxious. I was a little worried about how I'd feel. It's like going into your first game. You just turn, easy and slow. It feels all right, so you work it up. It feels great," stated Orr after his first workout. Coach Sinden would like Orr to play a game or two before the playoffs. Orr, being Orr, would like to play a bit more than that if it is physically possible.

The next scheduled game for the B's was Wednesday night at Madison Square Garden in New York. In a close game, Johnny Bucyk's thirtieth goal of the season at 15:27 of period 3 provided the difference as the Bruins beat the Rangers 2–1.

On Saturday night, the Bruins continued to have trouble at Maple Leaf Gardens as the Leafs, behind pudgy Bruce Gamble, shut out the B's 3–0. Gamble made thirty-one saves to record the shutout. Boston left Toronto immediately after the game and headed home for an encounter with the first place Canadiens.

In what proved to be a historic St. Patrick's Day night, the Bruins clinched a playoff spot for the first time since 1959. The Canadiens were leading the Bruins by a 1–0 count late in the third period when the Bruins exploded for three quick goals in a matter of two minutes. Fred Stanfield lit it up at 17:39, followed by Derek Sanderson, who scored the game winner at 18:45. Phil Esposito clinched it with an empty netter at 19:39 to wrap up the playoff spot as the B's went on to a 3–1 win over Les Habitants.

After a three-day rest, the Chicago Blackhawks invaded the Boston Garden. Unknown to the Hawks, they were about to be ambushed by an eight-goal onslaught by the Bruins. Led by Eddie Shack's two goals and Gerry Cheevers twenty-one saves, the Bruins outgunned the Hawks 8–0.

With Orr scheduled to return to action in Detroit, a summary of the team's performance without him was as follows:

Games Played	Wins	Losses	Ties
17	10	6	1

Frank Mahovlich scored two goals to lead the Wings to a 5–3 victory. Orr returned to the Bruins' lineup and saw limited action as the B's continued to ready themselves for the playoffs.

As the Bruins headed into the last week of the season, they were two points behind the second place Rangers and three points ahead of fourth-place Chicago. First up would be the New York Rangers on Johnny Bucyk Night. Among the gifts received by the Chief were a new car, a diamond ring, and a boat. He then assisted on one-third-period goal scored by Phil Esposito, but the Bruins were defeated by the Rangers, 5–4.

In a preview of the first round matchup for the Bruins, the team traveled to Montreal, where they squeaked by the Canadiens, 2–1, on goals by Ken Hodge and Eddie Shack.

The following night, the Bruins closed out the season against the defending Stanley Cup Champion and "out of the playoffs" Toronto Maple Leafs. The Leafs rolled on to an easy 4–1 victory over the B's.

For the first time since the 1958–59 season, the Boston Bruins would participate in the Stanley Cup Playoffs. Their opponent in the opening round would be the Montreal Canadiens.

Some notable quotes on Orr from various figures around the NHL:

From Gordie Howe of the Detroit Red Wings: "What's his best move? I'd say his best move is putting on those skates."

Rod Gilbert of the rival New York Rangers paid probably the highest compliment when he iterated, "He's everything everybody says he is. I can only wish he was on our team."

Harvard University and Olympian star Bill Cleary credited Orr's hockey sense due to anticipation skills. "When Orr is chasing the puck in the defensive zone, he's looking both sides and behind him as he retreats, checking out the whole team. He'll have an offensive play in his head before he retrieves the puck."

Phil Goyette of the Rangers said many defensemen "have a weak skating side but not Bobby. He moves with ease. On offense, he can shift a guy right out of his pants, but on defense, he is very quick and steady on his feet."

Jean Ratelle, also of the Rangers, said, "Defensively, he has all the moves. I always have to be careful with him because he can block my shot and get the puck away from me on the same move."

New York Times hockey writer Gerry Eskanazi quipped, "Orr is one of the transcendental athletes. When he is on the ice, it is his game—not because he dominates it but because he seems to have invented it."

Coach Sinden had been quoted as saying Orr has four speeds. General Manger Milt Schmidt insists he has three speeds. Fellow defenseman Ted Green believed Orr has eighteen speeds of fast and doesn't believe he has seen them all. His ability to change speeds just adds to his deceptiveness.

Milt Schmidt expressed the happiness about Orr throughout the Bruins' organization. "Bobby's only twenty, a long way from his peak. He's still growing and will get a lot stronger. He won't hit his peak until he is twenty-seven or twenty-eight."

As the regular season wound down, *Boston Globe* staff writer Chris Lydon wrote a feature story about Orr. The headline, designed to grab the reader's attention, succeeded in spades: "Don't ask what Orr can't do—ask what he can do" (Milt Schmidt).

Lydon concluded: Ponder this hockey fans. Orr will still be getting better in 1975. If he is as durable as Gordie Howe, he'll still be a star in 1990.

March 1968					Orr's Stats				
					Game		Season		
Date	Venue	Versus	W-L-T	Score	G	A	G	A	PTS
3	Boston	St. Louis	W	9–3	DNP		11	20	31
6	Chicago	Blackhawks	W	5–3	DNP		11	20	31
7	Toronto	Philadelphia	W	2–1	DNP		11	20	31
10	Boston	Detroit	L	7–5	DNP		11	20	31
13	New York	Rangers	W	2–1	DNP		11	20	31
16	Toronto	Maple Leafs	L	3–0	DNP		11	20	31
17	Boston	Montreal	W	3–1	DNP		11	20	31
21	Boston	Chicago	W	8–0	DNP		11	20	31
18	Los Angeles	Kings	W	6–5	DNP		11	20	31
21	Minnesota	North Stars	L	5–3	DNP		11	20	31
24	Detroit	Red Wings	L	5–3	0	0	0	11	20
28	Boston	New York	L	5–4	0	0	0	11	20
30	Montreal	Canadiens	W	2–1	0	0	0	11	20
31	Boston	Toronto	L	4–1	0	0	0	11	20

1967–1968 Final Standings

Eastern Division

	W	L	T	PTS	GF	GA
Montreal	42	22	10	94	236	167
New York	39	23	12	90	226	183
Boston	37	27	10	84	259	216
Chicago	32	26	16	80	212	222
Toronto	33	31	19	76	209	176
Detroit	27	35	12	66	245	257

Western Division

	W	L	T	PTS	GF	GA
Philadelphia	31	32	11	73	173	179
Los Angeles	31	33	10	72	200	224
St. Louis	27	31	16	70	177	191
Minnesota	27	32	15	69	191	226
Pittsburgh	27	34	13	67	195	216
Oakland	15	42	17	47	153	219

April 1968 Playoffs

The Bruins returned to the playoffs for the first time since 1959 as they opened up the playoffs in Montreal. Claude Provost's goal at 14:40 of the third period helped Montreal to a 2–1 victory over the Bruins in game 1 played on April 4. This was the first playoff game of Orr's career. Numerous playoff games were postponed due to the assassination of the Reverend Martin Luther King on April 4.

Game 2 was played two nights later at the Forum. Montreal's Jacques Lemaire fired home two goals as the Canadiens beat the Bruins again, this time by a 5–3 margin. Orr earned his first playoff assist on Ted Green's second-period goal at 13:06.

The first playoff game in Boston since April 7, 1959, ended in the same result, a loss for the Bruins. This time, Montreal spanked the B's 5–2 with five different Habs, Jean Beliveau, Claude Provost, Ralph Backstrom, John Ferguson, and Dick Duff, scoring goals. For the third consecutive game, the Bruins were outshot, this time by a 33–27 margin. Orr recorded his second assist of the playoff series with his helper on Eddie Westfall's first-period goal.

For the fourth game in succession, the Bruins opened the scoring only to suffer the same results as the previous three contests, this time a 3–2 Montreal win behind two goals and one assist from Claude Larose. The Bruins went quietly in four straight games as the Canadiens would continue all the way to their fifteenth Stanley Cup championship.

April 1968 Playoffs					Orr's Stats				
					Game		Season		
Date	Venue	Versus	W-L-T	Score	G	A	G	A	PTS
4	Montreal	Canadiens	L	2–1	0	0	0	0	0
6	Montreal	Canadiens	L	5–3	0	1	0	1	1
9	Boston	Montreal	L	5–2	0	1	0	2	2
11	Boston	Montreal	L	3–2	0	0	0	2	2

Orr won his first Norris Trophy as the league's outstanding defenseman while Derek Sanderson won the Calder Trophy as the top rookie of the 1967–1968 season. This was the second year in a row that a Bruin had won the Calder Trophy as Orr had won the trophy the previous season.

Orr was quite honest about his selection as the league's top defenseman. "That's what you call a real steal," said Orr, who did not expect to win it due to the number of games he missed this season. "But it was a thrill for me to win it, and I hope to have a bigger impact next year when we win the Stanley Cup," insisted Orr. Orr was also named to the first All-Star team.

As in the previous season, Orr did not have to be protected in this year's draft due to the fact that he still had junior eligibility left. Orr was scheduled to be the Director of the Camp Milbrook Hockey Camp located at the Cohasset (MA) Winter Gardens.

During the playoffs, Orr told his attorney Alan Eagleson that his knee was bothering him. With that in mind, Orr had another operation on his ailing knee. Due to fluid buildup in the joint, Orr was confined to bed for ten days. Because he could not run his Camp Milbrook hockey camp, he recruited Harry Sinden, John McKenzie, Derek Sanderson, and Eddie Johnston to run the boys' camp in his stead.

View from the Balcony

The Bruins, losers for eight straight seasons, began to make some rumblings, not only around the league but in the city of Boston. To begin with, the Bruins made the big trade with Chicago, sending away fan favorites Gilles Marotte and Pit Martin. Along with Phil Esposito, Ken Hodge, and Fred Stanfield obtained from the Blackhawks, the rambunctious Eddie Shack was obtained from the Toronto Maple Leafs. With a distinctly different look to the team, the Bruins introduced some new sights around the Garden. The building received a fresh coat of paint, and the Bruins were welcomed back home with new dressing room quarters for both themselves and the visiting teams, which included a new western sector comprised of Oakland, Los Angeles, Minnesota, St. Louis, Pittsburgh, and Philadelphia.

The Bruins also introduced a new home and road uniform kit. The home jersey featured a base color black with gold shoulder yokes to go along with white-and-gold trim. The black pants and white socks were worn with both home and road jerseys.

The Bruins traditionally traveled from their locker room, down a long corridor, and entered the rink at center ice adjacent to their bench. Starting this season, the team would enter the ice at the same location as the Zamboni in the east end of the arena, just under the ledge where organist John Kiley played his favorite hit tunes.

The first indication that this season might be different occurred in the second home game, a 6–2 romp over Montreal when newly acquired Phil Esposito fired home four goals in the game.

The Bruins had been kicked around for years by their N.H.L. brethren. Payback time had arrived with the Blackhawks getting particular attention when the B's blasted them by scores of 7–2, 6–0, and 8–0.

St. Patrick's Day was a particularly enjoyable day as they not only defeated the Montreal Canadiens 3–1 but qualified for the playoffs for the first time since the spring of 1959.

Although the Bruins went out four in a row to the Canadiens in the postseason, they began to show that they would be reckoned with moving forward and for the foreseeable future.

Derek Sanderson expressed some opinions shared by many: "Bobby Orr was the best player I ever saw. He used to curl around the net, and everybody, like a magnet, would be sucked into him. And they would watch him, mesmerized, and he'd sneak behind them, and he'd find you at center ice, had more breakaways than you could shake a stick at. You know, he was just a brilliant playmaker, and the next thing you know, you'd look up, and he'd be with you! Somehow he got by everybody. He was just the best, without question."

Top Hockey Stories from 1968

Stanley Cup Champions	Montreal Canadiens
Art Ross Trophy	Stan Mikita, Chicago Blackhawks
Hart Trophy	Stan Mikita, Chicago Blackhawks
Lady Byng Trophy	Stan Mikita, Chicago Blackhawks
Vezina Trophy	Gump Worsley and Rogatien Vachon, Montreal Canadiens
Calder Trophy	Derek Sanderson, Boston Bruins
Smythe Trophy	Glenn Hall, St. Louis Blues
Norris Trophy	Bobby Orr, Boston Bruins
Masterton Trophy	Claude Provost, Montreal Canadiens
Calder Cup Champions	Rochester Americans
Memorial Cup Champions	Niagara Falls Flyers
NCAA Hockey Champions	Denver

Top Sports Stories

World Series Champions	Detroit Tigers
Super Bowl III Champions	New York Jets (game played on 1/12/1969 at Orange Bowl, Miami, Florida)
NBA Champions	Boston Celtics

Kentucky Derby Winner   Forward Pass
NCAA Football Champions   Ohio State (10-0-0)
NCAA Basketball Champions   UCLA
1968 Winter Olympics are held in Grenoble, France. The USSR wins Olympic Gold with a 6-1-0 record.

1968–1969

pull the shades!

WE'RE THE CLASSIC EXAMPLE

It's 1968:

Orr Nominated For Top Award

All That 'Glittered' Was Bruins

Impossible Dream—On Ice

CHAPTER 3

1968–1969: The Final Stumbling Block

THE BRUINS WERE BACK IN the playoff hunt after a successful 1967–1968 season, which included a third-place finish and a spot in the Stanley Cup Playoffs. Although the players and fans were disappointed that the team lasted only four games in the first round, the Bruins' trajectory seemed to be full bore ahead. The 1968–1969 offseason provided significant hope for the future.

August 7, 1968: Boston, Massachusetts

For the second time in two days, a Bruin signed a three-year contract. First, it was Phil Esposito signing on the dotted line. On August 7, Orr had the honors of adding his signature to a new agreement with Boston. "I suspect this will be a trend with us. I'm sure that Esposito and Orr are the first three-year contracts that the Bruins have signed," said Bruins' president Weston Adams.

According to Adams and Orr's attorney Alan Eagleson, the only part of the rumored contract that was true was that it was for three years. "The reported figures have been greatly exaggerated. There are no bonuses for winning the Stanley Cup, making the playoffs, team position at the end of the year, points, or goals. Life insurance is not included in the contract, nor does it differ in respect from insurance of all NHL players. Although the Bruins would be pleased to see Orr continue his education, no mention of it is made in the contract," said Eagleson.

In mid-August, Dr. John Palmer, who, along with Dr. Robert Jackson, had operated on Orr's knee back in June, opined that Orr should be ready for training camp on September 14. Palmer examined Orr's knee before declaring the operation was a success.

It was now time for Orr to give his thoughts on various subjects surrounding himself and the Boston Bruins. On his new three-year contract: "I understand why fans are interested. I am myself when I read about ball players and golfers. Sometimes it bothers me a little. I wouldn't go up to another fellow and ask him what he makes. Actually, I think there are only six people who really know my salary."

On his injuries: "I know there are people who say that I am injury-prone. The way that some of these things happened, the result would have been the same. Heck, Gordie Howe had things happen to him when he was a young player, and he's going into his twenty-third season."

On winning the Norris Trophy: "It felt great, and I was grateful. But I felt I had a terrible year. How many games did I play, 46? To tell the truth, I played lousy in the playoffs. Not very many of us were very good. Certainly I wasn't. We can all play better than that."

About the coming season: "The first thing is I want to play every game, and I hope I am over these injuries. I am anxious to get started, but I know it's best to take it a little easy. This is a good team, and it doesn't depend on any one man, not me or anyone else."

On long range ambitions: "I don't think of that. I just want to concentrate on us winning this season, all the way through the Stanley Cup. I don't see any reason why we can't finish first."

The *1969 Hockey Annual* featured a story about Stan Waylett, the trainer for the Minnesota North Stars. Waylett was the trainer with the Oshawa Generals when Orr reported to the team at age fourteen. Orr told the story that Waylett would always get mad at him because he refused to tape his sticks. Waylett reiterated that it was a sore spot for him. Waylett said, "I don't know why he wouldn't tape it. It was one of those mental things. All the tape does is prevent the stick from breaking. Orr said that the tape weighed the stick down, but how much are four or five extra raps of tape going to weigh?"

Orr was still using little to no tape on his sticks. "I still get in trouble over it. I guess it's all in my head," said Orr.

September 1968

The Bruins opened training camp on September 14 in London, Ontario, and played eight exhibition games against NHL opponents. As the regular season schedule pointed out, weekday night home games would start at 8:00 p.m., Sunday tilts start at 7:30 p.m., and afternoon games would commence at 2:00 p.m.

The Bruins named four alternate captains for the 1968–1969 season. The four were Orr, Esposito, Bucyk, and Eddie Westfall.

Back at the home base of the Boston Garden, things continued to change. While fans of a certain era had always understood that the number (13,909) meant that the Boston Garden was playing to a capacity crowd, in this season, the capacity number increased 14,642.

The 13,909 attendance figure was established after the 1942 Cocoanut Grove night club fire, which killed 492 people, 32 more than the authorized capacity.

The fact that the Bruins continued to fill the Garden was not lost on the arena's other tenant, the Boston Celtics. Jon Washington, Public Relations Director of the Los Angeles Kings, after conversing with Celtics General Manager Red Auerbach, noted this quote from the redhead: "The Bruins were out or it for ten years, yet they played to capacity crowds every game. The Bruins' fans have to be the greatest sports fans anywhere in the world… dammit!"

October 1968

On the Monday before the season began, doctors gave Orr permission to play in the opener against Detroit. With Orr playing, the only Bruin not available for action was defenseman Ted Green, who was refusing to honor the second year of the two-year contract he signed the year before.

For the third season in succession, the Bruins opened up at home against the visiting Detroit Red Wings. Orr earned an assist on Phil Esposito's second-period goal as the Bruins toppled Detroit, 4–2. Orr earned a first-period minor penalty for falling on the puck in the crease. On the ensuing power play, Gordie Howe scored for the Red Wings.

On Sunday night, the Philadelphia Flyers invaded the Garden and came away losers, 3–2. It was an uneven effort by the B's as evidenced by Orr's postgame comments. "For the first period and most of the second, they had us running around, and too many of us were trying to do things individually."

The Bruins headed out on their first western swing of the campaign. In the opener before a cozy gathering of only 4,270 fans at the Oakland-Alameda County Coliseum, the B's edged the Seals by a 2–1 margin. Orr assisted Bucyk on his second-period power play goal that turned out to be the game winner.

The next night in Los Angeles, the Kings edged the Bruins 2–1. Although Orr did not register any points, he did manage to earn two minor penalties as the Bruins suffered their first loss of the young season.

The Bruins headed to Pittsburgh for a Saturday night encounter with the Penguins. Five different B's scored goals, including Orr's first of the season as they routed the Penguins, 5–1.

On October 24, the Bruins suffered their second loss of the season as the Blues tipped them by a 2–1 margin at Boston Garden. Two of the three goals on the evening were scored by Parry Sounders, Orr for Boston and Gary Sabourin for St. Louis. Orr's goal was his second of the season. On a separate sartorial note, thieves broke into the St. Louis dressing room and stole five of the Blues' game jerseys.

The B's visited Toronto for a Saturday night clash with the Leafs and were blanked by Johnny Bower 2–0. It was the nineteenth consecutive game without a Boston win in Toronto dating back to November 27, 1965.

After two consecutive losses, the Bruins came with their A game and defeated the defending Stanley Cup champion Montreal Canadiens, 4–2 at the Boston Garden. Orr was held off the score sheet and assessed a two-minute minor in the first period.

The Bruins headed out on a brief midwestern road trip to Minnesota and Detroit. On Wednesday night at the Met Center in Bloomington, the B's edged the North Stars 4–2. Orr assisted on Fred Stanfield's second-period goal. The team headed to Detroit right after the game for a Halloween matchup with the Red Wings.

In spite of Orr's third goal of the season, the Bruins went down to defeat at the hands of the Red Wings. Frank Mahovlich's three goals helped pace Detroit to the 7–5 victory. Gordie Howe's three assists gave him nine hundred helpers for his career.

During the pregame warm-ups, a practice shot by Orr almost killed goaltender Eddie Johnston. The durable Johnston was the last goaltender to play a complete NHL season as he played all seventy contests during the 1963–64 campaign. It is hard to believe by today's standards, but Johnston had not yet worn a mask in a game, leaving his face unprotected when Orr's shot struck him near his temple.

Johnston was rushed immediately to a hospital where blood clots were found. His condition was so critical a Roman Catholic priest was summoned to Johnston's side. He was hospitalized for eighteen days, but it took another eight weeks before Johnston recovered. Upon his return to action, he was fitted with a mask, which he wore for the remainder of his career.

The Bruins finished the first month of the season tied for second place with the Chicago Blackhawks. Both teams were behind the Canadiens.

October 1968					Orr's Stats				
					Game		Season		
Date	Venue	Versus	W-L-T	Score	G	A	G	A	PTS
11	Boston	Detroit	W	4–2	0	1	0	1	1
13	Boston	Philadelphia	W	3–2	0	0	0	1	1
16	Oakland	Seals	W	2–1	0	1	0	2	2
17	Los Angeles	Kings	L	2–1	0	0	0	2	2
19	Pittsburgh	Penguins	W	5–1	1	0	1	2	3
24	Boston	St. Louis	L	2–1	1	0	2	2	4
26	Toronto	Maple Leafs	L	2–0	0	0	2	2	4
27	Boston	Montreal	W	4–2	0	0	2	2	4
30	Minnesota	North Starts	W	4–2	0	1	2	3	5
31	Detroit	Red Wings	L	7–5	1	1	3	4	7

November 1968

In their first contest of November, the Bruins faced the Blackhawks at Boston Garden. Orr scored his fourth goal of the season to lead the Bruins four-goal second-period attack that eventually blossomed into a 5–3 Boston victory.

On Wednesday evening, Orr's two assists helped pace the Bruins to a 7–1 victory over the Philadelphia Flyers at the Garden. He was also assessed a third-period two-minute penalty for closing his hand on the puck. The Bruins then enjoyed a respite of three days before facing the St. Louis Blues in Boston on Sunday.

In a game marked by a stick-swinging incident between Ted Green and Bob Plager of the Blues and a donnybrook between the teams, they finally played a hockey game but had to settle for a 1–1 tie. The Bruins were then off for games in Toronto and Philadelphia.

Derek Sanderson's late third-period goal helped the Bruins to a 1–1 tie in Toronto. The next evening, the team visited the Flyers at the Spectrum in Philadelphia.

After playing catch up in Toronto, the Bruins repeated the scripts in Philadelphia except in this game, the ending was different as the B's lost to the Flyers by a 4–2 margin. Orr was involved in two fights with former Bruin Gary Dornhoefer. He handled Dornhoefer in both bouts but was also assessed a ten-minute misconduct after the third period fight and was essentially out of the game for the last eight-and-one-half minutes of action. After the game, Orr expressed frustration. "He speared me twice. I don't mind anyone wanting to fight, but when they go to me with the stick, that's something else again. He's gone for me twice, but three times and he's out." The next day, Orr's right hand, sore from the pounding on Dornhoefer, was x-rayed. The results were negative.

On Sunday evening, Orr scored his fifth goal along with his eighth assist as the Bruins defeated the Seals, 6–3. He was also assessed a ten-minute misconduct in the first period after berating referee Bob Sloan for not calling a tripping infraction against him. Orr's two assists helped the Bruins defeat the Los Angeles Kings 4–1 at the Boston Garden on the 21st. The Bruins would host the Rangers and Leafs over the coming weekend.

In the Saturday night contest, the B's swamped the New York Rangers 5–1 in a game at the Boston Garden. Orr assisted on Fred Stanfield's second-period goal.

The next evening, the Maple Leafs visited the Garden as the Bruins fired forty-two shots on former B's goaltender Bruce Gamble and long-time Leaf Johnny Bower. The Boston club easily defeated the Leafs, 7–4. Phil Esposito's three goals were the deciding factor in the win. Gamble was the victim on two of the goals while Bower let in Esposito's final tally. Next up for the B's was a midweek contest along the Mississippi River against the Blues.

On the 27th at the Arena in St. Louis, the Bruins opened up a two-goal margin in the first period only to lose the lead in the third period and settled for a 4–4 tie. Jimmy Roberts of the Blues scored two third-period goals to tie the game.

For the second consecutive Saturday night, the Bruins entertained the Rangers in Boston. Unlike the previous Saturday, the Rangers pumped thirty-nine shots on Gerry Cheevers and came out with a 4–1 victory over the Bruins.

The Bruins ended November in third place, two points behind front-running Montreal and one point in arrears of the New York Rangers.

November 1968							Orr's Stats		
	Game			Season					
Date	Venue	Versus	W-L-T	Score	G	A	G	A	PTS
3	Boston	Chicago	W	5–3	1	1	4	5	9
6	Boston	Philadelphia	W	7–1	0	2	4	7	11
10	Boston	St. Louis	T	1–1	0	0	4	7	11
13	Toronto	Maple Leafs	T	1–1	0	0	4	7	11
14	Philadelphia	Flyers	L	4–2	0	0	4	7	11
17	Boston	Oakland	W	6–3	1	1	5	8	13
21	Boston	Los Angeles	W	4–1	0	2	5	10	15
23	Boston	New York	W	5–1	0	1	5	11	16
24	Boston	Toronto	W	7–4	0	0	5	11	16
27	St. Louis	Blues	T	4–4	0	0	5	11	16

December 1968

Thanks to Gerry Cheevers's twenty-seven saves and shorthanded goals by Dallas Smith and Eddie Westfall, the Bruins blanked the North Stars at Boston Garden, 4–0. It was the Boston's first shutout since the previous March 21 when they white-washed Chicago by an 8–0 score.

Phil Esposito scored two goals in a 2–2 tie against the Montreal Canadiens at Boston on December 5. The unusual aspect of this game was that both goals were scored on Phil's brother Tony, who was minding the nets for the Habs in his first NHL game. Brother Tony stopped thirty-six shots, and Gerry Cheevers had thirty-five saves in the tie. Orr earned his thirteenth assist on Esposito's tying goal.

In Saturday's tilt at the Garden, the Bruins swept past the Red Wings, 4–1. Orr assisted on Johnny Bucyk's second-period goal. Orr also received a fighting major when he became entangled with Wings' forward Frank Mahovlich in the second period. The Bruins were now off to Chicago for a Sunday night engagement with the Blackhawks.

In what might be called an embarrassment, the Blackhawks rolled out to a 5–0 lead by the midway point of the second period in a game at Chicago Stadium on the 8th. Ken Hodge and Orr both scored before the end of the second period to narrow the gap, but it was too little too late as the Bruins lost to Chicago, 7–5. Bobby Hull with three goals and Dennis Hull with two goals paced the attack for the Hawks.

On Wednesday night, the Bruins and Rangers met at Madison Square Garden. Ken Hodge's third-period goal brought the B's a 2–2 tie with the Broadway Blueshirts. The Bruins headed home for weekend games with the Blackhawks and Penguins.

In the team's next game on December 14, Orr fired home three goals as the Bruins romped over the Chicago Blackhawks, 10–5. This was the first three-goal game in Orr's career. The Bruins' goaltender on this evening was Joe Junkin, who played his only career NHL game. Dave Dryden (brother of future nemesis Ken) was the victim of the Bruins' onslaught.

The three goals that Orr scored were his seventh, eighth, and ninth of the season. He also added two assists for his first five-point game. When he scored his third goal at 10:06 of the second period, the game was held up for ten minutes as the ice had to be cleared of about fifty hats, none of which were of any use to Orr as he did not wear hats.

The list of previous Bruins' defensemen to score the "trick":

Eddie Shore on February 24, 1931, at Philadelphia	Boston Bruins (5), Philadelphia Quakers (1)
George Owen on February 11, 1932, at Boston	Montreal Maroons (7), Boston Bruins (4)
Flash Hollett on November 21, 1943, at Montreal	Montreal Canadiens (13), Boston Bruins (4)
Dit Clapper on February 17, 1945, at Boston	Boston Bruins (6), New York Rangers (1)

In the Sunday game against Pittsburgh, the Bruins scored half of the goals that they had scored the previous evening, but it was still enough for the B's to defeat the visiting Penguins, 5–3. Phil Esposito had his second three-goal game on the season. Boston closed out the four-game home stand with a contest against the Los Angeles Kings on the 19th. Bucyk and Ron Murphy each scored two goals, and Orr had two assists as the Bruins defeated the Kings, 6–4.

In what was described as a classic, the Bruins and Canadiens engaged in a 0–0 deadlock at the Montreal Forum. Gerry Cheevers with thirty-four saves and Tony

Esposito with forty-one saves earned the shutouts. The teams would return to Boston for a rematch on Sunday night.

With the 0–0 game on December 21 in the books, it should be noted that the previous 0–0 game involving Boston occurred on November 30, 1963, when the Bruins and Canadiens also engaged in a scoreless tie. In that game, also played at the Montreal Forum, Eddie Johnston of the B's and Charlie Hodge of the Canadiens were the goaltenders of record.

The first 0–0 game in Bruins' history occurred on December 1, 1927, when Boston and Pittsburgh Pirates knotted up in a game played at Duquesne Gardens in Pittsburgh. Goaltenders in that contest were Hal Winkler of the B's and Roy Worters of Pittsburgh.

If the previous evening provided spectacular goaltending, this game had a plethora of scoring, first by Montreal and then by the Bruins. The Canadiens moved out to a 3–0 first period lead before Phil Esposito struck at the 18:00 mark. Early in the second period, Henri Richard put the Habs ahead 4–1 before the Bruins pushed back and scored the next five goals to go ahead 6–4, and then finally settling for a 7–5 victory over Montreal. When Orr scored his tenth goal of the season to put the Bruins ahead of Montreal in the scintillating win, Derek Sanderson had this to say about his teammate: "A super goal. That kid ain't human. I sit on the bench and watch him all the time. Having a guy like him on a club gives everyone a big lift. I hope he can play until he's fifty-six." The goal was Orr's one-hundredth career point.

After the loss, Montreal's woes continued as the bus taking the team to the airport was broken into, and many players lost personal items. After the intense action over the weekend with Montreal, the Bruins hosted the Oakland Seals for a Christmas night meeting. The previous Christmas, the Bruins and Seals staged a donnybrook, but this game could best be described as a sleeper. The Seals, behind two goals by Bill Hicke, beat the Bruins 3–1. Orr assisted on the Bruins' lone goal, his nineteenth helper of the campaign. The Bruins now headed out on a four-game road trip to St. Louis, Detroit, Minnesota, and New York.

On the first game of the trip, the Bruins blitzed the Blues, 6–2. Ken Hodge had two goals while Orr assisted on Wayne Cashman's second-period goal. The next evening, the Bruins appeared at the Olympia in Detroit and took on the Red Wings. Detroit opened up a 3–0 lead early in the second period before the Bruins came back with three of their own goals scored by Esposito, Hodge, and Grant Erickson. Erickson's goal was his only one of his career. The Bruins and Wings settled for a 3–3 tie.

Boston moved up from third into second place, one point behind Montreal as the 1968 portion of the schedule closed.

December 1968					Orr's Stats				
					Game		Season		
Date	Venue	Versus	W-L-T	Score	G	A	G	A	PTS
1	Boston	Minnesota	W	4–0	0	1	5	12	17
5	Boston	Montreal	T	2–2	0	1	5	13	18
7	Boston	Detroit	W	4–1	0	1	5	14	19
8	Chicago	Blackhawks	L	7–4	1	0	6	14	20
11	New York	Rangers	T	2–2	0	0	6	14	20
14	Boston	Chicago	W	10–5	3	2	9	16	25
15	Boston	Pittsburgh	W	5–3	0	0	9	16	25
19	Boston	Los Angeles	W	6–4	0	2	9	18	27
21	Montreal	Canadiens	T	0–0	0	0	9	18	27
22	Boston	Montreal	W	7–5	1	0	10	18	28
25	Boston	Oakland	L	3–1	0	1	10	19	29
28	St. Louis	Blues	W	6–2	0	2	10	21	31
29	Detroit	Red Wings	T	3–3	0	0	10	21	31

January 1969

The Bruins opened the New Year with a solid 4–2 victory over the Rangers in New York. The win forged them into a first place tie with Montreal. Orr had his eleventh goal and an assist in the game. The team then moved on to Minnesota for a meeting with the North Stars on the 4th. Phil Esposito's two goals helped the Bruins to a 2–2 tie with the Stars.

After the four-game road trip, the Bruins returned home to meet the Toronto Maple Leafs. After a fight-filled first period, the Bruins had goals from Stanfield, Green, and Hodge and went on to defeat the Leafs by a 3–2 score.

Next up on the agenda would be the Bruins in Montreal on Saturday night. John McKenzie's two goals plus singles from Orr, Green, Hodge, and Esposito propelled them to a 6–3 victory at the Forum. The next night it was back to the Boston Garden for a game with the Penguins.

Esposito earned five assists while Hodge and Murphy scored two goals each as the Bruins motored into first place with an 8–4 thumping of Pittsburgh at the Garden. Orr had two assists, upping his point total to 38.

Next up for the Bruins were the Maple Leafs and a Wednesday night game at the great arena on the corner of Church and Carlton Streets in Toronto. The Bruins gave up two late goals and squandered a 5–3 lead before settling on a 5–5 tie.

The next evening, the Bruins hosted the North Stars at Boston Garden. Ken Hodge hit for his nineteenth and twentieth goals of the season as the Bruins walked away with a 5–1 win over Minnesota. Orr was held off the score sheet for the second consecutive game.

The Bruins and Flyers were set to meet for the third time this season, this time at the Spectrum on Saturday afternoon. Former Bruin farmhand Doug Favell started in net for the Flyers. Defenseman Ted Green scored two first-period goals and the Bruins went on to a 5–3 victory. Orr had an assist on Green's first goal of the game.

On Sunday night, Toronto visited the Garden. In an unusual move, Coach Punch Imlach of the Maple Leafs started five defensemen to try and blunt the high flying Bruins. In the first 5:12 of the game, the Bruins earned five minor penalties. The Leafs did manage one power play goal. However, the Bruins, behind Orr's thirteenth goal scored a 5–3 victory over the Leafs.

Cheevers, Orr, Green, and Esposito represented the Eastern Division at the twenty-second All-Star Game played in Montreal on January 21. This was the first "East versus West" All-Star Game format. The game ended in a 3–3 tie. Orr wore jersey number 2 in the contest due to Montreal's Beliveau having seniority with the number 4.

After the All-Star extravaganza, there was much talk about Orr. Here are a few of the quotes and quips from various people associated with the National Hockey League:

"He is absolutely the greatest player I have seen come into the league in my 12 years. He has shouldered great responsibility with Boston right from the start at the age of 18. He has all the natural attributes—skating, desire, shot and head. He has had good coaching but many of the things he does, nobody can teach him. They were there all along" (Bobby Hull).

"Hustle is the big thing in this game, and Bobby Orr really has that. If he has any weaknesses, I haven't discovered them" (Gordie Howe).

"You must realize that this man plays as a forward as much as a defenseman" (Jean Beliveau).

"Orr's biggest asset is the way he moves the puck. He skates better than most forwards and he has a wonderful sense of anticipation" (Tim Horton).

"He is so mobile that he recovers from just about any mistake he might make" (Doug Harvey).

"He has a tremendous shot and he has a great variety in the way he shoots at you" (Glenn Hall).

"He has a new move in every game" (Gerry Cheevers).

"We all know how good he is. He deserves everything but, the best I can say is what a good kid he is" (Ted Green).

Elmer Ferguson, who had covered hockey in Montreal since the inception of the NHL in 1917, said, "I have never seen anyone, with any team, who can lift his team as Orr does. I never thought I'd see the likes of Eddie Shore with Boston, but I'm thinking now this boy is better in so many of the things he does."

Shore himself had this assessment on Orr. "I don't know that I ever saw another man who was as good as Orr in gauging the speed of the man to whom he is passing."

After the All-Star break, the Bruins moved into the Detroit Olympia. Ken Hodge scored both goals for the Bruins in a 2–2 tie with the Red Wings. The Olympia appeared to be a good location for Hodge since he had now scored six goals in Detroit this season. Orr had an assist on Hodge's second-period power play goal. The Bruins headed home for weekend games with West Division teams St. Louis and Minnesota.

On Saturday night, Gerry Cheevers stopped all nineteen shots, and Hodge had two more goals as the Bruins defeated the Blues, 4–0. Orr had two assists in the game.

When the B's faced the North Stars at Boston Garden, they were going for their fourteenth consecutive undefeated game. Esposito, Bucyk, Hodge, and McKenzie potted single goals to negate Claude Larose's two goals as the Bruins defeated the Minnesota, 4–3.

The Bruins flew out to the West Coast, where they met the Oakland Seals on Wednesday night. Eddie Westfall's goal with seventeen seconds left in the game earned Boston a 3–3 tie with the Seals. Orr assisted Westfall on the game-tying goal. The B's met the Kings in Los Angeles the following night.

In a wild affair on the 30th, the Bruins, after running up a 7–2 lead, held on for a 7–5 win over the Los Angeles Kings. Derek Sanderson had three goals for the B's, while Eddie "the Jet" Joyal had two goals for the Kings. Orr twisted his knee when it got caught in a rut on the ice at the Forum. He missed the next nine games due to the injury.

The Bruins, thanks to going undefeated in January and extending their unbeaten streak to sixteen games, finished the month on top of the Eastern Division.

January 1969					Orr's Stats				
					Game		Season		
Date	Venue	Versus	W-L-T	Score	G	A	G	A	PTS
2	New York	Rangers	W	4–2	1	1	11	22	33
4	Minnesota	North Stars	T	2–2	0	0	11	22	33
9	Boston	Toronto	W	3–2	0	1	11	23	34
11	Montreal	Canadiens	W	6–3	1	1	12	24	36
12	Boston	Pittsburgh	W	8–4	0	2	12	26	38
15	Toronto	Maple Leafs	T	5–5	0	0	12	26	38

16	Boston	Minnesota	W	5–1	0	0	12	26	38
18	Philadelphia	Flyers	W	5–3	0	1	12	27	39
19	Boston	Toronto	W	5–3	1	0	13	27	40
23	Detroit	Red Wings	T	2–2	0	1	13	28	41
25	Boston	St. Louis	W	4–0	0	2	13	30	43
26	Boston	Minnesota	W	4–3	0	1	13	31	44
29	Oakland	Seals	T	3–3	0	1	13	32	45
30	Los Angeles	Kings	W	7–5	0	0	13	32	45

February 1969

The Bruins opened February with the team holding Orr out of action due to the knee injury. Coach Sinden had underestimated the severity of the injury, stating that for precautionary reasons, he would likely miss only one game.

The Bruins' unbeaten streak, now at eighteen games, continued with wins over Detroit (4–2) and Chicago (7–2). Due to the uncertainty of Orr's condition, Bruins' President Weston Adams denied there was anything wrong with Orr's knee. "There is nothing seriously wrong with Bobby according to the information that I have from our medical department. We never at any time considered his injury serious."

General Manager Milt Schmidt had this to say about Orr's absence from the lineup. "I have not withheld any information on Bobby. I have reported on everything I have been told by the doctor. The matter is just what I've said all along. We have to proceed on a day-to-day basis."

As time wore on, Orr made the decision to return home and recuperate in Parry Sound. While home, Orr visited Dr. Palmer in Toronto, who reported that he should stay off the ice for five days and then start skating with the idea he would be able to play in a game in another five days.

The Bruins' undefeated streak ended at eighteen games as they lost to the Blues in the Mound City, 3–1 on February 6. The streak extended from December 28 through February 5 with the B's winning thirteen games and tying five. As they continued without Orr, they went on to meet the Flyers in Philadelphia (a 6–5 win), and tie the Seals (3–3) at Boston Garden.

After an altercation with Larry Hale of the Philadelphia Flyers, Esposito was assessed a misconduct penalty for shoving and hitting Referee Bob Sloan. The incident would be reviewed by NHL President Clarence Campbell.

Only 7,704 fans showed up for the February 9 game at Boston Garden, a 3–3 tie with the Oakland Seals. A raging snowstorm was occurring in Boston, keeping the crowd well below capacity for the evening.

In the last home game before a six-game road trip, the Bruins stomped on the Blackhawks 7–3. Hodge with three goals, Esposito with two goals, and Stanfield's one goal paced the Boston attack. The trade that had brought the trio to Boston two years before was continuing to pay dividends.

In the road trip opener, the Bruins lost to the Canadiens, 3–1 on the 15th. The next afternoon and for the second time in twenty hours, the Bruins went down to defeat, this time to the Blackhawks in Chicago, 5–1. Five different Hawks—Doug Mohns, Bobby Hull, Jim Pappin, Howie Young, and Andre Boudrias—tallied goals for the winners in the afternoon contest.

The day after the loss to Chicago, it was officially learned that Esposito would be suspended for two games due to the incident with referee Sloan in Philadelphia on February 8.

In mid-February, Orr began light skating with the team at the Watson Rink on the Harvard University campus. He had been out since January 30. The Bruins' losing streak hit three games, this defeat coming at the hands of the Pittsburgh Penguins, 3–0. Pitt goaltender Joe Daley notched the victory over the Bruins.

The team suffered their worst defeat of the season in a February 23 game at New York as they were blasted by the Rangers, 9–0, their fourth consecutive loss. The B's played without the suspended Esposito, but Orr returned to the lineup after his nine-game absence. The Rangers' ninth goal was scored by rookie and future Bruins' great Brad Park. It was his first career goal.

The Bruins ended their four-game losing streak when they visited Los Angeles and defeated the Kings, 4–2. Orr earned his first two assists since January 29 as he helped on McKenzie's nineteenth and twentieth goals of the season. The next evening, the Bruins met the Seals in Oakland. Orr scored his first goal since January 19 while Bucyk netted two goals in the B's romp over the Seals, 9–0. The Boston finished the six-game road trip with a 2–4 record and headed back to Boston for a three-game home stand.

The Bruins ended the month tied in points for first place with the Montreal Canadiens. The Habs, with two more wins, sat atop of the Eastern Division.

February 1969					Orr's Stats				
	Game			Season					
Date	Venue	Versus	W-L-T	Score	G	A	G	A	PTS
2	Boston	Detroit	W	4–2	DNP		13	32	45
5	Chicago	Blackhawks	W	7–2	DNP		13	32	45
6	St. Louis	Blues	L	3–1	DNP		13	32	45
8	Boston	Philadelphia	W	6–5	DNP		13	32	45
9	Boston	Oakland	T	3–3	DNP		13	32	45
11	Boston	Chicago	W	7–3	DNP		13	32	45

15	Montreal	Canadiens	L	3–1	DNP		13	32	45
16	Chicago	Blackhawks	L	5–1	DNP		13	32	45
19	Pittsburgh	Penguins	L	3–0	DNP		13	27	40
23	New York	Rangers	L	9–0	0	0	13	32	45
26	Los Angeles	Kings	W	4–2	0	2	13	34	47
27	Oakland	Seals	W	9–0	1	1	14	35	49

March 1969

After the Rangers ran up a 2–0 lead, the Bruins scored seven consecutive goals on route to an 8–5 victory over New York. Orr had two goals, but the story of the game was Phil Esposito notching his ninety-ninth point of the season breaking the mark of 97 points held by Bobby Hull of Chicago during the 1965–1966 season.

The next evening, Esposito had two goals, and Eddie Johnston made nineteen saves as the Bruins downed the Penguins at the Garden, 4–0. Orr had two assists to up his point total to 54.

The Bruins and Red Wings played to a 2–2 tie on Boston Garden ice on the 5th. Orr had one assist on the tying goal scored by McKenzie.

Three nights later, the teams met again, this time in Detroit. Despite Orr's seventeenth goal of the season, the Bruins fell to the Red Wings, 7–4. Bruce MacGregor had two goals for Detroit while the Bruins failed on four power play opportunities.

Back at the Garden on Sunday night, the Bruins hosted the Los Angeles Kings. Hodge scored his thirty-seventh and thirty-eighth goals, and Orr copped his eighteenth as the Bruins knocked off the Kings, 7–2. The Bruins headed out for a three-game road trip to Minnesota, Philadelphia, and Toronto.

A couple of statistical milestones were achieved in Minnesota as the Bruins and North Stars played to a 3–3 draw. Esposito's two assists brought him to a total of sixty-eight for the season, one better than the previous record holders, Stan Mikita of Chicago and Dickie Moore of Montreal. Orr had his nineteenth goal while also earning his fifty-ninth point, equaling the total accumulated by Pierre Pilote of Chicago during the 1964–65 season.

Two nights later in Philadelphia, the B's fell to the Flyers at the Spectrum, 2–1. They then moved on to Toronto for the first game of a home-and-home series with the Maple Leafs.

In the lid-lifter at Maple Leaf Gardens, Toronto scored five third-period goals and defeated the Bruins, 7–4. The Bruins had not won a game in Toronto since November 27, 1965, a stretch of twenty-two games. Orr did earn an assist on Ken Hodge's thirty-ninth goal but also earned a five-minute major, the result of a third-period fight with Pat Quinn. He also recorded his sixtieth point to establish a new record for points by defenseman. The old record was held by Pierre Pilote of Chicago.

On the back end of the "home and home" the next evening in Boston, the Bruins spotted the Leafs a two-goal lead but rumbled back with eight consecutive second-period goals and squashed the Toronto sextet by an 11–3 score. Derek Sanderson led the attack with three goals. The Bruins had an astounding eight second-period goals and added fourteen assists tying a twenty-five-year record for points (22) in a single period. Hodge had two goals, and Garnet "Ace" Bailey netted his first two career goals. Of the 27 accumulated points by the Bruins, Orr surprisingly did not register a goal or assist.

Orr spent his last night as a twenty-year-old scoring his twentieth goal of the season. It was the winning goal in a 3–2 victory over the Penguins and tied the record for defensemen. The record was previously held by former Bruin "Flash" Hollett when he was a member of the 1944–45 Detroit Red Wings. It was Orr's second game-winning goal of the season.

The Bruins came away with a 5–5 tie against the Chicago Blackhawks at the Boston Garden the next evening in a game that produced great drama. To begin with, the Bruins moved out to a 4–0 lead early into the second period. Ron Murphy had two goals for Boston. Just as suddenly, the Blackhawks scored the next five goals to take the lead late in the game. Bobby Hull had two power play goals. The first tied the game at 17:19 of the third period, and the second put the Hawks ahead at 17:32. Esposito, McKenzie, and Orr were all serving two-minute minor penalties when the two Chicago power play goals were scored.

The Bruins pulled goaltender Gerry Cheevers for the extra attacker. With one second remaining on the Garden clock, Orr tipped a Bucyk shot past Denis DeJordy to salvage the tie. It was Orr's twenty-first goal of the season, breaking the record of twenty goals. To make the event sweeter, it was Orr's twenty-first birthday. It's was on to Chicago for a Saturday night rematch at the Stadium.

Referee Art Skov signals goal. Orr celebrates his record-
breaking twenty-first marker of the season. Others in picture
are Ken Hodge (8) and Pat Stapleton (12) of Chicago.

When the Bruins defeated the Blackhawks 5–3, they knocked Chicago out of the playoffs for the first time in eleven years. Esposito scored two goals for the winners, his forty-sixth and forty-seventh, matching the record for goals by a center shared with Montreal's Jean Beliveau. The next afternoon, the Bruins played the Rangers in a nationally televised game from Madison Square Garden.

In the daytime tilt, Ranger defensemen Jim Neilson with two goals and Rod Seiling with a single marker paced the Broadway Blueshirts to a 4–2 win. The Rangers fired forty-six shots on Boston goaltender Gerry Cheevers.

As the Bruins rolled into the last week of the season, they were four points behind Montreal with three games left on the schedule. On Thursday night at Boston Garden, the Bruins hosted the Rangers. Spotting the New Yorkers a two-goal lead, the Bruins came back with two of their own in the middle stanza. Orr's minor/misconduct penalties enabled the Rangers to end the second period with a 3–2 lead. John McKenzie's twenty-eighth goal at 6:47 of the third period enabled the Bruins to come back and earn a 3–3 tie.

With first place on the line, the Bruins played the Montreal Canadiens in a home-and-home set to end the campaign. In the Saturday night game in Montreal, five different Canadiens scored goals and led Montreal to a 5–3 victory clinching first place in the process. Orr earned his forty-third assist and final point of the season on Hodge's forty-third goal.

In the season finale on Sunday afternoon, Esposito scored his forty-eighth and forty-ninth goals of the year as the Bruins edged past Montreal, 6–3. Ted Harris and Orr continued their feud with a lively second-period bout. The Bruins ended the season three points behind the Canadiens.

March 1969					Orr's Stats				
					Game		Season		
Date	Venue	Versus	W-L-T	Score	G	A	G	A	PTS
1	Boston	New York	W	8–5	2	1	16	36	52
2	Boston	Pittsburgh	W	4–0	0	2	16	38	54
5	Boston	Detroit	T	2–2	0	1	16	39	55
8	Detroit	Red Wings	L	7–4	1	0	17	39	56
9	Boston	Los Angeles	W	7–2	1	0	18	39	57
11	Minnesota	North Stars	T	3–3	1	1	19	40	59
13	Philadelphia	Flyers	L	2–1	0	0	19	40	59
15	Toronto	Maple Leafs	L	7–4	0	1	19	41	60
16	Boston	Toronto	W	11–3	0	0	19	41	60
19	Pittsburgh	Penguins	W	3–2	1	1	20	42	62
20	Boston	Chicago	T	5–5	1	0	21	42	63
22	Chicago	Blackhawks	W	5–3	0	0	21	42	63
23	New York	Rangers	L	4–2	0	0	21	42	63
27	Boston	New York	T	3–3	0	0	21	42	63
29	Montreal	Canadiens	L	5–3	0	1	21	43	64
30	Boston	Montreal	W	6–3	0	0	21	43	64

1968–1969 Final Standings

Eastern Division

	W	L	T	PTS	GF	GA
Montreal	46	19	11	103	271	202
Boston	42	18	16	100	303	221
New York	41	26	9	91	231	196
Toronto	35	26	15	85	234	217
Detroit	33	31	12	78	239	221

Chicago	34	33	9	77	280	246

Western Division

	W	L	T	PTS	GF	GA
St. Louis	37	25	14	88	204	157
California	29	36	11	69	219	251
Philadelphia	20	35	21	61	174	225
Los Angeles	24	42	10	58	185	260
Pittsburgh	20	45	11	51	189	252
Minnesota	18	43	15	51	189	270

April 1969 Playoffs

The three thousand tickets available for the opening round of the playoffs against Toronto were scooped up at the Boston Garden box office in less than two hours.

In the opener, the Bruins throttled the Leafs at Boston Garden, 10–0. Esposito had four goals and two assists. The six points tied the record for most points in a playoff game held by Dickie Moore of the Montreal Canadiens in a game against Boston on March 25, 1954. Bucyk and Sanderson had two goals each. The game was marred by an injury to Orr, who was laid out by Toronto defenseman Pat Quinn's hit. Quinn was assessed a five-minute major penalty for his indiscretion and instantly became public enemy number one in the eyes of Bruins' fans. Orr was taken to the Massachusetts General Hospital for overnight observation, and x-rays taken proved negative.

March 1969					Orr's Stats				
					Game		Season		
Date	Venue	Versus	W-L-T	Score	G	A	G	A	PTS
1	Boston	New York	W	8–5	2	1	16	36	52
2	Boston	Pittsburgh	W	4–0	0	2	16	38	54
5	Boston	Detroit	T	2–2	0	1	16	39	55
8	Detroit	Red Wings	L	7–4	1	0	17	39	56
9	Boston	Los Angeles	W	7–2	1	0	18	39	57
11	Minnesota	North Stars	T	3–3	1	1	19	40	59
13	Philadelphia	Flyers	L	2–1	0	0	19	40	59

15	Toronto	Maple Leafs	L	7–4	0	1	19	41	60
16	Boston	Toronto	W	11–3	0	0	19	41	60
19	Pittsburgh	Penguins	W	3–2	1	1	20	42	62
20	Boston	Chicago	T	5–5	1	0	21	42	63
22	Chicago	Blackhawks	W	5–3	0	0	21	42	63
23	New York	Rangers	L	4–2	0	0	21	42	63
27	Boston	New York	T	3–3	0	0	21	42	63
29	Montreal	Canadiens	L	5–3	0	1	21	43	64
30	Boston	Montreal	W	6–3	0	0	21	43	64

April 2, 1969. In the above photo, an injured Orr receives help from Ken Hodge.

April 2, 1969. Toronto players come to the rescue of Pat Quinn after the Orr hit.

Jim Dorey of the Maple Leafs was serving a penalty at the time of the incident. "I was in the penalty box right when it happened. I saw it all. And you know Pat, they might say it's a dirty hit. He's six feet four, six feet five. You know if you're tense, you sort of get your back up a little bit. So that's how he hit Orr. He wasn't a low hitter, and he was just a big, big guy, and he didn't bend over. He was just stiff. And it might have looked like he caught him in the head intentionally, but it wasn't. It was just the way Quinn checked."

When Referee John Ashley sent Quinn to the penalty box, the fans tried to get their revenge by smashing the glass behind the Toronto sin bin. The Leafs' bench raced to Quinn's rescue as the melee ensued. Quinn was finally escorted to the Toronto dressing room. Ashley handed out 132 minutes in penalties, including thirty-two minutes to former Bruin Forbes Kennedy for his antics during a third-period brawl with Cheevers and McKenzie. Kennedy set a playoff record for most penalties with eight, receiving four minors, two majors, a ten-minute misconduct, and a game misconduct totaling thirty-eight minutes. The record stood for eleven years before being tied by Pittsburgh's Kim Clackson on April 14, 1980, set at Boston Garden.

Game 2 was played the next evening in the same venue, the Boston Garden. Orr returned to action in this game, adding an assist in the 7–0 whitewashing of the Leafs. The Boston Police Department added fifteen extra officers to their normal contingent. After organist John Kiley finished the Canadian and American national anthems, the crowd started chanting, "We want Quinn! We want Quinn!" The chants of "Get him! Kill him!" continued throughout the game.

This contest was much calmer than game 1 with only fighting majors handed out to Don Awrey and Larry Mickey of the Leafs. However, the results were basically the same. Bucyk had his third and fourth goals of the series, and Esposito had his fifth goal in two games to pace the Boston victory. The teams headed to Toronto for games 3 and 4 over the weekend. As preparations for these games proceeded, scribes out of Toronto wondered if the Leafs could win a period.

In game 3, Eddie Westfall opened the scoring with a shorthanded goal to lead the Bruins to a 4–3 victory. Orr had two assists including a helper on Derek Sanderson's game winner at 2:52 of the third period. The victory marked the first Boston victory in Toronto over a stretch of twenty-two games dating back to November 27, 1965.

The Leafs entertained the Bruins on Sunday night in game 4 of the series with Boston being up three games to none. Just as in game 3, the B's opened the scoring with a shorthanded goal, this one by Sanderson. Like game 3, Derek scored the winning goal as the Bruins downed the Maple Leafs 3–2. The series ended with a four-game Boston sweep over Toronto. Immediately following the game, the Maple Leafs fired their coach and general manager, Punch Imlach, after four Stanley Cup championships in eleven years. The Bruins would now go on to meet their nemesis from Montreal in the Stanley Cup semifinals.

In game 1 at Montreal, Sanderson continued on his hot streak as he scored both goals, including a shorthanded goal to give the Bruins a 2–0 lead going into period three. However, two goals, including the tying goal by Jean Beliveau at the 19:04 mark of the third stanza enabled the Canadiens to catch the Bruins in regulation. The overtime lasted just forty-two seconds as Ralph Backstrom scored the winning goal and gave the Habs a 1–0 lead in the best of seven series.

Game 2, again in overtime, followed the pattern of game one. The Bruins out-played Montreal for most of the game only to relinquish the lead late in the contest and then outright lost in overtime, 4–3. This time, the winner was scored by rookie Mickey Redmond at 4:55 of the first overtime. For the third game in succession, Orr was held off the score sheet.

The series turned to Boston Garden for games 3 and 4. In game 3, Gerry Cheevers earned his third shutout of the playoffs as he stifled the Canadiens with thirty-four saves, and the Bruins went on to beat the Habs going away, 5–0. Esposito had a hand in all five goals (two goals and three assists), and Orr had two assists in the Boston romp.

Game 4 was much closer and certainly more dramatic. The Bruins got two shorthanded goals, one by Westfall and one by Sanderson. Orr scored his first ever playoff goal, the game winner as the Bruins downed Montreal 3–2 and tied the series at two games apiece. The goal came against Canadiens' goaltender Rogie Vachon. Game 5 moved back to Montreal. Sanderson suffered a charley horse in game 4 and would be lost for game 5.

In game 5, Montreal moved out to a 3–0 lead over the Bruins before they scored two goals in a little over three minutes in period 2. Both Boston goals were scored by Hodge, one on the power play with an assist to Orr. These two scores were Boston's only offense for the night as the Bruins went down to defeat by a 4–2 margin. The Montreal win gave the Habs a 3–2 series lead with game 6 to be played in Boston.

Game 6 in Boston would be the last game of the season for the up and coming Bruins as the Canadiens nipped the B's in double overtime, 2–1. Jean Beliveau scored the winner at the 11:28 mark of the second overtime. It was Beliveau's first ever game-winning overtime goal in his fifteen-year career. The Bruins' home loss was their first in twenty-two games but came at an inopportune time for the team as they were eliminated from the 1969 playoffs. The winning Canadiens would eventually go on to defeat the St. Louis Blues in the Stanley Cup finals.

April 1969 Playoffs					Orr's Stats				
					Game		Season		
Date	Venue	Versus	W-L-T	Score	G	A	G	A	PTS
2	Boston	Toronto	W	10–0	0	1	0	1	1
3	Boston	Toronto	W	7–0	0	1	0	2	2

5	Toronto	Maple Leafs	W	4–3	0	2	0	4	4
6	Toronto	Maple Leafs	W	3–2	0	0	0	4	4
10	Montreal	Canadiens	L	3–2 (OT)	0	0	0	4	4
13	Montreal	Canadiens	L	4–3 (OT)	0	0	0	4	4
17	Boston	Montreal	W	5–0	0	2	0	6	6
20	Boston	Montreal	W	3–2	1	0	1	6	7
22	Montreal	Canadiens	L	4–2	0	1	1	7	8
24	Boston	Montreal	L	2–1 (OT)	0	0	1	7	8

Phil Esposito led all playoff scorers with eighteen points while Derek Sanderson established a new N.H.L. record with three shorthanded goals. Weston Adams Sr. stepped down as president of the Bruins as Weston Adams Jr. took over the presidency. Bobby Orr won the Norris Trophy and Phil Esposito, the Hart Trophy. Bruins radio announcer Bob Wilson would be leaving Boston's radio team to join KMOX in St. Louis.

View from the Balcony

For the first time in team history, the Bruins reached the 100-point mark while finishing a mere three points behind first place Montreal in the final standings. The improvement of the team continued in an upward trajectory and a couple of Bruins' bounces might have lifted the team into the final round. It was not to be as the Canadiens again prevailed in a grueling six game series.

The regular season established many team records as the Bruins became the first team in NHL history to score 300 goals in a season, finishing with 303. Phil Esposito broke the record for assists in the season with seventy-seven while becoming the first player in N.H.L. history to score 100 points. Esposito and Orr would continue to set records in the coming years.

At this point, the Stanley Cup seemed inevitable, although the Bruins suffered a heartbreaking loss to close the 1969 playoffs. In retrospect, this should have been the first of a string of championships for a team that seemingly looked unbeatable. The dynasty never developed, although it would be difficult to argue against the brilliance of a team that seemingly had everything.

As the decade of the '60s wore on in greater Boston, hockey interest continued to grow. The Bruins had a long history of devoted fans, but with the arrival of Orr, it made the hockey fans mainstream. The Metropolitan District Commission (MDC), the state agency responsible for recreation, beaches, and parklands in greater Boston, went on an extensive rink-building binge. Seemingly overnight, rinks began to pock-mark metropolitan Boston, many still open to this very day. Led by Bobby Orr, it would be hard to argue against the influence that he and the resurgent Bruins had on the region.

Sports talk radio was also in its infancy with shows like *Voice of Sports* on WHDH radio featuring local writers gabbing about the chief topics of the sports week. Another interesting program featured the iconoclastic Eddie Andleman, Mark Witkin, and Jim McCarthy on *The Sports Huddle*, which began on WBOS-FM but became so popular that it moved to a regular three-hour session each Sunday night on both WHDH radio and WBZ radio.

The Bruins' radio stations of the era were WHDH radio 850 and WBZ, radio 1030 on the dial. For the first time in memory, a two-hour sports talk program would be broadcast Monday through Friday with host Guy Maniella on WBZ radio. It was Boston's first sports radio call in show with Maniella and the Bruins mutually benefiting from the added exposure. It was difficult to understand that during this period in Boston's sports history, the Bruins would be the number one team in the city, but they were. The Celtics were still winning championships, the Red Sox had the dramatic 1967 "Impossible Dream," and the Patriots were still known as the Boston Patriots. But here were the once moribund, inept, sometimes comatose, but always lovable Bruins dominating the airwaves and newspaper spaces like rock stars.

And then there was TV38. Channel 38 was one of two independent UHF stations on the Boston television dials. The station was originally owned by the Archdiocese of Boston but was sold to Storer Broadcasting in 1966. The other UHF station was channel 56 owned by Kaiser Broadcasting. In 1966, channel 56 bought the rights to televise Bruins road games for one season. After the first season, the station management, not impressed with the Bruins' ratings, did not renew the broadcast contract. Channel 38, needing programming to fill the day, stepped in, and the rest is history. With the Garden selling out every night, fans were demanding to see the Bruins live on television, and that is what they got. During the height of their popularity, one million homes were tuning into games on TV38. Fans of a certain age will remember the opening notes of the song "Nutty" by the 1960s instrumental group the Ventures. It was the theme song heard at the beginning of Bruins' telecasts for many years. Street hockey games all over Boston were serenaded by screeching kids humming "Nutty" before their opening face-offs.

Top Hockey Stories from 1969

Stanley Cup Champions	Montreal Canadiens
Art Ross Trophy	Phil Esposito, Boston Bruins
Hart Trophy	Phil Esposito, Boston Bruins
Lady Byng Trophy	Alex Delvecchio, Detroit Red Wings

Vezina Trophy	Jacques Plante and Glenn Hall, St. Louis Blues
Calder Trophy	Danny Grant, Minnesota North Stars
Smythe Trophy	Serge Savard, Montreal Canadiens
Norris Trophy	Bobby Orr, Boston Bruins
Masterton Trophy	Ted Hampson, Oakland Seals
Calder Cup Champions	Hershey Bears
Memorial Cup Champions	Montreal Junior Canadiens
NCAA Hockey Champions	Denver

NHL increases the regular season schedule to seventy-six games.

Top Sports Stories

World Series Champions	New York Mets
Super Bowl IV Champions	Kansas City Chiefs (game played on 1/11/1970 at Tulane Stadium, New Orleans, Louisiana)
NBA Champions	Boston Celtics
Kentucky Derby Winner	Majestic Prince
NCAA Football Champions	Texas (11-0-0)
NCAA Basketball Champions	UCLA

1969–1970

CHAPTER 4

1969–1970: Mission Accomplished

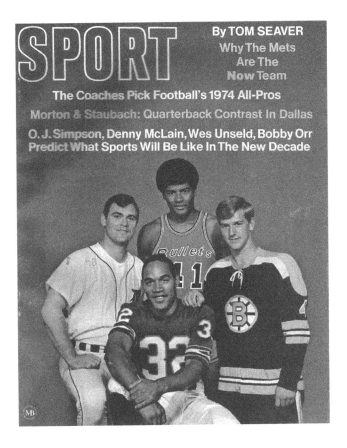

SPORT

By TOM SEAVER
Why The Mets
Are The
Now Team

The Coaches Pick Football's 1974 All-Pros

Morton & Staubach: Quarterback Contrast In Dallas

O.J. Simpson, Denny McLain, Wes Unseld, Bobby Orr
Predict What Sports Will Be Like In The New Decade

BOBBY ORR MISSED THE BEGINNING of training camp to attend a panel discussion in New York City for *Sport Magazine*. The panel included Orr, Denny McLain of the Detroit Tigers, Wes Unseld of the Baltimore Bullets, and O.

J. Simpson of the Buffalo Bills. The article resulting from the discussion appeared in the December 1969 issue. The cover of the magazine featured the four panelists.

In off-season personnel moves, Tommy Williams and Barry Gibbs were dispatched to Minnesota on May 7. In return, they received Minnesota's first pick in the 1969 entry draft (Don Tannahill). On the 14th, the B's traded Eddie Shack along with Ross Lonsberry to the Los Angeles Kings for right winger Ken Turlik and two future draft choices. The choices turned out to be Ron Jones in the 1971 draft and Andre Savard in the draft of 1973.

The Bruins lost Glen Sather and Grant Erickson in the NHL draft while they picked up Billy Speer from the Pittsburgh Penguins.

Boston would be playing eleven exhibition games this season. Training camp opened on September 11 in London, Ontario. The opening exhibition game in Montreal featured the seemingly annual donnybrook between the Bruins and Habs.

Earlier in the same game, Phil Esposito pushed referee Ken Bodendistel while protesting a minor penalty. Esposito was later fined $250 by NHL President Clarence Campbell.

Weston Adams, chairman of the Boston Bruins, ordered that the team's farm club, the Oklahoma City Blazers, wear helmets to protect their players from head injuries. The Bruins also filed a motion with the NHL Rules Committee to make the wearing of helmets mandatory no later than January 15. The motion defeated, 11–1, with Adams the only dissenting vote.

Former Bruin great and Hockey Hall of Famer Eddie Shore was named the tenth winner of the Lester Patrick Trophy for his outstanding contributions to hockey in the United States.

1969–70 Preseason

The September 21 match between the Bruins and St. Louis Blues at Ottawa turned tragic when Bruins' defenseman Ted Green was involved in a stick-swinging duel with Wayne Maki of the Blues. Green suffered a fractured skull and had to have emergency surgery. Green was suspended for thirteen games while Maki was suspended for thirty days. Both players were also assessed $300 in fines. Green would miss the entire 1969–70 season due to the injury.

In addition to uncomfortable chest pains, Orr suffered an injury described as slightly pulled ligaments of the right knee. He was ordered off skates for at least a week of training camp.

In office news, Orr signed an endorsement contract to promote Yardley the purveyor of men's grooming products. Advertisements would regularly appear in the *Hockey News* and other publications.

October 1969

The Bruins were set to begin a seven-month odyssey that, in the end, would become a part of Boston sports' lore. With the temperatures inside Boston Garden hovering around eighty degrees, the Bruins and New York Rangers ushered in the 1969–70 schedule. Fred Stanfield and John McKenzie scored power play goals and lifted the Bruins to a 2–1 victory over the Rangers. Orr assisted on both goals.

On Wednesday evening, the Bruins hosted the Oakland Seals. Orr collected three more assists as the Bruins walked away with an easy win, 6–0. It was the first three-assist game in his career. Gerry Cheevers stopped seventeen shots to earn the shutout. The Bruins headed out to Pittsburgh for their first road game of the early season, the first half of a home-and-home weekend.

After running up a first-period 3–0 lead, the Bruins had to settle for a 3–3 tie at the Igloo. Orr earned his fifth assist on Wayne Cashman's first-period goal.

Back in Boston the next evening, Gerry Cheevers made his second start of the season and recorded his second consecutive shutout, this time a 4–0 whitewashing of the Penguins. Cheevers faced twenty-six shots while Orr scored his first goal in the victory. The Bruins embarked on a five-game road trip to Minnesota, Oakland, Los Angeles, Toronto, and Montreal.

The Bruins squeaked by the North Stars, 3–2, in game 1 of the western/eastern swing. Orr recorded the Gordie Howe hat trick as he scored a goal in the first period, engaged in a fight with former teammate Billy Goldsworthy, and assisted on a third-period goal by Phil Esposito. It was then on to Oakland and a Friday night meeting with the Seals.

Cheevers' shutout string of 151 minutes, 26 seconds was broken when the Seals' Joe Hardy scored Oakland's first goal at the 11:26 mark of the second period. However, the Bruins, behind two Esposito goals and three assists from Orr, tipped the Seals, 4–2. The three assists included the one hundredth of his career. The Bruins moved down the coast for a Saturday night game with the Kings. In a tight affair, the Bruins trimmed the Kings, 3–2, in Los Angeles. Orr earned two more assists in the victory as the Bruins headed back east to finish off the five-game road swing.

"I never saw him play before, and I just as soon hope to never see him again. It's almost hard to believe. The stats sheet says he had three shots, but he was responsible for fifteen others. Don't think for a minute that it is inconceivable that this man might come up with 100 points if he stays healthy" were the words of King's Coach Hal Laycoe. Laycoe had played with the Bruins in the 1950s.

As Boston headed into Toronto, the specter of twenty-two straight regular season games without a win at Maple Leaf Gardens hovered over the team. This game would be no exception. The Leafs had goals from Murray Oliver, Jim McKenney, Ron Ellis, and Dave Keon to hand the Bruins their first loss of the season, 4–2. Orr, although earning a minor penalty, was held off the score sheet for the first time this season.

October 1969					Orr's Stats				
					Game		Season		
Date	Venue	Versus	W-L-T	Score	G	A	G	A	PTS
12	Boston	New York	W	2–1	0	2	0	2	2
15	Boston	Oakland	W	6–0	0	3	0	5	5
18	Pittsburgh	Penguins	T	3–3	0	1	0	6	6
19	Boston	Pittsburgh	W	4–0	1	0	1	6	7
22	Minnesota	North Stars	W	3–2	1	1	2	7	9
24	Oakland	Seals	W	4–2	0	3	2	10	12
25	Los Angeles	Kings	W	3–2	0	2	2	12	14
29	Toronto	Maple Leafs	L	4–2	0	0	2	12	14

November 1969

The Bruins opened November on All Saints' Day in Montreal, and the way they played, none of the saints were with the team. The Canadiens throttled the B's in the one-sided 9–2 Montreal victory. Mickey Redmond had two goals for the Habs as they poured forty-nine shots on the B's goaltender Eddie Johnston. Orr was credited with one assist in the game on McKenzie's third-period goal. The Bruins wrapped up the five-game road trip at 3 wins and 2 losses.

Program from November 1, 1969 (Bruins at Montreal)

The next evening back in the cozy confines of the Boston Garden, the Bruins tangled with the Maple Leafs. They twice squandered two goal leads and settled for a 4–4 tie with Toronto. Esposito had two goals on the night while Orr tallied three assists.

The St. Louis Blues visited Boston on Wednesday night. In this contest, the Bruins gave up a two-goal lead once, then fell behind 4–3 before a Jim Harrison marker earned the B's a 4–4 tie with the Blues. For only the second time this season, Orr was held off the score sheet. The Bruins continued their uninspired play as they lost to Detroit, 3–2, and were now in the midst of a four-game winless streak. Orr did earn an assist on Garnet Bailey's first goal of the season.

In a rare Monday night game, the Bruins hosted the Oakland Seals. McKenzie and Bucyk each notched two goals, and Orr added three assists to lead the Bruins to an 8–3 victory over the visiting Oakland sextet. The Bruins had an astounding sixty-three shots on goal in the victory.

Orr poke-checks Billy Hicke (9) of Oakland as goaltender Eddie Johnston follows puck, and Gerry Ehman of the Seals looks to pick up the loose biscuit.

The Zamboni ice resurfacing machine, operated at the Boston Garden since 1954 and the first NHL venue to use the contraption, was replaced with a new Zamboni introduced during the November 10 game against Oakland. The original machine, number 21 had been operated by Lelo Grassa, who was well-known for his "tipping of the hat" as he entered and exited the rink. Grassa, the original operator of number 21, had the pleasure of navigating the new number 500 on this evening.

Lelo Grassa

Defenseman Rick Smith's first career NHL goal helped propel the Bruins to a 3–1 win over the Detroit Red Wings at Boston Garden. The Bruins scored two goals, one minute and thirty-two seconds apart in the third period to seal the deal. Orr had an assist on the final goal by Esposito.

The Bruins mid-November slump continued as they relinquished another two-goal lead and fell to the Rangers at Boston Garden, 6–5. Orr had his third and fourth goals of the season in the losing effort. This was the first home ice loss since Christmas of 1968. The unbeaten home streak lasted twenty-five games.

The next evening, the Los Angeles Kings visited the Garden. Stanfield had two goals, and Orr garnered four assists as the Bruins breezed by the Kings, 7–4. This was the first four-assist game in his career.

Eric Nesterenko scored both Chicago goals as the Bruins, and Hawks played to a 2–2 tie at Chicago Stadium. Nesterenko's tying goal was scored after Chicago pulled their goalie in the last minute and potted with just ten seconds left in the game. Orr had an assist on Stanfield's second-period goal and a unanimous decision in a fight with Chicago firebrand Keith Magnuson. The redheaded Chicago defenseman's aggressive and gritty play inspired the wrath of both Orr and Bruins' fans.

Despite firing forty-nine shots on Montreal goaltender Rogatien Vachon, the Bruins had to settle for a 2–2 tie in a November 23 meeting at the Boston Garden.

Three days later, the Bruins' woeful record against the Eastern Division continued in a downward spiral as they were blanked by the Rangers at Madison Square Garden by a score of 3–0. At this point in the season, the Bruins were 2-5-3 against the East. Orr did earn a major penalty when he became involved in a first-period fight with the Rangers' Dave Balon.

November 15, 1969, Orr and Dave Balon (17) engage in
first-period fisticuffs at Madison Square Garden.

The Bruins came back to life as they defeated the Philadelphia Flyers 6–4 at the Boston Garden on Thanksgiving night. Orr had two goals for the B's in the win. Boston had forty-one shots on ex-farmhand Doug Favell. "Boston is the only city I know where they celebrate Thanksgiving by thanking the Lord for a hockey player," stated Flyers' coach Vic Stasiuk.

On the 29th, Derek Sanderson's power play goal at 18:35 of the third period enabled the Bruins to come from behind and earn a 2–2 tie with the Canadiens at the Montreal Forum. The Bruins and Maple Leafs met at Boston Garden on Sunday night. Orr's power play goal in the first period helped the Bruins to a 4–1 victory over the Maple Leafs. The Bruins ended November with a 5-4-5 record and in third place behind New York and Montreal.

November 1969					Orr's Stats				
					Game		Season		
Date	Venue	Versus	W-L-T	Score	G	A	G	A	PTS
1	Montreal	Canadiens	L	9–2	0	1	2	13	15
2	Boston	Toronto	T	4–4	0	3	2	16	18
5	Boston	St. Louis	T	4–4	0	0	2	16	18
8	Detroit	Red Wings	L	3–2	0	1	2	17	19
10	Boston	Oakland	W	8–3	0	3	2	20	22
13	Boston	Detroit	W	3–1	0	1	2	21	23
15	Boston	New York	L	6–5	2	0	4	21	25
16	Boston	Los Angeles	W	7–4	0	4	4	25	29
21	Chicago	Blackhawks	T	2–2	0	1	4	26	30

23	Boston	Montreal	T	2–2	0	0	4	26	30
26	New York	Rangers	L	3–0	0	0	4	26	30
27	Boston	Philadelphia	W	6–4	2	1	6	27	33
29	Montreal	Canadiens	T	2–2	0	0	6	27	33
30	Boston	Toronto	W	4–1	1	1	7	28	35

December 1969

As December dawned, they faced the Red Wings at the Olympia in Detroit. The Bruins opened a 3–0 lead and then a 4–2 margin before succumbing to two third-period Detroit goals and settling for a 4–4 tie. Orr earned two assists to bring his total to thirty.

On Saturday night at the Garden, the Chicago Blackhawks provided the opposition for the Bruins. Ken Hodge scored the first two goals of the game, which proved to be all the Bruins needed as they glided past the Hawks, 6–1. Orr had one assist in the game. The Minnesota North Stars moved into the Garden on Sunday night.

Orr began writing a column for the *Boston Sunday Globe*. His first installment published on December 7 discussed the recent outbreak of physical encounters between players and referees.

The Bruins and Stars played to a 2–2 tie, but that was not the story of the game. Orr's left knee was injured in the third period when he blocked a shot by ex-mate Billy Goldsworthy. The extent of his injury was not disclosed, and he remained in question until Wednesday evening's game in New York.

Early in the day on the 10th, the Bruins obtained Wayne Carleton from the Toronto Maple Leafs for rugged center Jim Harrison. Carleton made his debut for Boston in that night's game at Madison Square Garden. In addition to assisting on Bucyk's first-period power play goal, Orr also had a second-period shorthanded marker. Unfortunately, the Rangers had three power play goals in addition to a shorthanded goal themselves and defeated the Bruins, 5–2.

The return matchup on Thursday night at Boston Garden featured newcomer Carleton scoring both Boston goals as the Bruins slid by the Rangers, 2–1. The team poured 49 shots on Eddie Giacomin, in goal for the New Yorkers.

Despite holding 2–0 and 3–1 leads, the B's had to fight back with two third-period goals to defeat the Flyers, 5–3, at the Spectrum in Philadelphia. Despite being blanked on the score sheet, Orr did manage nine minutes in penalties, which included a two-minute high-sticking minor and a fighting major when he became involved with Philadelphia's Earl Heiskala in the second period. The Bruins returned to Boston after the game to prepare for Sunday night's tilt with the Pittsburgh Penguins.

Gary Doak's first goal of the season, an unassisted score, was the margin of difference as the Bruins slipped by the Penguins at Boston Garden, 2–1.

The team traveled to St. Louis to meet the Blues on Thursday night. After building a 2–0 first-period lead, Boston had to settle for a 3–3 tie. With a penalty called against Noel Picard at 4:51 of the third period, Jim Lorentz capitalized off an Orr rebound for his second score of the game.

The Bruins defeated the Penguins 6–4 at Pittsburgh on December 20. Orr recorded five assists for the first time in his career. The five points matched the five points (three goals and two assists) Orr garnered on December 14, 1968. Bucyk had two goals in the affair. Defenseman Don Awrey scored his only goal of the season.

In Orr's *Sunday Boston Globe* column, he commented on the current crop of NHL players he also competed against in junior hockey, which included Mickey Redmond and Serge Savard of Montreal, Jim McKenney of Toronto, Danny Grant and Danny O'Shea of Minnesota, Andre Lacroix of Philadelphia, and teammates Wayne Cashman and Wayne Carleton.

In the Sunday night game at the Garden, Orr scored his ninth goal of the season, but the Bruins couldn't hold off the Canadiens and lost by a 2–1 count.

Christmas night featured the Los Angeles Kings at the Garden. Esposito and Hodge fired home two goals apiece, and Orr scored his tenth goal along with an assist as the Bruins easily rolled past the Kings, 7–1. Boston had twenty first-period shots on goal, but Gerry Desjardins, in the Los Angeles net, stopped them all. They warmed up in the second period and fired home six goals to take control of the game.

Orr's goal was shorthanded at 4:13 of the second stanza. At 7:55, he received a fighting major along with Bill "Cowboy" Flett of Los Angeles. After serving his penalty, he assisted on Johnny Bucyk's seventeenth goal at 16:44 of the second period and once again completed the Gordie Howe hat trick. The B's embarked on a five-game road trip to Philadelphia, Detroit, Los Angeles, Oakland, and Toronto.

In the start of the five-game road trip, Orr fired home a shorthanded first-period goal and added three assists to lead the Bruins to a 5–4 victory over the Flyers. This was Orr's first ever goal in Philadelphia.

The Bruins spent New Year's Eve in Detroit. Wings Captain Alex Delvecchio (who did not have a goal in his first thirty games) scored his first two goals of the season as the Red Wings easily defeated the Bruins, 5–1, at the Olympia. Orr was held off the score sheet for the first time in six games, although he did pick up a minor penalty for hooking at 9:00 of the second period. Boston ended the 1969 half of the schedule in second place behind the New York Rangers.

December 1969					Orr's Stats				
					Game		Season		
Date	Venue	Versus	W-L-T	Score	G	A	G	A	PTS
4	Detroit	Red Wings	T	4–4	0	2	7	30	37
6	Boston	Chicago	W	6–1	0	1	7	31	38

7	Boston	Minnesota	T	2–2	0	0	7	31	38
10	New York	Rangers	L	5–2	1	1	8	32	40
11	Boston	New York	W	2–1	0	0	8	32	40
13	Philadelphia	Flyers	W	5–3	0	1	8	33	41
14	Boston	Pittsburgh	W	2–1	0	0	8	33	41
18	St. Louis	Blues	T	3–3	0	1	8	34	42
20	Pittsburgh	Penguins	W	6–4	0	5	8	39	47
21	Boston	Montreal	L	5–2	1	0	9	39	48
25	Boston	Los Angeles	W	7–1	1	1	10	40	50
28	Philadelphia	Flyers	W	5–4	1	3	11	43	54
31	Detroit	Red Wings	L	5–1	0	0	11	43	54

January 1970

In Orr's latest *Boston Sunday Globe* column, he wrote that wearing helmets made sense, though he himself would never wear one. He also mentioned the owner of the St. Louis Blues, Sid Salomon, and how the Blues treat players "like people, not peons." The Blues were known for rewarding the team with various perks, such as making sure that players, if possible, spent Christmas with their families and enjoyed season ending vacations at the Solomon estate in Florida.

The Bruins spent the next week in California with games at Los Angeles and Oakland. In Los Angeles, Ken Hodge had two goals, including the one hundredth of his career, while Orr assisted on the Bruins' first and last goals as the B's downed the Kings, 6–2. The Bruins moved to Oakland and a midweek game with the Seals. Bucyk fired home two goals, including his three hundredth NHL goal, and the Bruins sailed past the Seals, 6–1. Orr had two assists in the game.

On Saturday night, the Bruins appeared on *Hockey Night in Canada* while trying to break a winless streak in Toronto that dated back more than four years. Although Orr was named the third star of the game while also scoring his twelfth goal, the B's still managed to lose to the Maple Leafs, 4–3. The Bruins ended the five-game road excursion at 3–2–0.

Back at the Boston Garden, the Bruins doubled up on the Seals with a 6–3 victory as Esposito fired home three goals. It was the first three-goal game by a Bruin player that season. Esposito scored one shorthanded, one on the power play, and one goal at even strength.

On top of being kept off the score sheet, Orr earned a ten-minute misconduct for questioning a call by Referee Art Skov.

On Thursday night, the Bruins hosted the Los Angeles Kings at the Garden. For the second consecutive game, the Bruins put up a six-spot as they trumped the

Kings, 6–3. Esposito had another two goals in the win, while Orr earned two assists. The Bruins opened up a 4–0 first-period lead, but the Kings came back with three straight goals before Esposito rallied with his two markers to wrap it up for the Bruins.

On Saturday night, the 17th, the Bruins lost a controversial 1–0 game to the Chicago Blackhawks at the Boston Garden. Gerry Pinder's goal at 7:39 of the second period was the only goal of the game. A brouhaha erupted when Referee Bill Friday declared Pinder's goal legal even though Friday was positioned near the blue line when the goal was scored. Replays of the event were inconclusive, although fans sitting at the Garden's east end insisted that the bulging of the net occurred when the butt end of Goaltender Eddie Johnston's stick struck a still camera mounted inside the Boston goal. The camera was being used by *Life Magazine*. The east end goal judge Tom Moon did not activate the goal light and was so sure of his judgment that he spent time shaking his head at Friday who refused to consult with him. The play ultimately cost the Bruins first place at the end of the season.

On the next night, the Montreal Canadiens came to Boston. After falling behind 3–2 at the end of two periods, the Bruins came back with four third-period goals as the B's knocked off the Habs, 6–3. Orr had his thirteenth goal to go along with an assist to lead the B's to the victory.

At the NHL All-Star Game, the East defeated the West 4–1. Orr appeared in his third straight All-Star Game but was held scoreless on the night. However, he was selected as third star of the game. The game was played in St. Louis, and Orr wore his traditional number 4 sweater. In the previous two games, Orr wore jerseys number 2 and number 5. The number 4 sweater had been worn by longtime Montreal great Jean Beliveau in previous games. Beliveau did not participate in the game, thus freeing up his number 4 jersey. Bucyk, Esposito, and McKenzie also represented the Bruins. The NHL announced that the 1971 game would be played at the Boston Garden.

This was an offering from Gerry Cheevers: "They say Bobby doesn't play defense. Heck, he makes hockey a forty-minute game for us. He's got the puck twenty minutes by himself. What better defense is there? If Orr has the puck, we're going to score—not the other guys."

After the All-Star Game break, the Bruins hosted the Philadelphia Flyers. The B's came back from three one-goal deficits and tied the Flyers on a goal by Esposito with six seconds left in the game. Orr assisted on the game, tying goal, as the Bruins peppered the Flyers with fifty-four shots.

In Orr's *Boston Sunday Globe* column, he defended teammate Phil Esposito's performance and constant criticism against him, calling it unfair and silly. Esposito's ability to score goals from the slot area had earned him the reputation as a "garbage man" although Bruins' fans saw Espo in a far different light. The Bruins and Rangers met to battle at Madison Square Garden on Saturday afternoon. Johnny Bucyk, with an assist from Orr and McKenzie, opened the scoring on the power play in the first period. After that, it was all Rangers. Jean Ratelle and Bob Nevin had two goals each, and the Rangers scored three power play goals while Bucyk was serving a major penalty for cutting Brad Park. The final score was 8–1 in favor of the Rangers.

The downtrodden Bruins returned home after the game to ready themselves for a Sunday night clash with the Penguins. Prior to the game, NHL President Clarence Campbell presented Esposito with the Art Ross Trophy and the Hart Trophy while Orr received the Norris Trophy, awards they won during the 1968–69 season. Orr tallied 176 points to top the Norris Trophy balloting. Runners up in the trophy race were Tim Horton of the Maple Leafs with 48 points and Ted Green of the Bruins with 27 points. In the game, Eddie Johnston turned aside thirty-four of thirty-five shots, and Orr deposited an empty net goal as the Bruins edged the Penguins, 3–1.

On Thursday night, the Minnesota North Stars entered the Garden. After the Bruins built up a 6–2 lead, they had to hold off the charging Stars before squeaking out a 6–5 win. Orr had a goal and three assists in the first period. Phil Esposito had his twenty-fifth and twenty-sixth goals in the contest. Ray Cullen had three goals for the North Stars.

The Bruins moved on to Montreal and a Saturday night encounter with the Canadiens. After spotting the Canadiens a 2–0 lead, the B's came back with two goals by Esposito and Orr's sixth as the teams battled to a 3–3 tie at the Forum. The Bruins ended January in second place behind the New York Rangers.

January 1970					Orr's Stats				
		Game		Season					
Date	Venue	Versus	W-L-T	Score	G	A	G	A	PTS
3	Los Angeles	Kings	W	6–2	0	2	11	45	56
7	Oakland	Seals	W	6–1	0	2	11	47	58
10	Toronto	Maple Leafs	L	4–3	1	2	12	49	61
11	Boston	Oakland	W	6–3	0	0	12	50	62
15	Boston	Los Angeles	W	6–3	0	2	12	51	63
17	Boston	Chicago	L	1–0	0	0	12	51	63
18	Boston	Montreal	W	6–3	1	1	13	52	65
22	Boston	Philadelphia	T	3–3	0	1	13	53	66
24	New York	Rangers	L	8–1	0	1	13	54	67
25	Boston	Pittsburgh	W	3–1	1	0	14	54	68
29	Boston	Minnesota	W	6–5	1	3	15	57	72
31	Montreal	Canadiens	T	3–3	1	1	16	58	74

A ditty called "That Wondrous Bobby" produced by RCA records was written by Charles Saba and performed by Allan Thicke. The reverse side of the record was "That Boston Dandy." Although Orr received a copy of the record from Mr. Saba, he had not been able to listen to it as he did not own a record player at the time. Thicke, a Canadian native, would later star in the television series *Growing Pains* and was a well-known actor, songwriter, and talk show host.

That Wondrous Bobby

Wondrous Bobby
Wondrous ways
Wondrous all-star when he plays
Born to be the nation's craze
Wondrous Bobby
Wondrous ways
Play a tune both loud and long
With a stick that can do no wrong
He'll snare a pass cruising by
Zoom right and let it fly
Precision plays can be found
And the praise is all around

Copyright, 1970, Dunbar Music of Canada, Ltd.

February 1970

The Bruins opened February with a nationally televised game with the Toronto Maple Leafs at the Boston Garden. The game featured a second-period bench-clearing brawl and thirteen goals, seven for Boston and six for the Leafs. The Bruins built up a 4–1 second-period lead only to have Toronto come back and tie the game. The Bruins then went up 6–4, but the Leafs came crawling back and tied the game early in the third session. John McKenzie's power play goal at 9:24 of the third period proved to be the game winner.

The bench clearing brawl was precipitated when Rick Ley of the Leafs left the Toronto bench to join the fray on the ice. The protagonists on the ice were McKenzie versus Brit Selby and Orr against old nemesis Pat Quinn. Orr, with a goal, two assists, and a fight earned yet another Gordie Howe hat trick.

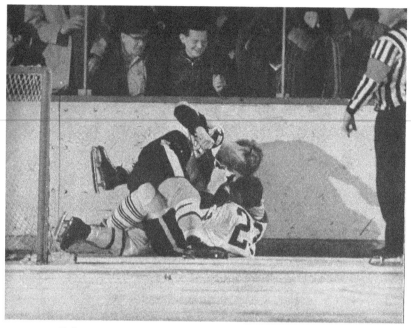

February 1, 1970, Boston Garden-Orr pummels Pat
Quinn to complete the Gordie Howe hat trick.

Twelve Bruins were fined $100. Eleven Leafs were fined $100. Two Leaf players were fined $200 (Rick Ley for leaving the bench and Brian Glennie for leaving the penalty box). And both franchises were levied $1,000 fines additionally.

The Bruins rode the rails to Chicago and were then ridden out of town on a rail after they succumbed to the Blackhawks at the Stadium, 8–4. Stan Mikita paced the Chicago win with one goal and four assists on the night. Sanderson had three assists for the B's in the loss. Although the Bruins traveled to Chicago by train, they returned to Boston via the air for their Thursday night game with the Flyers.

The Bruins, led by Orr's two goals and an assist, defeated Philadelphia at the Boston Garden 5–1. The story of the game was the benching of the slumping Ken Hodge and Wayne Carleton, although Carleton did dress for the game. Hodge, miffed and ordered to watch the game, left the building.

The Bruins met the Detroit Red Wings at Boston Garden on Saturday night. Orr's twentieth goal of the season was not enough to offset two goals by Garry Unger as the B's and Red Wings played to a 2–2 tie.

In the last home game before a six-game road trip, the Bruins hosted the St. Louis Blues. Don Marcotte scored three goals and McKenzie had two as they slid past the Blues 7–1. The game featured the return to Boston of Wayne Maki, who was involved in the stick-swinging incident with Ted Green during the preseason. Maki was lustily checked by various Bruins throughout the game while being booed continuously by Garden patrons. The team was now off to St. Louis, Pittsburgh, Oakland, Los Angeles, Minnesota, and Chicago.

Bobby Orr was the official greeter at the opening of the International Boat Show at the Prudential Center in Downtown Boston on February 7 and 8.

In the lid-lifter of the road trip, the Bruins met the Blues in St. Louis. McKenzie's late third-period power play goal lifted Boston to a 3–2 victory over the Blues. Orr had two assists in the contest. The Bruins moved on to Pittsburgh for a Saturday night game with the Penguins. Boston defeated Pittsburgh 3–0 and moved into a first place tie with New York. Orr had his twenty-first goal of the year while Gerry Cheevers stopped all thirty-five shots in goal for the B's.

McKenzie's twenty-first goal of the season allowed the Bruins to come from behind and tie the Seals in Oakland, 3–3. Orr had an assist on Bucyk's twenty-third goal of the year. The team moved on to Los Angeles for the next night's game.

Orr broke his own record when he scored his twenty-second goal in the first period of the 5–5 tie with the Kings at the Los Angeles Forum. Wayne Rutledge was the victim of the goal. McKenzie had two goals, but the Bruins had to come back from 5–4 deficit to tie the Kings on a goal by Eddie Westfall.

The B's headed back east as they prepared to meet the North Stars in Bloomington on the 21st. Orr had two goals and an assist as the Bruins defeated the Stars, 4–2.

The next afternoon, the Bruins met the Blackhawks in a nationally televised game from the Chicago Stadium. The B's opened the scoring at the 0:39 mark of the first period, but the Hawks scored four consecutive goals and easily defeated the Bruins, 6–3.

The team returned home from the six-game road jaunt to face the New York Rangers. The Bruins rolled out to a fast 3–0 lead in the first period and then a 4–1 lead early in the second before the Rangers tightened the game 4–3 at the end of the second stanza. Fred Stanfield's third-period power play goal iced the 5–3 victory for the Bruins.

Gerry Cheevers turned aside twenty-eight shots as the Bruins blanked the Chicago Blackhawks, 3–0, at the Boston Garden. The win put Boston one point behind the New York Rangers for the top spot in the Eastern Division.

February 1970					Orr's Stats				
					Game		Season		
Date	Venue	Versus	W-L-T	Score	G	A	G	A	PTS
1	Boston	Toronto	W	7–6	1	2	17	60	77
4	Chicago	Blackhawks	L	8–4	0	0	17	60	77
5	Boston	Philadelphia	W	5–1	2	1	19	61	80
7	Boston	Detroit	T	2–2	1	0	20	61	81

8	Boston	St. Louis	W	7–1	0	1	20	62	82
11	St. Louis	Blues	W	3–2	0	2	20	64	84
14	Pittsburgh	Penguins	W	3–0	1	0	21	64	85
17	Oakland	Seals	T	3–3	0	1	21	65	86
18	Los Angeles	Kings	T	5–5	1	1	22	66	88
21	Minnesota	North Stars	W	4–2	2	1	24	67	91
22	Chicago	Blackhawks	L	6–3	0	2	24	69	93
26	Boston	New York	W	5–3	0	0	24	69	93
28	Boston	Chicago	W	3–0	0	0	24	69	93

March 1970

The Bruins continued playing good hockey and moved into first place with a 3–1 victory over the St. Louis Blues at Boston Garden. The win put the B's one point ahead of the Rangers and vaulted them into first place in the Eastern Division. Orr had his twenty-fifth goal of the season, scored while on the power play. The Bruins had a return engagement with the Blues on Wednesday night in St. Louis.

In the road half of the home-and-home series for the Bruins, the Blues built up a 3–0 lead and never looked back as they defeated Boston by a 3–1 margin in a game played at the St. Louis Arena. Boston's lone tally was scored with twenty-five seconds remaining in the game. The team then moved on to Philadelphia.

Simon Nolet garnered his first career three-goal game, and ex-Bruin Gary Dornhoefer scored two goals as the Bruins and the Flyers settled for a 5–5 tie in an afternoon game at the Spectrum. Boston came back from a 3–1 deficit to go ahead 5–3 only to have the Flyers come back with Nolet, completing the hat trick with goals late in the second period and midway through the third period. Orr earned on assist on McKenzie's third-period goal.

In a nationally televised Sunday afternoon game, McKenzie and Hodge scored first-period goals, and it proved to be enough as the Bruins blanked the Canadiens, 2–0. Orr assisted on both Boston goals while Eddie Johnston made twenty-five saves as the B's continued to hold on to first place in the Eastern Division.

At Chicago Stadium on the 11th, the Bruins and Hawks played to a rare 0–0 tie. Eddie Johnston earned his second consecutive shutout, making thirty-two saves. Tony Esposito made twenty-four saves in the Chicago net.

For the twenty-fifth straight regular-season game at Maple Leaf Gardens, the Bruins came out on the short end of a 2–1 loss to Toronto. Boston fired forty-two shots on Bruce Gamble but were only able to pierce his armor once on a Bucyk power play goal in the first period.

The next evening back at the Garden, Orr had his twenty-sixth and twenty-seventh goals of the season and contributed two assists, but the Bruins were only able to grab a 5–5 tie against the Detroit Red Wings. Frank Mahovlich had his thirty-first and thirty-second goals in the game for Detroit. Orr's second goal of the night was shorthanded, his fourth "shortie" of the season. Orr continued his assault on the record books as he became the first defenseman to record 100 points in a season.

March 15, 1970, Orr slips the puck past Detroit netminder Roy Edwards.

The Bruins prepared for a first-place showdown against the Chicago Blackhawks on March 19 by holding a practice at Harvard University's Watson Rink on the campus in Cambridge. The weekday workout attracted over two thousand fans.

The Bruins edged the Hawks 3–1 on goals by Johnny Bucyk, his twenty-eighth and twenty-ninth and Sanderson's fourteenth. Eddie Johnston came within four minutes and forty-four seconds of shutting down the Hawks, but Dennis Hull spoiled the shutout.

The Bruins readied for a home-and-home series with the Minnesota North Stars. In the Saturday afternoon game in Bloomington, the Stars scored a 5–4 victory in spite of Orr's twenty-eighth goal of the season. He also garnered two assists in the contest, with Sanderson potting two goals in the losing effort.

Back in Boston on Sunday night, the Bruins blanked the North Stars in the return matchup at Boston Garden, 5–0. Orr's twenty-ninth and thirtieth goals of the season, along with two assists, paced the Boston attack. Johnny Bucyk scored his thirtieth. As the Bruins moved into the last two weeks of the season, they held a one-point lead over the Chicago Blackhawks.

The Bruins moved into Madison Square Garden for a Wednesday night game with the Rangers. Sanderson's second-period shorthanded goal helped the B's to a 3–1 victory. The win helped the Bruins maintain a three-point lead over Chicago. Due to the nationwide air traffic controller strike, the Bruins were forced to travel back and forth to New York by bus for that March 25 game with the Rangers.

For the second consecutive weekend, Boston was involved in a home-and-home matchup, this time the Detroit Red Wings providing the opposition. In the Saturday matinee at Boston Garden, it took Orr's third-period goal, scored with less than four minutes on the clock, to salvage a 5–5 tie. The B's gave up a 3–1 lead, only to fall back 4–3 and then 5–4 before Orr's thirty-first goal of the season knotted the game. In addition to the two goals, Orr also had two assists in the contest. The four points in the game gave Orr 101 on the season, thus becoming the first defenseman in NHL history to record 100 points. The B's and Wings would meet the next afternoon at the Olympia in the Motor City.

Alex Delvecchio's third-period power play goal lifted the Wings into a 2–2 tie with the Bruins. Orr assisted on both Boston goals, but the resulting tie enabled the Chicago Blackhawks to vault into a tie for first place with the Hawks owning the tie breaker (more wins) in the standings.

With a snowstorm raging back east, the Bruins were not able to fly back to Boston, forcing them to sleep over in Dearborn, Michigan. They moved on to Windsor, Ontario, located across the river from Detroit, where they would fly to Montreal for the first of the final three games of the year.

March 1970					Orr's Stats				
					Game		Season		
Date	Venue	Versus	W-L-T	Score	G	A	G	A	PTS
1	Boston	St. Louis	W	3–1	1	0	25	69	94
4	St. Louis	Blues	L	3–1	0	0	25	69	94
7	Philadelphia	Flyers	T	5–5	0	1	25	70	95
8	Boston	Montreal	W	2–0	0	2	25	72	97
11	Chicago	Blackhawks	T	0–0	0	0	25	72	97
14	Toronto	Maple Leafs	L	2–1	0	0	25	72	97
15	Boston	Detroit	T	5–5	2	2	27	74	101
19	Boston	Chicago	W	3–1	0	0	27	74	101
21	Minnesota	North Stars	L	5–4	1	2	28	76	104
22	Boston	Minnesota	W	5–0	2	2	30	78	108
25	New York	Rangers	W	3–1	0	1	30	79	109
28	Boston	Detroit	T	5–5	1	2	31	81	112
29	Detroit	Red Wings	T	2–2	0	2	31	83	114

April 1970

Despite a losing effort in Montreal, the Bruins retained a first place tie with Chicago. The final score in Montreal was 6–3 in favor of the Habs. Phil Esposito had two goals (his forty-first and forty-second), while Orr registered his thirty-second goal of the season in the loss.

For the third weekend in a row, the Bruins were involved in a home-and-home set, this time with the Maple Leafs. After twenty-five games without a victory in Toronto, the Bruins finally disposed of the Leafs with a solid, 4–2 victory at Maple Leaf Gardens. Orr had his thirty-third goal in the victory.

In the season finale at Boston Garden, the Bruins again bested Toronto, this time by a 3–1 count. Orr had an assist on McKenzie's second-period goal.

April 1970					Orr's Stats				
					Game		Season		
Date	Venue	Versus	W-L-T	Score	G	A	G	A	PTS
1	Montreal	Canadiens	L	6–3	1	2	32	85	117
4	Toronto	Maple Leafs	W	4–2	1	1	33	86	119
5	Boston	Toronto	W	3–1	0	1	33	87	120

1969–1970 Standings

Eastern Division

	W	L	T	PTS	GF	GA
Chicago	45	22	9	99	250	170
Boston	40	17	19	99	277	216
Detroit	40	21	15	95	246	199
New York	38	22	16	92	246	189
Montreal	38	22	16	92	244	201
Toronto	29	34	13	71	222	242

Western Division

	W	L	T	PTS	GF	GA
St. Louis	37	27	12	86	224	179
Pittsburgh	26	38	12	64	182	238

Minnesota	19	35	22	60	224	257
Oakland	22	40	14	58	169	243
Philadelphia	17	35	24	58	197	225
Los Angeles	14	52	10	38	168	290

April 1970 Playoffs

The Bruins and New York Rangers were set to meet in the Stanley Cup Playoffs for the first time since 1958. The best of seven series opened in Boston on Wednesday night, April 8.

Phil Esposito's three goals led the way as the Bruins trounced New York, 8–2, in the opening game of the 1970 playoffs. Boston also scored two shorthanded goals on the same penalty with Esposito and Sanderson scoring forty-four seconds apart.

After falling behind 2–1 in game 2, the B's stormed back with four straight goals and defeated the Rangers in game 2 by a score of 5–3. The B's, with a 2–0 game advantage, headed to New York for games 3 and 4 to be played over the weekend.

Madison Square Garden organist Eddie Layton played "Talk to the Animals" in getting the capacity crowd of 17,250 worked up for game 3. Wayne Cashman set a Bruins' record with thirty-two minutes in penalties in a wild, 4–3 loss to the Rangers at Madison Square Garden. Derek Sanderson was thrown out of the game after a first period free for all involving all the players on the ice. The game took an unusually long three hours and six minutes to play; 174 penalty minutes were called with 138 minutes called in the first period alone. The Rangers got back in the series with the 4–3 victory.

On the next evening, the Rangers moved out quickly as Rod Gilbert scored two goals in the first five minutes of a 4–2 victory for New York. Bruins goaltender Eddie Johnston played his only game in the playoffs. With the series all knotted up, the teams moved back to Boston for the pivotal fifth game.

Prior to game 5, a moment of silence was held for the astronauts aboard Apollo 13, which had lost power while attempting to land on the moon. The oxygen tank of the command module had exploded, preventing the Apollo from landing on the moon. Despite extreme hardships on the crew, the spacecraft was able to return to Earth on April 17. After an early Orr goal, the Rangers came back with two goals and took a 2–1 lead heading into the third period. Esposito then came up big with two goals, one at 2:20 and the other at 7:59. The Bruins survived two New York power plays late in the third period and won the game, 3–2.

When the Bruins arrived at the Newark, New Jersey, airport prior to game 6, the bus driver responsible for taking the B's to their New Jersey hideaway caused the Bruins angst when he could not find the location of the team's hotel.

In game 6, Boston finally eliminated the Rangers by a score of 4–1. Orr scored two goals in the win to raise his total to seven goals for the playoffs. This broke the record for goals scored in the playoffs shared by Earl Seibert of Chicago in 1938 and Red Kelly of Detroit in 1954.

A frustrated Rod Gilbert of the New York Rangers just couldn't believe it. "That Orr, he is impossible. Hockey is a team game, right? One man is not supposed to beat a whole team, right? But what else can I say? You saw it. One man beat the Rangers in this series."

In the other east division series, the Chicago Blackhawks knocked off the Detroit Red Wings, so it would be the Bruins and Chicago in the Division finals. Chicago, having finished in first place, received home advantage for the first two games of the series. In the opener of the semifinal round, Esposito fired home three goals against younger brother Tony, who was tending the twine for the Blackhawks. The Bruins moved on to a 6–3 victory.

Game 2 was also the Bruins' victory as Orr, McKenzie, Marcotte, and Esposito found the back of the net in the 4–1 win. The Bruins, with the next two games at home, held a 2–0 lead in the series.

With the series now in Boston, the thought of a sweep started to creep into the minds of the local fandom. In game 3, the Hawks were leading 2–1 after the first period, but the B's went to work and scored the game's next four goals in the 5–2 victory, giving Boston a stranglehold on the series. Bucyk netted two of the goals for Boston. Gerry Cheevers won his fifth straight playoff game for the Bruins.

Game 4 would prove to be the most competitive game of the series. After Don Marcotte's shorthanded goal and John Bucyk's even strength marker, the Bruins took a 2–0 lead into the first intermission. As Dennis Hull was leading the charge with two goals, the Chicagoans scored three consecutive times and took a 3–2 lead before Stanfield's goal at 15:40 of the second stanza tied up the game at the end of the second period, 3–3. Orr's cousin Bryan Campbell put the Chicago sextet ahead again at 4:10 of the third. At 15:19, Ken Hodge tied up the game with assists to Cashman and Esposito.

With the clock winding down to less than two minutes in the game, Fred Stanfield lasered a perfect pass to McKenzie breaking in on the right wing. As his shot dented the net behind Tony Esposito, the crowd erupted into a frenzy. When the Bruins killed off the remaining time in the game, it had earned the right to be in the Stanley Cup finals for the first time since 1958. Pandemonium reigned inside and outside the old barn on Causeway Street, but there was still unfinished business before they could quaff from the Cup. The Stanley Cup finals were now set as the Bruins would meet the St. Louis Blues.

During the 1960s and into the '70s, one of the pleasures of attending a game at the Boston Garden was seeing the flags of the six teams, the so-called Original Six hanging in the Garden's rafters. The New York Rangers and Toronto Maple Leafs banners were set on blue background. Chicago, Detroit, and Montreal had red fields. Boston's flag was gold, black, and white. The set remained in the "heavens" even after the 1967 expansion. Sometime in January of 1970, a brave (but probably crazy) soul decided to move up in the girders and pilfered Chicago's handsome ensign. The logo on the red field bore resemblance to the early 1950s Blackhawks circle emblem. Life and games continued at the Boston Garden, albeit without Chicago's pennant.

During the postgame handshakes and with the crowd delirious with happiness, the Chicago Blackhawks flag that had been missing for weeks was, and without notice, suddenly unfurled from the second balcony on the north side of the building. Upon seeing the spectacle, the building seemingly shook with joy. When the playoffs returned to the Garden for games 3 and 4 of the Stanley Cup finals against St. Louis, Chicago's colors were proudly hanging from its rightful place among the heavenly girders.

| **April 1970 Playoffs** | | | | | Orr's Stats | | | | |
| Date | Venue | Versus | W-L-T | Score | Game | | Season | | |
					G	A	G	A	PTS
8	Boston	New York	W	8–2	2	1	2	1	3
9	Boston	New York	W	5–3	0	1	2	2	4
11	New York	Rangers	L	4–3	1	0	3	2	5
12	New York	Rangers	L	4–2	1	0	4	2	6
14	Boston	New York	W	3–2	1	1	5	3	8
16	New York	Rangers	W	4–1	2	0	7	3	10
19	Chicago	Blackhawks	W	6–3	0	2	7	5	12
21	Chicago	Blackhawks	W	4–1	1	0	8	5	13
23	Boston	Chicago	W	5–2	0	1	8	6	14
26	Boston	Chicago	W	5–4	0	1	8	7	15

May 1970 Playoffs

The Stanley Cup finals series opened in St. Louis on May 3 with the Blues hosting the B's. In game 1, Bucyk's hat trick led the Bruins in a 6–1 thrashing of the Blues. Ernie Wakely surrendered two of Bucyk's three goals while Jacques Plante gave up one. Wakely had replaced Plante in goal for St. Louis after Plante had been felled by a Fred Stanfield slap shot earlier in the game.

When the Bruins defeated the Blues in game 2 of the finals on May 5 at St. Louis, Orr recorded two assists to bring his total of points to 18 for the playoffs, a record for a defenseman in one playoff year. Orr's points broke the record formerly held by Tim Horton of Toronto in 1962. Gerry Cheevers went on to record his eighth straight playoff victory. The teams moved back to Boston for games 3 and 4.

Game 3 was played on Thursday night, May 7, in the Boston Garden. Frank St. Marseille scored a power play goal, but it would be the Blues' only goal of the game as the Bruins won going away, 4–1. Wayne Cashman scored two of the four Boston goals in the victory

Mother's Day, May 10, 1970, was a day that any Bruins' fan at the time would have etched in their conscience forever. It would be remembered and celebrated each spring. With Dan Kelly calling the game on CBS television and Fred Cusick at the microphone on WBZ radio, the call of the goal conjures up a time of our lives when anything seemed possible. Many of us were all barely out of our teenage years, still suffering from acne and greasy hair. The Vietnam War was going full tilt. There was unrest in the country as four students at Kent State University were killed by National Guardsmen. But in Boston, it was a beautiful, warm early spring afternoon.

Rick Smith of the Bruins gave the B's an early 1–0 lead, but St. Louis, playing their best game of the series, came storming back with Red Berenson lighting the lamp at 19:17 of the first period and Gary Sabourin of the Blues scoring at 3:22 of the second stanza. Sabourin's goal would be the first scored by a player from Parry Sound, Ontario, on this afternoon. Phil Esposito tied the game for Boston with a goal from the slot at 14:22 of period 2.

Early in the third, Larry Keenan of the Blues made it 3–2 with a goal at the nineteen-second tick. The score stayed in St. Louis' favor until Johnny Bucyk finished off a terrific rush and tied the game at 3–3 with just under seven minutes left in regulation.

It was a very sultry afternoon in the Garden as the teams prepared for overtime. The upper reaches of the Garden had concession stands in all four corners. Bottled beer was cracked open and poured into Dixie cups. A shovel of ice chilled the Coca-Cola, but not for long. As the final period began, many fans were still below the stadium on the Garden concourse, waiting in a long line to use the always overcrowded restrooms or still waiting for their cool libation. And suddenly at 5:10 p.m., the Bruins' checking line of Sanderson, Westfall, and Carleton, was sent out to start the overtime. The defense paring was Awrey and Orr. As the puck moved into the St. Louis zone, it rimmed around the net to the right wing boards. Orr kept the puck in the zone and passed it up to Sanderson standing behind the goal line to the left of Glenn Hall, in goal for the Blues. At the forty-second mark, as Orr was cruising in front of the St. Louis goal, he received a pass from Sanderson and knocked it past Hall for the overtime winner, and the celebration began.

The 4s were wild.
The Bruins scored four goals in the game.
The fourth goal was scored by number 4 Bobby Orr.

Orr's goal was scored while being tripped by Noel Picard, number 4 of the Blues.

The goal was scored in the fourth period (first overtime) of the game.

The goal was scored at the forty-second mark.

The victory marked the fourth Stanley Cup championship in Bruins history.

Derek Sanderson (number 16 is 4 squared) assisted on Orr's goal

Orr's goal was also the second goal scored by a player from Parry Sound, Ontario, on this day. It was Orr's first goal of the finals.

With the winning of the Conn Smythe Trophy as MVP of the playoffs, Orr, for the first time in NHL history, won four major awards. They were the Art Ross Trophy as top scorer, Hart Trophy as MVP of the regular season, Norris Trophy as best defenseman and the aforementioned Conn Smythe Trophy. Orr had a point in all fourteen playoff games for a playoff consecutive-point scoring record. Counting the final eight games of the regular season, he had at least one point in twenty-two straight games.

A historical footnote to the Stanley Cup final is recorded on this beautiful May day. This was the last time that the original bowl of the Stanley Cup was used. In the summer of 1970, it was retired to the Hockey Hall of Fame in Toronto.

May 1970 Playoffs					Orr's Stats				
	Game			Playoffs					
Date	Venue	Versus	W-L-T	Score	G	A	G	A	PTS
3	St. Louis	Blues	W	6–1	0	1	8	8	16
5	St. Louis	Blues	W	6–2	0	2	8	10	18
7	Boston	St. Louis	W	4–1	0	1	8	11	19
10	Boston	St. Louis	W	4–3 (OT)	1	0	9	11	20

In the midst of the 1970 Stanley Cup playoffs, newspapermen were complaining about how Bobby Orr had made life so difficult for them. "How many different ways can you describe his greatness?" (*Hockey Stars of 1971*, Stan Fischler).

"Orr is at least hockey's sixth dimension. He revolutionizes his game as Babe Ruth did, as Bill Russell did. He plays a game with which I am not familiar. Orr plays hockey in a way that makes old timers feel like dinosaurs" (Larry Merchant, *New York Post*).

Fleetwood Records of Revere, Massachusetts, releases "Goal Bruins," a 33 rpm vinyl record chronicling the 1969–70 season.

"In my opinion, Gordie Howe was the greatest player of all time, but Orr was just a step away" (Glenn Hall).

"If you're going to get scored on, I don't mind as long as it's Bobby Orr. To my mind, he was the greatest hockey player in the world" (Noel Picard).

"I don't remember anything about the game except the last goal" (Red Berenson).

"Looking back, I was fortunate enough to play in Bobby Orr's prime. He was the best. He was the only player who could singlehandedly take control of a game" (Tim Ecclestone).

"As long as it's Bobby Orr, that's okay. If it would have been a fourth-line guy, I'd feel kind of bad, but not if it's Bobby Orr. It was an honor to be on the ice with him" (Jean Guy Talbot).

"If it wasn't for me, Bobby would never have scored that goal. I let in three bad goals during the game. I think I could have had a couple of them. All I had to do is stop one of them, and we would have won in regulation" (Gerry Cheevers).

The Goal by Andrew Podneiks (the above quotes)

"I never thought I'd be saying this but I always thought Howie Morenz was the greatest player I ever saw and now, I've got to change my mind. There's never been one to equal Orr" (King Clancy—Toronto Maple Leafs).

When the Bruins won the Stanley Cup on May 10, the breakdown of birthplaces of the players was as follows:

- Ontario, 21
- Quebec, 9
- Alberta, 2
- Manitoba, 2
- Saskatchewan, 1
- England, 1

The city of Montreal (4) represented the most players dressed for the deciding Stanley Cup game. It was followed closely by Toronto (3) and Parry Sound (3). The three Parry Sound players were Orr along with the Blues' Terry Crisp and Gary Sabourin. It is amazing that a small town of about six thousand residents would produce three National Hockey Leaguers to appear in this deciding game for the Cup. The three were all born within the space of five years.

"First of all, I felt he had a tendency to go on the offensive too much, but I can't think of a time when he couldn't get back with his fantastic speed to take care of his defensive job. The second thing I wanted to be shown was whether he could control the tempo of a game. That's the mark of a great defenseman, like Doug Harvey, and I thought it could only come from experience. But Bobby can do that too. He can speed things up or slow them down anytime he feels like it. He may be the only guy who was born experienced" (Harry Sinden).

"A few people knocked Orr and Gretzky and Guy Lafleur as being ineffective defensively, which just made me shake my head. When my teams played against Orr and Gretzky—and Lafleur was on my side—much of the time when they were on the ice, they had the puck. It's difficult for the opposition to score in that situation and that seems like rather good defense to me. And if they didn't have the puck, they were the best at stripping it from the opposition" (Scotty Bowman).

View from the Balcony

The Gallery Gods, the special fans that populated the second balcony at Boston Garden, were considered the most passionate and knowledgeable patrons of the Bruins with their lineage going back to the building of the Garden. They understood the twenty-nine years of frustration. They had not seen a Cup winner since months before the onset of American involvement in World War II. As the team took hold of the lowest rungs of the NHL standings in the early 1960s, management promised that a savior was on the way, a player that would make old-timers forget Eddie Shore and Milt Schmidt. They even showcased him at the Boston Garden on a couple of occasions while he was still in junior hockey.

In October 1966, Orr arrived, and as a small child will stumble before it walks, the B's with Orr stepped backward and went from fifth place in the standings to last place. But in the spring of 1968, after eight straight seasons out of the play-offs, Boston qualified for the postseason. Although the series against Montreal ended quickly, the taste of the tournament gave rise to the B's lasting two rounds in 1969, again being knocked out by the Canadiens. It might be that the better team did not win the 1969 Stanley Cup, but the combination of frustration and anticipation led to high expectations with the onset of the 1969–1970 campaign. The frustration all ended on that glorious Mother's Day of 1970. With Orr imitating Nureyev, he sealed the deal at the forty-second mark of the first overtime period beating Blues' goaltender Glenn Hall and sending the city of Boston into a controlled frenzy. It had been a mere 10,620 days between Cup championships. When the Bruins won the Cup in 1941, they celebrated it with a banquet at the Copley Plaza Hotel. In 1970, over one hundred thousand fans crowded the City Hall Plaza and joined the team in celebration of a Stanley Cup win. Orr, without having to die, was granted immediate sainthood by the local hockey mavens.

Top Hockey Stories from 1970

Stanley Cup Champions	Boston Bruins
Art Ross Trophy	Bobby Orr, Boston Bruins
Hart Trophy	Bobby Orr, Boston Bruins
Masterton Trophy	Pit Martin, Chicago Blackhawks
Lady Byng Trophy	Phil Goyette, St. Louis Blues
Vezina Trophy	Tony Esposito, Chicago Blackhawks
Calder Trophy	Tony Esposito, Chicago Blackhawks
Smythe Trophy	Bobby Orr, Boston Bruins
Norris Trophy	Bobby Orr, Boston Bruins
Calder Cup	Champions Buffalo Bisons
Memorial Cup Champions	Montreal Junior Canadiens
NCAA Hockey Champions	Cornell

Top Sports Stories

World Series Champions	Baltimore Orioles
Super Bowl V Champions	Baltimore Colts (game played on 1/17/1971 at Orange Bowl, Miami, Florida)
NBA Champions	New York Knickerbockers
Kentucky Derby Winner	Dust Commander
NCAA Football Champions	Nebraska (11-0-1), Texas (10-1-0) and Ohio State (9-1-0)
NCAA Basketball Champions	UCLA
World Cup Winner	Brazil over Italy

A happy Orr beams following the game. TV38 announcer
Don Earle is pictured on the lower right.

The goal from a slightly different angle: Referee Bruce Hood (5) signals Orr's
Stanley Cup winning goal. St. Louis Blues defenseman Jean Guy Talbot is seen on
the outside edge behind the net. Glenn Hall is the goaltender, and Noel Picard is
seen in front of Hall. Linesman Ron Ego is seen in the background behind Orr.

Two things happen when a goal is scored. The goal judge flicks on the light while the referee signals a goal has been scored. The National Hockey League assigned the minor officials (official scorer, game timekeeper, penalty timekeeper, and goal judges) to the contest. During the playoffs, the NHL assigned the minor officials, and for this Stanley Cup game, the officials came from the New York Rangers.

Official scorer: Louis Crovat
Game timekeeper: Robert McGowan
Penalty timekeeper: Edward Aubel
East goal judge: Arthur Reichert
West goal judge: Saul Maslow

The Bruins traditionally defended the west goal in the first and third periods. Since the game was in overtime (fourth period), the Blues were defending the west goal. Photos of the goal seen from the front of the net show the west goal judge to be Saul Maslow. So when the question "Who flicked on the light when Orr scored the winning goal?" is asked, the answer is Saul Maslow.

NATIONAL HOCKEY LEAGUE

OFFICIAL REPORT OF MATCH

Boston — vs — Saint Louis

Played in Boston Garden, Boston Rink, Date May 10th 1970

HOME CLUB		Y or N		VISITING CLUB		Y or N
No.				No.		
30	Cheevers	Y	Goal	1	Hall	Y
1	Johnston	N	Sub-Goal	31	Wakely	N
4	Orr	Y	Defense	3	Talbot	Y
10	R. Smith	Y	"	4	Picard	Y
20	D. Smith	Y	"	5	Bob Plager	Y
24	Speer	N	"	12	Talbot (A)	Y
25	Doak	Y	"	13	Bill Plager	Y
26	Awrey	Y	"			
				6	Roberts (A)	Y
7	Esposito (A)	Y	Forward	7	Berenson (A)	Y
8	Hodge	Y	"	9	St Marseille	Y
9	Bucyk (A)	Y	"	10	Goyette (A)	Y
11	Carleton	Y	"	11	Sabourin	Y
12	Cashman	Y	"	12	Crisp	Y
16	Sanderson	Y	"	14	Ecclestone	Y
17	Stanfield	Y	"	15	McCreary	Y
18	Westfall (A)	Y	"	18	Reimer	Y
19	McKenzie	Y	"	20	McDonald	Y
21	Marcotte	Y	"	21	Bordeleau	Y
22	MacGregor	Y	"	22	Gray	Y

Game starting time 7:05 P.M. First period ended at 3:15 P.M. Second period started at 3:17 P.M. and ended at 3:52 P.M. Third period started at 4:13 P.M. and ended at 4:52 P.M. Overtime started - 5:09 ended 5:10

Won by Boston Score 4 to 3

Official Scorer Lynne Grove Game Timekeeper Reg McGowan

Penalty Timekeeper Ed Cembal

Goal Judges Anthony Rizzolot — Sam Marlow

Linesmen Matt Pavelich — Ron Ego

REMARKS:

Signed D. Hood

Lynne Grove Referee / Official-Scorer

SPECIAL INSTRUCTIONS

1969-1970 BOSTON BRUINS . . . STANLEY CUP CHAMPIONS

First Row: (l. to r.) Gerry Cheevers, Milt Schmidt, General Manager, Coach Harry Sinden, Ed Johnston, Weston W. Adams, Chairman, Weston W. Adams, Jr., President, Tom Johnson, Asst. Gen. Mgr., 1970-71 Coach, John Adams.
Second Row: Dan Canney, Trainer, Bill Lesuk, Bobby Orr, Wayne Cashman, Eddie Westfall, Phil Esposito, Don Awrey, Don Marcotte, John Bucyk, Fred Stanfield, John Forristall, Asst. Trainer.
Third Row: John McKenzie, Ron Murphy, Dallas Smith, Derek Sanderson, Wayne Carleton, Ken Hodge, Bill Speer, Garnet Bailey, Gary Doak, Jim Lorentz, Rick Smith.

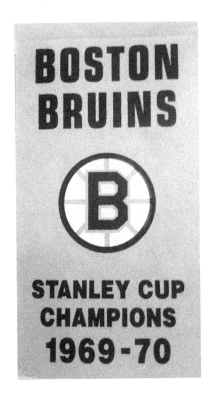

CHAPTER 5

1970–1971: The Dynasty Ends

D URING THE 1969–70 SEASON, ORR had moved into a rented home on Carolann Road in suburban Lynnfield. He was frequently seen in his front yard, talking to groups of kids. Neighbors noticed. "A star, friend, neighbor, an inspiration to youth, a high scorer both in the rink and in the hearts of the townspeople of Lynnfield," read the plaque Orr received at a testimonial dinner held in his honor on May 30. Proceeds from the event went to local children to attend hockey camps. More than five hundred locals attended the event, including teammates Eddie Johnston, Ken Hodge, and Eddie Westfall. One sad note as a moment of silent prayer was said in honor of ex-Bruin goaltender Terry Sawchuck, who had passed away the previous day in New York.

The big news of the off-season was Coach Harry Sinden's decision to leave the Bruins four days after winning the Stanley Cup. Sinden accepted an executive position with the Sterling Homex Company of Rochester, New York, a leader in the field of industrial homes. Two weeks after Sinden's resignation, the Bruins named Tom Johnson to succeed him. He became the twelfth coach in team history.

May 14, 1970, Bruins Coach Harry Sinden shakes hands with General
Manager Milt Schmidt after resigning as coach of the Bruins.

Orr was set to embark on a full schedule for the summer of 1970. He was among
several Canadian athletes who met Prince Charles at a gathering in Ottawa. "Bobby
Orr Day" was held in Parry Sound on July 4. Orr's good friend, Father Francis Chase
of Sacred Heart Parish in Watertown, Massachusetts, gave the invocation. Among
the gifts received by Orr was an oil portrait done by Larry Johnson of the *Boston
Globe* and a copy of the bill authorizing the building of the Bobby Orr Recreation
Center in Parry Sound. Bobby Orr Pizza in Oshawa also opened that summer. The
franchise was a division of Champs Food Service of Winnipeg, Manitoba.

Orr's hockey stick, signed by all his teammates, sold for $1,000 at the Channel
2 auction. Channel 2 was and continued to be the local public broadcasting station
in the city of Boston. Orr was continuing his involvement in the Bobby Orr–Mike
Walton Hockey School located in Orillia, Ontario. Cost of a one-week stay at the
camp was $125.

Orr and John McKenzie were one of the twenty-four teams competing in the
American Airlines NHL Players' Association golf tournament in Toronto from June
5 to 28. One other Boston tandem consisting of Eddie Johnston and John Bucyk
would also compete in the tourney that was worth $12,000. Orr was honored at
the American Academy of Achievement awards dinner in Dallas, Texas. Also receiving awards that evening were Henry M. Watts, president of the Muscular Dystrophy
Association, Walter Lantz, the creator of the Woody Woodpecker cartoon, and actor
John Wayne.

Alan Eagleson, attorney for Orr, reported that the star defenseman was spending over $15,000 a year sending autographed pictures to his fans. Eagleson explained
that Orr could not deduct this expense from his Canadian income tax obligations.

The Bruins would open training camp on September 10 in London, Ontario. The Stanley Cup would make a reappearance in Boston for nine days beginning September 23. The chalice would be on display at the State Street Bank and Trust main lobby along with the stick that Derek Sanderson used to assist on Bobby Orr's Stanley Cup game-winning goal.

The Bruins opened up the exhibition schedule with a 7–5 loss to the Chicago Blackhawks in a game played in London, Ontario. Orr injured his right wrist when he was jammed into the boards, but x-rays were negative. He would miss at least the next two exhibition games. As his wrist remained sore, it was speculated that he may have tendinitis. Hockey fans in Quebec City, expecting an appearance by Orr for a scheduled exhibition game with the Flyers, protested loudly to the Flyers' and the club's minor league affiliate, the Quebec Aces, management about his absence. The B's lost the contest 2–1. Similar incidents of fan dissatisfaction were expressed in Kitchener, Ontario (New York Rangers farm location), and at Madison Square Garden, where Orr also missed action.

The Bruins hosted the Montreal Canadiens in a home exhibition game on October 4. Orr had an assist on a late goal by Bucyk. Of note in this exhibition game was the Montreal goaltender, one Ken Dryden, who spent most of the season with the AHL Montreal Voyageurs. A former B's draft pick, Dryden, would play a major role against the Bruins the following spring.

As the Bruins opened the 1970–71 season, the expectations were high that the B's would make another strong run at the Stanley Cup. Anticipation was so high that the regular season seemed like a mere formality. With the addition of two new clubs, the Vancouver Canucks and the Buffalo Sabres, Boston would now embark on a seventy-eight-game schedule, up from the seventy-six-game schedule they had played the previous two seasons. The B's lost Stanley Cup members Gary Doak to Vancouver and Jim Lorentz to Buffalo. Doak was a former roommate of Orr during his first season with the cub.

"Bobby Orr: The Canadian Game" was shown on the Bruins' local outlet, Channel 38. The sixty-minute special was filmed by the Canadian Broadcasting Company over the final two months of the 1969–70 campaign. The film debut in Canada received rave reviews.

October 1970

The Bruins opened the season with a 7–3 victory over the visiting Detroit Red Wings. Orr assisted on a first-period goal by Bucyk but later had to leave the game after he was hit by the Wings' Frank Mahovlich. He suffered a charley horse in the Sunday night opener but was expected to fly to Los Angeles as the Bruins headed out for an early season West Coast swing.

Ironically, Eddie Westfall suffered the same injury when he was hit by Detroit defenseman Bobby Baun. In Orr's case, he was rushed to the Massachusetts General Hospital for precaution. Westfall hobbled out of the Garden on his own accord.

In the road opener at Los Angeles, Orr was credited with two second-period assists, and Phil Esposito registered a hat trick as the Bruins won a high-scoring 8–5 victory over the Kings. Bruins' games from the West Coast, Oakland, Los Angeles, and Vancouver were televised live back to Boston on WSBK (TV 38). This was the first time this was done by any team on the east coast.

Two nights later, the Bruins appeared in Oakland to meet the rechristened California Golden Seals, who were now clad in white skates. The club was now under the ownership of Charlie Finley, the flamboyant insurance salesman who also owned the Oakland Athletics baseball team. Orr notched his first two goals of the season in the 5–1 Bruins' victory.

The Bruins played their first ever game in Vancouver, British Columbia, on the 18th. Canucks' fans got their first look at Boston's twenty-two-year-old superstar as the B's skated away with a 5–3 victory.

Upon the team's return to Boston, a political dust up was awaiting Orr. Boston City Councilor Louise Day Hicks's campaign was handing out the 1970–71 Bruins' schedule with a picture of Orr alongside Mrs. Hicks. Running for Congress in the Massachusetts Ninth Congressional District, Hicks was accused of using the photo as a political endorsement. Orr's attorney, Alan Eagleson, stated that Orr's only financial involvement to date is a contribution to the Kevin White for Congress campaign and to his close friend, State Treasurer Bob Crane.

LOUISE DAY HICKS AND BOBBY ORR
BRUINS 1970 DAY
Boston City Hall
Signed Hon. L. Day, 1782 Columbia Rd. South Boston

BRUINS
1970 - 1971
SCHEDULE
ELECT ATTORNEY ELECT
LOUISE DAY
HICKS
TO THE
UNITED STATES CONGRESS

For the second straight game, Orr was held scoreless as the Bruins and Blackhawks tied at 3–3 in a game at the Boston Garden. An unusual penalty was called at the start of the game as Referee Bruce Hood issued a minor bench penalty against the Hawks for an "infraction of the starting lineup." Coach Billy Reay of Chicago had Gerry Pinder starting on right wing instead of Cliff Koroll, who was in the submitted starting lineup card.

Next into Boston was the Philadelphia Flyers, who took a first-period lead of 2–0 before the Bruins answered back with four consecutive goals. Although Orr was again held off the score sheet, he did manage to earn a five-minute major after a bout with Philadelphia's Larry Hillman. Ted Green scored his first goal after sitting out the 1969–70 season. He received an elongated ovation from the sellout crowd. After six games, the Bruins stood at 5-0-1.

The Bruins traveled out to Detroit for a Thursday night encounter with the Red Wings. Despite Orr assisting on Esposito's seventh goal of the campaign, the Bruins went down to defeat by a count of 5–3. Awaiting next was a Halloween night encounter with their close rival, the New York Rangers.

The Boston Garden was full of anticipation in the renewal of the great Boston—New York rivalry. After a scoreless first period, the Bruins unloaded with three consecutive goals as they coasted to a 6–0 win over the hated New Yorkers. Orr scored his third goal of the season to go along with three assists to lead the Bruins' charge. Eddie Johnston was credited with the whitewash.

October 1970					Orr's Stats				
					Game		Season		
Date	Venue	Versus	W-L-T	Score	G	A	G	A	PTS
11	Boston	Detroit	W	7–3	0	1	0	1	1
14	Los Angeles	Kings	W	8–5	0	2	0	3	3
16	California	Seals	W	5–1	2	0	2	3	5
18	Vancouver	Canucks	W	5–3	0	0	2	3	5
22	Boston	Chicago	T	3–3	0	0	2	3	5
25	Boston	Philadelphia	W	4–3	0	0	2	3	5
29	Detroit	Red Wings	L	5–3	0	1	2	4	6
31	Boston	New York	W	6–0	1	3	3	7	10

November 1970

For the second night in a row, the Bruins shut out the opposition 5–0. This time, the victims were the Minnesota North Stars. Gerry Cheevers got the assignment in goal for Boston, while Orr was credited with an assist on a third-period goal by McKenzie.

Going into the Thursday evening encounter with the St. Louis Blues, the Bruins had gone twenty-nine straight games, including playoffs, undefeated at home. The last time the Blues had been in town, May 10, the Bruins hoisted the Stanley Cup after Orr's brilliant flying goal in overtime. The shutout tables were turned in this one as the scoreless streak of 163 minutes and 53 seconds was broken by Frank St. Marseille of the Blues, who went onto a 2–0 victory over the B's. The last home loss for Boston occurred on January 17 of the previous season when they lost to Chicago, 1–0, on a disputed goal.

The Bruins then headed to Pittsburgh for a Saturday night tilt with the Penguins. A late goal by Ken Hodge salvaged a 2–2 tie. After the game, it was right back to Boston and a Sunday night contest with Les Habitants.

With Orr compiling three assists and six different Bruins finding the back of the net, the Bruins coasted to a 6–1 victory over Montreal on November 8, but that wasn't the story of the night. A first-period bench clearing donnybrook spilled over into the stands. The major combatants were Guy Lapointe, Claude Larose, and Terry Harper for the Habs and Ken Hodge, Don Awrey, and Wayne Cashman for the Bruins. Amazingly, Derek Sanderson and Phil Roberto engaged in fisticuffs that carried into the stands near the Montreal bench, but both players managed to avoid the penalty box. Referee John Ashley apparently did not notice Sanderson and Roberto as he was busy with the other players scattered over the Boston Garden ice.

November 8, 1970, Bruins-Habs brawl.

In the inaugural visit by the Vancouver Canucks to the Boston Garden on the 10th, the Bruins slipped by them 6–3. Orr scored his fourth goal and added an assist in the contest. Despite two assists by Orr, the Bruins lost at Toronto on the 14th by a score of 3–2. The Bruins headed back to the Hub immediately following the game to meet the California Golden Seals on Sunday evening.

Orr scored the first tally of the game, but Gary Smith in goal for Charlie Finley's Seals stopped forty-one of forty-two shots to defeat the Bruins 2–1. The game was not without controversy as it appeared that Bruins' defenseman Dallas Smith had tied the game in the third period. However, Referee Bryan Lewis waved the goal off-ruling against the goal judge by claiming that the puck did not enter the net.

The Bruins moved onto Minnesota for a Wednesday night encounter with the North Stars. Orr's three assists propelled the Bruins to a win as they doubled up on the Stars by an 8–4 score. The next encounter would be in the City of Brotherly Love on Saturday where they faced the Flyers. Orr extended his current point scoring streak to six games with an assist on Don Marcotte's third-period goal as the Bruins defeated the Flyers by a score of 5–2.

The next evening back in Boston, the Bruins would be facing the Pittsburgh Penguins. Orr opened the scoring with his sixth goal of the season as the B's downed the Penguins 4–2.

On Tuesday night in St. Louis, the B's squandered a two-goal lead and had to settle for a 5–5 tie. Tim Ecclestone's goal with forty-eight seconds left in the third period brought the Blues even at five. Orr assisted on two second-period goals and now had twenty-six points on the season.

Thanksgiving night 1970 was celebrated with a visit from the Chicago Blackhawks. Orr's first-period goal and assist sparked the Bruins to a 3–0 lead. The Hawks closed the gap with two early third-period goals, but it wasn't enough as the B's defeated the Chihawks, 3–2. Orr's point streak now stood at nine games.

Waiting was a Saturday afternoon tilt in Manhattan with the New York Rangers. Orr scored his eighth goal of the season and assisted on Don Marcotte's third-period goal, but again, the Bruins give up a late score by Bob Nevin and had to settle for a 3–3 draw. The helper raised his career total of assists to 200.

To close out November, the Bruins returned to the Garden for a Sunday night match with the Toronto Maple Leafs. Orr assisted on the third-period game-winning goal by Eddie Westfall, and then Orr added an empty netter, his ninth of the season as the Bruins downed Toronto by a 4–2 score.

November 1970					Orr's Stats				
	Game			Season					
Date	Venue	Versus	W-L-T	Score	G	A	G	A	PTS
1	Boston	Minnesota	W	5–0	0	1	3	8	11
5	Boston	St. Louis	L	2–0	0	0	3	8	11
7	Pittsburgh	Penguins	T	2–2	0	0	3	8	11
8	Boston	Montreal	W	6–1	0	3	3	11	14
10	Boston	Vancouver	W	6–3	1	1	4	12	16
14	Toronto	Maple Leafs	L	3–2	0	2	4	14	18
15	Boston	California	L	2–1	1	0	5	14	19
18	Minnesota	North Stars	W	8–4	0	3	5	17	22
21	Philadelphia	Flyers	W	5–2	0	1	5	18	23
22	Boston	Pittsburgh	W	4–2	1	0	6	18	24
24	St. Louis	Blues	T	5–5	0	2	6	20	26
26	Boston	Chicago	W	3–2	1	1	7	21	28
28	New York	Rangers	T	3–3	1	1	8	22	30
29	Boston	Toronto	W	4–2	1	1	9	23	32

December 1970

The Bruins headed out for a three-game road swing through Chicago, Buffalo, and Montreal, starting out with the Blackhawks. In spite of Esposito's three goals, the Bruins lost to Chicago 4–3. Orr assisted on Esposito's first goal of the game and was later banished from the game after earning a five-minute major fighting penalty when he became involved in a fight with archrival Keith Magnuson late in the third period. The Orr scoring streak had now reached twelve games.

The Bruins invaded the Aud in Buffalo, their first ever appearance in western New York. The B's needed two late third-period goals to earn a tie with the Sabres. Orr scored his tenth goal, a shorthanded effort, and added his twenty-fifth assist to extend his scoring streak to thirteen games. He suffered a minor hip injury but would play in the next game. Two nights later, the Bruins entertained all the Dominion of Canada as they were highlighted on *Hockey Night in Canada* from Montreal.

Orr assisted on Esposito's second-period goal, helping him keep his point scoring streak alive. The Bruins defeated the Canadiens, 4–2. Orr also earned a five-minute major resulting from a fight with the Habs Marc Tardif.

The following evening, the team was back at Boston Garden. Esposito notched another hat trick as the Bruins doubled up on Pittsburgh, 6–3. Orr's left hip continued to bother him, and he was limited to seven shifts but managed to add two assists in his brief appearances. Next up for the Bruins were the Buffalo Sabres at the Garden on Thursday evening. Orr would command three days of rest before this game to help with his ailing hip.

Orr seemingly benefitted from the rest as attested by his eleventh goal and three assists, helping the Bruins thump the Sabres 8–2 on the 10th. Bucyk scored two goals and four assists in the Bruins' win. Bucyk played in his one thousandth NHL game and received a $1,000 bill from Bruins President Weston Adams Jr. It was also Buffalo's first ever visit into the Boston Garden. Orr would be carrying a sixteen-game scoring streak on to Philadelphia for a Saturday matinee.

Gerry Cheevers stopped 33 Flyers' shots, and the Bruins blanked Philly, 1–0, in a game played at the Spectrum. Orr's scoring streak was halted at sixteen games. The contest was marred by a brawl behind the penalty box involving Derek Sanderson, who was serving a two-minute minor for hooking. A fan allegedly spit on Sanderson, and the fighting erupted.

The next evening, the Red Wings would be visiting Boston, and another Orr scoring streak ensued. He scored his twelfth goal and added two assists as the Bruins knocked off Detroit, 6–2. Esposito registered another three-goal game as he scored his twenty-fourth, twenty-fifth and twenty-sixth of the season. Orr's three-point night brought him up to three hundred career points.

Orr then added three assists to bring his total to thirty-six as the Bruins edged the Kings 6–4 in Boston on the 16th. Before the game, Orr received the Grecian Urn that he was awarded for being named the *Sports Illustrated* Man of the Year. He became the second Boston-based player, Carl Yastrzemski, of the Red Sox in 1967 being the first to receive the honor.

The Bruins headed to the Mound City, St. Louis, for a Saturday night game against the Blues. Orr had an assist as the Bruins easily skated by the Blues, 7–1. They headed back to Boston immediately after the game and would face the Minnesota North Stars at the Garden the next night.

For the second consecutive game, the Bruins put a seven spot on the scoreboard and defeated the Stars, 7–2. McKenzie fired home the hat trick, Sanderson scored a shorthanded goal, and Orr notched an assist as the Bruins won their eighth straight game, their longest-winning streak in fourteen years.

Next up for the Bruins would be the Red Wings in Detroit. Two first-period goals were all the B's needed as they defeated the Wings, 2–1. Orr assisted on Stanfield's game winner as the Bruins extended their winning streak to nine games.

On Christmas night in Boston, the B's would be taking on the Penguins at the Garden in the first of a home and home series. After spotting Pittsburgh two goals, the Bruins pumped in six straight and went on to an 8–4 victory. Orr had one assist and extended his point streak to six games. Orr was assessed a ten-minute misconduct by Referee Dave Newell after he protested a tripping call against Sanderson in the second period.

On the next evening, the Penguins managed to snap Boston's ten-game winning streak and defeated the Bruins by a 4–2 margin. The Pittsburgh sextet mounted a 4–0 lead into the middle of the third stanza before the Bruins scored two late goals with Orr and Sanderson both scoring their thirteenth. The 13,050 in attendance was the largest crowd to witness a game at the Igloo since the Penguins entered the league in 1967.

Orr's goal and three assists led the way as the Bruins topped the North Stars in Bloomington, Minnesota, 6–2. Orr had now scored in eight straight games and reached the New Year's holiday with fourteen goals and forty-four assists.

December 1970					Orr's Stats				
					Game		Season		
Date	Venue	Versus	W-L-T	Score	G	A	G	A	PTS
2	Chicago	Blackhawks	L	4–3	0	1	9	24	33
3	Buffalo	Sabres	T	4–4	1	1	10	25	35
5	Montreal	Canadiens	W	4–2	0	1	10	26	36
6	Boston	Pittsburgh	W	6–3	0	2	10	28	38
10	Boston	Buffalo	W	8–2	1	3	11	31	42
12	Philadelphia	Flyers	W	1–0	0	0	11	31	42
13	Boston	Detroit	W	6–2	1	2	12	33	45
16	Boston	Los Angeles	W	6–4	0	3	12	36	48
19	St. Louis	Blues	W	7–1	0	1	12	37	49
20	Boston	Minnesota	W	7–2	0	1	12	38	50
23	Detroit	Red Wings	W	2–1	0	1	12	39	51
25	Boston	Pittsburgh	W	8–4	0	1	12	40	51
26	Pittsburgh	Penguins	L	4–2	1	1	13	41	54
30	Minnesota	North Stars	W	6–2	1	3	14	44	58

January 1971

The euphoria that enveloped the Bruins in 1970 continued as the hockey scene moved into 1971. The B's, seemingly on top of the world, would continue their regular season domination of the rest of the National Hockey League. The Bruins spent New Year's Eve in Buffalo, New York. The holiday celebration continued for them as they pasted the host Sabres by a score of 9–4. McKenzie, Hodge, and Stanfield all scored twice while Orr earned two assists in the blowout before a packed audience of 10,527 at the Buffalo Auditorium.

The four-game road trip ended in Philadelphia with Bucyk firing home three goals and Orr netting his fifteenth goal of the season as the Bruins whipped the Flyers, 5–1. Orr also garnered an assist as his point streak had now reached ten games.

In television news, it was announced by WSBK (TV 38) that the remainder of the Bruins' West Coast games would be televised live and not on twenty-four-hour delayed tape as had been done previously. Much of the interest in the team, and thus eyeballs watching the telecasts, was credited to Bobby Orr.

The B's first home contest of the 1971 portion of the schedule also marked the halfway point in the season. The Vancouver Canucks visited the Garden for the occasion. Orr had a goal and an assist as the Bruins nipped the Canucks by a 6–4 margin. The next day, the Boston squad headed out to Chicago for a Saturday night contest with the Blackhawks. The Bruins let 2–1 and 3–2 margins slip away as the Chicagoans scored two late second-period goals and defeated the B's, 4–3. The winning goal for the Blackhawks was scored by Bobby Hull, his twenty-fourth of the season. The loss ended the Bruins four-game winning streak, but Orr's scoring streak was extended to twelve games.

The Bruins had scant, little time to brood over the loss as they were due back in Boston for a Sunday night tilt with the Golden Seals. In that game, Hodge and Bucyk scored two goals each as the B's bested the Seals by a 7–4 score. Orr extended his point streak to thirteen games with an assist on a second-period goal by Westfall.

The B's enjoyed three days off as they waited for a visit from the Los Angeles Kings on Thursday evening. The story on this game was Phil Esposito, who notched his fifth hat trick of the season to break an NHL record. Wayne Carleton bagged two goals, and Orr counted four helpers as the B's trounced Los Angeles by a 9–5 score. The Canadiens of Montreal were home waiting for a Saturday night matchup with the B's.

A crowd of 18,804, a new Montreal Forum record left happily as the Canadiens defeated the Bruins by a 4–2 margin. Orr scored his seventeenth goal of the season, and former Bruin farmhand Phil Myre stopped thirty-seven shots in the Montreal victory. The old attendance record of 18,794 was set when the B's visited Montreal six weeks prior on December 5.

Sunday was not a day of rest for Toronto goalkeeper Bruce Gamble, who despite his forty-five saves, still managed to let in nine goals as the Bruins trounced the Leafs 9–1 at Boston Garden. This was the third game in the last eight in which the B's had scored nine goals. Orr netted a goal, his eighteenth and an assist, his fifty-fifth of the season. With eight of the next nine games at home, the Bruins would now enjoy a brief respite as the NHL took time off for the twenty-fourth All-Star Game.

A four-day lull in the schedule allowed the Bruins time to author a letter requesting better treatment for prisoners of war in Vietnam. Also during the break, the

NHL announced that six Bruins had been selected to the All-Star Game to be held in Boston on January 19. The six were Orr, Esposito, McKenzie, Bucyk, Westfall, and Hodge.

24th ANNUAL
NATIONAL HOCKEY LEAGUE
All-Star Game

1971

EAST

JANUARY 19

WEST

· BOSTON GARDEN ·
BOSTON, MASSACHUSETTS

$1 97 CENTS
.3: Sales Tax

January 19, 1971, program from the twenty-fourth
annual National Hockey League All-Star Game

The All-Star Game was played at the Boston Garden on Tuesday night, the 19th, and was the first such affair ever held in Boston. Former B's bench boss Harry Sinden came out of retirement for one night to coach the East squad while Scotty Bowman handled the West team. Detroit Red Wings great Gordie Howe competed in his twenty-second All-Star Game. Speculation had it that Bowman would use the "shadow" strategy to contain Orr (his fourth straight appearance) in this game but later conceded that it just wouldn't happen in this contest.

In the game, the West defeated the East by a score of 2–1. Bobby Hull and Chico Maki of the Blackhawks scored for the West while Yvan Cournoyer of Montreal provided the East's only goal. After the break, the Bruins hosted the Chicago at the Garden.

The All-Star banquet was held at the Sheraton Hotel in Boston on
January 18, 1971. Phil Esposito, Brad Park, Orr, and Tony Esposito are
in the foreground. In the back are NHL President Clarence Campbell,
Weston Adams of the Bruins (partially seen), Bill Wirtz of Chicago, David
Molson of Montreal (partially seen), and Bill Jennings of New York.

Orr's nineteenth goal helped pace the B's to a 6–2 victory over the Blackhawks
on the 23rd. Six different Bruins scored in the game as Boston solidified their hold
on first place.

The following evening was Ted Green Night at the Garden as the Bruins and
their fans (along with the visiting Canadiens) honored Green on his comeback. After
the pregame ceremonies, the Bruins continued their winning ways with a 4–2 win
over the Habs. Orr fired home his twentieth goal of the season to go along with two
assists. Next up for the Bruins would be the Rangers and a midweek encounter at
Madison Square Garden.

Esposito assisted on both Boston goals, but the Bruins could only manage a 2–2
tie with New York. Orr's consecutive point scoring streak ended at eighteen games.
The point streak had begun on December 13.

Back in Boston Garden for a game with the Philadelphia Flyers, Orr started a
new streak with two assists as the Bruins toppled the Flyers by a 6–2 score. Hodge
scored two goals to pace the Bruins' victory. The game also marked the eighty-third
straight sellout at home.

The Bruins closed out the month at home with a game against the St. Louis
Blues on Sunday the 31st. For the second straight game, they managed to pump home

six markers with two of the goals scored by Orr. For good measure, he tacked on an assist on a Derek Sanderson goal. The game marked the first afternoon contest since the May 10 Stanley Cup winning game. The second goal by Orr was the one hundredth of his career. It also was the first time that a defenseman scored twenty-plus goals in three consecutive seasons. The contest was shown on the CBS television network although not in its entirety. With a little over eight minutes gone in the game, CBS cut away from the broadcast to televise the Apollo 14 moon shot. Channel 5, which was showing the game, was barraged by irate fans. Walter Cronkite, the venerable CBS anchor, made a belittling reference to the "little thing like a moon shot being allowed to interfere with a hockey game" as he gave the 6–0 score.

After the game, it was announced that the Bruins were involved in a three-team trade. The ball started rolling several days earlier when the B's traded winger Danny Schock to the Philadelphia Flyers. On Saturday, the Flyers sent Bernie Parent and a 1971 second-round pick to the Maple Leafs for goaltender Bruce Gamble, forward Mike Walton, and a first round pick in that year's draft. The Bruins then dealt Rick MacLeish to Philadelphia for Walton. He was a partner in the Orr-Walton Sports Camp in Ontario, and upon his arrival to Boston, he temporarily moved in with Orr.

The boxing world had an impending "large bout" featuring Mohammed Ali versus Joe Frazier to be held at Madison Square Garden. Each fighter would receive $2.5 million dollars, and the fight would be shown in theaters and closed circuit television. Among the distributors were United Artists theaters and the Loew's theater group. Hollywood entertainers Andy Williams and Sergio Mendes were distributing throughout the south and Midwest while Orr would be part of the group distributing in Canada.

The Philadelphia Sportswriters Association honored Orr as the professional athlete of the year. Notre Dame quarterback Joe Theismann was honored as the amateur athlete of the year.

January 1971					Orr's Stats				
					Game		Season		
Date	Venue	Versus	W-L-T	Score	G	A	G	A	PTS
1	Buffalo	Sabres	W	9–4	0	2	14	46	60
3	Philadelphia	Flyers	W	5–1	1	1	15	47	62
7	Boston	Vancouver	W	6–4	1	1	16	48	64
9	Chicago	Blackhawks	L	4–3	0	1	16	49	65
10	Boston	California	W	7–4	0	1	16	50	66
14	Boston	Los Angeles	W	9–5	0	4	16	54	70
16	Montreal	Canadiens	L	4–2	1	0	17	54	71
17	Boston	Toronto	W	9–1	1	1	18	55	73

23	Boston	Chicago	W	6–2	1	0	19	55	74
24	Boston	Montreal	W	4–2	1	2	20	57	77
27	New York	Rangers	T	2–2	0	0	20	57	77
28	Boston	Philadelphia	W	6–2	0	2	20	59	79
31	Boston	St. Louis	W	6–0	2	1	22	60	82

February 1971

Brooks Robinson of the Baltimore Orioles won the twenty-first annual Hickok Athlete of the Year Award presented in Rochester, New York. In second place was George Blanda of the Oakland Raiders, followed by Orr in third. The Hickok Athlete of the Year included a diamond-encrusted belt, awarded by the Hickok Belt Company of Rochester.

The Bruins continued on their nine-out-of-ten games at home stretch when they faced the Los Angeles Kings to open the month of February. Orr had two goals and one assist to pace the Bruins to a 7–3 victory over the visitors from the City of Angels.

Esposito scored his one hundredth point of the season, the second season in a row he had accomplished the feat as the Bruins nudged past the Buffalo Sabres 4–3 at the Garden. Orr was held scoreless in the game for only the eighth time this season. The Minnesota North Stars would provide the opposition on Sunday night at the Garden. The Stars were spotted a three-goal lead after one period. The Bruins made a comeback, scoring three of the next four goals but had to come from behind to manage a 4–4 draw with the Stars. The tie broke a streak of nineteen straight wins at home. Orr recorded his sixty-second assist on a goal by Hodge early in the third period. He also managed to fire thirteen shots on net but was repulsed on every shot by the Gumper, Lorne Worsley, who was in goal for Minnesota. One last home game was scheduled before the B's embarked on a six-game road trip.

The Bruins, behind five assists from Hodge, defeated the New York Rangers 6–3. Orr had two goals, his twenty-fifth and twenty-sixth of the season to buttress the attack as the Bruins now moved to a nine-point lead in the East Division.

The first game of the six-city tour started in St. Louis. Westfall's three goals were the difference as the Bruins stifled the Blues by a 5–3 score.

On a rare Sunday afternoon game in Toronto, the Bruins rolled past the Leafs by a 5–1 count. The game was broadcasted nationwide in both Canada and the United States. After being shutout in St. Louis, Orr came back with two assists against the Leafs. The Bruins then headed to the West Coast to meet the Canucks, Seals, and Kings.

Despite Orr's goal and two assists, Rosaire Paiement's third goal of the game at 19:13 of the third period lifted Vancouver to a 5–4 victory over the Bruins. It was the B's first loss in thirteen games. On Friday night, Boston would meet the Seals in Oakland in game 4 of their annual February road trip.

It was a game of Eddie's. Eddie Westfall's record tying seventh shorthanded goal and Eddie Johnston's twenty-sixth saves backstopped the B's to a 5–0 shutout of the Seals. Orr had a goal and three assists in the contest. After the game, it was onto Los Angeles for a Saturday night tilt with the Kings.

The Bruins hopped out to a quick 3–0 first period lead only to see it dissipate in the third period as the Kings defeated the Bruins 5–4 before a sellout crowd of 16,005. This full house broke the attendance record of 15,577 established in 1968. Mike Byers's goal at 19:19 of the third period sealed the comeback for Los Angeles. Orr was credited with a first-period assist on a goal by Hodge. The Bruins headed back to Boston on Sunday but would only be there a day before taking off for Buffalo and the final game of the road trip.

The wrap up in Buffalo, including a 6–3 win, produced some revisions to the NHL Guide and Record book. Bucyk recorded his 350th career goal. Orr scored his 100th and 101st points of the season, becoming the first player in NHL history to have two consecutive 100-point seasons. With Esposito already over the 100-point mark, the Bruins became the first team to produce two 100-point players in a season.

The Bruins returned home for a two-game set with both Vancouver and Toronto on the schedule. On Thursday evening, the Canucks scored the first two goals of the game in the first period. Over the next two periods, Boston pumped home six straight strikes and went on to an 8–3 win over Vancouver. Although Orr was held scoreless, he did pick up fighting majors in the first and third period. Both bouts were against former Niagara Falls Flyer Rosaire Paiement. The seeds of a feud between Orr and Paiement Canucks were also planted in this February 25 game.

Paiment had this to say about Orr: "Bobby is a good fighter. Fighting is sort of my game. I cut him up twice in Boston in one game. The first time I tried to check him, he came right after me. I grabbed his sweater, and I didn't expect anything to happen when he tried to sucker-punch me. He threw the first punch but missed me completely. I didn't miss him. In the third period, he jumped me in the corner. He wanted to fight again. I cut him good over the eye again. But Bobby's such a good skater and stick-handler. That's his biggest asset. He's got all the ability in the world. The kid's got everything."

In the same game, Westfall's twentieth goal of the season earned him a new Porsche, the gift of a neighbor of Westfall's. The Porche dealer, Dick Hegarty, promised him a car if he reached the milestone. It was Westfall's first twenty-goal season in the NHL.

The Bruins closed out the February portion of the schedule with a Sunday afternoon nationally televised game against the Toronto Maple Leafs. The B's ran out to a 4–0 lead only to see the Leafs come back with three consecutive goals to make it a squeaker with Boston prevailing 4–3. Orr, after being held scoreless against Vancouver, picked up two assists to bring his point total to 103.

| February 1971 | | | | | Orr's Stats | | | | |
| | | | | | Game | | Season | | |
Date	Venue	Versus	W-L-T	Score	G	A	G	A	PTS
3	Boston	Los Angeles	W	7–3	2	1	24	61	85
6	Boston	Buffalo	W	4–3	0	0	24	61	85
7	Boston	Minnesota	T	4–4	0	1	24	62	86
9	Boston	New York	W	6–3	2	1	26	63	89
11	St. Louis	Blues	W	5–3	0	0	26	63	89
14	Toronto	Maple Leafs	W	5–1	0	2	26	65	91
16	Vancouver	Canucks	L	5–4	1	2	27	67	94
19	California	Seals	W	5–0	1	3	28	70	98
20	Los Angeles	Kings	L	5–4	0	1	28	71	99
23	Buffalo	Sabres	W	6–3	1	1	29	72	101
25	Boston	Vancouver	W	8–3	0	0	29	72	101
28	Boston	Toronto	W	4–3	0	2	29	74	103

March 1971

The Bruins opened up the month of March with a whitewashing of the North Stars in Minnesota. Eddie Johnston made twenty-two saves to record the win, and Orr came up with two first-period assists to pace the victory.

Two nights later at the Garden, the B's unloaded on the California Seals, 7–0. Gerry Cheevers stopped thirty-two shots while goaltender Gary Smith of the Seals faced sixty-three shots on net. Smith made fifty-six saves, quite a night's work in the losing effort. Saturday night, the Bruins would be in the Steel City for a game with the Penguins.

Orr scored his thirty-first goal of the campaign, and the Bruins' winning streak was extended to six games as the B's topped the Pens, 6–3, in a game played at the Igloo. Phil Esposito netted goals 54, 55, and 56 of the season as the Bruins earned their forty-seventh victory, breaking the record of forty-six wins held by both themselves and Montreal.

The team returned home after the game to meet the St. Louis Blues on Sunday night. After spotting the Blues a one-goal lead, the B's, behind Orr's thirty-second goal scored four straight and upended St. Louis, 4–1. The team headed out on a four-game road swing, which included their last visit to the West Coast.

Orr's two goals and one assist lifted the Bruins to an easy 8–1 victory over the California Golden Seals. Esposito fired home his fifty-eighth goal of the season, tying him with former teammate Bobby Hull for most goals in a single season.

Espo managed to tie the record in just sixty-six games. Orr's goals raised his season total to thirty-four, breaking his own record of thirty-three, set the previous season. The record-breaking goal was scored at the fifty-six-second mark of the third period against Chris Worthy in net for the Seals.

The next evening, the Bruins exploded for seven more goals as they defeated the Los Angeles Kings by a 7–2 score. In this contest, Esposito broke the single-season goal scoring record by registering his fifty-ninth and sixth goals of the campaign. He also scored his 127th point, breaking his record of 126 set in the 1968–69 season. Orr also enjoyed one goal and three assists in the victory. After the dust settled, Orr had set a new record for points by a defenseman 123, eclipsing the mark of 120 that he had set the season before.

There was an interesting note from Jim Murray, columnist of the *Los Angeles Times* who wrote that "they gave a parade to Roger Maris after his magic moment of breaking Babe Ruth's home run mark while Phil Esposito had to look for a ride home."

Next up, the Vancouver Canucks hosted the B's on Saturday night at the Pacific Coliseum. On this road trip, Boston managed to score eight goals at Oakland and seven in Los Angeles the following night. In Vancouver, the third stop, the number dwindled to six goals, but still the B's came away with a 6–3 victory over the Canucks. Orr managed to assist on four of the goals as the Bruins earned to their tenth straight victory. With the fifty-first victory, the B's broke the record of fifty wins in a season. The twenty-first road win also beat the NHL record of twenty road wins held by the 1951–52 Red Wings and the 1957–58 and 1968–69 Canadiens. The Bruins now moved on to a home and home series with the Detroit Red Wings.

The B's completed the four-game road trip at the Detroit Olympia. Despite the team launching forty-eight shots on Roy Edwards in the Detroit net, Orr managed only one assist, but the B's trounced the Red Wings by an 11–4 score. Bucyk scored his forty-ninth and fifth goals of the year to join Rocket Richard, Boom Boom, Bobby Hull, and Phil Esposito in the fifty-goal club. Wayne Carleton and Rick Smith also potted two goals each in the romp.

Two nights later, the clubs met in the Boston Garden for the back half of the home-and-home set. McKenzie rapped home three goals, and the Bruins again romped over the Wings 7–3. Orr had one assist to extend his point-scoring streak to ten games.

With the Philadelphia Flyers in town for a Saturday night contest, there was much to be happy about. It was Bobby's twenty-third birthday, and to celebrate, he scored his thirty-sixth goal. Even more importantly, the Bruins clinched first place and won the Prince of Wales Trophy for the first time in thirty years. It was the Boston's thirteenth straight victory.

The next night, the expansion Buffalo Sabres arrived at the Garden for a Sunday night tilt. Former Bruin Eddie "the Entertainer" Shack registered his fifth career hat trick, and the Sabres defeated the Bruins, 7–5. Esposito's shorthanded goal was the twenty-second "shortie" for the B's this season. Orr's thirty-seventh goal brought the

B's within one goal late in the game, but it wasn't enough as Boston lost for the first time in fourteen games.

In a tight game played at the Chicago Stadium on the 24th, the Blackhawks, on a second-period goal by Bobby Hull, nipped the Bruins, 2–1.

The Bruins and New York Rangers would now meet in a home-and-home series on the next to last weekend of the schedule. At the Boston Garden on Saturday night, the Rangers rolled out to five consecutive goals and coasted to an easy 6–3 victory. The five first-period goals were the most given up by Boston in any one period this season.

The next evening in New York, the Rangers extended the Bruins' losing streak to four games as they defeated the B's 2–1. Esposito scored his sixty-ninth goal of the season, but for the second straight game, Orr was held off the score sheet, albeit with limited ice time. After the game, the Rangers' Vic Hadfield was quoted as saying that the Bruins "were not prepared for the playoffs." As it turns out, Hadfield was quite prophetic in his assessment.

The last week of the season would finish with three games, one in Montreal, one in Toronto, and the season finale back home in Boston against the Canadiens.

In Montreal on Wednesday night, the Bruins scored two goals in all three stanzas as they tipped the Habs by a 6–3 margin. Orr recorded one assist in the game.

March 1971					Orr's Stats				
					Game		Season		
Date	Venue	Versus	W-L-T	Score	G	A	G	A	PTS
2	Minnesota	North Stars	W	6–0	0	2	29	76	105
4	Boston	California	W	7–0	1	3	30	79	109
6	Pittsburgh	Penguins	W	6–3	1	3	31	82	113
7	Boston	St. Louis	W	4–1	1	2	32	84	116
10	California	Seals	W	8–1	2	1	34	85	119
11	Los Angeles	Kings	W	7–2	1	3	35	88	123
13	Vancouver	Canucks	W	6–3	0	4	35	92	127
16	Detroit	Red Wings	W	11–4	0	1	35	93	128
18	Boston	Detroit	W	7–3	0	1	35	94	129
20	Boston	Philadelphia	W	5–3	1	2	36	96	132
21	Boston	Buffalo	L	7–5	1	0	37	96	133
24	Chicago	Blackhawks	L	2–1	0	0	37	96	133
27	Boston	New York	L	6–3	0	0	37	96	133
28	New York	Rangers	L	2–1	0	0	37	96	133
31	Montreal	Canadiens	W	6–3	0	1	37	97	134

April 1971

The Bruins traveled by train to Toronto for their final road game of the year. The B's exploded for eight goals including three by former Leaf Wayne Carleton. Esposito also added two goals, his seventy-second and seventy-third of the season. Orr managed to tally three assists in the contest. His assist on Hodge's goal was Orr's one hundredth of the season. The Bruins swept by the Leafs, 8–3.

The Bruins, behind Esposito's seventy-fourth, seventy-fifth, and seventy-sixth goals defeated the Montreal Canadiens in the season finale at the Boston Garden. Orr registered two assists in the contest. On this evening, Canadiens' superstar Jean Beliveau played his last regular season game.

The Bruins rewrote the NHL record book as they set thirty-seven new marks, which included nineteen individual and eighteen team records. Orr recorded a plus/minus of a stunning 124, which still stands forty-seven years later.

The Bruins captured four major NHL awards—Bucyk's Lady Byng Trophy, Esposito's Art Ross Trophy, and Orr's Hart and Norris Trophies.

April 1971					Orr's Stats				
					Game		Season		
Date	Venue	Versus	W-L-T	Score	G	A	G	A	PTS
3	Toronto	Maple Leafs	W	8–3	0	3	37	100	137
4	Boston	Montreal	W	7–2	0	2	37	102	139

1970–71 Standings

Eastern Division

	W	L	T	PTS	GF	GA
Boston	57	14	7	121	399	207
New York	49	18	11	109	259	177
Montreal	42	23	13	97	291	216
Toronto	37	33	8	82	248	211
Buffalo	24	39	15	63	217	291
Vancouver	24	46	8	56	229	296
Detroit	22	45	11	55	209	308

Western Division

	W	L	T	PTS	GF	GA
Chicago	49	20	9	107	227	184
St. Louis	34	25	19	87	223	208
Philadelphia	28	33	17	73	207	225
Minnesota	28	34	16	72	191	223
Los Angeles	25	40	13	63	239	303
Pittsburgh	21	37	20	62	221	240
California	20	53	5	45	199	320

Playoffs, April 1971

The Bruins opened their defense of the Stanley Cup with a 3–1 victory against the Montreal Canadiens at the Boston Garden. Orr began the scoring with a first-period power play goal. The Habs started rookie goaltender Ken Dryden who ended up making thirty-nine saves in the contest. Orr was hit with a ten-minute misconduct penalty by referee John Ashley. He was protesting a minor holding a call on him midway through the third period when he was assessed the penalty.

Aril 7, 1971, Orr argues with Referee John Ashley over a minor holding call.

Game 2 was played the next evening at the Garden. Tom Johnson switched goaltenders, replacing Gerry Cheevers with Eddie Johnston. Yvan Cournoyer opened the scoring with a goal early in the first period. The Bruins, behind Orr's goal and three assists, scored five straight goals to take a 5–1 lead into the latter stages of the second period.

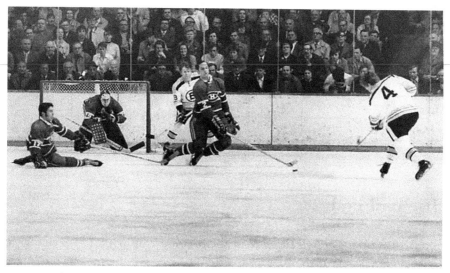

Orr fires a shot on net. Bruin John McKenzie looks for the rebound.
Number 17 is Phil Roberto, number 2 is Jacques Laperriere,
and the goaltender waiting on the volley is Ken Dryden.

The Canadiens came back to life when veteran Henri Richard scored a goal at 15:33 of the second period to squelch the Bruins' runaway express. Derek Sanderson's trip of Richard after the Pocket Rocket scored seemed to ignite the Montrealers. Then Captain Jean Beliveau had two quick strikes early in the third period as the Canadiens would score six consecutive goals and go on to stun the B's 7–5.

On Saturday night at the Forum, the noose began to tighten around the necks of the B's. After Esposito scored an early first-period goal, Montreal's Frank Mahovlich scored two goals to pace the Habs to a 3–1 victory. Gerry Cheevers's record of eleven straight playoff wins was broken with the loss.

Game 4 was the next evening, again at the Forum. Orr set a playoff record for defensemen with three goals as the Bruins beat the Canadiens 5–2. Orr became the first defenseman to score three goals in a playoff game. The series was now dead-locked at two games apiece. Game 5 would be played Tuesday night at the Garden.

The Bruins fired fifty-six shots on Ken Dryden, and he managed to stop for-ty-nine of the volleys as the Bruins coasted to a 7–3 victory over the Canadiens. Orr recorded three assists in the contest. The Bruins needed just one victory to cement the series. Game 6 would be played in Montreal on Thursday night.

While Orr managed to rack up nine minutes in penalties, including a five min-ute major for fighting with Peter Mahovlich of the Habs, the Bruins got kicked in the gut and lost to the Canadiens by an 8–3 score in Montreal. Mahovlich scored twice as Montreal ran away with the victory. The win set up a game seven scheduled for Sunday afternoon at the Boston Garden.

April 18, 1971, Boston Garden, disconsolate players. *Left to right:* Don Marcotte, Bobby Orr, Phil Esposito, Ken Hodge, Wayne Cashman.

A day of infamy for the Boston franchise occurred on a cold, rainy, and gloomy Sunday afternoon in Boston. The fans had not been prepared for the unmitigated disaster that was about to be bestowed on them. Ken Hodge's first-period goal at 6:50 gave the B's an early 1–0 lead. The affair would go downhill from that point. Frank Mahovlich scored his sixth playoff goal at 14:48 to tie the game. Rejean Houle put the Habs ahead for good three minutes later. J. C. Tremblay's second-period goal and Frank Mahovlich's second of the game early in the third period sealed the Bruins' fate as they were eliminated from the playoffs, the final score 4–2.

"They'll be taking shots at Tom Johnson," said Orr after the contest. "Tom's a damn good coach. We lost because we didn't play hockey, not because of coaching." Orr also predicted a Montreal-Chicago Stanley Cup final series. Days later, while accepting the Norris and Hart Trophies, Orr said he would gladly "swap them for the Stanley Cup."

> After the experience in the playoffs, they'll be no turning back this time. I think we'll finish in first place again, and then I think we'll go all the way. I think we'll be a better team for what we went through after the way we lost. I don't think we really ever thought that Montreal could beat us that way. But we know we will have to work harder. Next year we'll think differently.

Finally, a reporter asked Orr what his off-season plans were. "I'm going home and practice hockey," replied Orr.

April 1971 Playoffs					Orr's Stats				
					Game		Season		
Date	Venue	Versus	W-L-T	Score	G	A	G	A	PTS
7	Boston	Montreal	W	3–1	1	1	1	1	2
8	Boston	Montreal	L	7–5	1	3	2	4	6
10	Montreal	Canadiens	L	3–1	0	0	2	4	6
11	Montreal	Canadiens	W	5–2	3	0	5	4	9
13	Boston	Montreal	W	7–3	0	3	5	7	12
15	Montreal	Canadiens	L	8–3	0	0	5	7	12
18	Boston	Montreal	L	4–2	0	0	5	7	12

Coach Al MacNeil of the Canadiens, "We gave Bobby Orr a lot of attention. We always do, plus we concentrated on stopping their big line. When the series started, the Bruins looked invincible. But the way the season went for them, I don't think they were ready for the hard skating and close checking game. I think this knocked them off-balance."

"I think Orr got tired in the long run. On our team, it was Beliveau, Laperriere, Frank, or Peter Mahovlich. You never knew who was coming up with the big effort" (Defenseman Terry Harper).

View from the Balcony

The dynasty was over after one season. How did it all go wrong? Were the Bruins too soft, too casual? Was the regular season too easy when every time a goal was needed, they could be scored in bunches? Was Dryden too good? Were the Canadiens the same team that they had beaten five out of six times in the regular season? Why did Coach Tom Johnson replace Gerry Cheevers in goal with Eddie Johnston in game 2 of the playoffs? Did the Bruins ever really recover from being up by four goals late in the second period only to lose going away to a suddenly speedier Montreal squad? When did Peter Mahovlich get this good?

All the regular-season heroics were for naught. The team that could have made a franchise statement didn't. Sure, they would win a cup in another year, but the string of championships awaiting them vanished like a fading sunset, leaving the fans in the darkness of night. The disappointment felt by the fandom was never fully alleviated. The potential to be Canadiens-like champions was there. In this regard, you came away with the understanding that players play for the moment, but fans worry every moment while they beg and cajole players to perform miracles that also vanish, like that fading sunset.

The wait for the start of the next season, a scant six months away, was excruciatingly long, but the clouds of disappointment would eventually lift, and the team would continue to strike fear in opponents. A few tweaks in the roster and a major trade the next February would bolster the team's run for the 1972 Cup.

Orr's superlative play would continue to provide fodder for observers of the hockey world. Ralph "Cooney" Weiland, a member of the Hockey Hall of Fame and the coach of the Harvard University hockey team, had a few thoughts on Orr in comparison with former teammate and opponent, Eddie Shore: "Wouldn't it be great to have Eddie and Bobby as defense partners? I'd love to coach them. I'd just say, 'Make sure one of you stays back, that you both don't rush.' They'd adjust to each other, and I'd sit on the bench and smile. I think I'd let Orr do more rushing. Orr, he's faster than Shore and a better stick handler. He breaks very quickly. He's the only guy in the league who goes into high gear from a standing start. That's a tremendous asset. He can pass, and he has a great shot. He's a remarkable hockey player."

"Both Shore and Orr have a quality you guys call color. When Shore rushed, the whole place stood up. You always expected something to happen, and it usually did. Orr, he lifts you out of your seat. When he carries the puck down the ice, goes around the defense and around the goal, and then makes a great pass, you see something of Shore."

What about Orr, a left-handed shot, playing right defense? "To begin with, he has more net to shoot at. A right-handed shot over there is aiming at the short side. A left-handed shot can move to his left and get more net to shoot at."

Weiland played with the Bruins on their 1929 and 1939 Cup winning teams while he coached Boston to the 1941 Stanley Cup championship.

Top Hockey Stories from 1971

Stanley Cup Champions	Montreal Canadiens
Art Ross Trophy	Phil Esposito, Boston Bruins
Hart Trophy	Bobby Orr, Boston Bruins
Masterton Trophy	Jean Ratelle, New York Rangers
Lady Byng Trophy	John Bucyk, Boston Bruins
Vezina Trophy	Ed Giacomin and Gilles Villemure, New York Rangers
Calder Trophy	Gilbert Perreault, Buffalo Sabres
Conn Smythe Trophy	Ken Dryden, Montreal Canadiens
Norris Trophy	Bobby Orr, Boston Bruins
Calder Cup Champions	Springfield Kings

Memorial Cup Champions	Quebec Remparts
NCAA Hockey Champions	Boston University

NHL added two new teams to the league. The Buffalo Sabres and the Vancouver Canucks joined the Eastern Division while the Chicago Blackhawks moved to the Western Division. The regular season schedule was increased to seventy-eight games.

Top Sports Stories

World Series Champions	Pittsburgh Pirates
Super Bowl VI Champions	Dallas Cowboys (game played on 1/16/1972 at Tulane Stadium, New Orleans, Louisiana)
NBA Champions	Milwaukee Bucks
Kentucky Derby Winner	Canonero
NCAA Football Champions	Nebraska (13-0-0)
NCAA Basketball Champions	UCLA

In their very first encounter on March 8, 1971, Joe Frazier defeats Muhammad Ali by dropping Ali to the canvas at the twenty-six-second mark of the fifth round in the Fight of the Century at Madison Square Garden.

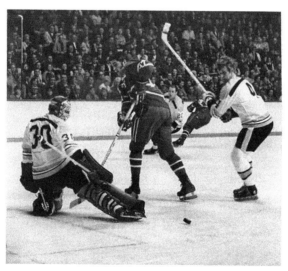

Gerry Cheevers kicks out shot by Montreal's Phil Roberto.
Bobby Orr chases puck near Boston goal.

April 8, 1971, Orr and Eddie Johnston thwart Montreal's
Guy Charron in game 2 of 1971 playoffs.

CHAPTER 6

1971–1972: Redemption

WITH THE BITTER DISAPPOINTMENT AFTER the early playoff ouster still stuck in everybody's craw, it was difficult to imagine spending the summer of 1971, explaining to family and friends what went wrong with the Bruins. No matter what happened, the Bruins could not redeem themselves until the Stanley Cup playoffs returned the following spring. At the moment, it seemed like an eternity. On a sad note, Orr's maternal grandfather, Gordon Steele, passed away in June.

To distract from the disappointment of the previous season's Stanley Cup playoff debacle, it was time to think about the contract status of Orr. He would need to be signed before the next campaign as his contract expired on June 1. Rumors had circulated since early February that contract negotiations were completed on a five-year one-million-dollar deal. There was little debate that Orr was worth that much to both the Bruins and the NHL.

At $200,000 a season, tax experts speculated that his burden in the United States and Canada could be as much as $125,000. Orr's attorney Alan Eagleson commented that "the aim is to see that Bobby keeps as much as possible."

In June, Clarence Campbell speculated the Bruins might have to trade one of their superstars to meet payroll. "Either they have to go up a dollar in their prices, get someone to erect a new arena, or sell off some of their stars." The question came up about Orr's worth. "Every cent he can get," said teammate Derek Sanderson.

"Whatever he's worth," said goaltender Gump Worsley of the Minnesota North Stars.

"At least $1 million over a five-year period," said Bruins' goalie Eddie Johnston. "More than that," according to Rod Gilbert of the New York Rangers.

"I can't measure it," quoted by Jim Pappin of the Chicago Blackhawks.

On August 26, the Bruins announced that he had signed a new five-year contract. Orr's attorney Alan Eagleson revealed that the contract had actually been signed in February.

This nugget from George "Punch" Imlach, general manager and coach of the Buffalo Sabres: "The thought has crossed my mind that Bobby Orr may have peaked as a hockey player."

In the Bruins' opening exhibition game, Orr scored a goal and an assist to lead the B's to a 5–3 win over the New York Rangers. The game was played before a full house of six thousand fans at the Treasure Island Gardens in London, Ontario.

On September 24, Orr filed a $100,000 suit against a Watertown, Massachusetts, sports company for using his name and image on clothing and pillowcases without his permission. Judge Reuben Lurie of Middlesex Superior Court issued the restraining order against Lubin's Rink and Bowling Supply Company. The company had asked permission to use Orr's name and picture but had never been granted the rights.

The suit was finally settled prior to the opening of the season. Max Lubin, owner of the company, was to sell the remaining inventory of goods. Orr would receive a 5 percent royalty on the remaining sales, and he ultimately received a payment of $2,500.

October 1971, the cover of *Hockey Times*

October 1971

As the 1971 playoff season ended in a loss, the opening of the 1971–72 regular season lid-lifter finished with a loss. This time, it was the New York Rangers that provided the opposition. The Rangers ran up a 4–0 lead after two periods before Esposito scored a third-period power play goal. The opening night final score: New York (4), Boston (1).

The Bruins road opener would be played on Wednesday night in Madison Square Garden. The Bruins turned the tables on the New Yorkers, sending thirty-five shots on beleaguered goalie Ed Giacomin. Six of the shots found the back of the net. Westfall had two of the goals while Orr had his first assist of the season on a goal by Stanfield as the Bruins skated by the Rangers, 6–1.

The following night, the B's were home to meet the second-year Buffalo Sabres. In this game, Esposito had two goals as the Bruins, for the second consecutive evening, fired home six goals in the 6–2 victory. Orr had his first goal of the season to go along with an assist. Next up would be the Toronto Maple Leafs at the Garden on Sunday night.

In this one, the Bruins rolled out to a 2–0 lead, but the Leafs fought back to tie the game early in the third period. The B's had to settle for a 2–2 finish. Orr earned an assist on Hodge's first-period shorthanded goal. The assist was the four hundredth point of his career. With Toronto garnering a point, it marked the first time since November 2, 1969, that the Leafs were able to manage any points against the Bruins in Boston.

The final home game before the West Coast swing would feature the Bruins and Detroit Red Wings on Wednesday night. Orr opened the scoring in the first period with his second goal of the young season and also added two assists in the same frame as the B's built up a 3–0 lead on the way to a 4–3 victory over the Wings.

Orr and Massachusetts Governor Frank Sargent put on a skating show at the Garden to publicize a November 22 exhibition game between the NCAA champion Boston University Terriers and the 1972 US Olympic team. The game would be held at the Boston Garden with ticket prices of $5, $4, $3, and $2.

The Bruins then headed for Oakland and a meeting with the Golden Seals on Friday night. In this tilt, Bucyk got his second and third goals of the season and paced the Bruins to a 5–1 win. Orr earned three assists in the game. The Bruins moved on up the coast to Vancouver for a Sunday afternoon date with the Canucks.

The Bruins had to come back from 3–1 deficit to defeat the Canucks in a tight game, 4–3. Orr scored his third goal of the season and added an assist in the game played before 15,570 at the Pacific Coliseum. The next game would be back east as the Bruins made their first appearance in the Montreal Forum on Wednesday night.

Outside of two assists by Orr, the Bruins crashed in a 5–2 loss to the Canadiens. The Habs garnered the first four goals of the game and easily beat the B's. Ken Dryden, now entrenched as Montreal's number one goaltender stopped twenty-eight of thirty shots directed his way. Montreal's Guy LaPointe had two goals for the

Montrealers. The loss snapped a six-game unbeaten streak for the Bostonians. The Bruins headed right out after the game for the next night's clash with the California Seals at the Garden, the second meeting between the clubs in less than a week.

For the second evening in a row, the Bruins lost, shut out by the Seals, 2–0. Gilles Meloche of the Seals stopped thirty-four shots in the whitewashing of the B's. Orr, who had matching minors with the Seals' Walt McKechnie in their previous contest the week before, expanded the minutes this time as they both earned third period fighting majors.

The Bruins closed out the first month of the regular season with a Halloween night contest against the Minnesota North Stars. Orr's opening goal, his fourth of the season, paced the B's to a 5–2 win over the visiting Stars. Sanderson and Hodge both had two goals while Orr earned two assists in the contest.

October 1971					Orr's Stats				
					Game		Season		
Date	Venue	Versus	W-L-T	Score	G	A	G	A	PTS
10	Boston	New York	L	4–1	0	0	0	0	0
13	New York	Rangers	W	6–1	0	1	0	1	1
14	Boston	Buffalo	W	6–2	1	1	1	2	3
17	Boston	Toronto	T	2–2	0	1	1	3	4
20	Boston	Detroit	W	4–3	1	2	2	5	7
22	California	Seals	W	5–1	0	3	2	8	10
24	Vancouver	Canucks	W	4–3	1	1	3	9	12
27	Montreal	Canadiens	L	5–2	0	2	3	11	14
28	Boston	California	L	2–0	0	0	3	11	14
31	Boston	Minnesota	W	5–2	1	2	4	13	17

November 1971

The Bruins opened the November portion of the schedule with a game against the St. Louis Blues. Reggie Leach and John Bucyk each scored two goals as the B's knocked off the Blues by a 6–1 margin. Orr was held off the score sheet save for a minor penalty in the first period. Boston headed out to the Motor City for a Saturday afternoon clash with the Red Wings.

Two third-period goals, one by Bucyk, the other by Esposito with an assist from Orr helped the Bruins edge Detroit by a 2–1 score. Gerry Cheevers stopped twenty-nine of thirty shots for the victory. After the game, Detroit General Manager Ned Harkness had this to say about Orr. "What a thrill it is to watch him when the Bruins have just four players on the ice. Orr took over the game. He was like a quarterback setting the players in the position he wanted them before he'd pass. And if the guys on the ice trying to cover him go to him, then he picks their pocket and makes them look foolish."

A disputed nongoal called against the Bruins with less than eight minutes to play was the basis for them losing to Montreal in a squeaker, 3–2, on the 7th. Orr did earn an assist on a second-period goal by Wayne Cashman. It was right back to Boston after the contest since the B's would be playing a traditional Sunday night game, this time against the Montreal Canadiens.

In a minor league note, the new AHL team, the Boston Braves, drew 14,031 fans on November 9 at the Boston Garden, an American Hockey League record. The game featured the Braves and Providence Reds. The popularity of the Braves stemmed from the hyperinterest in the Boston region brought on by the Bruins and, more specifically, Orr. It would be difficult to overstate his influence.

The Bruins moved on to a Wednesday night encounter with the Blackhawks at the Chicago Stadium. Second-period power play goals by the Hull Brothers lifted the Chihawks to a 3–1 victory over the B's. With consecutive losses to brood over, the Bruins were right back in action the following evening as the California Seals came into Boston, the beginning of a five-game home stand. After spotting the Seals an early 1–0 lead, the Bruins behind Phil Esposito's two goals (one shorthanded), defeated the Seals, 5–2.

The B's enjoyed a couple of days off before a Sunday night visit from the Los Angeles Kings. The time off must have done some good as the Bruins humiliated the Kings by a score of 11–2. Orr had his second career hat trick to go along with three assists. Mike Walton and Phil Esposito each tallied two goals in the rout.

The third straight West Coast visitors, this time the Vancouver Canucks, invaded the Garden for a Thursday night game. Orr tallied two more goals, and Eddie Johnston made twenty-two saves as the Bruins shut out Vancouver, 5–0. Vancouver forward Ron Stewart, a former Bruin, was sitting on the bench when a Vancouver clearing pass was deflected by Orr right into Stewart's face. He was taken to Massachusetts General Hospital, where he was treated for a broken jaw.

The final two games of the home stand featured the Blackhawks on Saturday night and the Blues on Sunday night. The Saturday tilt was a low-scoring affair as the Bruins tipped the Hawks, 2–1. Orr assisted on both Boston goals. The Bruins did not draw any penalties in the game.

In the Sunday night affair, Orr's hockey camp partner Mike Walton scored two goals as the B's broke away from a tight game in the third period and coasted to a 6–2 win over St. Louis. Orr recorded an assist on the first goal of the night by Bucyk.

With Thanksgiving week now upon the Bruins, they faced a home-and-home encounter with the Philadelphia Flyers, Wednesday in Philly, and Thanksgiving night back in the Garden. In the Thanksgiving Eve affair, the Bruins held on for their sixth straight win as McKenzie and Esposito provided all the goals needed in a 2–1 Bruins' win. Orr extended his point-scoring streak to five games.

After football and turkey, it was time for hockey at the Garden. Orr was involved in all four scores (one goal, three assists) as the Bruins edged the Flyers, 4–2, for their seventh consecutive win. Orr's goal proved to be the game winner. For the first time in over two weeks, the Bruins hit the road, this time a contest in St. Louis on Saturday night.

In a high scoring, back and forth game, the Bruins and Blues played to a dead-locked 6–6 game. Orr had his eleventh goal of the season plus two assists. He also added to his collection of Gordie Howe hat tricks when he was involved in a fight with the Blues' Floyd Thompson.

November 1971					Orr's Stats				
					Game		Season		
Date	Venue	Versus	W-L-T	Score	G	A	G	A	PTS
4	Boston	St. Louis	W	6–1	0	0	4	13	17
6	Detroit	Red Wings	W	2–1	0	1	4	14	18
7	Boston	Montreal	L	3–2	0	1	4	15	19
10	Chicago	Blackhawks	L	3–1	0	0	4	15	19
11	Boston	California	W	5–2	0	0	4	15	19
14	Boston	Los Angeles	W	11–2	3	3	7	18	25
18	Boston	Vancouver	W	5–0	2	1	9	19	28
20	Boston	Chicago	W	2–1	0	2	9	21	30
21	Boston	St. Louis	W	6–2	0	1	9	22	31
24	Philadelphia	Flyers	W	2–1	0	1	9	23	32
25	Boston	Philadelphia	W	4–2	1	3	10	26	36
27	St. Louis	Blues	T	6–6	1	2	11	28	39

December 1971

The Bruins opened December on *Hockey Night in Canada* from Toronto. Five different players scored for the Bruins as they defeated the Leafs, 5–3. The Bruins scored four goals in the third period to overcome a 2–1 Toronto lead. The main charge occurred during a one-minute and fifty-three-second span of the third stanza when Reggie Leach, Dallas Smith, and Esposito scored for the B's. As a testament to his brilliant play and without even having scored a goal, Orr was still the voted "first star" of the game. The current unbeaten streak extended to nine games

The next night back in Boston, the Bruins faced the Pittsburgh Penguins. After a scoreless first period, Orr scored his twelfth goal of the season to pace the Bruins to a 5–3 victory over the Pens. Orr also contributed an assist on one of Hodge's two goals. The Bruins now headed off on a three-game West Coast swing.

In the road opener at Los Angeles, the Bruins extended the unbeaten streak to eleven games as they defeated the Kings 5–3. The final score was the third successive game that finished with a 5–3 outcome, all games in favor of the B's.

The Bruins moved up the Pacific coast for a Saturday night tilt with the Vancouver Canucks. Orr scored his thirteenth goal of the season as the B's won going away, 6–2. Esposito had two goals in the contest. The unbeaten streak was now twelve games. The road trip continued in Oakland the next evening.

The twelve-game unbeaten streak came to an end. Boston native Bobby Sheehan opened the scoring for the Seals, and ex-Bruin Wayne Carleton's goal put the nail on the coffin as the Seals defeated the B's, 4–2.

The Bruins faced their chief competitors, the New York Rangers, who were in town for a Thursday night game. Paced by Orr's opening goal at 1:47 of the first period, Boston scored seven consecutive markers and moved on to an easy 8–1 victory. Eight different players scored for the Bruins as they beat both Rangers' goaltenders Eddie Giacomin and Gilles Villemure for four goals each.

"That goal was the key play of the game. It was fantastic play by a great player. We just let him skate almost eighty feet without laying a hand on him. He gave us that little shift from his forehand to his backhand, and his goal gave them the momentum," Emile Francis, coach of the New York Rangers, commented on Orr after the Bruins defeated the Rangers 8–1 on the 16th.

The weekend ahead would feature a home-and-home series with the Pittsburgh Penguins. The Saturday night game would be played at the Igloo in Pittsburgh. McKenzie scored twice as they edged the Penguins 4–3. The next evening at the Garden, the Bruins went up 2–0 in the first period only to have the Penguins come back with a couple of goals in the second period. The game ended in a 2–2 tie.

As the team moved to Buffalo on the night before Christmas Eve, the Bruins had to settle for a 4–4 tie with the Sabres. Hodge's third-period goal, assisted by Orr, proved to be the game-tying goal.

Christmas night 1971 featured the Bruins and Philadelphia Flyers in what would be the last scheduled December twenty-fifth game for the Bruins. Henceforth, agreements between the league and the players determined that no games would be played on this holiday. In the game, the B's spotted Philadelphia a 1–0 lead, but Orr scored his fifteenth goal in the opening minute of the second period, which led to four other Boston goals, and the B's toppled the Flyers, 5–1.

The final home game before a seven-city road trip featured the Toronto Maple Leafs on Sunday night. Hodge, with one assist from Orr, scored the first and last goal of the game as the Bruins defeated the Leafs, 3–1, at the Boston Garden. The road trip opened at the Chicago Stadium, where Orr racked up a goal and three assists to help the Bruins defeat the Blackhawks 5–1.

The 1971 portion of the schedule closed the next evening with a matchup at the Metropolitan Center in Bloomington, Minnesota, between the Bruins and North Stars. Despite being outshot by the Stars, the B's hung on to earn a 2–2 tie. Orr added an assist on Esposito's thirtieth goal.

December 1971					Orr's Stats				
					Game		Season		
Date	Venue	Versus	W-L-T	Score	G	A	G	A	PTS
4	Toronto	Maple Leafs	W	5–3	0	1	11	29	40
5	Boston	Pittsburgh	W	5–3	1	1	12	30	42
8	Los Angeles	Kings	W	5–3	0	0	12	30	42
11	Vancouver	Canucks	W	6–2	1	0	13	30	43
12	California	Seals	L	4–2	0	0	13	30	43
16	Boston	New York	W	8–1	1	1	14	31	45
18	Pittsburgh	Penguins	W	4–3	0	0	14	31	45
19	Boston	Pittsburgh	T	2–2	0	0	14	31	45
23	Buffalo	Sabres	T	4–4	0	1	14	32	46
25	Boston	Philadelphia	W	5–1	1	1	15	33	48
26	Boston	Toronto	W	3–1	0	1	15	34	49
29	Chicago	Blackhawks	W	5–1	1	3	16	37	53
30	Minnesota	North Stars	T	2–2	0	1	16	38	54

January 1972

The Bruins' seven-game road swing continued with the first game of the 1972 portion of the season, a tilt at Madison Square Garden in New York. Orr's seventeenth goal of the season opened the scoring as the Bruins built up a 4–0 lead and continued on to defeat the Broadway Blueshirts, 4–1. Bucyk had two goals in the affair. Amazingly, the Bruins only recorded fifteen shots on net with Gilles Villemure stopping 11 of the blasts. In the previous two contests against the New Yorkers, the Bruins had outscored the Rangers 12–2 but had been outshot by the Rangers 79–43.

Game number 4 of the trip took the B's to Maple Leaf Gardens in Toronto. Although they only had twenty-seven shots on goal, two of the shots beat forty-three-year-old Leaf goalie Jacques Plante. Meanwhile at the other end of the rink, Eddie Johnston stopped all twenty-nine of Toronto's salvos as the Bruins shutout Toronto, 2–0. Orr's eighteenth goal of season opened the scoring in the first period and proved to be all the goals the B's needed for the win. With the victory, the Bruins extended their unbeaten streak to ten games, and they were looking to extend it to eleven games as they traveled to Buffalo the next night to take on the Sabres.

The Bruins, with three power play goals, defeated the Sabres at the Auditorium in Buffalo 5–2. Orr had his nineteenth goal to go along with his fortieth and forty-first assist. The Bruins moved into first place behind the idle New York Rangers. They had been dominating in their previous twenty-four games with only one loss and four ties to go along with nineteen wins.

The Bruins headed for a Saturday night matchup in St. Louis. The latest unbeaten streak fell to the wayside as the Blues, behind two goals from Garry Unger and Gary Sabourin, defeated the B's, 5–3. Phil Esposito scored his thirty-third and thirty-fourth goals of the season in a losing Boston effort.

With the All-Star Game looming on the horizon, the squads were being voted on, and to no one's surprise, Orr was a unanimous first All-Star. Esposito also joined him while defenseman Dallas Smith was voted to the second team. The midwinter exhibition would be played in Bloomington, Minnesota, on January 25.

The Bruins enjoyed a four-day respite before the final game of the road trip. The Igloo in Pittsburgh was the location, and the Penguins were the opposition for this Wednesday night meeting. As is often the case, the visiting team at the end of a long road trip might come up empty in the enthusiasm category. This may have been the case as the Bruins held on to a 2–2 tie with the Penguins. Orr did add his forty-second assist on a first-period goal by Bucyk.

The next evening, the team came home to Boston for their first home game in eighteen days. The Bruins and Kings matched third-period goals as the game ended in a 1–1 tie.

It was a Saturday night, and the Chicago Blackhawks would be invading the Garden in the first of two weekend home games. Phil Esposito's two goals against brother Tony and Sanderson's shorthanded goal lifted the B's to a 4–2 victory. Orr assisted Marcotte on his first goal of the season.

The next night, the Detroit Red Wings came into town. The first period was scoreless but was more than made up for in the subsequent two periods. Sanderson scored three goals, and Hodge hit for two as the Bruins crushed the visitors 9–2. This was the largest goal outburst since the Bruins blitzed the Los Angeles Kings for eleven goals on November 14.

For the second time in ten days, the Bruins were in St. Louis. The ending was different this time as Gerry Cheevers stopped all twenty-five shots and the Bruins blanked the Blues, 2–0. This was Cheevers first shut out of the season, and Orr picked up his forty-fifth assist on Esposito's thirty-eighth goal.

With a Saturday *Hockey Night in Canada* game looming, the Bruins headed for Montreal and a game with the Canadiens. Unfortunately, a sudden strike by cameramen and technicians of the CBC caused a cancellation of the telecast, both in Canada and back home on TV38. A wild and wooly game ensued. Going into the contest, the Habs had not lost at home in twenty-two previous outings (nineteen wins, three ties). The Canadiens jumped out to a 2–0 lead until late in the first period when Bucyk scored his twentieth goal on the power play.

The Bruins then scored five second-period goals, including a power play score and a shorthanded marker. Stanfield had two of the goals, and Westfall had the shorthanded score. Orr scored his twentieth of the season to lead off the third period, and the Bruins defeated Montreal by a score of 8–5.

The final game before the brief All-Star break was the next night in the Boston Garden as the Bruins hosted the Buffalo Sabres. A third-period goal by Dallas Smith enabled the Bruins to pull out a 3–3 tie. Orr was held scoreless in the affair.

Next stop on the schedule would be the NHL. All-Star Game being played at the Met in Bloomington, Minnesota. The Boston star contingent consisted of Orr, Esposito, Dallas Smith, and McKenzie.

In the game, the East tipped the West by a score of 3–2. Esposito scored the game winner with an assist from Orr and Smith. Hard to fathom, but it was the first point for both Esposito (five games) and Orr (four games) in All-Star competition.

On Thursday night, the Bruins opened a home-and-home series with the Philadelphia Flyers at Boston Garden. Behind Esposito's three goals, Boston defeated the Flyers by a margin of 4–2. Orr assisted on Espo's third goal.

The back half of the series was Saturday afternoon in Philadelphia. Different location but same score as the Bruins downed the Flyers 4–2. Four different Bruins, Reg Leach, Sanderson, Cashman, and Esposito scored for the B's. The unbeaten streak reached nine games with the victory.

On Sunday night back at the Garden, the Bruins met the St. Louis Blues for the third time in the month of January. Orr fired home his twenty-first goal of the season, a shorthanded tally, and added three assists as the B's defeated the Blues, 5–2. Thirty-five seconds after Orr's "shortie," Sanderson also scored a shorthanded goal.

January 1972					Orr's Stats				
					Game		Season		
Date	Venue	Versus	W-L-T	Score	G	A	G	A	PTS
2	New York	Rangers	W	4–1	1	0	17	38	55
5	Toronto	Maple Leafs	W	2–0	1	1	18	39	57
6	Buffalo	Sabres	W	5–2	1	2	19	41	60
8	St. Louis	Blues	L	5–3	0	0	19	41	60
12	Pittsburgh	Penguins	T	2–2	0	1	19	42	61
13	Boston	Los Angeles	T	1–1	0	0	19	42	61
15	Boston	Chicago	W	4–2	0	1	19	43	62
16	Boston	Detroit	W	9–2	0	1	19	44	63

18	St. Louis	Blues	W	2–0	0	1	19	45	64
22	Montreal	Canadiens	W	8–5	1	1	20	46	66
23	Boston	Buffalo	T	3–3	0	0	20	46	66
27	Boston	Philadelphia	W	4–2	0	1	20	47	67
29	Philadelphia	Flyers	W	4–2	0	0	20	47	67
30	Boston	St. Louis	W	5–2	1	3	21	50	71

February 1972

The Bruins motored into February with a contest at Madison Square Garden. Orr scored his twenty-second goal. Phil Esposito knocked home his forty-fourth, and the Bruins shut out the Rangers, 2–0. Gerry Cheevers was called upon to make thirty-eight saves in the contest to earn the victory. The win was the third Boston victory at Madison Square Garden this season.

The next night, the Minnesota North Stars were at the Garden. The B's poured forty-seven shots on goal and connected for six markers as the Bruins defeated the Stars, 6–1. The Bruins had two goals within the first 1:44 of the first period and coasted to the win. Orr had three assists, including one in collaboration with goaltender Eddie Johnston on Bucyk's second-period power play goal.

Next up was a Saturday afternoon contest with the visiting Detroit Red Wings. Orr fired home his twenty-third goal of the season as the B's trimmed the Wings, 3–2. Westfall had two goals, including his fifth game winner of the season. The win extended the Bruins' undefeated streak to thirteen games.

The Bruins now headed to Buffalo for a Sunday night game with the Sabres. Coach Tom Johnson had this to say about his Bruins: "We were out-hit, out-skated, out-hustled, and out-everythinged." You can also add *outscored* as the Sabres scored the first six goals of the game and embarrassed the Bruins, 8–2. Former Bruin Jim Lorentz had two goals for the winners. Orr had one assist on the Bruins' first goal by Mike Walton late in the second stanza. The Bruins would now have a few days to mull over this disastrous event. The unbeaten streak ended at thirteen games.

If the Bruins' fans were worried about Sunday's debacle at Buffalo, by Thursday, it had been all but forgotten. Orr's twenty-fourth goal of the season and Fred Stanfield's fifteenth and sixteenth goals propelled the Bruins to a 9–1 shellacking over the visiting Vancouver Canucks. Cheevers extended his personal unbeaten streak to twenty games. Orr also had three assists to give him fifty-seven on the season.

The newly created World Hockey Association held its initial draft in Anaheim, California, on February 12 and 13; and 1,073 players were drafted among the twelve WHA franchises. Current Bruin players drafted included the following:

Miami: Carol Vadnais, Derek Sanderson
Winnipeg: Ted Green
Dayton: Phil Esposito, Bobby Orr
New England: Eddie Johnston, Gerry Cheevers, Johnny Bucyk, Eddie Westfall
Los Angeles: Wayne Cashman, Ken Hodge, Fred Stanfield
Calgary: Dallas Smith
Ontario: Nick Beverley, Don Awrey, Terry O'Reilly
Edmonton: Garnet Bailey
Chicago: Don Marcotte
Quebec: John McKenzie

In a related matter, Orr's attorney, Alan Eagleson was the featured speaker at the Massachusetts Society of Certified Public Accountants dinner meeting in Newton, Massachusetts. Eagleson suggested that if a player could advance himself by jumping to the newly formed World Hockey Association, he would recommend that they do it.

The rematch against the Sabres happened on Saturday afternoon with the B's swearing revenge. Five different Bruins scored including Orr with his twenty-fifth of the season as the Bruins defeated the Sabres, 5–1. The Bruins pummeled the Sabres' goal with fifty-five shots.

Twenty-four hours later, the Montreal Canadiens made an appearance at the Garden. Ken Dryden stopped thirty-nine shots as the Habs, and B's play to a 2–2 draw. Wayne Cashman scored both Boston goals while Orr was kept off the score sheet. The Bruins had one more home game before embarking on a six-game road trip.

That test was Tuesday night against the California Seals. Paced by Orr's record-tying four assists in one period, the B's dumped the Seals by a 6–3 margin. This record was originally set by Buddy O'Connor of the Montreal Canadiens on November 8, 1942. Since O'Connor's record, nine other players had recorded four assists in a period before Orr's feat. Sanderson and Walton had two goals apiece in the win. Orr and former teammate Wayne "Swoop" Carleton exchanged third-period blows and earned fighting majors. The Bruins were now off on a six-game road swing to Philadelphia, Minnesota, Chicago, Vancouver, Oakland, and Los Angeles.

The road trip opened on Thursday night at the Spectrum in Philadelphia. Phil Esposito scored his forty-seventh, forty-eighth, and forty-ninth goal of the season; and Orr added his twenty-sixth as the B's downed the Flyers by a score of 4–1.

On Saturday night in Minnesota, the Bruins defeated the North Stars, 6–4. Boston was paced by two shorthanded goals on the same penalty. The goals by Sanderson and Orr were fifty-seven seconds apart in the second period. Immediately after the game, the B's headed for Chicago, where they would play an afternoon tilt the next day.

If there was any question about Orr's head being in the game, the following anecdote concerning his shorthanded goal serves as evidence. Orr had a wide-open net to the left of Minnesota's Gump Worsley but held it for a longer period than thought necessary. Orr's explanation was "We had to kill off more penalty time." He made it sound so reasonable.

Before twenty thousand loyal Chicago fans, the B's defeated the Blackhawks 3–1. This was the second home loss of the season for the Hawks. The other loss, on December 29, also came at the hands of the Bruins. Esposito had two goals while Orr garnered his sixty-fifth assist.

Next game for the Bruins was a Tuesday night engagement in Vancouver with the Canucks. In this one, the Bruins eked out a 4–3 win highlighted by Derek Sanderson's sixth shorthanded goal of the season. Sanderson's goal was scored while Orr was in the penalty box.

The next evening, the Bruins were in Oakland to take on the Golden Seals. Prior to the game, the B's announced the acquisition of Seals' defenseman Carol Vadnais along with minor leaguer Don O'Donoghue. The Bruins sent Rick Smith, Reggie Leach, and Bob Stewart west to the Seals. In Carol Vadnais' last game with the Seals on February 20 against St. Louis, he registered a hat trick.

With the acquisition of Vadnais on February 23, Bruins' fans made a comical reference to the 1969 movie *Bob & Carol & Ted & Alice*, which starred Natalie Wood, Robert Culp, Elliott Gould, and Dyan Cannon. Soon after the trade, Garden fans hung the following sign from the face of the first balcony honoring their defense corps of Orr, Ted Green, Carol Vadnais, and Dallas Smith:

Bob, Ted, Carol, and Dallas

As for the game, in what was a classic barn burner, the Bruins came back from a 6–1 deficit and defeated the Seals, 8–6. Stanfield led the way with three goals. Orr had a goal, his twenty-eighth and four assists.

In the final game of the month and the last contest of the six-game road trip, the Bruins found themselves in Los Angeles for a game with the Kings. A sellout crowd of 16,005 greeted the combatants on that Saturday evening. The Kings had averaged 8,675 fans per game during the 1971–1972 season, so a visit from Bobby Orr and company was welcome news to the accountants. The Bruins stomped out to a quick 3–0 lead, giving the team ten straight goals over the last two games. Orr had his twenty-ninth goal and seventieth assist to lead the way as they crowned the Kings by a 5–4 score. The win, the seventh in a row, also extended their unbeaten streak to ten.

February 1972					Orr's Stats				
					Game		Season		
Date	Venue	Versus	W-L-T	Score	G	A	G	A	PTS

2	New York	Rangers	W	2–0	1	0	22	50	72
3	Boston	Minnesota	W	6–1	0	3	22	53	75
5	Boston	Detroit	W	3–2	1	0	23	53	76
6	Buffalo	Sabres	L	8–2	0	1	23	54	77
10	Boston	Vancouver	W	9–1	1	3	24	57	81
12	Boston	Buffalo	W	5–1	1	1	25	58	83
13	Boston	Montreal	T	2–2	0	0	25	58	83
15	Boston	California	W	6–3	0	4	25	62	87
17	Philadelphia	Flyers	W	4–1	1	0	26	62	88
19	Minnesota	North Stars	W	6–4	1	2	27	64	91
20	Chicago	Blackhawks	W	3–1	0	1	27	65	92
22	Vancouver	Canucks	W	4–3	0	0	27	65	92
23	California	Seals	W	8–6	1	4	28	69	97
26	Los Angeles	Kings	W	5–4	1	1	29	70	99

March 1972

With the end of the season on the horizon, the Bruins started the month of March with a home game against the Vancouver Canucks. Phil Esposito notched his third three-goal game of the season, and Eddie Johnston earned his fourth assist of the season. Orr had his thirtieth goal and seventy-first assist of the season to lift him over the 100-point mark for the third season in a row. In addition, Orr received a five-minute major for a second-period fight with the Canucks' Rosaire Paiement. This was Orr's second Gordie Howe hat trick of the season. The Bruins defeated the Canucks 7–4. The win marked the twenty-fourth consecutive game at home without a loss.

The Bruins moved on to Detroit for a Saturday night game at the Olympia. Cashman scored his ninteenth and twentieth goals of the campaign as the Bruins edged the Red Wings, 5–4.

Back home in Boston, the home unbeaten streak ended at twenty-four games as the Los Angeles Kings shut out the Bruins, 2–0 on the 5th. Gary Edwards made thirty-eight saves in goal for the Kings.

After spotting the North Stars 2–0 and 3–1 leads, the Bruins came back and defeated the North Stars in Bloomington, 5–4. Ace Bailey manufactured two goals while Orr had two assists. Doug Roberts of the Bruins scored his first goal of the season in the win. Gerry Cheevers extended his personal undefeated streak to twenty-seven games.

The upcoming weekend schedule consisted of a home-and-home series with the Pittsburgh Penguins. Saturday night's game was at the Igloo in Pittsburgh. After

Sanderson scored a shorthanded goal, the Penguins scored four consecutive goals en route to a 6–4 victory over the Bruins. Orr scored his thirty-first goal to go along with two assists. His three points gave him a total of five hundred for his career.

The next evening back at the Boston Garden, the Bruins went up 3–0 in the first period. However, the Penguins came back and scored four of the last five goals of the game. Orr's thirty-second goal prevented the Bruins from dropping two straight games as Boston and Pittsburgh played to a 4–4 tie.

In a scheduling oddity, the Bruins headed back to the West Coast for a single game at Los Angeles. The Kings, who had shut out the Bruins in Boston a little over a week before, were in for a thumping as the B's behind Orr's thirty-third goal of the season routed the Kings by an 8–3 margin.

Back at home for the next four games, the Bruins hosted Minnesota on Sunday night. Esposito fired home three goals, and Orr scored his thirty-fourth of the season as the Bruins coasted past the North Stars, 7–3. The game was marred by a second-period slashing/spearing incident involving Wayne Cashman of the Bruins and Dennis Hextall of the Stars. Cashman was suspended by the league for three games.

On Thursday night, the Rangers and Bruins met for the final time in the regular season, this tilt at Boston Garden. Archbishop Humberto Medeiros, the Vicar of Boston, saw his first hockey game, and it was a good one. Bucyk had two goals, and Orr scored his thirty-fifth as the Bruins dumped the Rangers, 4–1. Gerry Cheevers was the star of the game stopping thirty-six of thirty-seven New York salvos.

The Bruins hosted the Blackhawks on Saturday night and the Montreal Canadiens on Sunday afternoon. In the Saturday night contest, Bobby Hull's forty-sixth goal of the season lifted the Blackhawks to a 5–5 tie with the Bruins. An unusual event happened when Hull scored. The fans at the Boston Garden rose and gave Hull a standing ovation on the occasion of his six hundredth career goal. After the game, Hull expressed his appreciation of the Boston fans. Esposito scored two goals, and Orr slipped home his thirty-sixth, a shorthanded tally in the middle of the second period.

The Montreal Canadiens visited the Garden less than sixteen hours later for a game with the B's played before a national television audience. Mike Walton scored his twenty-sixth and twenty-seventh goals of the season as the Bruins took out the Canadiens by a score of 5–4. Orr had one assist in the contest.

The Bruins headed out for their final road swing of the year with games at Detroit, Toronto, and Montreal. In the Detroit game, Orr scored his thirty-seventh goal to tie the record he set the previous season, but the B's bowed to the Red Wings, 6–3.

The next night in Toronto, the Bruins lost their second consecutive game, a 4–1 decision by the Leafs. Orr played briefly but left the game early due to a sore left knee. He left for Boston to be examined while the rest of the team stayed in Toronto. Gerry Cheevers's thirty-two-game unbeaten streak was broken in the loss to the Leafs. He had compiled a record of 24-0-8 during the streak. The Bruins headed for Montreal by train and the final road game of the season.

March 1972					Orr's Stats				
					Game		Season		
Date	Venue	Versus	W-L-T	Score	G	A	G	A	PTS
2	Boston	Vancouver	W	7–3	1	1	30	71	101
4	Detroit	Red Wings	W	5–4	0	0	30	71	101
5	Boston	Los Angeles	L	2–0	0	0	30	71	101
8	Minnesota	North Stars	W	5–4	0	2	30	73	103
11	Pittsburgh	Penguins	L	6–4	1	2	31	75	106
12	Boston	Pittsburgh	T	4–4	1	0	32	75	107
16	Los Angeles	Kings	W	8–3	1	0	33	75	108
19	Boston	Minnesota	W	7–3	1	3	34	78	112
23	Boston	New York	W	4–1	1	0	35	78	113
25	Boston	Chicago	T	5–5	1	1	36	79	115
26	Boston	Montreal	W	5–4	0	1	36	80	116
28	Detroit	Red Wings	L	6–3	1	0	37	80	117
29	Toronto	Maple Leafs	L	4–1	0	0	37	80	117

April 1972

In the last road tilt of the regular season, the Bruins visited the Montreal Forum to play the Canadiens in a rare Saturday afternoon contest. The Canadiens scored the first five goals of the contest en route to a 6–2 drubbing of the Bruins. Both Orr and Esposito were sidelined for the game.

In the season finale, the Bruins raked the Leafs by a 6–4 count. Three B's scored their first goals of the season: Don Awrey, Ted Green and Terry O'Reilly. In pregame festivities, Orr received the Dufresne Trophy as the outstanding player in home games. The Gallery Gods presented the Eddie Shore Trophy to Sanderson as the Gallery's favorite player.

At the season closed, an unidentified Bruin proclaimed, "Whenever we got careless during the regular season, there was always the nightmare of April 1971 to put us back on track."

With a total of 117 points, Orr became the first player in NHL history to record three consecutive 100-point seasons. By winning the Hart Trophy, Orr became the first player in NHL history to be named the most valuable player for three straight seasons. He was only the second defenseman to win the award, the last being Eddie Shore in 1938.

The Bruins would then prepare for the opening round of the playoffs against the Toronto Maple Leafs, which was set to open on Wednesday night in Boston.

April 1972					Orr's Stats				
					Game		Season		
Date	Venue	Versus	W-L-T	Score	G	A	G	A	PTS
1	Montreal	Canadiens	L	6–2	DNP		37	80	117
2	Boston	Toronto	W	6–4	DNP		37	80	117

Meanwhile, forty miles south of the Boston Garden in Providence Rhode Island, Orr's influence prompted Reds' owner George Sage to contemplate moving his AHL team's games away from their traditional Sunday night berth in deference to the Bruins. The B's broadcast all their games on channel 38 and could be seen in Providence on most Sunday nights.

1971–72 Final Standings

Eastern Division

	W	L	T	PTS	GF	GA
Boston	54	13	11	119	330	204
New York	48	17	13	109	317	192
Montreal	46	16	16	108	307	205
Toronto	33	31	14	80	209	208
Detroit	33	35	10	76	261	262
Buffalo	16	43	19	51	203	289
Vancouver	20	50	8	48	203	287

Western Division

	W	L	T	PTS	GF	GA
Chicago	46	17	15	107	256	166
Minnesota	37	29	12	86	212	191
St. Louis	28	39	11	67	208	247
Philadelphia	26	38	14	66	220	258
Pittsburgh	26	38	14	66	200	236

| California | 21 | 39 | 18 | 60 | 216 | 288 |
| Los Angeles | 20 | 49 | 9 | 49 | 206 | 305 |

April 1972 Playoffs

The Bruins opened the first round of the playoffs at home against the Toronto Maple Leafs on Wednesday night. Esposito scored two late first-period goals to lift the Bruins to a 5–0 victory over the Leafs. Cheevers made twenty-seven saves in the win while Orr garnered two assists. On his ailing knees, he had this to say, "Physically, I felt good, I felt fine. When you win 5–0, everything is fine. But this is only one win, only one. We won the first game last year too, I remember. There is still a long way to go."

Game 2 was scheduled for the next night at Boston Garden. The Bruins pulled out to a 2–0 first period lead before the Leafs tied it up on two early second-period goals. Bucyk put the Bruins up 3–2 to end the frame. Guy Trottier tied the game up for Toronto at the 9:42 mark of the third period, sending the game into overtime. Orr had an assist on Esposito's first-period goal. He almost ended the game with ten seconds left, but Toronto goaltender Bernie Parent made a diving poke check to prevent the goal. Early in the first overtime, ex-Bruin Jim Harrison knocked home the game winner to tie the series at one game each.

Jim Harrison of Toronto watches Orr in front of an empty
Boston net in this 1972 playoff game at Boston Garden.

Game 3 was played on Saturday night at Maple Leaf Gardens. Orr had a goal and an assist, and Eddie Johnston came up with thirty saves as the Bruins blanked the Leafs by a score of 2–0. The victory was Johnston's first in four Stanley Cup appearances. Orr played thirty-four minutes and twenty-eight seconds in the contest and was named the first Star of the Game.

On the lighter side, Sanderson showed up for the game sans mustache. He took much grief from his mates. The next evening, the two teams were back at it. After the Bruins opened the scoring, the Toronto sextet had leads of 3–1 and 4–2, which were eliminated by three third-period Boston goals. Goals by Westfall shorthanded along with singles by Esposito and Hodge, propelled the B's to the 5–4 victory and a 3–1 series lead.

Orr's left knee continued to be fodder for the press. The *Boston Globe's* Will McDonough stated that Orr seems to be bothered when he moves quickly to his right, and he avoided situations that would cause him to push off on his left knee. Fellow *Globe* writer Harold Kaese noted that "if Orr's has a sore knee, everybody should have one."

Game 5 was back in Boston on Tuesday evening. Hodge's third-period goal broke up a 2–2 stalemate, and the Bruins defeated Toronto 3–2 and won the quarter-final round of the playoffs. He had scored the winning goal for the second consecutive game. Orr had one assist in the clincher as the Bruins now waited for the winner of the St. Louis–Minnesota series. That wait would last one week before the second round commenced.

For the second time in three seasons, the Bruins met the St. Louis Blues in the playoffs. This time around, it was the semifinal round, which opened up in Boston on Tuesday, April 18. After spotting the Blues a 1–0 lead early in the first period, the Bruins, behind Fred Stanfield's three goals, coasted to a 6–1 victory. Orr, with one assist, had the helper on Stanfield's third goal.

Game 2 was played on Thursday evening at the Garden. If the Bruins coasted to a win in the first game, their second game victory should be considered a moon shot victory with the final score being 10–2. Bucyk had his second career playoff hat trick, and Westfall had two goals in the debacle. The game was so one-sided fans began chanting "Bring in the Braves," a reference to the American Hockey Leagues' Boston Braves. By the end of the game, more than half of the 14,995 on hand had left for parts unknown. Orr did manage two assists in the contest.

In off-the-ice news, Bruins General Manager Milt Schmidt announced that no Bruin would be allowed to play in the Canada-Russia series scheduled for September. St. Louis GM Sid Abel, who agreed with Schmidt on the upcoming exhibition, asked Bruins' coach Tom Johnson for a little help. "Have some of your players, like Orr, put their skates on backwards, will you?"

The series moved on to St. Louis for game 3 on Sunday night. The Bruins' goal total was down, but not by much as they again beat up on the Blues, this time by a

7–2 margin. In this contest, McKenzie and Walton both had a pair of goals to lead the B's to the triumph. After Boston fell behind 1–0, Westfall scored a shorthanded goal, the first of seven consecutive Bruins' goals. Orr managed one assist in the game.

Tuesday night's game at the St. Louis Arena would prove to be the closest contest of the series. Bucyk and Esposito both deposited two goals as the Bruins defeated the Blues 5–3 and swept the series four games to none. With three assists, Orr set the record for assists with fifteen in the playoffs. The old record of fourteen assists was set by Pat Stapleton of Chicago and Jean Claude Tremblay of Montreal in 1971.

Orr's knee troubles had been noticed by other players. Barclay Plager of the Blues had this observation: "But I know Orr isn't right. We sat down on the ice there one time, and we just looked at each other. And I said, 'Are you hurting?' He said, 'Yes.' No matter what, if he had only one leg, he'd still be the greatest thing out there. Orr just controlled the game tonight, and he's controlled all four games."

General Manager Milt Schmidt also announced that Orr would have knee surgery after the Stanley Cup playoffs had finished. The Bruins would now play the New York Rangers in the Stanley Cup finals to begin on Sunday afternoon, April 30.

After Dale Rolfe of the Rangers opened the scoring, the Bruins popped in five straight goals to take a 5–1 lead midway through the second period. Hodge had three of the goals. When Don Awrey entered the penalty box at 16:44 of the first period, the Bruins went to work as they managed to score two shorthanded goals on the same penalty. Sanderson at 17:29 and Hodge at 18:14 were the scorers. After Hodge completed the hat trick, the Rangers came back to score four consecutive goals and tie the game at 5–5 by the midpoint of period 3. That's when Ace Bailey, motoring down the left wing, swung around defenseman Brad Park to score the winner at 17:44 of the third period, which gave the B's a 6–5 victory over the New Yorkers. Orr had an assist on the Hodge, second-period goal. "I thought I had him. I figured I had him by the boards, and there was no way he could go around me," said Park. One of Bailey's teammates uttered, "If Ace Bailey played regularly, he'd be a thirty-goal scorer."

April 1972 Playoffs					Orr's Stats				
					Game		Season		
Date	Venue	Versus	W-L-T	Score	G	A	G	A	PTS
5	Boston	Toronto	W	5–0	0	2	0	2	2
6	Boston	Toronto	L	4–3 (OT)	0	1	0	3	3
8	Toronto	Maple Leafs	W	2–0	1	1	1	4	5
9	Toronto	Maple Leafs	W	5–4	0	3	1	7	8
11	Boston	Toronto	W	3–2	0	1	1	8	9

18	Boston	St. Louis	W	6–1	0	1	1	9	10
20	Boston	St. Louis	W	10–2	0	2	1	11	12
23	St. Louis	Blues	W	7–2	0	1	1	12	13
25	St. Louis	Blues	W	5–3	0	3	1	15	16
30	Boston	New York	W	6–5	0	1	1	16	17

May 1972

Game 2 of the finals was played on Tuesday night at the Garden. Hodge's goal during a two-man power play advantage propelled the B's to a 2–1 squeaker over New York. The two-man advantage lasted for ten seconds, and the Bruins capitalized after seven seconds of the five-on-three. Orr notched his seventeenth playoff assist on the first-period goal by Johnny Bucyk.

The game was marred by a discrepancy in the game clock. Coach Emile Francis of the Rangers claimed that the clock continued to run for four seconds during the last minute of play in the game. He was overruled by the officials. Veteran Garden timekeeper Tony Notagiacomo was working the game clock. The minor officials for the game assigned by the NHL were from Montreal. The backup timekeeper supervised the game clock with a stopwatch. Referee Art Skov supported the timekeeper in the controversy. Game 3 was scheduled for Thursday evening at Madison Square Garden.

The Rangers took game 3 by a 5–2 margin. Orr's goal scored at 1:10 of the second period was his seventeeth career playoff goal, breaking the record of sixteen held by Red Kelly when he was with the Detroit Red Wings. Brad Park and Rod Gilbert both had two goals in the Rangers' victory. Park became the first player in Stanley Cup history to score two power play goals in one period. Game 4 would be played on Sunday afternoon in Manhattan.

The Bruins edged the Rangers in the game at Madison Square Garden, 3–2. The first period featured fights involving Bobby Rousseau and Derek Sanderson with Gene Carr taking on Don Awrey. Then at 16:15, McKenzie and Glen Sather fought while Brad Park and Orr also drew five minute majors for their fisticuffs. Orr scored two first-period goals and assisted on Marcotte's second-period shorthanded goal, giving him a record twenty-two points for a defenseman in one playoff year. He set the previous mark of 20 points in 1970.

After the game, Phil Esposito was quoted as saying, "If the Rangers think they are going to beat us three in a row, they're full of crap. And you can spell that *K-R-A-P*... That's Park spelled backwards."

With the Bruins now ahead three games to one, anticipation of a cup triumph loomed over Boston Garden for game 5. However, the Rangers delayed the celebration with a solid 3–2 win over the Bruins as the New Yorkers' Bobby Rousseau struck twice in the third period to overcome a 2–1 deficit and sent the series back to New York.

It was a Thursday night, May 11, and after losing out on the cup and a potential dynasty in 1971, the Bruins came back and took the Stanley Cup with a 3–0 victory in game 6. Orr's power play goal at 11:18 of the first period, propelled the B's to the franchise's fifth Stanley Cup. Wayne Cashman, with two goals, and Gerry Cheevers' thirty-three saves cemented the Boston victory. It was a hard-fought game with six fighting majors included in the contest. Orr received a ten-minute misconduct in the first period to go along with his game totals of one goal and one assist. After the game, Orr said, "It was a great feeling winning the cup the first time, but it was sweet this time, too, especially winning it here. Cheesie and Eddie J. have been great for us all the way."

After the final buzzer and congratulatory handshakes and hugs with his mates, Orr and Brad Park of the Rangers formed the handshaking line between the teams. After going through the line, Orr headed for the Rangers' bench to shake hands with losing coach Emile Francis. Wayne Cashman and Ted Green refused to shake hands with the Broadway Blueshirts.

The dressing room scene after the game was more subdued and less raucous than 1970, perhaps because the game was played on the road. Again, Orr was surrounded by the media and was saying, "I'm thirsty. Will somebody give me a ginger ale? This was our best game because we had to play our best." Orr then described his first goal (and game winner) to the audience of media types. "You have to be careful on a move like that, or they will catch you flatfooted. They almost caught me on that goal. I wasn't shooting, really. I was trying to pass in front to anyone who might be there to deflect it." Orr had spun away from Bruce MacGregor before firing the puck some thirty feet towards the net. The puck whizzed past Rangers' netminder Gilles Villemure into the far corner of the cage.

Johnny Bucyk opined, "This is the best of the Bruins teams. But personally for me, the thrill isn't as big as it was in 1970. The first time you win is always the best."

Orr became the fourth player to score two Stanley Cup winning goals, joining Toe Blake, Jean Beliveau, and Henri Richard of the Montreal Canadiens in this category.

Orr also confirmed that he was scheduled for an operation, probably in June.

The Rangers' assessment of the series could be summed up by New York Captain Vic Hadfield. "We played them pretty even—except they had Bobby Orr." Hadfield concluded, "You want to know what turned this game around? It was the same thing that turned the whole series around—Bobby Orr." Rangers' forward Jack Egers had this to say: "Orr was the best player I ever saw. He's also the classiest. He was a classy guy, but so were guys like Gilbert and Ratelle. Orr, Ratelle, and Gilbert carried themselves on and off the ice like you wish you would have."

Twice during game 4 at Madison Square Garden, Orr had to be taken out to the dressing room to have treatment on his injured knee. Despite the pain, he managed to score two goals in the Bruins 3–2 victory. Said Rangers coach Emile Francis: "He was playing hurt, real hurt, and it was so obvious. But he did the job and won the game for them." Brad Park joked, "I wish I was hurt like that." Park, who was considered the next-best backliner after Orr, also had this to say: "There's a standing joke on the Rangers. The guys tell me I better hurry up if I'm going to catch up with Bobby Orr, but they all know I will never catch up." Orr, who won the Norris Trophy in 1972 for a record fifth consecutive season, garnered 204 of a possible 210 points. Park finished second in the voting with 117 points followed by Bill White of Chicago with 25.

In addition to winning the Norris, Orr won the Hart Trophy as the league's MVP for a record-setting third straight season, becoming the first player to accomplish this feat.

Gilles Villemure played eight seasons with the New York Rangers and was a right-handed catching goaltender had this to say after the series: "Bobby was the one who opened up the game. You know, like all defensemen in the sixties were, that I remember, they were all defensive defensemen. They were low-scoring games, but he came in and opened everything up. Oh, he was the best, the best I've seen anyway."

Foes and friends had observations about Orr. "There are players, there are stars, there are superstars, and then there is Bobby Orr," so said Serge Savard of the Montreal Canadiens.

"They should have another league for him to play in," iterated Bobby Clarke of the Philadelphia Flyers.

Terry O'Reilly of the Boston Bruins in a passing thought said, "They should pass him around from team to team each year, just to keep things fair."

"Bobby Orr would be the man. He is a master of his craft, a virtuoso. Ted Williams was the brash one, was a more exciting personality than Bobby Orr, the shy one, but in their professions, they are comparable performers," said Harold Kaese of the *Boston Globe.*

"In my thirty-six years in the NHL, Bobby is the greatest player I have ever seen in the past, the greatest player in the present, and if anyone greater should show up, I just hope the Good Lord has me around to see him and let him be a Bruin," said General Manager Milt Schmidt. In 2016 on the eve of his ninety-eighth birthday, Schmidt said this to Kevin Paul Dupont of the *Boston Globe*: "The best player I've ever seen. No question about it. None. The players are all bigger and faster now. But if Bobby Orr played today, forget it, he'd make them sick."

May 1972 Playoffs					Orr's Stats				
					Game		Season		
Date	Venue	Versus	W-L-T	Score	G	A	G	A	PTS
2	Boston	New York	W	2–1	0	1	1	17	18
4	New York	Rangers	L	5–2	1	0	2	17	19
7	New York	Rangers	W	3–2	2	1	4	18	22
9	Boston	New York	L	3–2	0	0	4	18	22
11	New York	Rangers	W	3–0	1	1	5	19	24

Orr won the Conn Smythe Trophy as playoff MVP, the first time any player had won this award twice. *Sport* magazine awarded Orr with a new Dodge Charger as the most valuable player of the playoffs. The Bruins were met by over ten thousand fans at Logan Airport when they arrived from New York after winning the series.

During the next day's city hall celebration, about fifteen thousand onlookers packed the Cambridge Street side of the Plaza to celebrate the Cup win. As the players tried to make their way back to the Garden, a short distance from the Plaza, the bus carrying them was encompassed by large crowds. Gerry Cheevers was quoted as saying, "Enthusiasm is great, but this is dangerous."

It would have been virtually unfathomable for anyone in attendance that day to entertain the thought that the Bruins would not experience another such celebration until Bobby Orr was sixty-three years old.

Each member of the Bruins received $17,500 in bonus money for winning the Stanley Cup. Chris Hayes and Garry Peters, who both had performed in the playoffs, did not have their names engraved on the Stanley Cup. The Cup was also engraved as "BQSTQN BRUINS," and the spelling error was not corrected until 1993.

Eddie Powers was the former president of the Boston Garden Arena Corporation, taking over from Walter Brown, who passed away in 1964. During his tenure, he booked all the shows into the Garden. He tells this vignette about Johnny Cash. "I had Johnny Cash here last year, and Bobby Orr turned out to be a fan of his. Orr asked me to introduce him to Cash. I told Cash, and Cash said 'Bobby who?' He never heard of him."

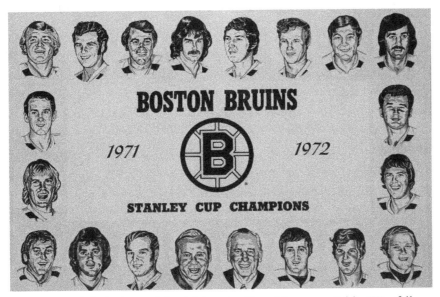

From top left clockwise: John Mckenzie, Don Marcotte, Eddie Westfall, Derek Sanderson, Fred Stanfield, Wayne Cashman, Johnny Bucyk, Carol Vadnais, Ted Green, Don Awrey, Gerry Cheevers, Bobby Orr, Phil Esposito, Milt Schmidt, Tom Johnson, Ken Hodge, Mike Walton, Eddie Johnston, Garnet "Ace" Bailey, Dallas Smith

View from the Balcony

After the playoff debacle of the previous season, the Bruins seemed to be on a mission of redemption. The fifty-four wins, down from the fifty-seven wins of 1970–1971, is still the second most in team history. The fifty-four wins were accomplished in the then seventy-eight-game schedule. After the 1971 series against the Canadiens, Orr was embarrassed enough for himself and his teammates. When asked about his summer plans, Orr replied, "I'm going to go home and practice playing hockey." Ultimately, his practice was rewarded.

The Bruins came out of the gate and compiled a 15-5-2 (32 out of 44 points) record through the first two months of the season. The team did not let up on the gas pedal throughout the season. Amazingly, the Bruins lost only three games in October, two games in November, one game in December, one game in January, one game in February, and then suffered through a rough patch in March, losing four games during the late winter / early spring portion of the schedule. In the fifteen playoff games played, the Bruins won twelve games on the way to their second Stanley Cup in three years.

The fans were thrilled again at the success of the team, but storm clouds were on the horizon. The World Hockey Association was no longer a twinkling in the WHA founders' eyes, as was NHL expansion to Atlanta and Long Island. Players would be lost in transactions, and the fear was that the team would be split apart. The dream of rattling off a string of championships was beginning to fade. So the moment of triumph for the discerning and oft time cynical fans was more like cloves on an aching tooth. There was relief, but the pain would soon return.

Integral parts of the championship teams, Gerry Cheevers, Derek Sanderson, Eddie Westfall, and John McKenzie would soon be gone. Management would ease out General Manager Milt Schmidt. Seats, hard to come by for the last few seasons, would now be available. But for the moment, life for Bruin's fandom was good.

Top Hockey Stories from 1972

Stanley Cup Champions	Boston Bruins
Art Ross Trophy	Phil Esposito, Boston Bruins
Hart Trophy	Bobby Orr, Boston Bruins
Masterton Trophy	Bobby Clarke, Philadelphia Flyers
Lady Byng Trophy	Jean Ratelle, New York Rangers
Vezina Trophy	Tony Esposito and Gary Smith, Chicago Blackhawks
Conn Smythe Trophy	Bobby Orr, Boston Bruins
Norris Trophy	Bobby Orr, Boston Bruins

Calder Cup Champions	Nova Scotia Voyageurs
Memorial Cup Champions	Cornwall Royals
NCAA Hockey Champions	Boston University

The NHL playoffs are amended in each division. The first-place team plays the fourth-place team, while the second-place team plays the third-place team.

Top Sports Stories

World Series Champions	Oakland Athletics
Super Bowl VII Champions	Miami Dolphins (game played on 1/14/1973 at Memorial Coliseum, Los Angeles, California)
NBA Champions	Los Angeles Lakers
Kentucky Derby Winner	Riva Ridge
NCAA Football Champions	USC (12-0-0)
NCAA Basketball Champions	UCLA

1972 Winter Olympics are held in Sapporo, Japan. The USSR wins the Gold Medal with a 4-0-1 record.

CHAPTER 7

1972–1973: The Long Drought Commences

WITH THE WINNING OF THE fifth Stanley Cup in team history, it was time to move on quickly. At the top of the list of things to do was Orr's ailing left knee. After a short vacation, he was scheduled to go under the knife at Massachusetts General Hospital sometime in June. "I talked to Bobby over the weekend," said Bruins' President Weston Adams Jr., "and he's consulted with the doctors. He told me he has some floating cartilage in his knee, which has caused it to lock from time to time. So rather than going on like that, he's decided to have the piece of cartilage removed. It doesn't sound like the type of thing that's going to take ninety days to recover from. I think he expects to be working out again in a month or so after surgery." This would be Orr's fourth knee operation.

Meanwhile, he was selected to his fifth postseason All-Star berth along with teammate Phil Esposito. Orr's total award money for the 1971–72 season totaled $25,500, which included his $15,000 share for winning the Stanley Cup.

While vacationing off Key Largo in Florida, Orr caught a forty-five-pound dolphin on board the Lorna, a boat owned by hotelier George Page, Orr's partner at the Branding Iron Restaurant in Boston. The restaurant was located at 75 Blossom Court behind the Massachusetts General Hospital.

In early June, Orr was operated on by Dr. Carter Rowe at the Massachusetts General Hospital. The operation lasted three hours, and Dr. Rowe claimed it was a success. Rowe described the operation an "overall cleanup" with several portions of cartilage and spurs being removed from the knee. However, the doctor recommended that no heavy skating be done before September, and when he did start, a brace should be worn. Orr would be confined to the hospital for seven to eight days and be required to use crutches for a few weeks after that.

Orr's attorney, Alan Eagleson claimed that Orr would be among the players representing Team Canada in the showdown series with the Russians scheduled for September. "He'll go to Russia even if it's to just carry the water bucket," declared Eagleson.

In early August, Orr reported that he would not be playing against the Russians due to the aftereffects of his knee operation. He would be skating at the Team Canada training camp but not be scrimmaging.

The brass back in Boston, Weston Adams Jr. and Milt Schmidt, expressed concern about Orr's workouts and whether Dr. Rowe was consulted on Bobby's knee. Rowe's instructions were that his training should be confined to simple exercises. Adams felt that he should not be playing whether it is with Team Canada or the Bruins until the knee was completely healed.

Finally, in late August, it was determined that he would not compete in the Canadian portion of the series, which was scheduled to open in Montreal on September 2.

After the completion of the first four games and the poor performance of Team Canada, it was hoped that Orr would be able to play the games played in Russia. He was deemed not ready and the concern for his availability for the season opener on October 8 was now in question.

As the home opener approached, Orr himself reported that his damaged knee was "not good" and "painful." As the Bruins got ready to defend the Stanley Cup, the team seemed headed into an uncertain future. Derek Sanderson, John McKenzie, and Gerry Cheevers were all gone to the new World Hockey Association. Harry Sinden had taken over as Managing Director with Milt Schmidt moving upstairs to an unspecified position. With Orr on the shelf, the team did seem to be wavering, and the early season goings would prove as much. For the first time in his career, he would miss opening night. It was later reported that Schmidt would be leaving the Bruins as the Adams family planned to sell the majority of its stock in the Bruins before the 1973–1974 season.

Cheevers, Awrey, Orr, Sanderson, Esposito, and Cashman were selected to participate for Team Canada in the series against Russia to be played in Canada from September 2 to 8 and in Moscow from September 22 to 28. Cheevers and Sanderson were not allowed to play because they had signed contracts with the new World Hockey Association.

McKenzie and Sanderson were now members of the Philadelphia Blazers of the WHA. Ted Green had signed on with the New England Whalers, who would play their games out of both the Boston Garden and Boston Arena. In light of McKenzie signing with the Blazers, the Bruins traded his NHL rights to the Philadelphia Flyers. With the Bruins filing suits in Suffolk Superior Court to prevent Cheevers and Sanderson from jumping to the WHA, the new circuit filed an anti-trust suit against the NHL. These court cases were later transferred to the Federal District Court in Boston.

Two new franchises were admitted into the NHL with the New York Islanders playing in the East Division and the Atlanta Flames joining the West Division. The B's lost Eddie Westfall in the draft to the Islanders. The Bruins would be holding training camp in London, Ontario, beginning September 12.

News reports claimed that Weston Adams Jr. had announced that the Boston Garden management was pondering the possibility of moving into a new building, possibly at Boston's South Station by 1975. The McNulty Company, designers of the Metropolitan Sports Center in Bloomington, Minnesota, had been hired to look into the feasibility of building a new arena. Reports out of Boston claimed that the Bruins were up for sale with channel 38 television being one of the prospective buyers. Orr's attorney, Alan Eagleson said that when he signed his next contract, he would like him to own a piece of the team.

October 1972

The Boston Garden seating capacity was increased to 15,003. To the dismay of many, the Bruins without Orr dropped their first two contests of the season. The losses included the home opener against Los Angeles and the road premier in Detroit.

After their first win of the season against the Islanders on Long Island, Orr was scheduled to play on the fifteenth against the Pittsburgh Penguins. However, it was decided that he was still not ready for game action. Coach Tom Johnson approached Orr while he was getting into his equipment. "I had a one-on-one with him. I don't feel he is quite ready just yet. I watched him skating on Friday. He was skating all right, perhaps, but he was not skating like Orr, and that was the important thing."

As the Bruins headed to Madison Square Garden for their first encounter of the season with the New York Rangers, it was apparent that Orr was still not ready to play. Prior to the game, teammate Mike Walton declared to Orr that the Bruins will win "one for the Gimper." However, without Orr, the Bruins were scuttled by the Rangers 7–1.

Orr made his 1972–73 season debut on Saturday, the 21st in Pittsburgh. The Bruins defeated the Penguins 4–2 with three of the four goals scored on the power play. Orr got his first minor (elbowing) penalty in the first period and had his first assist on Ken Hodge's power play goal in the second frame. The following night back at the Boston Garden, the B's, in spite of Orr's first goal of the season allowed a 3–1 lead to collapse and lost to the Vancouver Canucks, 5–4.

The team headed to Buffalo to face the surprising first place Sabres. Boston was leading by a 2–0 score after the first period but surrendered two goals in the second period and settled for a 2–2 tie. Thirty-three-year-old rookie goaltender Ross Brooks made his NHL debut and stopped thirty-four of the thirty-six shots directed his way.

In Boston the next day for a game with Chicago, Orr headed to Dr. Carter Rowe's office for a reevaluation of his left knee. Attending the meeting was Orr, Coach Tom Johnson, and Managing Director Harry Sinden. Although his knee was declared medically sound, it was decided that his knee had not advanced to the point where he should even be playing limited minutes. Prognosis was that Orr would be out anywhere from two to eight weeks.

Without Orr in the lineup, the Bruins finished the month of October with a loss to Chicago (6–3) and wins over the Maple Leafs (3–2) and the Islanders (9–1). In the 9–1 win over the Islanders and old friend Eddie Westfall, left winger Johnny Bucyk scored his four hundredth career goal while Greg Sheppard celebrated his first career hat trick. Future Islander great Billy Smith was the victim of the onslaught.

October 1972					Orr's Stats				
					Game		Season		
Date	Venue	Versus	W-L-T	Score	G	A	G	A	PTS
8	Boston	Los Angeles	L	4–2	DNP		0	0	0
11	Detroit	Red Wings	L	4–3	DNP		0	0	0
14	New York	Islanders	W	7–4	DNP		0	0	0
15	Boston	Pittsburgh	W	8–4	DNP		0	0	0
18	New York	Rangers	L	7–1	DNP		0	0	0
21	Pittsburgh	Penguins	W	4–2	0	1	0	1	1
22	Boston	Vancouver	L	5–4	1	0	1	1	2
25	Buffalo	Sabres	T	2–2	0	1	1	2	3
26	Boston	Chicago	L	6–3	DNP		1	2	3
28	Toronto	Maple Leafs	W	3–2	DNP		1	2	3
29	Boston	NY Islanders	W	9–1	DNP		1	2	3

November 1972

The Bruins began November on a West Coast swing through Los Angeles, Oakland, and Vancouver. After a loss in LA, the Bruins moved up the coast and blew a three-goal lead and had to settle for a 6–6 tie in Oakland. In the Seals' game, Ross Brooks surrendered three goals to Joey Johnston. The B's moved onto Vancouver, where they managed a 4–2 victory on the 5th.

Back in Boston, the Massachusetts Lottery was about to award a million-dollar prize to a lucky contestant for the eighth time. Making the presentation was Robert Crane, the treasurer of the Commonwealth of Massachusetts. On the dais with Crane was Orr, who announced the winner, Helen and David Sullivan of Brockton, Massachusetts. Although Mrs. Sullivan got to kiss Orr, her husband had to borrow a dime to phone his parents with the good news.

At about the same time, Orr's attorney, Alan Eagleson, stated that Orr would probably be out until the first of the year. Both Orr and Sinden denied the report. In spite of not playing, Orr spent time working out at the Colonial Country Club in Lynnfield, Massachusetts, under the watchful eye of trainer Gene Berde, who was famous for rounding Boston Red Sox superstar Carl Yastrzemski into shape. It was reported that Orr's ideal playing weight for his return to action was between 185 and 187 pounds.

In the November 9th 8–3 victory over Detroit at Boston Garden, Johnny Bucyk scored his 1,000th NHL point. After missing nine games, Orr returned to action on November 18 at Long Island. To make life sweet, Orr scored the first goal of the game on his first shot in a 7–3 win over the Islanders. "It was a coincidence, strictly a coincidence," claimed Orr. Although it was reported that he would see limited action, Orr actually racked up twenty-three minutes of playing time.

The next night back in Boston, the Bruins entertained the Maple Leafs. Orr assisted on Greg Sheppard's first-period goal but was critical of his overall play, saying, "No, I wasn't tired, I just played like a blooming midget, a blooming jerk." Toronto coach John McLellan had a different take on the subject of Orr. "He looked like he had never been out of the lineup. I don't know why they had to save him until just before we were coming to town." The Bruins toppled the Maple Leafs, 6–5.

On Thursday night, the Bruins hosted California at the Garden. Orr had his first multiple goal game of the season with two goals as the B's edged the Seals, 4–2. The next night in Atlanta, goaltender John Adams played his first game of the year and earned career shutout number one in white washing the Flames, 4–0. Orr had his fifth goal of the season in the first period. This was the Bruins' first ever visit to the Omni in Atlanta, Georgia.

Back in Boston on Sunday night to meet the Philadelphia Flyers, Orr had a two-point game (one goal, one assist) as the B's bested the Flyers, 6–4. Orr's goal at 19:32 of the first period brought this reaction from his rookie season roommate Joe Watson now playing the backline for Philadelphia. Orr traded passes with Gregg Sheppard, and as he raced toward the goal waiting for Sheppard's pass, Watson held onto Orr "for dear life. I couldn't believe he could still make the play" as Orr deposited the backhander behind Doug Favell. "He looks like the same Orr to me."

On Wednesday night at the Forum in Montreal, the B's six-game winning streak came to an end, although the unbeaten streak was extended to seven games as the Bruins and Canadiens played to a 3–3 tie.

Rumors were floating that Orr's attorney, Alan Eagleson, had bought a 42 percent interest in the Bruins. The rumors were denied by Clarence Campbell, president of the NHL, and Bruins' President Weston Adams Jr. The other fluttering rumor was that the Bruins' TV 38 partner, Storer Broadcasting, was sniffing around the edges of buying the team since there was now increasing interest in cable television.

One last test for the month of November would be the next evening in western New York as the Bruins would clash with the Buffalo Sabres. The B's, who were led by Orr's two goals and two assists, came from behind and defeated the Sabres by a count of 5–4.

November 1972					Orr's Stats				
					Game		Season		
Date	Venue	Versus	W-L-T	Score	G	A	G	A	PTS
2	Los Angeles	Kings	L	5–2	DNP		1	2	3
3	California	Seals	T	6–6	DNP		1	2	3

5	Vancouver	Canucks	W	4–2	DNP	1	2	3
9	Boston	Detroit	W	8–3	DNP	1	2	3
12	Boston	Montreal	L	5–3	DNP	1	2	3
16	Boston	St. Louis	W	4–0	DNP	1	2	3
18	New York	Islanders	W	7–3	1	1	2	3	5
19	Boston	Toronto	W	6–5	0	1	2	4	6
23	Boston	California	W	4–2	2	0	4	4	8
24	Atlanta	Flames	W	4–0	1	1	5	5	10
26	Boston	Philadelphia	W	6–4	1	1	6	6	12
29	Montreal	Canadiens	T	3–3	0	0	6	6	12
30	Boston	Buffalo	W	5–4	2	2	8	8	16

December 1972

The Bruins started December as they ended November, with a victory, this time over the New York Islanders 5–1. The unbeaten streak had now reached nine games. Orr had two assists in the contest. Eddie Johnston shut out the Blues for the second time this season, and Orr assisted Don Marcotte on a first-period goal as the Bruins defeated the Blues at Boston Garden, 5–0.

The Boston Garden Arena Corporation, owners of the Boston Bruins and the Boston Braves and the Storer Broadcasting Company, announced an agreement to merge through a stock exchange. Under the merger plan, each share of Garden-Arena stock would be exchanged for 1.6 shares of Storer stock. The agreement was announced on December 7.

The unbeaten streak was extended to eleven games as the Bruins defeated the Flyers, 4–3 at the Spectrum in Philadelphia. Orr had an assist on Phil Esposito's seventeenth goal of the season—a goal that turned out to be the game winner.

The next evening back at Boston Garden, the Bruins throttled the Seals by an 8–4 score. Ken Hodge had three goals in the contest, and Orr had one assist as the team's unbeaten streak reached an even dozen games. Marshall Johnston of the Seals fired home three goals in the Seals' losing effort.

On December 11, Orr would headline the Unity Youth Services Building fundraiser at the Hynes Auditorium in downtown Boston. All members of the 1970 and 1972 Stanley Cup champions would be present, and filmed highlights of those playoffs were shown.

Bruins' fans of that era may remember the Wayne Cashman-Jim Schoenfeld battle in which the players crashed through the end boards precipitating in a brawl. It happened in Buffalo on December 13 in a 7–3 Sabres thrashing of the Bruins. The game also included a bench clearing brawl at the conclusion of the match. The fisticuffs continued until late in the game when O'Reilly, Orr, and Vadnais were thrown out the contest. Referee Bob Myers handed out 141 minutes in penalties. For the sixth time in Orr's career, he achieved the trio of a goal, an assist, and a fight. In the first period, he assisted on Ken Hodge's power play goal. The second period showed Orr scoring a goal at the 8:31 mark. For the remainder of the game, Orr would rack up major penalties after two altercations with Schoenfeld, and he earned a game misconduct at 18:01 of the third period.

With the unbeaten streak broken, the Bruins chartered back to Boston for a game with the New York Rangers the next night. A four-goal output in the second period fueled by Cashman's two goals, and Orr's two assists propelled the B's to a 4–2 victory. They outshot the Rangers, 55–24.

For the second time in eight days, the Bruins were back in the City of Brotherly Love. Orr's two assists extended his scoring streak to eight games, and the Bruins defeated the Flyers, 5–3. Ken Hodge and Gregg Sheppard each tallied two goals. The team now headed to western Pennsylvania and a date with the Pittsburgh Penguins.

The Bruins came out on top of the Penguins 3–2 at the Igloo. An interesting event occurred late in the second period. Orr had apparently scored his tenth goal of the season, but it was waved off when referee Art Skov said he had blown the whistle stopping play. When Orr blew his stack, he received a ten-minute misconduct and a game misconduct, thus ending his evening of play.

The Red Wings were next up at the Boston Garden. The B's had thirty-eight shots on net and connected on eight of them. Orr had two assists in the game but sat out much of the third period with lingering flu symptoms.

In the last game before Christmas and an upcoming five-game road trip, the Bruins defeated the Atlanta Flames, 3–1. Orr's ten-game scoring streak ended when he was held off the score sheet by the tight checking Flames.

Bobby Orr became engaged to Peggy Wood on Christmas Day, though no wedding date was announced. Miss Wood, a teacher from Ft. Lauderdale, Florida received a 3.5 carat diamond ring.

In the back half of the home and home series, the Bruins met the Flames at the Omni on the 27th. No change in the scoring from the previous game as the Bruins won again, 3–1. Orr was held off the score sheet for the second consecutive game, although he did pick up a minor penalty in the third period.

The Bruins moved into the Met Center in Bloomington, Minnesota, where they would face the North Stars on the 29th. Orr's tenth goal was all that the Bruins needed as Eddie Johnston earned his third shutout of the season and the B's defeated the Stars, 2–0.

It was announced by Brian O'Neill, the NHL's Executive Director, that Orr would be fined $100 for leaving the bench during the wild altercation with the Buffalo Sabres on December 13.

December 1972					Orr's Stats				
					Game		Season		
Date	Venue	Versus	W-L-T	Score	G	A	G	A	PTS
3	Boston	NY Islanders	W	5–1	0	2	8	10	18
7	Boston	St. Louis	W	5–0	0	1	8	11	19
9	Philadelphia	Flyers	W	4–3	0	1	8	12	20
10	Boston	California	W	8–4	0	1	8	13	21
13	Buffalo	Sabres	L	7–3	1	1	9	14	23
14	Boston	NY Rangers	W	4–2	0	2	9	16	25
17	Philadelphia	Flyers	W	5–3	0	2	9	18	27
19	Pittsburgh	Penguins	W	3–2	0	1	9	19	28
21	Boston	Detroit	W	8–1	0	2	9	21	30
23	Boston	Atlanta	W	3–1	0	0	9	21	30
27	Atlanta	Flames	W	3–1	0	0	9	21	30
29	Minnesota	North Stars	W	2–0	1	0	10	21	31

January 1973

In the first game of 1973, the Bruins moved into the Pacific Coliseum for a game with the Canucks. Orr tied a league record by assisting on six goals as the Bruins coasted to an 8–2 victory. Phil Esposito had the hat trick as the Bruins peppered Bruce Bullock, in goal for Vancouver with fifty-three shots. The six assists tied the record held by Babe Pratt of the Toronto Maple Leafs set on January 8, 1944, and equaled by Pat Stapleton of Chicago on March 30, 1969.

The Bruins moved onto St. Louis for their next encounter against the Blues. Despite Orr's eleventh goal, the B's eight-game winning streak came to an end as St. Louis upended the Bruins, 4–2. Orr's goal was the 163rd of his career, breaking the record of goals for defenseman held by Red Kelly. The goal was scored against St. Louis's Jacques Caron.

In what can only be described as a freaky accident, forward Mike Walton suffered jaw, neck, and leg injuries in addition to receiving over one hundred stitches during the trip to St. Louis. Walton was injured when he accidentally fell through a plate glass door of the team's hotel.

In a nationally televised game from the Chicago Stadium, the Bruins and Blackhawks played a back-and-forth, seesaw game that the Hawks finally won 5–4 on a power play goal by Dan Maloney at 19:09 of the third period. Orr was serving a minor penalty at the time of the goal. He did have three assists in the game.

After the five-game road trip, the Bruins returned to the Garden where they would host the Minnesota North Stars. Since the Stars joined the league in 1967–68, a span of fourteen games, they had not won a game in Boston. In this contest, Ken Hodge, with an assist from Orr and Bucyk, fired home his twenty-third goal as the Bruins and North Stars skated to a 1–1 tie. Rookie center Richie Leduc made his debut with the Bruins in this game. Leduc had been attending the game as a spectator but was quickly pressed into action as Gregg Sheppard came down with the flu just prior to game time.

Saturday night was *Hockey Night in Canada*, and the B's were at Maple Leaf Gardens for a tilt with Toronto. Orr's two assists helped Boston register a 4–1 win over the Leafs.

The next night at Boston Garden, the Bruins avenged the December 13 loss at Buffalo and blasted the Sabres 6–0 behind four goals by Phil Esposito.

The Islanders visited the Garden on Thursday night, and it resulted in the most unusual and shocking game of the year. New York ran out to a 5–0 lead by the 17:46 mark of the first period. The Bruins did make a comeback but it was too little, too late as the first-year Isles defeated the Bruins 9–7. Orr managed three assists in the game, but the combination of goaltenders Eddie Johnston and John Adams made only nineteen saves on twenty-eight shots. Bucyk had a big night scoring four goals in a losing effort. On Saturday night in Pittsburgh, the Bruins lost their second straight game as Jim Rutherford, and the Penguins shut out the B's, 3–0.

Back in Boston on Sunday night, Wayne Cashman notched his first career three-goal game, a "pure" hat trick and sent the Bruins to a 5–2 victory over the California Seals. Cashman's three consecutive goals were scored in the second period. Orr managed two assists in the contest.

In a midweek contest at Madison Square Garden, the Bruins lost to the Rangers, 4–2. The loss was the third defeat in the previous four games and was compounded further when the Bruins were defeated by the Red Wings at Boston Garden the next evening, also by a 4–2 margin. Orr was credited with an assist on both Boston goals in the loss to Detroit. The second assist was the four hundredth of his career.

After the game, the players held a closed door meeting to hash out their problems. Up to this point, for the month of January, the Bruins record was a less-than-stellar 4-6-1. A Saturday night contest with the Chicago Blackhawks loomed for the team that seemed to be heading in reverse.

With the crowd chanting, "Bring back Derek, we'll chip in the salary," and booing the home team, the Bruins lost to Chicago by a 4–2 score. With the team now in complete tailspin and having lost five of their last six games, changes seem inevitable. Garnet "Ace" Bailey was benched one game for making an obscene gesture toward the crowd following the 4–2 loss.

For the second consecutive Sunday, Cashman deposited three goals as the Bruins shaded the Los Angeles Kings, 6–5. Orr also had his twelfth goal as the B's broke their three-game losing streak. The team finished January with a dismal 5-7-1 record.

With the All-Star Game at Madison Square Garden set for Tuesday night, the Bruins sent Orr, Smith, Esposito, Hodge, and Coach Tom Johnson to represent the East Division. Coach Johnson was subdued when assessing Orr's play during the game. Orr started the evening by falling on his backside during the pregame introductions. His play during the game left Johnson to remark, "I don't know what's wrong with Bobby. He's not favoring his knee. He's just playing below average hockey."

Orr, who was on the ice for all four of the West's goals, agreed with the analysis. "The smartest thing the coach did all night was getting me and Dallas Smith off the ice." As for his faux pas during the intro, Orr said, "I don't think I've ever been so embarrassed. I don't know what is wrong with me. I'm not thinking properly, and it shows in my play. Who knows, I probably tripped over myself. I have two left feet, you know."

Orr Nominated to Gillette Award List

Orr was the lone New England area athlete nominated to the Gillette Cavalcade of Champions Award list. The other nominees included the following:

Baseball:	Dick Allen (Chicago White Sox)	Basketball:	Kareem Abdul-Jabbar (Milwaukee Bucks)
	Johnny Bench (Cincinnati Reds)		Wilt Chamberlain (Los Angeles Lakers)
	Steve Carlton (Philadelphia Phillies)		Jerry West (Los Angeles Lakers)
Football:	Larry Brown (Washington Redskins)	Golf:	Jack Nicklaus
	Franco Harris (Pittsburgh Steelers)		Gary Player
	Earl Morrall (Miami Dolphins)		Lee Trevino

Other male professionals: Muhammad Ali
Stan Smith

Male amateurs: Frank Shorter
Mark Spitz
Bill Walton

Woman athletes: Chris Evert
Billie Jean King
Mickie King

| January 1973 | | | | | Orr's Stats | | | | |
| | | | | | Game | | Season | | |
Date	Venue	Versus	W-L-T	Score	G	A	G	A	PTS
1	Vancouver	Canucks	W	8–2	0	6	10	27	37
4	St. Louis	Blues	L	4–2	1	0	11	27	38
7	Chicago	Blackhawks	L	5–4	0	3	11	30	41
11	Boston	Minnesota	T	1–1	0	1	11	31	42
13	Toronto	Maple Leafs	W	4–1	0	2	11	33	44
14	Boston	Buffalo	W	6–0	0	0	11	33	44
18	Boston	NY Islanders	L	9–7	0	3	11	36	47
20	Pittsburgh	Penguins	L	3–0	0	0	11	36	47
21	Boston	California	W	5–2	0	2	11	38	49
24	New York	Rangers	L	4–2	0	0	11	38	49
25	Boston	Detroit	L	4–2	0	2	11	40	51
27	Boston	Chicago	L	4–2	0	0	11	40	51
28	Boston	Los Angeles	W	6–5	1	2	12	42	54

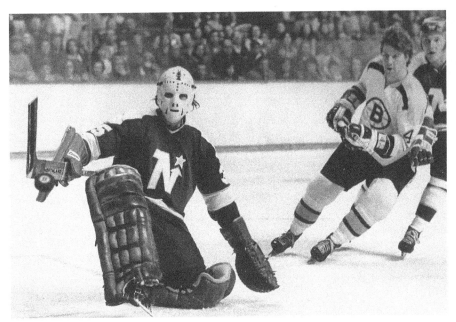

January 11, 1973. Orr fires on future teammate Gilles Gilbert of Minnesota while being shadowed by former mate Bill Goldsworthy in game at the Boston Garden.

February 1973

After the All-Star Game, the Bruins began the second half of their six-game home stand with a contest against the Maple Leafs. Esposito potted his thirty-first, thirty-second and thirty-third goals of the season, and Orr netted his thirteenth goal to go along with three assists as the B's buzzed past the Leafs, 5–2.

On Saturday night, it would be the New York Rangers on Boston Garden ice. The spark provided by the win over Toronto was quickly extinguished by the New Yorkers. After taking a 3–2 lead early in the second period, the B's gave up five consecutive goals and lost to the Rangers, 7–3. Orr had a goal and assist in the losing contest. Walt Tkaczuk of the Rangers tucked three past Eddie Johnston in the New York win.

The home stand ended the next evening as the new heavyweights of the NHL, the Philadelphia Flyers, came to town. Although the B's played better than they had recently, they still had to settle for a 2–2 tie. Orr managed an assist on Greg Sheppard's fifteenth goal at the 11:23 mark of the first period. Orr also picked up a five-minute major due to an altercation with Philadelphia defenseman Andre "Moose" Dupont.

The next day, the other shoe dropped. Manager Harry Sinden axed Tom Johnson and replaced him with Braves' coach Bep Guidolin. Many of the players responded to the firing:

"It should have been one of us. They got the wrong guy" (Phil Esposito).

"We let him down, he didn't let us down" (Wayne Cashman).

"It's a shame. The guy got fired because we weren't playing as we should for him. Maybe they should have fired some of us. But that's the way it goes. If everything is going good, the players get the credit. When things go bad, the coach gets the blame. Perhaps we just didn't have the guts to play well for him" (Bobby Orr).

This was the third time in team history that the Bruins replaced their coach in midseason. Milt Schmidt replaced Lynn Patrick during the 1954–55 season, and Schmidt replaced Phil Watson during the 1961–62 campaign. Johnson's replacement, Bep Guidolin, was familiar with much of the Bruins' roster as Bobby Orr, Wayne Cashman and Nick Beverly played for Bep when he coached the Oshawa Generals of the OHA. Terry O'Reilly, Doug Roberts, Fred O'Donnell, and Ross Brooks spent time with the Braves under Guidolin's tutelage.

With the six-game home stand now in the rearview mirror and the team entrusted to new coach Guidolin, the Bruins were off to Minnesota and a game with the North Stars on the 7th.

Phil Esposito's two goals lifted the Bruins past the Stars, 3–2. Orr assisted on Esposito's thirty-fifth goal of the season as the B's won in Guidolin's debut as Boston's coach. On Saturday afternoon, the Penguins reported to the Garden for a game with the B's.

Mike Walton's three first-period goals helped the Bruins ice Pittsburgh 6–3. Orr scored his fifteenth goal to go along with an assist and a second period fighting major earned in a bout with future teammate Darryl Edestrand. The game also marked the return of prodigal son Derek Sanderson wearing number 27 after his brief stint in the WHA.

With Derek back in the fold, the paying off a five-year-old bet was now consummated. Orr and Derek Sanderson had bet $1,000 that they would be the first to walk the aisle in matrimony. With Orr having announced his engagement, Derek paid up. The loot, arriving in the Bruins' dressing room, was a cool 990 one-dollar bills and 1,000 pennies to bring the total to $1,000. The next evening, Ross Brooks stopped all twenty-two shots fired by the Los Angeles Kings as the Bruins shut out the Kings 2–0.

In the final home game before an extended six-game road swing, the Bruins hosted the Vancouver Canucks. Bucyk and Greg Sheppard scored two goals each, and Orr registered three assists as Boston defeated the Canucks by a 7–3 margin. They opened the road trip on a positive note as Boston defeated the Flyers in Philadelphia, 3–1. Orr scored his sixteenth goal and assisted on two others playing a remarkable forty minutes. "He was our quarterback. He played more than he would ordinarily, but that's what we plan to do in our big games," said Coach Guidolin. This was the fourth straight season that the Bruins had not lost at the Spectrum. They continued on to Minnesota for their second game of the road trip.

Guidolin had more comments on Orr. "He's going good. He'll be rested when it's necessary, but there is never any difficulty about that. Bobby Orr is one of those guys that communicate well, and he'll let me know if he really needs rest. Mostly, though, my theory is that a tired Orr is better than another rested player in crucial situations."

After five straight victories under Guidolin, the B's finally let down and were stomped by the Minnesota North Stars, 5–2 in Bloomington. Danny Grant scored three goals for the victors.

The next evening at the Chicago Stadium, Sanderson scored his first goal since returning from the WHA, a shorthanded goal, and Orr had his seventeenth as the Bruins slid by the Hawks, 4–1.

The Bruins now headed off to the NHL's northwest outpost and an encounter with the Canucks. In a game of ebbs and flows, the Canucks rolled out to a 4–0 lead. The Bruins got the next five and went ahead 5–4. Vancouver got the next two to go ahead 6–5. The B's scored the final two goals and finally defeated the Canucks, 7–6. Boston's goals were scored by seven different players, including Orr's eighteenth of the season. Three of the Boston goals were on power plays.

Boston moved down the coast for a contest with the Seals in Oakland. The Bruins screamed out to a 6–0 lead and rolled on to a 6–2 victory. Orr earned one assist in the contest. On Saturday night, the Los Angeles Kings hosted the Bruins before a full house of 16,005 fans at the Fabulous Forum. Bucyk netted three goals to lead the B's to a 7–5 victory over the Kings as Boston closed out their road trip with a 5–1 record.

February 1973					Orr's Stats				
					Game		Season		
Date	Venue	Versus	W–L–T	Score	G	A	G	A	PTS
1	Boston	Toronto	W	5–2	1	3	13	45	58
3	Boston	NY Rangers	L	7–3	1	1	14	46	60
4	Boston	Philadelphia	T	2–2	0	1	14	47	61
7	Minnesota	North Stars	W	3–2	0	1	14	48	62
10	Boston	Pittsburgh	W	6–3	1	1	15	49	64
11	Boston	Los Angeles	W	2–0	0	0	15	49	64
13	Boston	Vancouver	W	7–3	0	3	15	52	67
15	Philadelphia	Flyers	W	3–1	1	2	16	54	70
17	Minnesota	North Stars	L	5–2	0	0	16	54	70
18	Chicago	Blackhawks	W	4–1	1	0	17	54	71
20	Vancouver	Canucks	W	7–6	1	1	18	55	73
21	California	Seals	W	6–2	0	1	18	56	74
24	Los Angeles	Kings	W	7–5	0	2	18	58	76

March 1973

Managing Director Harry Sinden issued an edict that barred any Bruin player from engaging in any outside activity or personal appearances until the end of the Stanley Cup playoffs. After the successful road trip, the Bruins returned home to face the St. Louis Blues. Speculation had it that the Bruins were looking at the opponent on Saturday night, the Montreal Canadiens, and just didn't take care of business on this night as the Blues downed the Bruins, 4–3. Orr had his nineteenth goal in the loss.

A record crowd of 18,960 fans jammed the Forum and watched the Habs humiliate the Bruins by a 5–1 score. The Canadiens scored five straight goals before Bucyk scored his thirty-third. Eddie Johnston was replaced in goal after the first period after letting in four of ten shots. Ross Brooks played the last two periods, saving sixteen of seventeen attempts by Montreal. Orr and Don Awrey were on the ice for three of the first four goals of the game. Orr was benched by Guidolin for the second period, although Bep later explained that "Bobby was injured so it wasn't a benching in the general sense." After the game, Sinden announced that the Bruins had acquired forty-four-year-old goaltender Jacques Plante from the Toronto Maple Leafs for future considerations. The future considerations turned out to be the first pick in the 1973 amateur draft. After the season, goaltender Eddie Johnston was sent to the Leafs as part of the deal.

The next afternoon, the Chicago Blackhawks made a matinee appearance at the Garden, and newly acquired Plante was in goal for the Bruins. Orr was sidelined with the injury he had sustained the previous evening. However, Esposito scored two goals, and Plante stopped all twenty-seven shots as the Bruins defeated the Blackhawks, 4–0. Leaving the ice, Plante raised his arms in the famous *V* for victory gesture.

The fandom was concerned about Orr's knee again. "Bobby doesn't like all the fuss about his knee," said Sinden after Orr canceled an appointment to have his knee examined. While the fans pondered if he was going to be plagued once again by a bad knee, Orr wondered when people were going to stop overreacting to his medical problems. Sinden continued, "We made an appointment for Bobby, and when he got up on Monday [after the Chicago game], he decided he didn't need the examination." Orr was expected to travel to the next game in St. Louis on Wednesday.

In Jacques Plante's return to St. Louis, the Bruins lost to the Blues, 5–2. Orr had an assist on Phil Esposito's forty-fifth goal. The Bruins moved onto to Atlanta for a Friday night game against the Flames. Orr's twentieth goal propelled the Bruins to a 3–2 squeaker over the Flames at the Omni in Atlanta. The B's traveled back to Boston for a Sunday tilt against the Canadiens.

The Habs came into the contest with a fifteen-game unbeaten streak. It would be the Bruins' first victory over Montreal that season, as they got goals from Esposito

(46), Fred O'Donnell (7), Bucyk (36), Doug Roberts (3), and Greg Sheppard (22). Orr also had two assists in the 5–3 Bruins' win.

There were 112 teams with 2,240 players in the first Bobby Orr New England Invitational Tournament held at Skate 3, located in Tyngsboro, Massachusetts. The tourney was held from April 16 to 21. The B's moved on to Long Island for a Tuesday night contest with the Islanders. Eddie Johnston stopped all twenty-two shots thrown at him to earn the 3–0 shutout win. The Bruins headed to western New York for a Thursday night game with the Sabres.

Orr scored his twenty-first and twenty-second goals, and the B's, behind Jacques Plante in goal, defeated the Sabres 4–1. The next night, the Bruins were in Detroit for a game with the Red Wings. The 5–4 victory over Detroit marked the fifth consecutive win as Wayne Cashman netted two goals in the contest. Doug Roberts, a native Michigander, scored the winning goal for the Bruins with eighteen seconds left in the game.

On Sunday, the Atlanta Flames invaded the Boston Garden. After Curt Bennett scored a first-period goal, the Bruins came back with seven straight goals for a 7–1 victory over the Flames. Bucyk had two goals while Orr had his twenty-third goal to go along with two assists in the win. Jacques Plante stopped twenty-two of twenty-three shots on the night. The key to the victory involved the Bruins killing off a five-on-three shorthanded situation in the first period. The two Boston players in the box were Esposito and Orr. During Atlanta's two-man advantage, the Flames mustered no shots on goal. Orr's three points elevated his career total to 600.

The Bruins hosted the North Stars at the Garden on Thursday night. Bucyk's thirty-eighth and thirty-ninth goals paced Boston to a 5–3 win and their seventh straight victory. The win also marked Plante's fifth victory in six starts. Orr had a goal and assist in the contest.

The New York Rangers were in the Garden for a Saturday afternoon matinee. Sheppard, Sanderson, and Esposito had goals, and Plante had his second shutout since joining Boston as the Bruins blanked the Rangers, 3–0. Orr had two assists and the first one, on Greg Sheppard's twenty-fourth goal, was also assisted by Plante. Their current winning streak reached eight games.

The next evening, the young Buffalo Sabres came into the Boston Garden. The Bruins won this one easily by a 6–1 score. Orr fired home his twenty-fifth and twenty-sixth goals to go along with an assist on Esposito's fiftieth goal in the first period. Orr was later tossed out of the game when he became the third man in during a fight between Mike Walton of the Bruins and Ron Busniuk of Buffalo. Ross Brooks, tending goal for the Bruins, remained the only undefeated goaltender in the league. Brooks' record was now eleven wins and three ties.

Olympic gold medal winner Mark Spitz was named winner of the Gillette Cavalcade of Champions Athlete of the Year for 1972. The winner in the professional category was Orr, who donated his $5,000 prize to the Bobby Orr Community Center Fund in Parry Sound, Ontario.

The Bruins clinched second place with a 6–3 victory over the Rangers in New York on the 28th. The highlight of the game was Esposito's four goals, which gave him fifty-five on the season. Orr had two assists, and Jacques Plante had twenty-six saves as the Bruins extended their winning streak to ten games.

In the final game of March, the Bruins were in Toronto to take on the Maple Leafs. Despite Orr scoring all three Boston goals, the team went down to defeat by a score of 7–3.

Bruins Managing Director Harry Sinden had this observation on Orr. "If Bobby is playing any differently, I don't believe you can attribute it too much to the knee. I suppose you have to allow for some subconscious reaction to fairly constant pain in the knee, but more important to me is the influence of maturity and increasing hockey intelligence."

"In his earlier seasons, Bobby was going hell-bent all the time. Now, he is not so physical or reckless, particularly with the puck. He paces himself to the situation, and he and Phil Esposito can pretty well combine to dictate the tempo of any game. The thing that I enjoy about him most of the time is his passing. He has become almost flawless, threading the needle with those passes and hitting a guy in stride," continued Sinden.

Scotty Bowman, coach of the Montreal Canadiens, added, "When I tell people to watch Orr, I tell them to watch his eyes continually. He knows where everyone is on the ice. He doesn't get the puck and look. He looks before he gets the puck."

| **MARCH 1973** | | | | | Orr's Stats | | | | |
| | | | | | Game | | Season | | |
Date	Venue	Versus	W-L-T	Score	G	A	G	A	PTS
1	Boston	St. Louis	L	4–3	1	0	19	58	77
3	Montreal	Canadiens	L	5–1	0	0	19	58	77
4	Boston	Chicago	W	4–0	DNP		58	77	61
7	St. Louis	Blues	L	5–2	0	1	19	59	78
9	Atlanta	Flames	W	3–2	1	1	20	60	80
11	Boston	Montreal	W	5–3	0	2	20	62	82
13	New York	Islanders	W	3–0	0	0	20	62	82
15	Buffalo	Sabres	W	4–1	2	0	22	62	84
16	Detroit	Red Wings	W	5–4	0	1	22	63	85
18	Boston	Atlanta	W	7–1	1	2	23	65	88
22	Boston	Minnesota	W	5–3	1	1	24	66	90

24	Boston	NY Rangers	W	3–0	0	2	24	68	92
25	Boston	Buffalo	W	6–1	2	1	26	69	95
28	New York	Rangers	W	6–3	0	2	26	71	97
31	Toronto	Maple Leafs	L	7–3	3	0	29	71	100

April 1973

With second place nailed down and the Bruins anticipating a first-round bout with the New York Rangers, the B's hosted the Canadiens in the season finale at the Boston Garden. Peter Mahovlich's two goals propelled Montreal to a 5–3 victory. Orr had an assist to give him seventy-two on the season as he finished with 101 points—his fourth straight 100-point season.

"I had heard of Bobby Orr when he was very young. He played with Parry Sound in my home town of Ganonoque, Quebec and I had seen him play when I was very young. I was actually at the game in which he was scouted by Wren Blair and Milt Schmidt in Ganonoque. I wasn't quite old enough to play in that game, but I remember the game because it was, I think, for a provincial championship or it was for a semifinal for a provincial championship. In a small town, that's a pretty big deal. So the small arena was just packed. There was a lot of buzz in the building about Bobby Orr, that's for sure," said Fred O'Donnell, who played 115 games for the Bruins over two seasons (1972–73 and 1973–74).

As a footnote, O'Donnell and Orr married their wives on the same day.

April 1973					Orr's Stats				
					Game		Season		
Date	Venue	Versus	W-L-T	Score	G	A	G	A	PTS
1	Boston	Montreal	L	5–3	0	1	29	72	101

1972–1973 Standings

Eastern Division

	W	L	T	PTS	GF	GA
Montreal	52	10	16	120	329	184
Boston	51	22	5	107	330	235
New York Rangers	47	23	8	102	297	208
Buffalo	37	27	14	88	257	219
Detroit	37	29	12	86	265	243

Toronto	27	41	10	64	247	279
Vancouver	22	47	9	53	233	339
New York Islanders	12	60	6	30	170	347

Western Division

	W	L	T	PTS	GF	GA
Chicago	42	27	9	93	284	225
Philadelphia	37	30	11	85	296	256
Minnesota	37	30	11	85	254	230
St. Louis	32	34	12	76	233	251
Pittsburgh	32	37	9	73	257	265
Los Angeles	31	36	11	73	232	245
Atlanta	25	38	15	65	191	239
California	16	46	16	48	213	323

1973 Playoffs

Prior to the opening of the playoffs, Mrs. Francis Sakoian of Arlington, one of the nation's top astrologers, worked up an astrological chart on Orr. Mrs. Sakoian was asked specifically about Orr's health—particularly his knees.

Mrs. Sakoian did not know who Orr was until she started doing research. "I found he had troubles with his knees in the past, and unfortunately, I think he will have the same kind of problem in the future."

The interesting aspect of Mrs. Sakoian's astrological study of Orr was how similar he was in many ways to John Havlicek of the Boston Celtics. Buttressing Sakoian's study was Dr. Michael Quaguelin, one of the most revered figures in the astrological world. The doctor had also done a study on the world's famous sports figures. He said, "Like Havlicek, Bobby is very competitive and wants to be at the forefront of whatever is going on. He has great willpower, self-confidence, and creativity. I've never seen him play, but he must have fantastic feet. His astrological sign shows great dancing feet."

While the Rangers stayed at the Thunderbird Motel and practiced at the Wallace Civic Center in Fitchburg, Massachusetts, they began to devise their game plan for the opening round against Boston. Fitchburg is about fifty miles northwest of Boston along Route 2, the Mohawk Trail. In preparation, the Rangers used an unusual tactic. In practices, Brad Park wore number 4 and acted as Orr, likely without the dipsy doodles. The Rangers practiced by checking Park and continued it into games against the real Orr. With only two points earned by Orr in the series, it would be hard to argue against the tactics.

The defense of their Stanley Cup championship began on Wednesday night, April 4, with games 1 and 2 at Boston Garden. After Doug Roberts opened the scoring for Boston, the Rangers pumped home six straight goals, including two by Brad Park and two by Walter Tkaczuk as the Rangers easily skated by the Bruins 6–2. Winger Ted Irvine of the Rangers was involved in two fights, one with Hodge in the first period and a tussle with Orr in the second stanza. While Orr was confined to the penalty box, the Rangers scored two goals and pulled away from the Bruins for the win. Irvine, who played one game with the Bruins during the 1963–'64 season, is the father of Chris Jericho, WWE star wrestler.

If game 1 was a stunner, game 2 seemed to show the Rangers of the playoffs were not the New Yorkers of the regular season. From Orr came this comment. "We were just not hungry enough for the puck. To them, it was like a piece of raw meat." With that in mind, the Rangers again topped the Bruins, this time by a 4–2 score. To make matters worse, Phil Esposito was sidelined for the rest of the playoffs with a torn medial ligament in his right knee caused by a hit from Rangers' defenseman Ron Harris.

On Saturday night, the playoffs moved to Madison Square Garden. Not only was it a change of venue for Boston, but there was a change in goal as Eddie Johnston replaced Jacques Plante. Greg Sheppard (two goals, one shorthanded), Fred Stanfield, and Mike Walton scored goals and led the way past the Rangers, 4–2. "We didn't come down here to lose. We all played like we should, but EJ had a big part in it," said Orr. Johnston had thirty-five saves on the night's work.

The next night, it was all Rangers as Eddie Giacomin stopped thirty-three shots on goal, as New York shut out the Bruins 4–0. The B's were now on the brink of elimination. Orr had not had a point in the first four games and briefly played right wing instead of right point on the Bruins' power play. It was the first playoff shutout victory for the Rangers since April 6, 1950, when goaltender Charlie Rayner blanked Montreal, 3–0.

On Tuesday, May 10, The Rangers exacted revenge from the previous year's finals. New York eliminated the Bruins from the Stanley Cup Playoffs with a 6–3 victory at Boston Garden. Orr got on the score sheet with a goal and an assist, but the B's were outplayed by the Broadway Blueshirts. Steve Vickers struck three times to lead the Rangers in the clinching victory. The Bruins only scored one power play goal in twenty chances during the five matches. After they were ousted by the Rangers, Cashman, Sanderson, and Walton refused to shake hands with the victorious New Yorkers.

Emile Francis's comments after the Rangers clinched the series: "I got the film of every game that we played against Boston that year. You could tell he [Orr] was having trouble, especially as the season went down. He was having trouble going back to get the puck. So before, when we attacked, we would dump it into the opposite corner. But now, with him having trouble going back, we started going right after him, better that he should be passing the puck to the other guy. You could just see him losing a step." Rangers' defenseman Ron Harris proudly stated, "When we beat out Boston, I thought I had played a great series. I never got a penalty, and I hit so many guys in the series. After the game, I was kind of late to get on the bus… Usually, I was the first guy on. As I was getting on, Bobby Orr was nearby, and he approached me and said, 'Ronnie, you played great.' He said, 'You're the reason we're not here anymore. You were the guy.'"

April 1973 Playoffs					Orr's Stats				
					Game		Season		
Date	Venue	Versus	W-L-T	Score	G	A	G	A	PTS
4	Boston	NY Rangers	L	6–2	0	0	0	0	0
5	Boston	NY Rangers	L	4–2	0	0	0	0	0
7	New York	Rangers	W	4–2	0	0	0	0	0
8	New York	Rangers	L	4–0	0	0	0	0	0
10	Boston	NY Rangers	L	6–3	1	1	1	1	2

Bobby Clarke of the Philadelphia Flyers was the 1972–73 winner of the Hart Trophy, emblematic of the Most Valuable Player in the National Hockey League. When asked if winning the trophy meant he was the best player in the NHL, Clarke responded thusly: "Are you kidding? If it went to the best, Bobby Orr would win it every year, hands down."

A few events occurred shortly after the Bruins were eliminated from the playoffs:

- Eddie Powers, vice president of the Bruins and the Boston Garden, passed away.
- Weston Adams Sr., former President of the Boston Bruins and the son of C.F. Adams, founder of the Bruins, passed away at age sixty-eight.
- Gary Darling replaced Red Sullivan as the new Director of Scouting.
- Jacques Plante left the Bruins for the Quebec Nordiques of the World Hockey Association.

On April 21, Milt Schmidt left the Bruins to become General Manager of the expansion Washington Capitals. It was announced that Red Sullivan would also be leaving the Bruins to take a position with the Capitals. Gary Darling was named the chief scouting director for the Bruins.

View from the Balcony

One round and out for the team favored to win the opening round of the playoffs surprised many observers. The late season surge colored the opinion that the Bruins were again the team to beat. Unfortunately, the seeds for the breakdown were planted during the 1971–72 campaign. Immediately after the Stanley Cup win, Orr needed surgery. The solid goaltending of Gerry Cheevers was lost when he signed with the Cleveland Crusaders of the World Hockey Association. Undervalued defensive forward Eddie Westfall was not protected in the expansion draft and was plunked by the newly formed New York Islanders. Derek Sanderson's marriage to the Philadelphia Blazers lasted eight games when he had enough of the new league and negotiated his way back to the Bruins. John McKenzie, the high-energy forward, also left for the Philadelphia Blazers of the WHA. The management of the team also started to change as Harry Sinden returned from private business and replaced General Manager Milt Schmidt to become the team's Managing Director. When the team faltered in January, Sinden replaced Tom Johnson with Armand "Bep" Guidolin. The team performed admirably at a 21-6-0 clip to finish second in the division.

However, the team lost Phil Esposito due to injury in the opening round of the playoffs while they were outscored 22–11. They never recovered and were easily ousted by the New Yorkers. Orr had experienced his least productive playoff since the spring of 1968. The hyperinterest in the team, where every play was dissected, started to wane. Fan favorites were allowed to leave. The American Hockey League's Braves could no longer fill the Garden when a third professional team, the New England Whalers of the WHA, took up residence on Causeway Street. The decades-long Stanley Cup drought was now officially underway.

Top Hockey Stories from 1973

Stanley Cup Champions	Montreal Canadiens
Art Ross Trophy	Phil Esposito, Boston Bruins
Hart Trophy	Bobby Clarke, Philadelphia Flyers
Masterton Trophy	Lowell MacDonald, Pittsburgh Penguins
Lady Byng Trophy	Gilbert Perreault, Buffalo Sabres
Vezina Trophy	Ken Dryden, Montreal Canadiens
Calder Trophy	Steve Vickers, New York Rangers
Conn Smythe Trophy	Yvan Cournoyer, Montreal Canadiens
Norris Trophy	Bobby Orr, Boston Bruins (sixth consecutive)
Calder Cup Champions	Cincinnati Swords

Memorial Cup Champions	Toronto Marlboros
NCAA Hockey Champions	Wisconsin
Avco/WHA Champions	New England Whalers

Two new teams are added to the league with the Atlanta Flames joining the West Division and the New York Islanders placing in the East Division. The Soviet National team and Canadian NHL stars played in the eight game Summit Series with the Canadians defeating the Soviets 4–3–1.

Top Sports Stories

World Series Champions	Oakland Athletics
Super Bowl VIII Champions	Miami Dolphins (game played on 1/13/1974 at Rice Stadium, Houston, Texas)
NBA Champions	New York Knickerbockers
Kentucky Derby Winner	Secretariat (also won the Triple Crown– Kentucky Derby, Preakness Stakes, and Belmont Stakes)
NCAA Football Champions	Notre Dame (11-0-0) and Alabama (11-1-0)
NCAA Basketball Champions	UCLA

CHAPTER 8

1973–1974: One Last Crack at the Cup

THE BRUINS ENTERED THE 1973–74 campaign celebrating their fiftieth season. The social event of the off-season occurred under seemingly clandestine circumstances on Saturday, September 8. Orr married Peggy Wood, originally from Michigan. The wedding was held at the Parry Sound Presbyterian church. The ceremony was conducted by Reverend Robert Crooks and was attended by Orr's sister Pat, his brother-in-law Gerry Murphy along with Crooks's wife and three children.

Orr arrived at training camp a scant two days after being married. "I've been running a couple of miles a day, and I'd rather skate than run." The newlywed Orr jokingly explained, "It was an excuse to get out of the house."

When the Bruins played Montreal in an exhibition game in Moncton, New Brunswick reporter Margaret Leahy noticed that the recently married Orr was not wearing a wedding ring. When asked, Orr replied, "It all happened so fast, we didn't have time to buy rings. We borrowed my parents' rings for the ceremony, and Peggy was ordering rings back in Boston." Almost going unnoticed was teammate Fred O'Donnell, who also got married on September 8.

With the goaltending situation in crisis, the Bruins traded center Fred Stanfield to the Minnesota North Stars for goaltender Gilles Gilbert. Eddie Johnston was sent to the Toronto Maple Leafs as the player to be named later in the deal that brought Jacques Plante to the Bruins in March. Plante had signed with the Quebec Nordiques of the World Hockey Association.

The Bruins signed first round draft pick Andre Savard and resigned defensemen Dallas Smith and Don Awrey. Forward Mike Walton left the Bruins and signed with the Minnesota Fighting Saints of the WHA. The Bruins opened training camp on September 17th in Fitchburg, Massachusetts.

Orr's attorney Alan Eagleson announced that he would offer Orr's services to every WHA team when Orr's contract expired after September 30, 1976. Orr reported that he would like to stay in Boston and would be willing to renegotiate his contract.

Don Awrey, a frequent defense partner of Orr for the previous six seasons, was signed to a new contract. In a surprise move, the Bruins then traded him to the St. Louis Blues for Jake Rathwell and a second round draft pick in 1974. Awrey had been feuding with Harry Sinden since the 1973 playoffs when he was benched. The Bruins named their first captain since the 1966–1967 campaign. Johnny Bucyk would wear the *C* on his jersey.

October 1973

In the season opener at Boston Garden, the Bruins knocked off the Vancouver Canucks by a 6–4 score. Esposito had three goals, including his four hundredth career goal in the second period. Orr was credited with the lone assist on Phil's 399th goal early in the first stanza. On a side note, the Bruins' record of 192 consecutive sellouts was shattered as the game attracted 14,523, roughly 500 fans short of capacity. The last nonsellout occurred during the 1969 season when a snowstorm struck Boston.

In the first road game of the season, the Bruins routed the Red Wings at the Olympia in Detroit. Esposito and Wayne Cashman each had two goals while Orr was credited with three assists as the Bruins downed Detroit, 9–4. The team headed back to Boston for a tilt with the Islanders on Sunday night.

The B's won their third straight and defeated the New York Islanders, 3–2 at the Garden. As an aside to the game, the city of Chelsea, Massachusetts, just over the Mystic Tobin Bridge from the Garden, experienced a general alarm fire that destroyed eighteen city blocks. Miraculously, nobody was killed. The fire had been complicated by the fact that the Tobin Bridge's upper deck (the bridge connects the Charlestown section of Boston with the city of Chelsea and was easily seen from the Garden) had been damaged and collapsed due to a truck accident in early September. North Shore travelers leaving Bruins' games had to find other routings to get to towns such as Chelsea, Revere, Saugus, Lynnfield, and North Shore communities.

The second road game of the season in Atlanta was marked by the first loss of the campaign. Esposito's two goals were not enough as the Flames tripped the Bruins, 4–3. Orr had two assists to bring his scoring streak to four games. Sunday night, the Bruins were back at the Garden for a game with Pittsburgh. Orr scored his first two goals of the season and added an assist as the Bruins belted the Penguins, 8–2. The game, scheduled for a 7:30 start, was delayed for thirty minutes due to the late finish of the Los Muchachos circus.

Despite Orr's third goal of the season, the Bruins bowed to the Blues in St. Louis. Bruins' center Rich Leduc broke his shoulder in the game and remained in St. Louis for observation. The B's headed back to Boston after the game and prepared for a Thursday night matchup with the Buffalo Sabres. Esposito and Chris Oddleifson fired home two goals each, and Orr had his fourth goal of the season as the Bruins throttled the Buffalo Sabres at the Garden by a score of 9–4.

For the second game in succession, Esposito had two goals, and Orr had an assist as the Bruins tipped Toronto, 3–2 in a *Hockey Night in Canada* contest played at Maple Leaf Gardens. In the first half of a home-and-home set with the Minnesota North Stars on the 30th, the teams played to a 3-all tie in Boston. Orr earned an assist on Johnny Bucyk's second-period goal. On Halloween night in Bloomington, goals by Esposito, Cashman, Hodge, Savard, and Orr propelled the B's to a 5–0 victory. Ross Brooks enjoyed his second career shutout, stopping all twenty-five shots fired toward him. Orr had at least one point in all ten of Boston's contests in October. The Bruins ended the month with a slim lead in the East Division over the Buffalo Sabres.

October 1973					Orr's Stats				
					Game		Season		
Date	Venue	Versus	W-L-T	Score	G	A	G	A	PTS
10	Boston	Vancouver	W	6–4	0	2	0	2	2
13	Detroit	Red Wings	W	9–4	0	3	0	5	5
14	Boston	NY Islanders	W	3–2	0	1	0	6	6
17	Atlanta	Flames	L	4–3	0	2	0	8	8
21	Boston	Pittsburgh	W	8–2	2	1	2	9	11
23	St. Louis	Blues	L	3–2	1	0	3	9	12
25	Boston	Buffalo	W	9–4	1	1	4	10	14
27	Toronto	Maple Leafs	W	3–2	0	1	4	11	15
28	Boston	Minnesota	T	3–3	0	1	4	12	16

November 1973

In a November article for *Sports Illustrated*, Esposito had this to say: "You can't compare Orr and me or Hull and me. They bring people to their feet. They are spectacular players. Orr is the best player in the game. I know it, and I admit it."

The Bruins' scheduled plane trip from Logan Airport in East Boston to Long Island was canceled due to the crash of a cargo transport plane. The replacement bus also had transmission problems but was finally able to make the trek to Uniondale.

This quote was from Orr: "I just hope that this isn't an indication of what might happen tonight." It turned out that Orr was quite prescient.

In the game at the Veteran's Coliseum, the Isles had six goals from six different players as they surprised the Bruins, 6–4. Orr did score his sixth goal of the season. The next evening, it was back at Boston Garden and a meeting with Charlie Finley's Oakland Seals. Esposito had two more goals as the Bruins toppled Oakland, 4–1. Orr had one assist in the contest, extending his consecutive point scoring streak to twelve games.

Despite Orr's seventh goal of the season, the Bruins were badly outplayed by the Rangers and succumbed to the New Yorkers onslaught in a game played at Madison Square Garden. The final score, 7–3, featured Brad Park's two goals in the Rangers win.

Instead of paying attention to the task at hand during the Rangers' game, the B's may have been looking ahead to their Thursday night game with the Canadiens. After the Bruins were knocked out of first place the previous evening in New York, they recaptured it in a playoff type game by beating the Habs, 2–1. Orr's extended point streak was now fourteen games as he assisted on Dave Forbes' game-winning goal in the second stanza.

On November 11, the Bruins scored four straight second-period goals, and they earned a 4–2 victory over the Vancouver Canucks. The four second-period goals were scored in nine minutes and twenty-nine seconds. Orr's eighth goal of the season extended his point scoring streak to fifteen games.

The Bruins moved on to Montreal to meet the Canadiens. In the sixteenth game of the season, Orr's point streak was finally broken, but the Bruins pulled out a 4–3 victory over Montreal. The next game on November 15 featured a phenomenal performance by Orr who scored three goals and four assists while the Bruins dumped the New York Rangers in Boston by a score of 10–2. His seven points were a record for a defenseman and fell one short of tying the record of eight points in a game set by Rocket Richard and Bert Olmstead. Orr quipped, "The three goals were really gifts, weren't they? The first one was off Eddie Giacomin's chest. The other two off of defensemen. I'm happy to take them though." Andre Savard also had two goals for the B's in the rout. Commenting on the turnaround after the Bruins loss the previous week in New York, Orr said, "Down there, we just didn't work. You don't get something for nothing. They kicked the dirt out of us down there. We knew if we wanted to beat them here, we'd have to work our butts off. After a few shifts, I had a feeling we would win, but not by a score like this. They're too good a team for that." Orr was on the ice for all ten Boston goals.

With four assists in the game, Orr brought his career total of helpers to 453, a new career mark for defensemen surpassing Hall of Famer Doug Harvey. The Bruins pinned an eight spot on the Red Wings, and Gilles Gilbert earned his first shutout as a Bruin as they vanquished the Detroiters, 8–0. Doug Grant was the unfortunate victim in the Detroit net. Orr had four assists in the contest.

The Bruins won their sixth straight as they defeated the Atlanta Flames, 5–2, at Boston Garden. Orr had two assists in the game as the team would now get a respite until Thanksgiving night when they hosted the Philadelphia Flyers.

Boston enjoyed the Thanksgiving holiday with a 4–2 win over the Flyers. Orr had two assists as the Bruins won their seventh game in a row. Phil Esposito had his twenty-second and twenty-third goals in the win. On Sunday night, the Bruins entertained the Los Angeles Kings. Orr scored his twelfth goal of the season, and the B's notched their eighth straight victory with a 3–1 victory over the Kings. It was on to Chicago for a Wednesday night encounter with the Blackhawks.

Boston and Chicago played to a 3–3 tie although the third Hawks' goal, scored by Dale Tallon, caused a huge uproar from the Bruins, who were thinking that the play was actually offside. In the ensuing argument over the call, Orr was handed a ten-minute misconduct penalty by Referee Lloyd Gilmour. "It wasn't anything I said," protested Orr. "I guess it was that I moved the puck toward the linesman [Ron Finn]." With the tie, the unbeaten streak had now reached nine games (8 wins, 1 tie).

November 1973					Orr's Stats				
					Game		Season		
Date	Venue	Versus	W-L-T	Score	G	A	G	A	PTS
3	New York	Islanders	L	6–4	1	0	6	13	19
4	Boston	California	W	4–1	0	1	6	14	20
7	New York	Rangers	L	7–3	1	1	7	15	22
8	Boston	Montreal	W	2–1	0	1	7	16	23
11	Boston	Vancouver	W	4–2	1	0	8	16	24
14	Montreal	Canadiens	W	4–3	0	0	8	16	24
15	Boston	NY Rangers	W	10–2	3	4	11	20	31
17	Boston	Detroit	W	8–0	0	4	11	24	35
18	Boston	Atlanta	W	5–2	0	2	11	26	37
22	Boston	Philadelphia	W	4–2	0	2	11	28	39
25	Boston	Los Angeles	W	3–1	1	0	12	28	40
28	Chicago	Blackhawks	T	3–3	0	0	12	28	40

December 1973

The Bruins opened December with a matchup against the New York Islanders. Despite the Islanders only receiving three minor penalties in the contest, the Bruins scored on two of the power play advantages, and they tipped the New Yorkers, 5–3. Orr scored his thirteenth goal of the season to go along with his twenty-seventh assist to key the Bruins' victory.

The next evening, the Bruins were in Philadelphia to meet the Flyers at the Spectrum. The Flyers held a 3–1 lead with eighty-two seconds left in the game, but Orr's goal at 18:38 and Esposito's score at 19:29 knotted the game at three apiece. The tie marked the twenty-fifth game in a row that the Flyers had not been able to beat Boston. Orr had a goal and an assist for the B's. On the 13th, Esposito and Hodge scored two goals each as the Bruins defeated the North Stars at the Garden, 4–2.

On Saturday night, the Vancouver Canucks came to Boston. Orr's sixteenth and seventeenth goals of the season to go along with Esposito's thirty-first and thirty-second of the campaign propelled the Bruins to a 7–2 victory over the Canucks.

The next evening, the Bruins beached the California Seals, 5–3. Orr had one assist in the game as the Bruins unbeaten streak reached fifteen games. The Penguins were next up at the Garden, and the Bruins would eke out a 6–5 victory over Pittsburgh. Orr had an assist on Hodge's twenty-third goal of the season, which turned out to be the game winner. After going undefeated for sixteen games, the Bruins finally lost one, falling to the Red Wings 4–2 at the Olympia in Detroit.

The next evening, the Bruins were back in Boston hosting the Toronto Maple Leafs. Old friend Eddie Johnston tended goal for the Leafs in his first visit back to Boston since being traded away the previous spring. The B's nipped Toronto by a 4–3 score. Orr had one assist in the contest.

The Bruins embarked on a five-game post-Christmas swing that began on the West Coast. After going undefeated in sixteen straight games, the Bruins lost for the second time in three games, this time to the Kings in Los Angeles by a 4–1 score. Orr managed to pick up a fighting major and a ten-minute misconduct penalty during the second period. For the third time since their inception, the Kings played to a sellout crowd on December 29. All three sellouts occurred when the Bruins were in town.

The next night in Oakland, the Bruins fired thirty-five shots, connecting on eight of them as they trounced the Golden Seals, 8–1. Bruins center Chris Oddleifson scored four goals in the game to pace the Bruins' victory. Orr had two assists in the contest and closed out the month with 55 points.

December 1973					Orr's Stats				
					Game		Season		
Date	Venue	Versus	W-L-T	Score	G	A	G	A	PTS
2	Boston	NY Islanders	W	5–3	1	1	13	29	42
8	Boston	Buffalo	W	5–2	1	0	14	29	43

9	Philadelphia	Flyers	T	3–3	1	1	15	30	45
13	Boston	Minnesota	W	4–2	0	0	15	30	45
15	Boston	Vancouver	W	7–2	2	3	17	33	50
16	Boston	California	W	5–3	0	1	17	34	51
20	Boston	Pittsburgh	W	6–5	0	1	17	35	52
22	Detroit	Red Wings	L	4–2	0	1	17	36	53
23	Boston	Toronto	W	4–3	0	1	17	37	54
29	Los Angeles	Kings	L	4–1	0	1	17	38	55
30	California	Seals	W	8–1	0	2	17	40	57

January 1974

The Bruins opened the New Year's Day holiday in Vancouver, British Columbia. Both teams had thirty-six shots on goal in a 2–2 draw. Orr had an assist on Esposito's thirty-sixth goal of the season. In the January 4 game at New York, Orr scored his eighteenth and nineteenth goals of the season, which were also the 199th and 200th goals of his career. The goals were scored against Peter McDuffe in net for New York. The 4–2 victory over the Rangers was played before a nationally televised audience from Madison Square Garden. For the first time, Orr's name appeared on the back of his sweater as that uniform feature began for the Bruins with this game.

Orr and company bussed to Long Island for a game with the Islanders the next night. Johnny Bucyk fired home three goals, and Orr had three assists as the Bruins defeated the Islanders by a 6–2 count. The Super Supper was held at the Chateau de Ville in Framingham, Massachusetts, on January 7, which featured a roasting of Orr and Esposito. The celebrities roasting the Bruins' stars were Frankie Fontaine (Crazy Guggenheim from *The Jackie Gleason Show*) and Bobby Morse (*How to Succeed in Business without Really Trying, Mad Men*).

The Bruins returned home to the Garden for games with Chicago and Montreal. On Thursday evening, they pulled out a 2–2 tie with the Hawks when Esposito scored the tying goal with forty-five seconds left in the game. Orr had his twentieth goal of the season—reaching that figure for the sixth straight season.

The Bruins' next contest was another nationally televised game at the unusual start time of 4:00 p.m. on Saturday. The undefeated home streak for the Bruins ended as the Canadiens went out to a quick 3–0 lead and never looked back, beating the Bruins by a 7–3 score. For Boston, it was best to forget this game as they headed straight out to Pittsburgh for a Sunday game with the Penguins. After the lackluster game on Saturday, the Bruins came back behind Esposito's two goals and Orr's three assists to defeat the Penguins 5–3.

On Wednesday night at Chicago Stadium, the Bruins notched three goals in the third period and came back from a 5–3 deficit to earn a 5–5 tie. For the second straight game, Orr had three assists. Saturday night was *Hockey Night in Canada* as a national television audience tuned in to see the Habs and B's play at the Forum. The Bruins were still stinging from the 7–3 loss the previous Saturday in Boston. With Ross Brooks tending goal, the Bruins got their revenge by throttling the Canadiens in a rout, 8–0. Brooks faced twenty-two Montreal shots. Don Marcotte's two goals and Orr's two assists paced the Bruins victory.

The next night back in Boston, the B's entertained Los Angeles. Ken Hodge scored two goals, and Orr had his twenty-first goal of the season as the Bruins trumped the Kings, 5–2. On Tuesday night, the Bruins met the Blues at the St. Louis Arena. Gilles Gilbert earned his second shutout of the season, and Marcotte scored the only goal in the contest as the Bruins extended their current unbeaten streak to five games with the 1–0 victory.

Two nights later, the Bruins met the Chicago Blackhawks at the Boston Garden. The simple story is that the Bruins lost to the Hawks, 2–1. The calls of Referee Wally Harris were questioned by the Bruins but unrest carried on into the stands. At the 14:54 mark of the second period, Derek Sanderson was tossed from the game for questioning Harris' work. With fifty seconds left in the contest, things got seriously out of hand. On the play in question, Orr was rushing over the Chicago blue line when he was tripped by defenseman Bill White. When the whistle blew, it turned out to be for an offside call rather than a tripping penalty on White. When Orr went ballistic, he was assessed a ten-minute misconduct penalty, effectively tossing him out of the game. To make matters worse, the Bruins were charged with a two-minute minor penalty.

At that point, debris began to rain from all over the Garden onto the playing surface. At 9:56 p.m., the game was temporarily suspended to give the bull gang a chance to clear the ice. Many of the fans thought that the game was forfeited and left the building. Initially, the bull gang refused to step on the ice since some of the missiles thrown on the ice included beer bottles. Finally, the cleanup was finished, and the game resumed at 10:32 p.m., a delay of thirty-six minutes. About three thousand diehards stayed for the final fifty seconds.

After the game, the Bruins refused to comment on the events, but Chicago's Stan Mikita had this to say. "I've been through a few things like that but never as bad as this. I never thought it would happen in Boston. But it shows how people can get when the big man [Orr] gets flattened, they want blood."

The Bruins moved to Long Island for a Saturday tilt with the Islanders. Ross Brooks saved all twenty-six shots fired his way as the Bruins shut out New York by a 4–0 score.

In a nationally televised game from Boston on the 27th, the Bruins overcame a 3–1 deficit and scored four straight goals to defeat the Flyers by a 5–3 margin. Orr had his twenty-second and twenty-third goals of the season to go along with an assist. However, a hit from Flyer's forward Bill Barber injured Orr's left leg, and he had to leave the game. Out of respect for Orr, Barber immediately went to Orr to apologize for the hit and to check on his condition. Due to the injury, Orr would miss the next four contests.

At the 19:35 mark of the second period, the Flyers' Dave Schultz received a ten-minute misconduct and a game misconduct. Watching the third period in civvies, Schultz had this to say about Orr: "I come out, and he scores. Then when he made that play for Hodge's goal, well, I went back into the dressing room and slammed the door. He is unbelievable. He is the game. I dunno, maybe there is a reason we haven't won against them [twenty-six in a row overall, not in the Boston Garden since November 12, 1967]. Maybe it's just Orr."

Due to the injury he suffered in the Philadelphia game, Orr would miss the All-Star Game in Chicago on Tuesday. Quipped East Division coach Scotty Bowman, "If any player really wanted to play in this game, it would be Bobby Orr. We know why he can't be here, and nobody is happy about it." Echoing Bowman was a Montreal writer who stated, "This really stopped being an All-Star Game on Saturday when Orr was hurt."

In the first game back after the All-Star Game, the Bruins hosted the Atlanta Flames at Boston Garden, their first game without Orr. Esposito scored his forty-fourth and forty-fifth goals of the season as the B's doused the Flames by a 4–2 margin.

Orr, who received the 1973 March of Dimes Humanitarian of the Year Award, had been named the 1974 Mass. Bay March of Dimes Special Events Chairman.

January 1974					Orr's Stats				
					Game		Season		
Date	Venue	Versus	W-L-T	Score	G	A	G	A	PTS
1	Vancouver	Canucks	T	2–2	0	1	17	41	58
4	New York	Rangers	W	4–2	2	0	19	41	60
5	New York	Islanders	W	6–2	0	3	19	44	63
10	Boston	Chicago	T	2–2	1	0	20	44	64
12	Boston	Montreal	L	7–3	0	0	20	44	64
13	Pittsburgh	Penguins	W	5–3	0	3	20	47	67
16	Chicago	Blackhawks	T	5–5	0	3	20	50	70
19	Montreal	Canadiens	W	8–0	0	2	20	52	72
20	Boston	Los Angeles	W	5–2	1	1	21	53	74
22	St. Louis	Blues	W	1–0	0	0	21	53	74

24	Boston	Chicago	L	2–1	0	1	21	54	75
26	New York	Islanders	W	4–0	0	1	21	55	76
27	Boston	Philadelphia	W	5–3	2	1	23	56	79
31	Boston	Atlanta	W	4–2	DNP		23	56	79

February 1974

The Bruins opened February without Orr in the lineup as they moved up to Toronto to face the Maple Leafs. Six different Leafs lit the lamp, and Toronto moved on to a 6–2 drubbing of the Bruins. The next night back in Boston, the Bruins survived a late rush from the Penguins and defeated Pittsburgh 5–4. Hodge had his thirty-fourth, thirty-fifth, and thirty-sixth goals of the season in the Boston win.

The speculation was that Orr would return for Thursday night's game with the St. Louis Blues. It was not to be as Orr missed his fourth straight game. However, the Bruins still managed to down the Blues, 5–3. After the game, it was announced that they had traded Chris Oddleifson and Fred O'Donnell to Vancouver for Bobby Schmautz.

When the Bruins shipped O'Donnell to Vancouver, he balked at reporting to the Canucks due to the fact that his wife was having their first child. The Canucks placed an ad in a Boston paper that read "Try us, you might like us." The ad was signed by Vancouver General Manager Phil Maloney. After nineteen days, O'Donnell reported to Vancouver only to tell Maloney that he had signed a contract with the New England Whalers of the WHA for the next season. Although O'Donnell was prepared to play with Vancouver for the rest of the season, Maloney told him to forget about it.

With the trade for Schmautz (who would wear number 17) and the departure of O'Donnell, Derek Sanderson, who had been wearing number 17, was able to reacquire his number 16, which he wore prior to signing with Philadelphia of the WHA.

Orr returned to the ice after missing four games with a knee injury. Upon his return, he chalked up three assists, and Carol Vadnais had two goals as the Bruins extended their unbeaten streak against the Flyers to twenty-seven games. The final score was 5–3 in favor of the Bruins in a game played at Boston Garden.

In the final home game before a six-game road trip, the Bruins met the Minnesota North Stars. With Gilles Gilbert making twenty-one saves, the Bruins shut out the Stars 4–0.

The road trip started in Oakland, where the Bruins defeated the Seals 9–6. The Bruins came back from a 4–1 deficit in the first period to win the game going away. Johnny Bucyk had his second hat trick of the season, and Orr contributed four assists in the contest. Phil Esposito also earned his 100th and 101st points of the season.

In Vancouver, Gregg Sheppard scored two goals, and Esposito notched career point number 1000 as the Bruins defeated the Canucks by a 4–2 score. The Bruins won their seventh straight as Don Marcotte scored two goals in a 5–2 win over the Kings at the Fabulous Forum in Los Angeles. Orr had one assist, which earned him his seven hundredth career point.

Esposito's three goals and Orr's twenty-fourth of the season helped the Bruins come from behind and earned a 5–5 tie with the North Stars in Bloomington, Minnesota. The tie game ended the Bruins seven-game winning streak.

Orr had his twenty-fifth goal of the season, and Ross Brooks won his thirteenth straight game as the Bruins defeated the Penguins at the Igloo, 6–2. Orr also had two assists in the contest. In the first ever nationally televised game from Buffalo, the Sabres knocked off the Bruins by a 3–2 score. Boston's unbeaten streak of nine was snapped as they lost for only the tenth time during this season.

When the Red Wings had visited Boston three months prior on November 17, the Bruins had shut out Detroit, 8–0. This time, the Wings did manage one marker, but the Bruins scored the other eight goals to defeat the visitors, 8–1. Goaltender Ross Brooks tied Tiny Thompson's NHL record with his fourteenth straight victory. Orr had two assists in the game, the second one on a goal by Terry O'Reilly, was his five hundredth regular season assist.

February 1974					Orr's Stats				
					Game		Season		
Date	Venue	Versus	W-L-T	Score	G	A	G	A	PTS
2	Toronto	Maple Leafs	L	6–2	DNP		23	56	79
3	Boston	Pittsburgh	W	5–4	DNP		23	56	79
7	Boston	St. Louis	W	5–3	DNP		23	56	79
9	Boston	Philadelphia	W	5–3	0	3	23	59	82
10	Boston	Minnesota	W	4–0	0	0	23	59	82
13	California	Seals	W	9–6	0	4	23	63	86
15	Vancouver	Canucks	W	4–2	0	0	23	63	86
16	Los Angeles	Kings	W	5–2	0	1	23	64	87
20	Minnesota	North Stars	T	5–5	1	1	24	65	89
23	Pittsburgh	Penguins	W	6–2	1	2	25	67	92
24	Buffalo	Sabres	L	3–2	0	0	25	67	92
28	Boston	Detroit	W	8–1	0	2	25	69	94

March 1974

The Bruins started March with a Saturday afternoon contest versus Red Wings at the Olympia in Detroit. The B's jumped out to a two-goal lead only to see the Wings jump back into the game, finally tying it 4–4 on a Red Berenson shorthanded goal in the third period. Despite three assists from Orr, the Bruins lost to the Maple Leafs at Boston Garden, 6–4. It was only the third loss on home ice that season.

The Bruins moved on to Atlanta, where they dropped their second straight game, 4–1, as Orr was held scoreless. Next up the Bruins faced Blues in St. Louis. For the third time that season, the Bruins shut out an opponent by an 8–0 score. This time, it happened at St. Louis on March 6 with Gilles Gilbert being credited with the shutout. Wayne Cashman netted three goals for the Bruins, and Esposito fired home his fifty-fifth and fifty-sixth goals.

The road trip continued with the Bruins facing the Kings in Los Angeles. Boston came back from a 4–2 deficit and tied the Kings, 4–4. Esposito's shorthanded goal, his second goal of the game and fifty-eighth of the season, tied the game at 17:49 of the third stanza. Orr netted his twenty-sixth goal of the season to go along with an assist on Espo's fifty-seventh goal in the first period.

In the last game of the road trip, the Bruins bowed to the Seals, 6–2 in Oakland. Former Bruin Reggie Leach had three goals for the opponents. Ross Brooks, in goal during the game, had his fourteen-game win streak snapped this game. After the game, a dressing room brawl between Derek Sanderson and Terry O'Reilly ensued. When Sanderson failed to board the flight back to Boston, he was fined $1,000 and suspended for the rest of the season by Bruins' management. This ended up being the Turk's last game in a Bruins' uniform.

Orr scored his one hundredth point for the fifth straight season as he was credited with an assist on Johnny Bucyk's third-period goal and the Bruins downed the Sabres at Boston Garden, 4–0. Gilles Gilbert pitched his second shutout in three games for the victory.

Boston met the Sabres in Buffalo two nights later. The B's fell behind early, 2–0, but came back on two goals by Esposito and Orr's twenty-seventh of the season as they edged the Sabres, 4–3.

The Maple Leafs entertained the Bruins on *Hockey Night in Canada* in Toronto on Saturday night. Esposito and Hodge each had two goals, and Orr was credited with one assist as the Bruins defeated the Leafs, 5–2. The following evening, Esposito scored two goals, and Orr had two assists as the Bruins downed the Rangers at Boston Garden, 5–2.

On Thursday night, the Bruins hosted the St. Louis Blues. For the third consecutive time that season, Gilles Gilbert blanked the Blues, this time, 7–0. Gilbert put aside all twenty shots directed toward him. Orr had his fifth career hat trick in addition to earning his fourth thirty-goal season, just a day after his twenty-sixth birthday. His three goals were scored against Wayne Stephenson (2) and Jimmy Watt (1). This was Watt's only appearance in an NHL game and lasted just twenty minutes. To have been scored upon by Bobby Orr in a goalie's only NHL appearance is surely a memory that would last him a lifetime.

After the game, St. Louis coach Lou Angotti thought his team played pretty well, but that too many of his players were admiring Orr. He signaled defensemen Barclay Plager, Ted Harris, and ex-Bruin Don Awrey. "His second goal was maybe his best since he had Esposito running interference for him, and he just stopped and shot," said Ted Harris. Awrey had this observation: "He's been playing as well as he ever has. You think he has shown you everything. Remember, he said that when he was twenty-two, and then he shows you something else."

The day before the St. Louis game, Orr had appeared at the Somerset (MA) Youth Hockey awards night but had other things on his mind. He was originally scheduled to meet a gravely ill sixteen-year-old Ronald Michaud of Fall River. When he got caught in Boston traffic, Fall River firefighters brought Ronald to the affair. Orr spent a half hour with Ron and promised to score against the Blues. Ronald upped the ante, asking Orr for a hat trick. In true Babe Ruthian manner, Orr made good on his promise, firing home three goals in the 7–0 win. The Atlanta Flames tipped the Bruins in a game played in Boston on Saturday, 4–3. Orr had one assist in the game. The B's now had a Sunday date with the Canadiens in Boston.

After the Bruins spotted Montreal a 2–0 lead, they came back with four consecutive goals on the way to a 6–3 victory over the Habs. Six different Bruins, Dave Forbes, Carol Vadnais, Andre Savard, Gregg Sheppard, Esposito, and Schmautz scored for Boston. On Wednesday night in New York, the Bruins tipped the Rangers, 3–2. Orr was credited with his eightieth assist of the season.

Next up for Boston was a Saturday night game at the Spectrum in Philadelphia. Despite Orr picking up two assists in the contest, the Bruins went down to defeat at the hands of the Flyers by a count of 5–3. The Philadelphia victory broke a winless streak of twenty-eight games against Boston dating back to March 13, 1969.

The Bruins exploded for five straight goals and breezed by the Detroit Red Wings, 6–1, in a game played at the Boston Garden on the final day of March. While the B's were killing second-period penalties, Coach Guidolin used Orr and Esposito up front as penalty killers.

March 1974					Orr's Stats				
					Game		Season		
Date	Venue	Versus	W-L-T	Score	G	A	G	A	PTS
2	Detroit	Red Wings	T	4–4	0	0	25	69	94
3	Boston	Toronto	L	6–4	0	3	25	72	97
5	Atlanta	Flames	L	4–1	0	0	25	72	97

6	St. Louis	Blues	W	8–0	0	0	25	72	97
9	Los Angeles	Kings	T	4–4	1	1	26	73	99
10	California	Seals	L	6–2	0	1	26	74	100
12	Boston	Buffalo	W	4–0	0	1	26	75	101
14	Buffalo	Sabres	W	4–3	1	1	27	76	103
16	Toronto	Maple Leafs	W	5–2	0	1	27	77	104
17	Boston	NY Rangers	W	5–2	0	2	27	79	106
21	Boston	St. Louis	W	7–0	3	0	30	79	109
23	Boston	Atlanta	L	4–3	0	1	30	80	110
24	Boston	Montreal	W	6–3	0	1	30	81	111
27	New York	Rangers	W	3–2	0	1	30	82	112
30	Philadelphia	Flyers	L	5–3	0	2	30	84	114
31	Boston	Detroit	W	6–1	0	2	30	86	116

April 1974

The Bruins, safely ensconced in first place, entered April with three games left on the schedule. In the second to last road game at Chicago, the B's held a 2–0 lead after two periods. However, in the third stanza, the Hawks, with Pit Martin scoring two goals, fired home six consecutive goals, and coasted past the Bruins, 6–2.

The last road game of the season was a *Hockey Night in Canada* special from the Montreal Forum. Frank Mahovlich scored three goals as the Canadiens defeated the Bruins, 6–2.

In the season finale on April 7 against Toronto at Boston Garden, the Leafs' Dave Keon, in his fourteenth National Hockey League season, received his first ever five-minute major for fighting when he was involved with Gregg Sheppard of the Bruins. Wayne Cashman netted three goals in Boston's 6–4 victory. Orr's two goals and four assists for six points helped propel the Bruins to the victory over the Leafs. It was the fourth time in his career that he had at least that many in a game.

Johnny Bucyk's consecutive game streak ended at 418 games. The streak had begun on January 23, 1969.

April 1974					Orr's Stats				
					Game		Season		
Date	Venue	Versus	W-L-T	Score	G	A	G	A	PTS
3	Chicago	Blackhawks	L	6–2	0	0	30	86	116
6	Montreal	Canadiens	L	6–2	0	0	30	86	116
7	Boston	Toronto	W	6–4	2	4	32	90	122

1973–74 Final Standings

Eastern Division

	W	L	T	PTS	GF	GA
Boston	52	17	9	113	349	221
Montreal	45	24	9	99	293	240
New York Rangers	40	24	14	94	300	251
Toronto	35	27	16	86	274	230
Buffalo	32	34	12	76	242	250
Detroit	29	39	10	68	255	319
Vancouver	24	43	11	59	224	296
New York Islanders	19	41	18	56	182	247

Western Division

	W	L	T	PTS	GF	GA
Philadelphia	50	16	12	112	273	164
Chicago	41	14	23	105	272	164
Los Angeles	33	33	12	78	233	231
Atlanta	30	34	14	74	214	238
Pittsburgh	38	41	9	65	242	273
St. Louis	26	40	12	64	206	248
Minnesota	23	38	17	63	235	275
California	13	55	10	36	195	342

Orr and Esposito tied for the Elizabeth Dufresne Trophy by being the top players during Bruins' home games, while Terry O'Reilly won the Gallery Gods Award. WBZ Radio 1030, broadcaster of Bruins' games awarded first, second, and third stars after every game. Top star of the season was Bobby Orr with 79 points, followed by Phil Esposito with 76 points and Gilles Gilbert with 61 points.

April 1974—Playoffs

April 1974 Playoffs					Orr's Stats				
					Game		Season		
Date	Venue	Versus	W-L-T	Score	G	A	G	A	PTS
10	Boston	Toronto	W	1–0	0	0	0	0	0
11	Boston	Toronto	W	6–3	0	1	0	1	1
13	Toronto	Maple Leafs	W	6–3	0	1	0	2	2
14	Toronto	Maple Leafs	W	4–3 (OT)	1	1	1	3	4
18	Boston	Chicago	L	4–2	0	1	1	4	5
21	Boston	Chicago	W	8–6	0	3	1	7	8
23	Chicago	Blackhawks	L	4–3 (OT)	0	0	1	7	8
25	Chicago	Blackhawks	W	5–2	0	0	1	7	8
28	Boston	Chicago	W	6–2	0	1	1	8	9
30	Chicago	Blackhawks	W	4–2	0	2	1	10	11

The Bruins opened the 1974 playoff season against the Toronto Maple Leafs at Boston Garden on the 10th. After scoring 349 goals in the regular season, the Bruins scored only one goal in the opening game of the playoffs. However, the goal was enough to win game one, 1–0. Gregg Sheppard's goal at 4:22 of the second period and Gilles Gilbert's thirty-five saves were the difference in the shutout for the Bruins. Orr earned a ten-minute misconduct penalty as the game clock expired.

In game 2, the Bruins doubled down on Toronto, 6–3. Six different Bruins had goals, and Orr had his first assist of the playoffs. Hodge, Schmautz, Bucyk, Cashman, Esposito, and Sheppard (empty net, shorthanded) were the goal scorers for the B's. The series moved to Toronto for the next two games on Saturday and Sunday.

In Toronto, Sheppard scored two goals to pace the Bruins to another 6–3 victory over the Maple Leafs. Orr had an assist on Andre Savard's second-period goal. Game 4 (and a possible Bruins' sweep) was scheduled for Sunday night in Toronto. Old friend Eddie Johnston was in goal for the Leafs. Hodge's overtime goal at 1:27 of the first overtime stanza helped the Bruins to a 4–3 victory and a sweep of the opening round of the playoffs. Orr scored his first goal of the playoffs to give the Bruins a 3–2 lead with a little over two minutes to play in the third period. Toronto's Inge Hammarstrom tied the game less than a minute later, which led to Hodge's game-winning goal. Terry O'Reilly scored his first career playoff goal in the game. Toronto fired forty-eight shots on goal compared to thirty shots by Boston. The

Bruins moved on to the second round of the playoffs and would meet the Chicago Blackhawks, starting on Thursday night at Boston Garden.

In game 1 of the semifinal series, which Bep Guidolin described as "the toughest game we lost all season," the Bruins were downed by Chicago 4–2 at the Garden. Tony Esposito, in goal for Chicago, stopped forty-six of forty-eight shots directed his way. John Marks's goal at 16:56 of the third period was the deciding goal in Chicago's victory.

In a nationally televised Sunday afternoon game at the Boston Garden, the Bruins slid past the Blackhawks, 8–6. Johnny Bucyk scored three goals and was assisted by Orr and Carol Vadnais on all his goals. With the series tied at one apiece, game 3 moved to Chicago.

When the series shifted to Chicago on April 23, the Blackhawks defeated the Bruins 4–3 as Jim Pappin scored the winner at 3:48 of overtime. Stan Mikita scored two goals for the Hawks, who overcame a two-goal deficit and tied the contest with forty-two seconds left on the clock.

Game 4 started with a bench minor to the Bruins. The penalty was earned by the Bruins when Chicago coach Billy Reay protested the appearance of Orr and Al Sims being in the Boston starting lineup. The lineup card issued to the official scorer listed Dallas Smith and Carol Vadnais as the starters. The Bruins killed the subsequent power play. Boston's well-balanced scoring attack featured five different goal scorers as they tied the series with a 5–2 victory at the Chicago Stadium. Goaltender Gilles Gilbert set a playoff record with his third assist. The series tied at two apiece, moved back to Boston Garden on Sunday.

Game 5 went to the Bruins, 6–2. A second-period, three-goal outburst that occurred in a matter of two minutes and forty-eight seconds gave the Bruins the win. Orr said, "You can't sit back and wait for Chicago. They handle the puck too well. You've got to check them, and you've got to come back because they always have somebody like Mikita waiting on the blue line to break in. They're a good club, a damn good hockey club."

Game 6 was played at the Chicago Stadium on Tuesday night. Don Marcotte's two goals and singles by Gregg Sheppard and Phil Esposito lifted the Bruins to a 4–2 victory and the elimination of Chicago from the playoffs. Orr had two assists in the victory. The Bruins moved on to the Stanley Cup finals against the Philadelphia Flyers.

May 1974 Playoffs

The Stanley Cup finals opened up at the Boston Garden on May 7. Orr's goal with twenty-two seconds on the clock lifted the Bruins to a 3–2 victory over the Flyers. "I'd like to tell you that I aimed it, but I didn't. The puck was rolling when it got to me, and I just shot it. It might have bounced, I don't know," said Orr.

Cashman and Sheppard scored the other goals for the Bruins. Now up one game in the finals, game 2 would be Thursday night in Boston.

If game 1 belonged to Orr, game 2 belonged to Bobby Clarke. After the Bruins went up 2–0, the Flyers came back to tie the game on a Moose Dupont goal with less than a minute to play in the game and the Flyers' goal empty. In the overtime, Clarke scored his second goal of the game to lift the Flyers past the B's, 3–2. With the series tied up at one game apiece, the teams moved on to Philadelphia for game 3.

For the third consecutive game, the Bruins scored the first goal. This time, it was their only goal as Philadelphia defeated the Bruins 4–1 and took a two-to-one series lead. The winning goal was scored by the man from Parry Sound, Ontario, but not the one Bruins' fans hoped for. It was former Bruin Terry Crisp who scored on a partial break after successfully killing a Flyers' penalty.

Game 4 started differently when the Flyers scored the opening two goals. The Bruins came back with two goals to tie it by the end of the first period. The second period was scoreless, but the Flyers scored two late third-stanza goals and went on to a 4–2 victory. Philadelphia was now one win away from Stanley Cup. Game 5 would be played in Boston on Thursday night.

Two goals by Orr and a shorthanded goal by Gregg Sheppard brought the Bruins back from the brink of elimination as the B's defeated Philadelphia 5–1 at Boston Garden. An NHL playoff record of forty-three penalties was assessed in the game. Bruins' General Manager Harry Sinden had this to say about Orr: "If you live to be one hundred years old, you'll never see a player like Orr. You can have one hundred Bobby Clarkes, I'll take one Bobby Orr. He made at least thirty moves tonight that I've never seen." With the series now at 3–2 in favor of the Flyers, the teams moved back to Philadelphia for game 6 at the Spectrum.

Bruins coach Bep Guidolin zapped his own players at the Stanley Cup luncheon in Philadelphia when he said, "It's nice to see the Flyers here. It's nice to see my team at the racetrack."

On May 19, Orr appeared in his last Stanley Cup finals game. The Flyers defeated the Bruins 1–0 in game 6 to win their first Stanley Cup. Kate Smith, for the second time in this season, performed "God Bless America" in person. Both appearances resulted in shutouts for the Flyers. A questionable call on Orr with 2:26 left in the game proved insurmountable as the Bruins failed to rally from the one-goal deficit. The only goal of the game was scored by Rick MacLeish at 14:48 of the first period. The Bruins fired thirty shots on goal with Bernie Parent stopping all of Boston's volleys.

Seven Flyers were prior members of the Bruins, including Bernie Parent, Joe Watson, Barry Ashbee, Terry Crisp, Gary Dornhoefer, Ross Lonsberry, and Rick MacLeish. Orr spent an incredible thirty-five minutes and nineteen seconds on the ice, which included an amazing fourteen minutes and twenty-eight seconds of play in the second period.

Flyers' coach Fred Shero had this assessment of the Bruins: "It may be Phil Esposito is a little tired although I can't pass judgment on that. They play those guys an awful lot all season. And we never keep one line out very long against Esposito's line. As for Orr, we just believe in overworking him, sending our centers in on him. The more Bobby has the puck, the harder he has to work and the more tired he gets. We have changed our tactics against Orr in this series."

Shero continued, "During the series we used to send a man in after Bobby and force him to pass to someone else. We thought it would be better to have someone else carrying the puck. But the mistake we made was once we let him pass the puck, we let him go free to take the return pass and then get back into the play. In this series, we send a man in after Bobby, but if he moves sideways, we try to slow up and prevent him from getting up ice quickly. Then if Orr passes the puck, we hit him to keep him out of the play. And if we can't hit him, the man with him stays in front of Orr so he can't get the puck back."

"I think New York is a better team than Boston. I know New York is a better team than Boston. Why? Because they have better players, but they are not as physical as Boston. Boston has more courage. That's why they're number one," summarized Shero.

Why didn't NHL opponents hit Orr more often? According to Bobby Clarke of the Philadelphia Flyers, "The reason is that he is so smart he never leaves himself in a position to get hit."

Jean Guy Talbot, former defenseman with Montreal, St. Louis, Minnesota, Detroit, and Buffalo had this to say: "The way the guy moves, with all the speed and quickness on his skates, puts the odds against an opponent anywhere on the ice. You make a move at him, and most of the time you're apt to be left there with your thumb in your mouth."

May 1974 Playoffs					Orr's Stats				
					Game		Season		
Date	Venue	Versus	W-L-T	Score	G	A	G	A	PTS
7	Boston	Philadelphia	W	3–2	1	1	2	11	13
9	Boston	Philadelphia	L	3–2 OT)	0	0	2	11	13
12	Philadelphia	Flyers	L	4–1	0	1	2	12	14
14	Philadelphia	Flyers	L	4–2	0	1	2	13	15
16	Boston	Philadelphia	W	5–1	2	1	4	14	18
19	Philadelphia	Flyers	L	1–0	0	0	4	14	18

Orr's winning of the Norris Trophy gave him thirteen NHL awards in his eight-year career, more than any player in history. The old record of twelve was held by Gordie

Howe of the Detroit Red Wings. Bep Guidolin resigned as Bruins coach and became the new coach of the expansion Kansas City Scouts. Guidolin was replaced by Don Cherry, who was the American Hockey League coach of the year with the Rochester Americans.

Harry Sinden was fined $1,000 by NHL President Clarence Campbell for "defamatory" remarks against referee Art Skov after the Bruins were defeated in game 6 of the Stanley Cup finals against the Philadelphia Flyers. Don Earle, the former voice of the Bruins, was the voice of the Philadelphia Flyers in 1974. He became the first broadcaster in history to call games for two different Stanley Cup winning teams.

View from the Balcony

From the ashes of the 1972–73 season, Harry Sinden made some astute moves and brought the Bruins back to the top of the Eastern Division and a return to the Stanley Cup finals. The acquisition of goaltender Gilles Gilbert solidified the goaltending position that had been weakened since Gerry Cheevers left for the WHA after the 1972 Stanley Cup win. Bobby Schmautz added feistiness, grit, and goals that were missing since the departure of John McKenzie. Orr, now in his eighth season, continued his spectacular play on the backline. For the seventh consecutive season, he captured the Norris Trophy as the league's best defenseman. He was also the only unanimous choice for the 1973–74 All-Star team. In addition to that, Orr led the league in points per game with an average of 1.65 per game. Phil Esposito (sixty-eight goals) and Ken Hodge (fifty goals) led the Bruins' resurgence. Defensive forward Don Marcotte chipped in twenty-four goals while tough as nails forward Wayne Cashman netted thirty goals. Graybeard left winger Johnny Bucyk added another thirty-one goals to the mix. Terry O'Reilly's presence on the ice opened up room for his teammates.

Trader Harry showed his prowess to jettison players no longer useful to the long term success of the Bruins. This willingness to ruffle players and their agents would prove to be one of Harry's legacies as he would manage the Bruins into the next century. On Harry's watch, the biggest trade in the team's history would be looming on the horizon.

Top Hockey Stories from 1974

Stanley Cup Champions	Philadelphia Flyers
Art Ross Trophy	Phil Esposito, Boston Bruins
Hart Trophy	Phil Esposito, Boston Bruins
Lady Byng Trophy	John Bucyk, Boston Bruins
Vezina Trophy	Bernie Parent, Philadelphia Flyers and Tony Esposito, Chicago Blackhawks (tie)
Calder Trophy	Denis Potvin, New York Islanders
Conn Smythe Trophy	Bernie Parent, Philadelphia Flyers
Norris Trophy	Bobby Orr, Boston Bruins
Jack Adams Award	Fred Shero, Philadelphia Flyers
Calder Cup	Champions Hershey Bears
Memorial Cup Champions	Regina Pats
NCAA Hockey Champions	Minnesota
Avco/WHA Champions	Houston Aeros

On May 12, former St. Louis Blues forward Wayne Maki passed away after a lengthy illness. Maki had been involved in a 1969 stick-swinging duel with former Bruins' defenseman Ted Green during an exhibition game at Ottawa.

The Minnesota North Stars fired General Manager Wren Blair after the 1973–74 campaign. Blair was best known as the scout who managed to ink Bobby Orr to a C form with the Oshawa generals, thus putting him into the Boston farm system. The C form was the document that linked a player to a team. Although a prospect could not sign the form if he was under eighteen years of age, a parent could sign the contract on the child's behalf.

Top Sports Stories

World Series Champions	Oakland Athletics
Super Bowl IX Champions	Pittsburgh Steelers (game played on 1/12/1975 at Tulane Stadium, New Orleans, Louisiana)
NBA Champions	Boston Celtics
Kentucky Derby Champion	Cannonade
NCAA Football Champions	Oklahoma (11-0-0) and USC (10-1-1)
NCAA Basketball Champions	North Carolina State
World Cup	West Germany defeats Holland

CHAPTER 9

1974–1975: The Bleeding Accelerates

WHEN BEP GUIDOLIN LEFT THE Bruins to coach the expansion Kansas City Scouts, the B's were left to ponder who would be their next coach. The search appeared to be very limited as Harry Sinden signed Don Cherry on June 13, 1974, less than a month after the Stanley Cup loss to Philadelphia. In his initial Boston press conference, Cherry promised that the Bruins would ice a tough squad.

When Cherry took the head coaching job with the Bruins, his eleven-year-old son Timothy had this to say: "Good… now I'll be able to meet Bobby Orr and Phil Esposito."

"So will I," answered his dad.

Cherry also added this story: "I met him [Orr] at the Hall of Fame in Toronto a couple of years ago, and he probably won't remember this, but he asked me to stand in front of him, to shield him from all the people who wanted his autograph. Some of them shoved me aside, and he signed them anyway."

It seemed that Orr took great delight in stressing the remarkable resemblance between Cherry and former Red Sox manager Dick Williams. Williams took over as manager of the California Angels in 1974. Orr had become friendly with Williams after he had rented the manager's house in Peabody during one baseball off-season. When Cherry stepped onto the ice one afternoon, he was wearing the blue-and-red cap of the Angels, a gift from Orr.

Dick Williams Harry Sinden, Don Cherry, and Tom Johnson

The Bruins trained at the Wallace Civic Center in Fitchburg, Massachusetts. During camp, Orr had this observation about this Bruins team's outlook for the coming season: "We had to be very disappointed by the way things happened last year. But we have one big thing going for us. We had great years from some of the younger guys like Al Sims, Andre Savard, Terry O'Reilly, and Gilles Gilbert. You know they'll be even better this year. Phil is in great shape, so am I and all the other guys."

The operation of the Bruins farm team, the Braves was suspended for a year. The Rochester Americans became be the B's number one farm club. The Bruins participated in the inaugural "Red Rooster Invitational Series" with the Providence Reds, New York Rangers, Nova Scotia Voyageurs, and the New England Whalers. The Bruins played the Rangers in the five-game series, which was sponsored by the Providence Reds.

In two exhibition games against the Montreal Canadiens, one featured a bench-clearing brawl in Montreal while the return match in Providence saw the teams combine for two hundred minutes in penalties.

The Kansas City Scouts and the Washington Capitals joined the NHL. The league was divided into two nine-team conferences with each conference fielding two divisions. The Bruins' new home was in the Adams Division of the Prince of Wales Conference. Joining the B's in the Division were Buffalo Sabres, Toronto Maple Leafs, and California Seals.

Former Bruins' General Manager Milt Schmidt, now GM of the fledgling Washington Capitals, had this to say about his number one draft choice Greg Joly: "He can do a lot of the incredible things Bobby Orr does." Joly ended up scoring twenty-one goals over 365 career games with the Washington Capitals and Detroit Red Wings.

During the midsixties doldrums surrounding the Bruins, two prospects kept the fandom hoping that things would be on the upswing. One of course was Orr. The other was his Oshawa teammate, goaltender Ian Young. He never made it due to a serious eye injury, and the NHL prohibited anyone with vision in only one eye from playing.

However, according to the Bruins' training camp roster, Young was one of the fourteen goalies vying for an NHL job. Young never did make the squad.

In the Bruins' first exhibition game of the season at Philadelphia, a rematch of the previous year's Stanley Cup finals, Orr injured his wrist and was listed day-to-day. Orr had this quip: "I probably played too much tennis this summer."

October 1974

The Bruins opened the 1974–75 season in Buffalo. In new coach Cherry's debut, the Bruins took it on the chin by a score of 9–5. Gilbert Perreault and line mate Rick Martin each had three goals in the Sabres win. After the game, Orr admitted, "We all stunk, and I was the worst offender." He was credited with one assist on Carol Vadnais's third-period goal.

In the home opener against the Toronto Maple Leafs, Ken Hodge's power play goal midway through the third period earned the Bruins a 3–3 tie. Orr assisted Hodge on his third-period power play goal.

The next game was a road game at the Stadium in Chicago. For the second time in three games, the Bruins were outclassed, this time by a 4–0 score. The game did provide some histrionics involving Orr. At the 14:21 mark of the third, a battle ensued between him and Chicago center Stan Mikita. Sticks were used, and the question was, "Who was the first to spear?" Mikita claims it was Orr. Orr said, "He's been playing that way for fifteen years, but I've never seen him the way he was tonight." Orr drew a double minor when he butt ended Mikita in the head. Orr admitted, "It was a cheap shot. He didn't deserve it." Tony Esposito earned the shutout for Chicago.

Derisively, Mikita said, "It shows you who's running the team. Cherry couldn't get him off at the end of the game." Cherry disagreed. After Orr came out of the penalty box, "I told him to stay out there as long as Mikita was out there. I just wish we had somebody go out after him. One of these nights, he's going to be wearing his helmet sideways."

On the next evening in Philadelphia, the B's gained a small measure of revenge with their first win of the season, a 4–1 victory over the Stanley Cup champions, Flyers. Esposito had two goals in the contest and had his third assist on the season. Ross Brooks, celebrating his thirty-seventh birthday, stopped thirty-three of thirty-four shots for the win. Orr told Coach Cherry after the win, "That's only the beginning. It'll be like that all the time now."

On Thursday night at Boston Garden, the California Seals were in town to provide the opposition. Five separate Bruins scored goals, and Orr had two assists, leading Boston to a 5–0 shutout. Gilles Gilbert stopped all sixteen shots fired his way. The crowd of 14,648 was the first nonsellout at the Boston Garden in forty-seven games.

Orr scored his first three goals of the season, but Carol Vadnais had to score the tying goal with the Bruins' net empty and thirty-two seconds left in the game for the Bruins to pull out a 5–5 tie with the Penguins at Pittsburgh. Vadnais's goal was scored on the power play while Jean Pronovost of the Penguins was in the penalty box. The Bruins had to overcome a two-goal deficit to earn the tie. It was Orr's sixth three-goal game of his career. The goals were scored against Gary Inness, who was tending goal for Pittsburgh. The next evening at the Boston Garden, the Bruins again had to climb back from two goals down and pull their goaltender in the final minute to even the score with the St. Louis Blues, 4–4. Orr scored the tying goal with thirty-four seconds left in the game.

Next up was the first ever visit to Boston by the new Kansas City Scouts, led by former Bruins' coach Guidolin. Bucyk and Esposito had two goals each, and Orr was credited with three assists as the Bruins trounced the Scouts, 8–2.

The Bruins invaded Bloomington, Minnesota, for a Wednesday night contest with the North Stars. For the fourth time in ten games, the Bruins had to settle for a tie as the B's and Stars were deadlocked at 3.

October 1974					Orr's Stats				
					Game		Season		
Date	Venue	Versus	W-L-T	Score	G	A	G	A	PTS
10	Buffalo	Sabres	L	9–5	0	1	0	1	1
13	Boston	Toronto	T	2–2	0	1	0	2	2
16	Chicago	Blackhawks	L	4–0	0	0	0	2	2
17	Philadelphia	Flyers	W	4–1	0	1	0	3	3
20	Boston	California	W	5–0	0	2	0	5	5
23	Pittsburgh	Penguins	T	5–5	3	1	3	6	9
24	Boston	St. Louis	T	4–4	1	2	4	8	12
27	Boston	Kansas City	W	8–2	0	3	4	11	15
30	Minnesota	North Stars	T	3–3	0	0	4	11	15

November 1974

The Bruins started the month of November on Long Island. Despite two goals from Esposito and two assists by Orr, the Bruins lost to the Islanders by a 3–2 count before a sellout crowd at the Nassau County Coliseum. Bobby Schmautz broke his right thumb in a fight with Ernie Hicke and was lost for thirteen games.

The next night, the Bruins were back at home to meet the Minnesota North Stars. Orr had his fifth goal of the season and nine other Bruins scored goals as they obliterated the North Stars, 10–1. Cesare Maniago, in goal for the Stars, was the victim of the 42-shot onslaught. "The Bruins came to bury Cesare, not praise him" (D. Leo Monahan of the *Boston Herald-American*).

On Tuesday night, the Bruins and Sabres played to a 2–2 tie. The Bruins had a five-on-three man advantage in the second period but could not score a goal. Orr did have an assist on Al Sims's first goal of the season. Two nights later, the Washington Capitals made their first appearance at the Garden and the first ever game between the two teams. For the second time in three games, the Bruins put up a ten-spot as Orr scored the hat trick and added three assists in the 10–4 win. On a historical note, Mike Marson of the Capitals, the second black player to perform in the NHL, made his first appearance in the Boston Garden. Marson had this to say about Orr: "That Orr is just amazing—unreal. I'm afraid I spent the evening watching him and Esposito for quite a while instead of playing against them." Orr's hat trick was the seventh hat trick of his career.

In the next game, a scene repeated many times during Orr's career, was witnessed by the capacity crowd at the Garden. It was early in the second period, and the Bruins were a man short killing a minor penalty to Carol Vadnais. Orr grabbed the puck on the right side of the defensive zone. With a change of pace, he moved by the Flames' Tom Lysiak. He sped into the offensive zone and skated around the net and put a backhander under the arm of former Bruin Bobby Leiter, who was sliding across the crease to help his goaltender Dan Bouchard. The goalie had vacated the front of the net to protect the other post, but the puck was already in the net. Typical of Orr and in an effort to not embarrass the Atlanta team, he put his head down and headed back to center ice for the ensuing face-off.

There were 15,003 fans and countless television viewers who were witness to this miraculous goal, his ninth of the season. The goal tied the score at one-all. By the end of the second period, the Flames had gone back up by a 3–2 margin. The Bruins countered in the third period on goals by Esposito and Wayne Cashman and finally doused the Flames, 4–3.

The Bruins were off to St. Louis for a Tuesday night game with the Blues. John Davidson, in goal for St. Louis, made thirty-two saves as the Blues nipped the B's, 4–3. Davidson was later known as a longtime hockey analyst in both the United States and Canada.

On Thursday night, Les Habitants of Montreal invaded the Garden. Orr scored his tenth goal of the season, but goaltender Ken Dryden of Montreal backboned the Canadiens to the 4–1 victory. This was the Bruins' first home loss of the season.

The Buffalo Sabres were next on the Saturday docket for the Bruins. In this game, Hodge, Al Sims, and Orr all scored two goals to pace the B's to a win over the Sabres. The Bruins gave up a 7–2 lead but held on for the 7–5 victory.

The next evening, the Bruins were at the Olympia in Detroit for a game with the Red Wings. Orr scored the first two Bruins' goals, both on the power play to lead the Bruins to a 5–2 win. After the game, Wings' coach Alex Delvecchio had this to say about Orr's performance: "That Orr, he is really something. I wish people wouldn't keep asking if he's as good as ever. He's better than I remember. I don't know of anybody who anticipates a play as he does, and he really motored several times tonight."

The California Seals visited the Garden on Thursday night where the Bruins squeaked out a 4–2 victory. Orr had one assist on the opening score by Dave Forbes. The Bruins knocked off the Rangers at Madison Square Garden on Saturday the 23rd. New York went out to an early 2–0 lead, but the B's stormed back with five straight goals to win going away. Orr had the first goal while Greg Sheppard managed two in the 5–2 Boston win.

As the team prepared to head for California, there was one more home game, this one a visit from the Vancouver Canucks. Don Marcotte and Esposito both had two goals as the Bruins rolled to a 7–4 win over the Canucks. The B's headed for the West Coast, and considering the lowly rank of the Seals, the Bruins were in a surprisingly tight game before inching out California by a 3–1 score. It was the sixth straight win for the Boston sextet.

After a couple of off days, the Bruins were in Los Angeles to meet the Kings. The six-game winning streak came to an end as the B's fired only twenty-three shots at Kings' goaltender Gary Edwards, who stopped them all in the 2–0 Los Angeles win.

November 1974					Orr's Stats				
					Game		Season		
Date	Venue	Versus	W-L-T	Score	G	A	G	A	PTS
2	New York	Islanders	L	3–2	0	2	4	13	17
3	Boston	Minnesota	W	10–1	1	3	5	16	21
5	Boston	Buffalo	T	2–2	0	1	5	17	22
7	Boston	Washington	W	10–4	3	3	8	20	28
10	Boston	Atlanta	W	4–3	1	1	9	21	30
12	St. Louis	Blues	L	4–3	0	0	9	21	30
14	Boston	Montreal	L	4–1	1	0	10	21	31
16	Boston	Buffalo	W	7–5	2	0	12	21	33
17	Detroit	Red Wings	W	5–2	2	0	14	21	35
21	Boston	California	W	4–2	0	1	14	22	36
23	New York	Rangers	W	5–2	1	2	15	24	39
24	Boston	Vancouver	W	7–4	0	1	15	25	40
27	California	Seals	W	3–1	0	2	15	27	42
30	Los Angeles	Kings	L	2–0	0	0	15	27	42

December 1974

The Bruins opened December at the Montreal Forum for a game with the Habs. The B's came back from a 4–1 deficit midway through the third period and scored three straight goals, two by Johnny Bucyk to come out with a 4–4 tie. Orr had two assists in the contest.

The next evening back at home, the Detroit Red Wings were the opposition. The B's fell behind 4–0 coming into the midpoint of period number 2. Although they got one back, the Wings ended the second stanza with a 5–1 lead. The B's scored three consecutive third-period goals, aided by two Orr assists, but the comeback fell short, and the Red Wings prevailed 6–4. Marcel Dionne had three goals for the Red Wings.

The B's hosted the Pittsburgh Penguins on the 8th at the Garden. Orr's winning goal at 13:33 of the third period propelled the Bruins to the 3–2 win.

The team headed to Kansas City on the 10th in their inaugural visit to western Missouri. For the second time in a matter of weeks, Marcotte and Esposito scored two goals apiece as the Bruins defeated the Scouts, 6–2. Orr was credited with two assists.

In a game before the Garden's smallest crowd in two seasons, 13,891 fans watched the Bruins knock out the Los Angeles Kings with a barrage of eight goals in an 8–1 conquest. Orr had his seventeenth goal of the season while Bucyk chipped in his ninth and tenth of the campaign.

In the second game of a five-game home stand, the Bruins shelled two Washington goaltenders (Ron Low and Michel Belhumer) in a 12–1 victory over the hapless Capitals. Orr and Marcotte had two goals apiece to pace the B's in the lopsided victory.

The next night, the Bruins welcomed the New York Islanders to the Garden. Orr had his twentieth goal of the year as Boston sailed to a 5–2 win over the Islanders. Dave Forbes had two goals, and Orr had his twenty-first as the Bruins extinguished the Atlanta Flames, 5–3, on the seventeenth. The game marked Boston's sixth consecutive victory.

The New York Rangers came into the Garden for the fifth consecutive Boston home game. The Rangers opened the scoring with two early first-period goals, but the Bruins came storming back as they pumped home nine consecutive goals and easily defeated the Rangers, 11–3. Esposito had three goals while Orr added a goal and three assists. The Rangers only managed sixteen shots in the game.

Two hat tricks were recorded in the Maple Leafs 8–4 victory over the Bruins on December 21 at Toronto. Esposito's three goals were negated by the three scores for Inge Hammarstrom of the Leafs. This was the second game in succession that the Boston center had scored three goals in a game. Orr assisted on two of the four Boston goals.

The next night, the Red Wings reported to the Boston Garden for a pre-Christmas tilt. Esposito had two goals, and Orr had his twenty-first score, but it took a

Marcotte goal at 19:10 of the third period for the Bruins to edge the Wings, 5–4. Esposito's second goal was the five hundredth of his career and earned him a standing ovation from the sellout crowd. Espo scored his five hundredth faster than any player in NHL history. This was also Phil's eighth goal in three games. The Bruins were now off on a five-game road trip. Orr's goal was the eight hundredth career point. At this juncture of his career, he had played 575 games.

In the first post-Christmas game, the Bruins brought their road show to the Oakland Coliseum and a game with the Seals. Dave Hrechkosy had two goals for the Oakland club, and the Seals slipped by the Bruins, 5–2.

In the final game of December and 1974, the Bruins moved into Vancouver to meet the Canucks. John Gould scored two goals for the Canucks as Vancouver defeated the B's by a 6–4 count. Orr had three assists on the four Boston goals.

December 1974					Orr's Stats				
					Game		Season		
Date	Venue	Versus	W-L-T	Score	G	A	G	A	PTS
4	Montreal	Canadiens	T	4–4	0	2	15	29	44
5	Boston	Detroit	L	6–4	0	2	15	31	46
8	Boston	Pittsburgh	W	3–2	1	0	16	31	47
10	Kansas City	Scouts	W	6–2	0	2	16	34	50
12	Boston	Los Angeles	W	8–1	1	1	17	35	52
14	Boston	Washington	W	12–1	2	2	19	37	56
15	Boston	NY Islanders	W	5–2	1	0	20	37	57
17	Boston	Atlanta	W	5–3	1	1	21	38	59
19	Boston	NY Rangers	W	11–3	1	3	22	41	63
21	Toronto	Maple Leafs	L	8–4	0	2	22	43	65
22	Boston	Detroit	W	5–4	1	1	23	44	67
27	California	Seals	L	5–2	0	0	23	44	67
28	Vancouver	Canucks	L	6–4	0	3	23	47	70
30	Los Angeles	Kings	L	2–0	0	0	23	47	70

January 1975

The Bruins started the 1975 portion of the schedule in Los Angles on the 2nd. In a fight-filled game at the Fabulous Forum, the Bruins rode out to a 3–0 lead and held on for a 5–2 victory over the Kings. Ken Broderick made his first start of the season stopping 24 of 26 Los Angeles shots.

The Bruins defeated the North Stars in Bloomington, 8–0, on January 4. Hodge had two goals, and Orr accumulated four assists in the win. However, the story of the game was an ugly incident between Dave Forbes of the Bruins and Henry Boucha of the North Stars.

In the fight between the two resulted in Boucha suffering a thirty-stitch cut to the eye. The injury was inflicted by the butt end of Forbes's stick. The Hennepin County attorney's office in Minneapolis launched an investigation and then indicted the Bruins' winger. Boucha underwent surgery to correct double vision in his right eye. The NHL suspended Forbes for ten games, the third longest suspension in the circuit's history. The four Bruins scheduled to play in the All-Star Game in Montreal, Orr, Esposito, Vadnais, and Bucyk threatened to boycott the game because of the suspension, but the players were talked out of it by Forbes.

In two previous games between the Bruins and Washington, the B's racked up a 22–5 margin in goals over the Capitals. In this game, the Bruins had to hold on just to gain a 3–3 tie at Washington. Orr did not play after the early moments of the second stanza due to a strained neck. This was the Boston's first visit to the nation's capital—though just outside DC in Landover, Maryland.

The first game after the road trip produced Esposito's thirty-eighth, thirty-ninth, and fortieth goals of the season as Boston downed Vancouver, 5–1. Orr's assist on Esposito's first goal of the game was his fifty-first of the season. Esposito's last goal of the game was the 507th of his career tying him with the great Jean Beliveau. Gary Smith (2) and Ken Lockett (1) were the victims of Esposito's three goals.

At the All-Star Game, an NHL first occurred when two female reporters were allowed in the dressing room for interviews. The reporters were Michelle St. Cyr of a Montreal radio station and Robin Herman of the *New York Times*. Orr, playing in his seventh All-Star Game, scored his first All-Star goal. Gary Smith of the Vancouver Canucks was the goaltender for the Campbell Conference. This would also be Orr's last appearance in an All-Star Game.

For the first time in over three months, the Bruins and Blackhawks met, this time at the Boston Garden. Orr opened up the scoring with his twenty-fourth goal, and the B's fired home four more while coasting to a 5–1 victory over the Hawks.

On Wednesday evening, the Bruins reported for duty at the Montreal Forum and a game against the Canadiens. Montreal moved out to a second period, 4–1 lead, before the Bruins attempted a late comeback. However, the Habs prevailed 5–3 although Orr did manage to register his twenty-fifth goal of the season.

The next night, Rogie Vachon of the Kings played like Ken Dryden played the previous night and helped Los Angeles to a 4–1 victory over the Bruins at Boston Garden. Orr earned an assist on Boston's only tally, a strike by Ken Hodge.

Orr scored his twenty-sixth goal of the season and added an assist, but the Bruins had to come back from a 4–3 deficit to tie the Penguins at the Civic Arena on Saturday afternoon.

The next evening back in Boston, Marcotte and Vadnais each tallied their one hundredth career goals, and the Bruins skated to a 6–3 victory over the Toronto Maple Leafs. Orr managed one assist for his eightieth point of the season.

In the previous two contests with Kansas City, the Bruins had outscored the Scouts by a cumulative 14–4. However, in this contest, Orr scored the first goal of the game at the 1:08 mark of the first period, and it looked like a rout could be on. Instead, the Scouts hit for the next three as Coach Guidolin exacted revenge against his former team by a score of 3–2 in a game played at the Boston Garden.

Orr's attorney Alan Eagleson denied a report that Orr would be seeking a 5-million-dollar contract when his current deal expired in 1976. "I have had friendly chats with Bruins' officials, and I told them I did not want to begin talking with them until June 1, 1976, when the deal expires." One report also claimed that Orr had a 2.5-million-dollar offer from the New England Whalers, but General Manager Jack Kelley pointed out that the World Hockey Association rights for Orr were owned by the Minnesota Fighting Saints.

The Bruins and Flyers met for a Saturday tilt at the Garden. Esposito had his forty-fourth and forty-fifth goals of the season while the B's had to settle for a 2–2 tie.

The next evening, the Bruins were in Kansas City to meet the Scouts for the second time in less than a week. In a troubling trend, they had to come from behind to earn a 3–3 tie with the lowly Scouts. Since the beginning of the month, the team had mounted a mediocre 5-3-4 record. Esposito managed to score his forty-sixth goal of the season in this contest.

Orr's third three-goal game of the season and his eighth career hat trick paced the Bruins 6–0 victory over the California Seals on January 30 at Boston Garden. Gilles Meloche got the neck burn while tending the nets for the Seals. Gilles Gilbert stopped all fifteen shots sent his way.

January 1975					Orr's Stats				
					Game		Season		
Date	Venue	Versus	W-L-T	Score	G	A	G	A	PTS
2	Los Angeles	Kings	W	5–2	0	1	23	48	71
4	Minnesota	North Stars	W	8–0	0	4	23	52	75
7	Washington	Capitals	T	3–3	0	0	23	52	75
9	Boston	Vancouver	W	5–1	0	1	23	53	75
11	Boston	Chicago	W	5–1	1	0	24	53	77
15	Montreal	Canadiens	L	5–3	1	0	25	53	78
16	Boston	Los Angeles	L	4–1	0	1	25	54	79
18	Pittsburgh	Penguins	T	4–4	1	1	26	55	81

19	Boston	Toronto	W	6–3	0	1	26	56	82
23	Boston	Kansas City	L	3–2	1	0	27	56	83
26	Boston	Philadelphia	T	2–2	0	0	27	56	83
27	Kansas City	Scouts	T	3–3	0	0	27	56	83
30	Boston	California	W	6–0	3	1	30	57	87

February 1975

The mini slump of January continued into February as the Maple Leafs skated to a 3–2 victory over the Bruins in Toronto. In the previous nine games, the Bruins were a paltry 2-4-3 and registered a lowly 7 out of 18 points.

In a nationally televised game the next day, Orr took part in all five Boston scores (one goal, four assists) as the Bruins leveled the Flyers by a score of 5–1. As an aside to the game, a crew from *60 Minutes* was on hand to do a story on violence in sports. To accommodate the filming crew, O'Reilly and Dave Schultz managed to get in a third-period tussle earning five-minute majors.

After the Bruins fell behind to Atlanta, 3–1, Orr and Vadnais scored thirty seconds apart in the third period to earn the Bruins a 3–3 tie with the Flames in a game played at the Omni in Atlanta. Atlanta's Richard Mulhern was quoted as saying in *Remembering Bobby Orr*, "We hated to check him. We respect him so much that we don't want to do anything to damage those knees."

The next night, the Bruins hosted the Minnesota North Stars. Orr had two assists as Boston slipped past the Stars by a 3–2 margin.

They then moved onto Detroit for a Saturday encounter with the Red Wings. In a game in which the Bruins scored eight times, surprisingly, Orr was not part of it. This night belonged to Esposito, who had four goals as the B's clipped the Wings by an 8–5 margin. Among Phil's four goals was his fiftieth goal of the campaign, turning that mark for the sixth consecutive season. Phil's four goals were scored against Jim Rutherford in net for Detroit.

In the last home contest before a six-game coast-to-coast sojourn, the Bruins whipped the New York Islanders, 5–1, behind Orr's goal and two assists.

On Wednesday night in Chicago, a game that might have been a harbinger of the need for a team makeover in the near future, the Bruins were embarrassed in an 8–3 loss to the Blackhawks. Jim Pappin of the Hawks scored three goals while Orr managed only one assist on Hodge's power play goal in the first session. It was now on to Buffalo for the next night's game with the Sabres. If the Bruins were to make any noise in catching first place Buffalo, this was the time.

As the Buffalo Auditorium crowd chanted, "Goodbye, Boston. We hate to see you go," the Bruins went down to defeat, 3–1. The only Boston goal was scored late in the game by Bobby Schmautz with Orr assisting on the power play. Incredibly,

Orr had only one shot on net, and Esposito had none. After the game, General Manager Harry Sinden made a brief appearance in the dressing room to express his displeasure with the team's effort but squelched any rumors of returning behind the bench. The road swing continued on to Philadelphia for a nationally televised game on Sunday afternoon.

The Flyers skated out to a quick 2–0 lead before the Bruins mounted a comeback to tie the game at 3 by the midpoint of the second period. Former Bruin Reggie Leach of the Flyers scored the game winner later in the period, and Boston suffered their third straight defeat 4–3.

The team moved out to Vancouver where the listing team ship was righted, at least for one night. Orr had his thirty-fourth goal of the season as they slipped by the Canucks, 3–1.

On Friday evening, the Bruins played the Seals at the Oakland Coliseum. Although Orr launched his thirty-fifth goal and Esposito hit for his fifty-third, they again came up short by a 6–4 count. Boston had now lost four of the first five games on the road trip.

In the road trip finale, the Bruins were thumped badly by the Kings in Los Angeles, 6–0. On top of being held scoreless, Orr picked up a five-minute major penalty during a late-game confrontation with old nemesis Terry Harper. The team headed back to Boston, ending the road trip 1–5.

In the first game after the disastrous excursion, the Bruins faced the Pittsburgh Penguins at the Boston Garden. After spotting the Penguins a 3–1 lead, the B's scored five of the next six goals to defeat the Penguins, 6–4. Six different Bruins scored goals with Orr adding two assists.

The Bruins sent Walt McKechnie to the Detroit Red Wings for Earl Anderson and Hank Nowak. In Nowak's first game for the Bruins, a February 25 encounter against the Pittsburgh Penguins, he was involved in two fights. One engagement was with Bob "the Battleship" Kelly while the other was with future NHL disciplinarian Colin Campbell. Nowak later scored the winning goal in the 6–4 victory.

The Bruins closed out February entertaining the Detroit Red Wings. Terry O'Reilly and Bobby Schmautz had two goals while Orr had his thirty-sixth goal as the B's downed the Wings 9–4 for their second straight win.

February 1975					Orr's Stats				
					Game		Season		
Date	Venue	Versus	W-L-T	Score	G	A	G	A	PTS
1	Toronto	Maple Leafs	L	3–2	0	0	30	57	87
2	Boston	Philadelphia	W	5–1	1	4	31	61	92
5	Atlanta	Flames	T	3–3	1	1	32	62	94

6	Boston	Minnesota	W	3–2	0	2	32	63	95
8	Detroit	Red Wings	W	8–5	0	0	32	63	95
9	Boston	NY Islanders	W	5–1	1	2	33	65	98
12	Chicago	Blackhawks	L	8–3	0	1	33	66	99
13	Buffalo	Sabres	L	3–1	0	1	33	67	100
16	Philadelphia	Flyers	L	4–3	0	2	33	69	102
18	Vancouver	Canucks	W	3–1	1	0	34	69	103
21	California	Seals	L	6–4	1	0	35	69	104
22	Los Angeles	Kings	L	6–0	0	0	35	69	104
25	Boston	Pittsburgh	W	6–4	0	2	35	71	106
27	Boston	Detroit	W	9–4	1	2	36	73	109

March 1975

To begin the month of March, the Bruins faced the Blackhawks. Gregg Sheppard's two goals and Orr's two assists propelled the Bruins to a solid 6–2 win in a game played at the Boston Garden.

Gilles Gilbert pitched a shutout and Hodge scored two goals as the Bruins shutout the Capitals in Landover, Maryland, 8–0. Orr's two assists lifted his assist total to seventy-five on the year.

In the next contest in Atlanta, the Bruins nipped the Flames, 4–2. Gilles Gilbert had thirty-eight saves, and Orr sealed the victory with an empty net goal with eight seconds left in the game. The goal was Orr's 250th goal in 607 career contests. The teams would meet again in Boston on Sunday.

Orr broke his own record for defensemen when he scored his thirty-eighth goal in a 5–2 victory over Atlanta. He also had three assists, and the team managed to net two shorthanded goals by Sheppard in their sixth consecutive win. On Vadnais' power play goal, Orr recorded his six hundredth career regular season assist.

Next up, the New York Rangers came to town for a Tuesday night soiree. Six different Bruins (Cashman, Savard, Sheppard, Vadnais, Esposito, Marcotte) scored goals, and Orr accounted for three assists as the Bruins knocked off the Rangers, 6–3, for their seventh straight win.

After the Bruins moved out to a 3–1 lead, the Penguins came back with four goals in a span of four minutes and thirteen seconds and defeated the Bruins 5–3, snapping their win streak. Orr earned an assist on Bobby Schmautz's first-period goal. Pierre Larouche had three goals for the Penguins in a game played at the Igloo in Pittsburgh.

Old friend Eddie Westfall's winning goal helped the New York Islanders trip the Bruins at Nassau County Coliseum, 3–1.

The next night, the Bruins and Blues matched up at the Boston Garden. Orr scored his thirty-ninth goal of the season on a first period power play, and the B's went on to beat the St. Louis, 7–2. He also contributed an assist as they snapped a two-game losing streak.

On their final visit to Montreal on Wednesday night, the Habs edged the B's by a 2–1 score. Esposito left the game early due to a strained knee ligament.

The Washington Capitals visited the Garden on Saturday night. Orr registered the hat trick (his fortieth, forty-first and forty-second goals of the season) as the Bruins crushed the Caps, 8–2. It was his fourth hat trick of the season, ninth of his career, and would turn out to be his last. With two weeks left in the campaign, this would prove to be the last regular season victory for the Bruins.

The next evening in New York, the Rangers topped the Bruins 7–5. Gregg Sheppard scored two goals for the B's, who then headed to St. Louis for a Wednesday night game with the Blues. Orr scored his forty-third goal of the season, but it would be the only Boston score as the Bruins fell 3–1. On Saturday night in Toronto, the Bruins and Leafs played to a 1–1 draw.

The next evening, the Bruins and Canadiens participated in a playoff-style game with Orr, his forty-fourth, and Esposito, his fifty-ninth, notching the Bruins goals in a hard fought 2–2 tie at the Boston Garden.

| **March 1975** | | | | | Orr's Stats | | | | |
| | | | | | Game | | Season | | |
Date	Venue	Versus	W-L-T	Score	G	A	G	A	PTS
2	Boston	Chicago	W	6–2	0	2	36	75	111
4	Washington	Capitals	W	8–0	0	2	36	77	113
7	Atlanta	Flames	W	4–2	1	0	37	77	114
9	Boston	Atlanta	W	5–2	1	3	38	80	118
11	Boston	NY Rangers	W	6–3	0	3	38	83	121
12	Pittsburgh	Penguins	L	5–3	0	1	38	84	122
15	New York	Islanders	L	3–1	0	0	38	84	122
16	Boston	St. Louis	W	7–2	1	1	39	85	124
19	Montreal	Canadiens	L	2–1	0	0	39	85	124
22	Boston	Washington	W	8–2	3	1	42	86	128
23	New York	Rangers	L	7–5	0	0	42	86	128
26	St. Louis	Blues	L	3–1	1	0	43	86	129
29	Toronto	Maple Leafs	T	1–1	0	0	43	86	129
30	Boston	Montreal	T	2–2	1	1	44	87	131

The *Hockey News* reported that player agent Alan Eagleson along with Orr and Esposito were interested in buying the Bruins. It was also speculated that Orr may have trouble getting the contract he desired due to club's overall decline in standing and popularity as evidenced by a decrease in attendance and plummeting television ratings.

April 1975

The Bruins fell prey to the Buffalo Sabres and lost 3–1 in a game played at the Boston Garden on April Fool's Day. In the final road game of the season at Buffalo, the Bruins were doubled up by the Sabres, 4–2. The Bruins woes continued as they were now winless in their previous six contests (0-4-2). Orr's playing time was limited to four power plays and eleven seconds at the end of the first period. Speculation was that Orr was injured. Coach Cherry responded that Orr was suffering a minor back spasm.

The winless skein reached seven games as the Bruins and Maple Leafs played to a 4–4 draw in the season finale at the Boston Garden. Orr scored his forty-fifth and forty-sixth goals of the season to go along with an assist. Orr was named the recipient of the Elizabeth C. Dufresne Trophy as the outstanding player in home games. It was the fifth time (1966–67, 1969–70, 1971–72, shared with Phil Esposito in 1973–74) that Orr had won the award. Orr was the only player to score against every NHL team this season.

April 1975					Orr's Stats				
					Game		Season		
Date	Venue	Versus	W-L-T	Score	G	A	G	A	PTS
1	Boston	Buffalo	L	3–1	0	0	44	87	131
3	Buffalo	Sabres	L	4–2	0	1	44	88	132
6	Boston	Toronto	T	4–4	2	1	46	89	135

1974–1975 Standings: Prince of Wales Conference

Adams Division

	W	L	T	PTS	GF	GA
Buffalo	49	16	15	113	354	240
Boston	40	26	14	94	345	245
Toronto	31	33	16	78	280	309
California	19	48	13	51	212	316

Norris Division

	W	L	T	PTS	GF	GA
Montreal	47	14	19	113	374	225
Los Angeles	42	17	21	105	269	185
Pittsburgh	37	28	15	89	326	289
Detroit	23	45	12	58	259	335
Washington	8	67	5	21	181	446

Clarence Campbell Conference

Patrick Division

	W	L	T	PTS	GF	GA
Philadelphia	51	18	11	113	293	181
New York Rangers	37	29	14	88	319	276
New York Islanders	33	25	22	88	264	221
Atlanta	34	31	15	83	243	233

Smythe Division

	W	L	T	PTS	GF	GA
Vancouver	38	32	10	86	271	254
St. Louis	35	31	14	84	269	267
Chicago	37	35	8	82	268	241
Minnesota	23	50	7	53	221	241
Kansas City	15	54	11	41	184	328

Game 1 of the opening round of the 1975 playoffs began in Boston on April 8. In game 1, Esposito scored three goals, Gregg Sheppard hit for two, and Orr picked up two assists as they scored the first seven goals and defeated the Blackhawks 8–2. Espo's first two goals were scored off brother Tony before he was pulled after the second period. His third goal was against Michel Dumas.

Game 2 was played at Chicago Stadium. Chicago moved out to a 2–0 first-period lead before the Bruins scored two in the second period. Dale Tallon's late second-period goal put the Hawks ahead 3–2, but Orr's third period shorthanded goal tied the game for the Bruins and forced the contest into overtime. Ex-Bruin Ivan Boldirev ended it at 7:33 of the first OT, and the Hawks defeated the B's, 4–3.

In the clinching game of the series, the Hawks moved out to a 3–0 lead and never looked back as they eliminated the Bruins in the opening round of the playoffs by a score of 6–4. The B's outshot the Hawks 56–19 in the clinching contest. Orr's final playoff point with the Bruins was an assist on Sheppard's goal at 18:58 of the second period. Despite outshooting Chicago a whopping 56 to 19, the Hawks outscored the B's 6–4.

April 1975 Playoffs					Orr's Stats				
					Game		Season		
Date	Venue	Versus	W-L-T	Score	G	A	G	A	PTS
8	Boston	Chicago	W	8–2	0	2	0	2	2
10	Chicago	Blackhawks	L	4–3 (OT)	1	2	1	4	5
11	Boston	Chicago	L	6–4	0	1	1	5	6

After the Stanley Cup opening series loss to the Chicago Blackhawks, Bruins' fans booed and littered the ice in disappointment over the play of the team. Rumors immediately started that Gerry Cheevers would be wooed back from the WHA and that All-Star center Phil Esposito would be dealt. The April 11 loss proved to be the final playoff game in Orr's career.

Orr became the first player in NHL history to win an individual award eight times as he was the recipient of the James Norris Trophy as the top defenseman in the league. It was also the last league award that Orr received.

On Patriot's Day 2075, the town of Concord, Massachusetts, will celebrate the nation's tricentennial. The residents of Concord in 1975 left a tube full of memorabilia to educate the future residents what life was like. A recording of life on Main Street, Concord, depicts traffic noise, a late winter afternoon at Sam's gas station, a television commercial, and a Bruins' game. The time capsule was placed in the pedestal of the Minuteman statue at the Revolutionary War battlefield. The cylinder also preserved microfilm letters from Lady Bird Johnson, Arthur Fiedler, Leverett Saltonstall, and Bobby Orr.

The *Boston Globe* ran a write-in contest to determine Boston's greatest all-time athlete. Finishing at the top of the list was Orr. Orr received a total of 550 first place votes to edge Ted Williams of the Red Sox with 354 points. In third place balloting was John Havlicek of the Celtics with 240 points.

View from the Balcony

The disappointment of another ouster from the playoffs, this time after three games, would have lasting effects on the Bruins. Attendance and television ratings were down. The buzz around town that the Bruins had created since they had become contenders was now a quiet murmur. The Bruins were three years out since their last Stanley Cup victory. Bobby Orr was ailing, and new coach Don Cherry seemed to be letting the inmates run the asylum as he may have been in awe of his charges. It took the lackluster performance of game 3 of the preliminary round to start to get management thinking that there may be internal problems with the team.

When did Cherry start to change his team? After the Bruins were eliminated in three games of the opening round against the Blackhawks, Cherry headed for Halifax, Nova Scotia on a scouting mission. "There I am, freezing, coming down with the flu, and I see Phil (Esposito) on TV. He's nice and tanned and telling how the club wasn't mentally prepared for the playoffs. I thought if a player isn't prepared for the Stanley Cup playoffs, no coach can help him. Right then, I decided to do things my way."

Changes would begin to percolate early next season, but it took a summer of soul-searching to build the case that the team had to change from the swashbucklers of the early '70s to the new, so-called lunch bucket teams of the late '70s. But like everything in life, change was inevitable, and it was no different in hockey. Teams can stagnate, and it appeared that the 1974–75 Bruins had stagnated.

Though Bobby Orr had scored a career-high forty-six goals and was only twenty-seven years old, it would have been difficult to foresee that his days as a dominant force in the NHL were essentially over.

Top Hockey Stories from 1975

Stanley Cup Champions	Philadelphia Flyers
Art Ross Trophy	Bobby Orr, Boston Bruins
Hart Trophy	Bobby Clarke, Philadelphia Flyers
Masterton Trophy	Don Luce, Buffalo Sabres
Lady Byng Trophy	Marcel Dionne, Detroit Red Wings
Vezina Trophy	Bernie Parent, Philadelphia Flyers
Calder Trophy	Eric Vail, Atlanta Flames
Conn Smythe Trophy	Bernie Parent, Philadelphia Flyers
Norris Trophy	Bobby Orr, Boston Bruins
Jack Adams Award	Bob Pulford, Los Angeles Kings

Calder Cup Champions	Springfield Indians
Memorial Cup Champions	Toronto Marlboros
NCAA Hockey Champions	Michigan Tech
Avco/WHA Champions	Houston Aeros

Two new teams, the Kansas City Scouts and the Washington Capitals, were admitted into the league. The teams were aligned into two 9-team conferences. The Prince of Wales Conference would host the Norris and Adams Divisions while the Clarence Campbell Conference would be made up by the Smythe and Patrick Divisions. The schedule was increased to eighty games.

Top Sports Stories

World Series Champions	Cincinnati Reds
Super Bowl X Champions	Pittsburgh Steelers (game played on 1/18/1976 at Orange Bowl, Miami, Florida)
NBA Champions	Golden State Warriors
Kentucky Derby Champion	Foolish Pleasure
NCAA Football Champions	Oklahoma (11-1)
NCAA Basketball Champions	UCLA

CHAPTER 10

1975–1976: Over So Fast

WITH THE PLAYOFF ELIMINATION FRESH in their minds, the Bruins went about the business of preparing for the 1975–76 season. In late May maneuvers, Phil Esposito and Terry O'Reilly signed multiyear contracts with the team.

Dave Forbes's trial for assault against Henry Boucha, stemming from the January 4 game at Minnesota, ended in a hung jury. The charges against Forbes were later dropped because the prosecutor in the case felt there was little reason to believe a jury would convict Forbes.

In other off-season news, an interview with Guy Maniella of WBZ radio's *Calling All Sports* talk show confirmed that Orr had met with the Minnesota Fighting Saints of the World Hockey Association. Orr said, "We have been talking with them a little bit, and they are very generous. But we are not going to make any moves until we talk with the Bruins... I still have a year left in my contract with Boston. I'm not going to give you figures from either Boston or Minnesota."

Bruins' Managing Director Harry Sinden said, "We were asked by Bobby a year ago not to discuss contract with him until it ran out in June 1976. We have honored that request. Orr is the most dynamic player to ever play the game, and if they [the WHA] have any hopes of salvaging their league, this is the kind of move they would make."

Orr continued, "I don't want to leave Boston, but you really have to sit down and think. It's a darn big business now." Sinden countered with, "We are going to do everything possible to keep Orr in Boston, but let's face it, there is only so much you can do."

In late August, the *Toronto Globe and Mail* reported that the signing of Orr by the Minnesota Fighting Saints was imminent. It was reported that Orr would receive a $1.5 million bonus and $300,000 per year for the next two years after his contract expired with the Bruins. Wayne Belisle, the owner of the Fighting Saints had this to say about a contract for Orr. "I told Alan Eagleson we could pay $250,000 a year for life. The only problem is that when he finishes his career, we'd have to shoot him. That's the only way we could afford it."

As contract talks continued to percolate, NHL President Clarence Campbell announced that the league would not help pay Orr's salary with the Bruins. The matter was brought up to compare WHA clubs contributing money to pay for Bobby Hull to jump to the Winnipeg Jets in 1972.

As August was turning into September, the sale of the Bruins from Storer Broadcasting to the Jacobs Brothers company, Sportsystems of Buffalo, New York, appeared inevitable. The negotiations were being closely watched by Eagleson and being used as leverage in negotiations between Orr and the Bruins.

On August 28, the sale of the team and Boston Garden to the Buffalo group was finalized. Rumor had it that a quid pro quo agreement was reached, where the NHL Board of Governors approved the sale of the Bruins only if Sportsystems signed Orr to a new contract, but in a matter of a few hours, the sale was complete. The NHL Board of Governors approved the sale, and contract negotiations with Eagleson commenced.

The price of the sale was $10,000,000. Almost immediately new paint was applied to the forty-eight-year-old Garden. Paul Mooney was appointed president of the Bruins by the Jacobs Brothers. When the season got underway, a new Garden policy took hold as the organ player performed crescendos to hype the crowd. Since this hyping had never been done before, each effort by the organist was greeted with boos, likely fueled greatly by booze.

After four days of training camp, Orr complained about discomfort in his left knee. After he was sent back to Boston, it was determined that he would have to go under the knife again. Dr. Carter Rowe performed the operation on Orr's knee. Estimation of his convalescence was six to eight weeks. He would be lost for the first twelve games of the 1975–76 season.

An exhibition game between the Bruins and Chicago Blackhawks, played in the Windy City, deteriorated into a bench clearing brawl that lasted about twenty minutes. Andy van Hellemond called 216 minutes in penalties. Thirty-one players left the benches to join the fracas and were assessed $100 fines.

The *Toronto Globe and Mail*, through Orr's attorney Alan Eagleson, reported that Orr's contract would not be affected by Canada's newly adopted wage and price controls. The law only applied to corporations with more than five hundred employees.

October 1975

The Bruins began the 1975–76 campaign without Orr in the lineup. He would miss all of October (nine games) and the first three games of November. The team got off to a less than scintillating start and finished October with a 4-3-2 record. They scored thirty-one goals while they allowed thirty goals for the month.

October 1975					Orr's Stats				
					Game		Season		
Date	Venue	Versus	W-L-T	Score	G	A	G	A	PTS
9	Boston	Montreal	L	9–4	DNP		0	0	0
12	Boston	NY Islanders	T	3–3	DNP		0	0	0
16	Detroit	Red Wings	T	2–2	DNP		0	0	0
18	New York	Islanders	W	5–2	DNP		0	0	0
19	Boston	Toronto	W	3–0	DNP		0	0	0
23	Boston	Kansas City	L	3–2	DNP		0	0	0
25	Montreal	Canadiens	L	6–2	DNP		0	0	0
26	Boston	Detroit	W	7–3	DNP		0	0	0
30	Boston	St. Louis	W	3–2	DNP		0	0	0

November 1975

The Bruins continued to flounder as the schedule moved into November. They were crushed by the Flyers in Philadelphia 8–1. Back in Boston, in what would be Phil Esposito's last home game, the Bruins downed the California Seals 5–0. The team then began a three-game road trip in Buffalo, where the Sabres blanked the B's, 4–0.

The team headed out west to Vancouver and an engagement with the Canucks on the 8th. However, there was some earth-shattering business conducted a day before the contest.

On November 7 in one of the most shocking trades, not only in hockey but in sports history, Phil Esposito and Carol Vadnais were traded to the New York Rangers for Brad Park, Jean Ratelle, and Joe Zanussi.

Harry Sinden's explanation of the deal: "In order to explain why I made the deal, I would have to infringe on the players involved, and I don't want to do that. They've just meant too much to me personally. We felt we had to move quickly. We weren't going anywhere as we were. We had to give up something good to get something good in return. That's why we traded as we did. Do you think it was easy… after all Phil has done for us?"

Still without a contract extension and returning from rehabilitation, Orr, along with newcomers Brad Park and Jean Ratelle, finally made their first appearance of the season at Vancouver on November 8. In spite of two assists, the Bruins fell to the Vancouver Canucks, 4–2. Rod Sedlbauer scored three goals in the Canucks victory. Dave Reece tended goal for Boston in the loss.

The next evening, the Bruins were in Oakland for a game with the Seals. Park and Ratelle scored their first goals with the Bruins while Bobby Schmautz had two goals, and Orr had three assists as the Bruins downed the Seals, 6–3.

In the first home game since the trade, the Bruins hosted the Minnesota North Stars. Gilles Gilbert pitched the shutout, and Orr scored his first goal of the season while Dave Forbes and Gregg Sheppard also scored two goals in the win. The last three goals by the Bruins were all scored while the team was shorthanded.

Orr scored his second goal of the season, and Brad Park had his first goal as a Bruin, and the team marched through Atlanta with a 5–3 victory. Park and Orr's goals were on the power play. While on an Atlanta radio sports talk show, Orr responded to a question by saying he did not think he would sign a new contract until sometime next year.

The next evening back in Boston, the Bruins edged the Kansas City Scouts by a 4–2 margin. The Orr-Park combination on the power play was starting to get some notice. Johnny Bucyk, who had seen a lot in his twenty-one seasons had this to say: "I've never seen two points covered like Park and Orr cover them." And this from Kansas City's Bep Guidolin: "You won't see any better-looking power play than theirs with Orr and Park at the points. It's the best you'll see in this league."

The Bruins moved on to the Motor City, where Orr scored his third goal while the B's and Wings played to a 3–3 draw. Detroit came back from a 3–1 deficit and tied the game with ten seconds left on the clock. The tying goal for the home team, scored by Mickey Redmond, happened while the Bruins were shorthanded, and the Wings had pulled their goaltender.

The next evening back on home ice, the Bruins played their second consecutive tie game and settled at two apiece with the New York Islanders. Orr managed one point when he assisted on Bobby Schmautz's second-period goal.

The Bruins played their third tie game in a row, this time a 3–3 final against the Toronto Maple Leafs at Boston Garden. Orr netted his fourth goal and assisted on Andre Savard's game-tying goal. Since his return to action on November 8, Orr had accumulated four goals and eleven assists. There was little in his performance so far this season to indicate that Orr's future with the Bruins was in serious jeopardy.

The Bruins broke the three-game tie streak when they upended the Los Angeles Kings, 4–2, in Boston. Orr had one assist on the game-winning goal by Doug Gibson. It was Gibson's first career goal. Ratelle did not play, and there was speculation that he was not happy playing in Boston.

The Bruins moved on to Madison Square Garden to take on the Rangers in what would be Orr's last game in a Boston uniform. His last assist as a Bruin came at

5:48 of the first period on a power play goal by Jean Ratelle. A secondary assist was credited to Ken Hodge. Orr's last goal as a Bruin, against John Davidson in goal for the Rangers, occurred at the thirty-fourth-second mark of the second period and was assisted by Ratelle. The final outcome of the game was a 6–4 Boston victory. Bobby Orr would never again wear the Bruins' crest in an NHL game.

Boston's next game would be a road contest in Chicago. As the Bruins were getting ready to depart for Chicago from Logan Airport, Orr reported to Coach Cherry that he had soreness in his left knee. "As soon as he spoke to me, I told him the best thing to do was stay in Boston and have the condition checked by Dr. Rowe." The examination of Orr's knee was not good.

Three days later, Orr would go under the knife for the fifth time on his left knee. He announced at that time that he did not intend to play the rest of the season. The reaction to Orr's latest operation was varied.

"I expect that Bobby will be skating within six or seven weeks. This is the first time he has suffered any condition on the outside of his left knee. All the other conditions have been on the inside. I would say that Bobby will definitely play very well again before the end of this season. No doubt about it in my mind" (Dr. Carter Rowe).

"If he has to go through this twice a year, I'm going to recommend that Bobby call it a career. He's financially secure. He's on the last year of his contract, so this kind of talk does not do any good for negotiations. But the hell with that. What matters is his health. Nobody should have to go through what he's been through. This definitely clouds Bobby's future" (Alan Eagleson).

"It's terrible to think of this happening to anybody, especially to a great guy like Bobby Orr, who is only twenty-seven years old. It is difficult to say what he means to this team and to this whole game. Just having him out there on the ice makes us all feel better" (Bobby Schmautz).

"I'm just sick about it. For a while, anyway, it'll be hard to think about it just from the hockey viewpoint. My immediate feeling is just what it would be about something like that happening to any friend. I received a call from Orr early on Saturday morning. He was getting ready to go into the operating room. He just wanted me to know about it from him. And you know another reason he called? He wanted me to be sure to wish the guys luck at the game here" (Don Cherry).

"If they have any brains, they'll keep him out the rest of the year. They can't gamble on his knee. It's criminal to even think about it" (Derek Sanderson of the St. Louis Blues).

"To be honest with you, I thought Bobby was playing on one leg. But he's so great, he can control it with one leg. If you put a wooden leg on him, he'll still play super hockey" (Phil Esposito of the New York Rangers).

"This operation was different" said Orr while showing a semicircular scar on the outside of his knee. "The earlier operation was to remove bone chips. This one was for cartilage on the outside of the knee."

November 1975					Orr's Stats				
					Game		Season		
Date	Venue	Versus	W-L-T	Score	G	A	G	A	PTS
1	Philadelphia	Flyers	L	8–1	DNP		0	0	0
2	Boston	California	W	5–0	DNP		0	0	0
5	Buffalo	Sabres	L	4–0	DNP		0	0	0
8	Vancouver	Canucks	L	4–2	0	2	0	2	2
9	California	Seals	W	6–3	0	3	0	5	5
13	Boston	Minnesota	W	6–0	1	2	1	7	8
15	Atlanta	Flames	W	5–3	1	2	2	9	11
16	Boston	Kansas City	W	4–2	0	0	2	9	11
19	Detroit	Red Wings	T	3–3	1	0	3	9	12
20	Boston	NY Islanders	T	2–2	0	1	3	10	13
23	Boston	Toronto	T	3–3	1	1	4	11	15
25	Boston	Los Angeles	W	4–2	0	1	4	12	16
26	New York	Rangers	W	6–4	1	1	5	13	18
29	Chicago	Blackhawks	T	4–4	DNP		5	13	18
30	Boston	Pittsburgh	W	4–2	DNP		5	13	18

November 1975—Boston Garden / Bobby Orr in His Last Month in a Bruins' Uniform

In the December 26 game at Buffalo, the Bruins spotted the Sabres a 2–0 lead, but the team came back scoring five straight goals en route to a 6–3 win. Cherry said of Orr, "Although he's not here, his spirit is still here... if we can just keep hanging around till he comes back." His voice trailed off.

Center Gregg Sheppard opined, "There is a difference in the club from the start of the season. And there is no question losing Bobby at the start of the season really hurt our morale. Then he came back about the time of the trade, and he was the one who pulled us together and got us started. Even though he is out now, he gave us the winning idea. And maybe we looked too much for him to do it all the time for us. Now, we are looking to ourselves."

Coach Cherry added, "I don't want anyone to forget it was Bobby who put us back on track in California. More than anyone else, he got us started."

As time wore on, contract talks percolated to a pitch. "I don't want to leave Boston, but if I had my choice, it would be Chicago," said Orr in what could be considered in retrospect to be prescient on his part. He continued, "Bill Wirtz [Hawks' owner] is a fine man and has a good record in both hockey and business. I'm just saying this if I had my choice. Other areas I would enjoy are Toronto and Montreal. Actually, any area where there is a definite change of seasons." Bobby Orr said this in the *Toronto Globe and Mail*, December 28, 1975. Orr was clearly contemplating a future in hockey beyond Boston.

In late January, the Bruins made a new contract offer to Orr that was rejected. It included the following:

- A salary of $295,000 for five seasons
- A payment of $925,000 on June 1, 1980, or 18.5 percent of the hockey club in lieu of the payment (Orr would later claim that he was not made aware of this provision)

Media accounts of the negotiations varied from paper to paper across the United States and Canada. In an April 18, 1976, column by Will McDonough of the *Boston Globe*, he stated that in the initial meeting between Orr and Jeremy Jacobs, the Sport System Chairman mentioned the possibility of part ownership of the Bruins for Orr.

As January turned into February, Tom Fitzgerald of the *Boston Globe* published a few pointers on the status of Orr's contract:

1. Under the terms of the standard players' contract that he signed in 1971, Orr is not required to play out an option year.
2. Orr will remain in Boston although this is by no means a certainty.
3. According to the five-year agreement last October between the owners and the NHL Players' Association, the Bruins would be entitled to "equalization or compensation" from any team signing Orr. But that of course might be subject to a legal challenge such as the NFL's Rozelle Rule challenged in a Minnesota court.
4. The negotiation committee for the Players' Association, which bargained with the owners, included Orr as a vice president and his attorney, Alan Eagleson, as executive director.

At the end of February, after three months of rehabilitation, Orr was working out with an eye to return on March 1. He was to go on the six-game road trip with the Bruins, which commenced on February 11 and ended on February 22. As the Bruins were getting ready to leave Boston, it was decided that Orr would stay back in Boston. Reasons given were that the team's road trip would be tiring and that ice would not be available in all the cities (Bloomington, Oakland, Chicago, Kansas

City, and two games in New York). It was felt that Orr could continue getting into game shape working out in the new gym at the Boston Garden.

In further contract news, reports out of Boston claimed that Alan Eagleson, Orr's attorney, would not accept a $300,000-plus-per-year salary, which would make Orr the highest-paid player in hockey. Eagleson continued, "If Mr. Adams still owned the Bruins, Orr would be signed by now."

In an Associated Press story out of Toronto, Eagleson stated that he had serious doubts about Orr signing with the Bruins. "The Bruins and their owner [the Jacobs Brothers] are not prepared to come close to what we are asking in the way of a contract, and that is unfortunate when you consider we are dealing with the greatest hockey player in the history of the game. Unless they sell the franchise to interests that are more oriented to the Boston scene and realize the value of Bobby, I can only speculate that we will not sign the contract they are offering."

As the Bruins approached the playoffs, a story appeared in the *Toronto Globe and Mail* stating that the chances of Orr returning to Boston are 1 in 100. Eagleson claimed that the contract offered to Orr is unsuitable and has "no security." Eagleson stated that Orr has been offered a "pay as you play" contract, which Eagleson opined could be in conflict with the collective bargaining agreement. Eagleson also mentioned that the Bruins were not entitled to compensation. The contract between the Players' Association and the NHL includes a compensation provision, which was hammered out by Eagleson as head of the Union.

On April 7, the Bruins released a brief statement that Orr would not be available for the 1976 Stanley Cup playoffs. Orr also stated the following: "This has been a very frustrating season for me. The 1976 Bruins are a fine team, and I regret that I have not been able to play with my teammates. The Bruins have been very good to me, and I was hoping to be ready for the playoffs, but the knee just isn't ready."

The Bruins denied that Orr's absence was a result of stalled contract negotiations. Coach Don Cherry went even further. "A couple of weeks ago, he came to me and said that if he was going to be ready, he'd really have to turn it on someday to see how the knee responded. So we scheduled a real hard scrimmage. Bobby looked all right, but the next day, there was aggravation in the knee." After that, Orr determined that he would not be able to play.

A May 7 article in the suburban *Lynn Item* claimed that the Bruins were about to trade Orr to the Blackhawks for John Marks, Phil Russell, and Ivan Boldirev. The Bruins denied the report since Orr had a no-trade contract.

In a June 4 report out of Toronto, Orr stated that he would not contest the Bruins' right to compensation if he signed with another NHL team.

In the *Lawrence Eagle-Tribune* of June 6, Orr admitted that he is "damaged goods" but that he will sign with either St. Louis or Chicago. The Blackhawks had reportedly offered Orr $500,000 for five years while the Blues offer was not divulged. Orr was quoted as saying, "To collect my pay, I would have to guarantee my 1974–

75 production. I don't think I'm in any position to guarantee that after my two operations this year. All I'm doing is telling the owners in advance who want to have me that they are purchasing damaged goods. I don't want any owner to think I'm in perfect condition."

Bruins' manager Harry Sinden denied that the Bruins' offer was tied to any performance level. Sinden continued, "Either I'm stupid or he is. One of us doesn't understand the offer. As I understand it, our offer does not have anything to do with 120 points or the 1974 performance. That is a bunch of crap."

Meanwhile, in Montreal, Eagleson confirmed that Orr's finances were solid. "I think I can safely say that Orr could sign a check for $2.5 million without a worry."

As the deadline for a deal drew near, the following points about the negotiations were made:

- Orr considered himself damaged goods.
- Orr's left knee might require a sixth operation
- If Orr considered himself physically unable to play, he might retire for a year and come back with the Canadian national team in the 1977 World Tournament.
- Orr said, "If I can't play, I won't accept the money."
- It was reported that three different contract proposals were offered to him by the Bruins:
  o $3.8 million over ten years
  o $1.75 million over five years
  o 18.6 percent ownership in the Bruins or the sum of $925,000 on June 15, 1980

William Wolbach from the Boston Corporation, a new member of the Bruins' Board of Directors, and Massachusetts treasurer Bob Crane both tried to intervene in the contact negotiations between the Bruins and Orr.

Rumors were surfacing that Orr would be playing for the Chicago Blackhawks after July 1. Reports indicated that a loophole in his contract would allow him to sign with another club without compensation. Also, it was rumored that Orr was not happy with the Jacobs Brothers, the team's new owners. Although the Bruins were interested in signing Orr before his latest knee operation, the negotiations on a new contract stalled while he was recovering from surgery. It was also reported that Bruins' ownership had nixed the idea of a five-year ($500,000 per year) contract for Orr.

Lloyd's of London refused to insure the contract for Orr claiming that his damaged knees were too big of a risk. Rather than staying in Boston, he returned to Parry Sound to rehabilitate. Brian O'Neill, Executive Director of the NHL, claimed that Orr's contract was covered by the five-year agreement between the league and the NHLPA and that the Bruins must be compensated if another team signed Orr.

1975–1976 Standings

Prince of Wales Conference

Adams Division

	W	L	T	PTS	GF	GA
Buffalo	48	15	17	113	313	237
Boston	46	21	13	105	339	240
Toronto	34	31	15	83	294	276
California	27	42	11	65	250	278

Norris Division

	W	L	T	PTS	GF	GA
Montreal	58	11	11	127	337	174
Los Angeles	38	33	9	85	263	265
Pittsburgh	35	33	12	82	339	303
Detroit	26	44	10	62	226	300
Washington	11	59	10	32	224	394

Clarence Campbell Conference

Patrick Division

	W	L	T	PTS	GF	GA
Philadelphia	51	13	16	118	348	209
New York Islanders	42	21	17	101	297	190
Atlanta	35	33	12	82	262	237
New York Rangers	29	42	9	67	262	333

Smythe Division

	W	L	T	PTS	GF	GA
Chicago	32	30	18	82	254	261
Vancouver	33	32	15	81	271	272
St. Louis	29	37	14	72	249	290
Minnesota	20	53	7	47	195	303
Kansas City	12	56	12	36	190	351

View from the Balcony

The Bruins went through a transformation unlike any other time in their history. The trade of Phil Esposito and Carol Vadnais was necessitated by Sinden's belief that Bobby Orr's career was in jeopardy. Park was considered the second best defenseman at the time of the trade and was an excellent offensive and defensive force at the blue line. Jean Ratelle, while not having the numbers that Esposito did, was nonetheless an excellent offensive and defensive center. Gerry Cheevers found his way back into the fold to solidify the goaltending position.

Under the tutleage of Don Cherry, the offensive juggernaut of past seasons was transformed into a tightly knit, defensive-minded team. Bobby Orr had played his last game as a Bruin. Initially, attendance dropped off slightly, then dramatically as the B's went through their metamorphasis.

Cherry, understanding that he no longer had the horses to compete with Montreal, Buffalo, and Philadelphia, changed the team's style of play. Defensive structure, goaltending, and special teams would be the formula to stay competitive. The loss of the stars would cost the franchise fannies in the seat, a fact that the team would have to accept for many years to come. Regardless, the changes would continue as the team resumed as one of the top-tier teams in the NHL.

The ten-year anniversary of a young phenom from Parry Sound making his debut with the Boston Bruins was approaching. Loyal Boston hockey fans would have to come to grips with the fact that Bobby Orr's tenure with the Bruins had expired. "All the lies they told about Bobby Orr were true" (Bruins' defenseman Ted Green).

Top Hockey Stories from 1976

Stanley Cup Champions	Montreal Canadiens
Art Ross Trophy	Guy Lafleur, Montreal Canadiens

Hart Trophy	Bobby Clarke, Philadelphia Flyers
Masterton Trophy	Rod Gilbert, New York Rangers
Lady Byng Trophy	Jean Ratelle, New York Rangers
Vezina Trophy	Ken Dryden, Montreal Canadiens
Calder Trophy	Bryan Trottier, New York Islanders
Conn Smythe Trophy	Reggie Leach, Philadelphia Flyers
Norris Trophy	Denis Potvin, New York Islanders
Jack Adams Award	Don Cherry, Boston Bruins
Avco/WHA Champions	Winnipeg Jets
Calder Cup Champions	Nova Scotia Voyageurs
Memorial Cup Champions	Hamilton Fincups
NCAA Hockey Champions	Minnesota

Top Sports Stories

World Series Champions	Cincinnati Reds
Super Bowl XI Champions	Oakland Raiders (game played on 1/9/1977 Rose Bowl, Pasadena, California)
NBA Champions	Boston Celtics
Kentucky Derby Winner	Bold Forbes
NCAA Football Champions	Pittsburgh (12-0-0)
NCAA Basketball Champions	Indiana

1976 Winter Olympics are held in Innsbruck, Austria. The Russians win the gold medal in hockey for its fourth straight Olympic title.

The Aftermath

IT DIDN'T LOOK RIGHT. IT had never looked right. It will never look right.

When "The Fours" restaurant opened on Canal Street across from the Boston Garden in 1976, one could look across the street from the pub and see the North Station Canal Street bump where the Green Line train would end its run and begin its exodus back into the bowels of the Boston subway system. Walking into the tavern, the clanging and screeching of the streetcars behind could not prepare the patrons for what they were about to witness. There it was, in the center of the bar just over the cash register amidst the plethora of memorabilia festooning every nook and cranny of this food, drink, and sports emporium. A picture of Bobby Orr wearing the regalia of the Chicago Blackhawks hung like a photo over a closed casket. How was this possible? Was it acceptable to call it a sacrilege? Had he somehow betrayed us? Could we now turn our back on him because he no longer wore the eight-spoked *B*? Did we have to change our allegiance to a team some one thousand miles to the west?

In the summer of 1975, the Jacobs Brothers, owners of the Sportservice Corporation of Buffalo, New York, were negotiating a deal to purchase the Boston Garden and the Boston Bruins from Storer Broadcasting. Approval for the $10 million transaction was predicated on whether the Jacobs would sign Orr to a contract extension. The signing of him with still a year to run on his current contract with the Bruins would cement their acceptance into the National Hockey League and had the added effect of keeping Orr from inking a deal with the rival World Hockey Association.

On August 28, the sale of the Bruins was approved by the NHL board of governors in the belief that Orr was set to re-sign. Negotiations on a new contract for Orr began immediately. Although talks on a new pact appeared to be moving along, his left knee, already operated on twice, was not cooperating. Prior to the first exhibition game of the 1975–76 campaign, he went under the knife again. While recuperating, problems with the contract continued to fester. When Lloyd's of London refused to guarantee the contract due to his knee woes, negotiations hit a serious snag and were stalled. Orr continued to rehab and joined the team early in November. Playing in ten games, he amassed 18 points on five goals and thirteen assists before his knee could no longer withstand the rigors of the NHL.

The promise of the arrival of Orr in 1966, tantamount to the anticipation of a child's Christmas morning, lived up to its billing. However, the end of his tenure in Boston was not known on November 26, 1975, the day he played his last game as a Bruin. Lawyers, owners, doctors, and accountants became the story line for followers of Orr. It was initially hard to feel his loss since we didn't know he was gone from our presence. Alan Eagleson let us know that if the Bruins weren't interested in Orr's services, others were.

"We are definitely interested in getting Orr, and I'm sure we're not the only ones" (Tommy Ivan, General Manager of the Chicago Blackhawks).

"Every team in hockey would be interested in getting Orr" (Sammy Pollock, General Manager of the Montreal Canadiens).

"We haven't given it a whole lot of thought. Frankly, I had hoped he would sign with the Bruins again. I think that would have been best for the league" (Ed Snider, owner of the Philadelphia Flyers).

"We're going to make an offer for Orr. Sure I'd like to have him. Anybody in hockey would be crazy if they didn't want him" (Emile Francis, General Manager of the St. Louis Blues).

"We are interested in Orr but we would have to be satisfied with his physical ability to come back and play" (John Zeigler, Vice President, Detroit Red Wings).

"I don't know if we are going to make an offer for Orr or not. There has been a lot of talk about us but none of it is true as far as I'm concerned" (Jake Milford, General Manager of the Los Angeles Kings).

But as rumors of his departure became fact, it was at first met with dead silence. Was this possible? On June 1, 1976, the improbable became reality.

June 1, 1976, Boston, Massachusetts

Orr's contract with the Boston Bruins expired, and he was eligible to become a free agent. However, in May of 1976, Orr secretly signed an agreement with the Chicago Blackhawks. It was executed in New Canaan, Connecticut, at the home of Ross Johnson, the president of Standard Brands and later of RJR Nabisco. The agreement called for a three-year contract commencing on June 1, 1976, and lasting until May 31, 1979. The salary would be $500,000 per year with options for another seven years at $500,000 per year. The agreement was signed by William Wirtz of Chicago and Bobby Orr and was witnessed by Johnson.

June 9, 1976, Montreal, Quebec

Alan Eagleson announced that Orr would be leaving Boston to sign with the Chicago Blackhawks. Eagleson bragged that Orr would be a millionaire by the time he was thirty. He claimed Orr had signed a guaranteed contract worth $3 million. He continued, "The Bruins effectively stopped negotiating with Bobby Orr on December 10, 1975, when he injured his knee."

June 24, 1976, Chicago, Illinois

In a public event at the Bismarck Theatre in Chicago, Orr signed a ceremonial $3,000,000-plus contract with the Blackhawks. Among the estimated two thousand in attendance were Chicago Mayor Richard Daley, Hawks owner William Wirtz and General Manager Tommy Ivan. Ivan originally signed Gordie Howe with the Detroit Red Wings, Bobby Hull with the Blackhawks, and now, Orr.

June 25, 1976, Boston, Massachusetts

Referring to the event in Chicago the previous day, Orr said from a podium of the 57 restaurant in Downtown Boston, "Yesterday was a very happy occasion. Here today, it is a very sad day. I just wanted this get-together because I didn't have a chance to see so many of you when I left in April. My years in Boston have been the greatest years of my life. I've never had a complaint, not a single complaint with the press, with the fans, not with anybody. It was a very difficult decision I had to make. Thank you for ten beautiful years."

In attendance at the affair were Phil Esposito, Eddie Johnston, Johnny Bucyk, Wayne Cashman, Ace Bailey, Dave Forbes, Bob Gryp, Ross Brooks, Bobby Schmautz, and Bruins' trainers Dan Canney, and John Forristall.

"It will feel very strange playing against the Bruins. I felt some of that when Espie went to the Rangers even though we didn't get to play against one another."

August 29, 1976, Boston, Massachusetts

The Boston Bruins released their 1976–1977 schedule. The Bruins' fans jotted down Thursday, November 4, when Orr and the Blackhawks meet each other for the first time since Orr's signing with Chicago. The game would be played at the Boston Garden

September 2, 1976, Ottawa, Ontario

Orr returned to the ice as a member of Team Canada in the Canada Cup series. He had three assists in Canada's 11–2 victory over Finland.

September 15, 1976, Montreal, Quebec

In the series finale, the Canadians defeated Czechoslovakia 5–4 in overtime. Orr was named the most valuable player in the tournament.

October 4, 1976, Chicago, Illinois

The Blackhawks defeated the Bruins 6–5 in an exhibition game played at Chicago Stadium. Although Orr, wearing the familiar number 4 on his Blackhawks white sweater did not register any points in the contest. This would mark the only time that he faced the Bruins while with the Hawks.

October 7, 1976, St. Louis, Missouri

Orr played his first official game as a member of the Chicago Blackhawks. He scored one goal and added an assist in the Hawks 6–4 victory over the Blues. Orr's goal was against Ed Staniowski. The game also marked the coaching debut for Emile Francis behind the St. Louis bench. The Cat had previously been with the New York Rangers.

October 24, 1976, Chicago, Illinois

Orr scored two goals in a 7–2 romp over St. Louis. Old friend Eddie Johnston was in net for the Blues. His first goal of the game, scored at the twenty-second mark, was Orr's nine hundredth regular-season point.

October 31, 1976, Chicago, Illinois

The Blackhawks defeated the Capitals 5–4. Orr injured his left knee and would not play in Thursday's encounter with the Bruins at Boston Garden.

January 27, 1977, Vancouver, British Columbia

Orr, due to his ailing left knee, played his final game of the 1976–77 campaign. He finished with four goals and nineteen assists for 23 points.

April 1977

Orr underwent the sixth operation on his left knee. He announced that he would take the entire next season off. He was named an assistant to Blackhawks General Manager and Coach Bob Pulford.

1977–1978

Did not play.

1978–1979

October 11, 1978, Landover, Maryland

Orr played his first game in twenty-one months. He did not register any points, but the Blackhawks defeated the Capitals 4–2 at Washington.

October 18, 1978, Chicago, Illinois

Orr assisted on a goal by John Marks at 4:13 of the first period in a 6–2 win over the Minnesota North Stars. It was the last recorded assist of Orr's career.

October 28, 1978, Detroit, Michigan

Orr scored his final goal and the final point of his career as the Blackhawks lost to the Red Wings, 7–2. The goal, at 14:42 of the third period, was surrendered by Rogie Vachon of the Wings.

October 29, 1978, Chicago, Illinois

Orr played the final game of his National Hockey League career in a 4–1 victory over the Montreal Canadiens. His minor penalty at 8:47 of the third period was his last entry in an NHL game summary. At this point in NHL history, Orr was the all-time leader in points-per-game average at .988

November 8, 1978, Chicago, Illinois

Orr said, "I know I'm going to have another operation. I have very little joint space in the knee. It's just bone on bone, and there are bone chips that break off. The doctor has told me I will need another operation. I feel discomfort after I skate. It's been five days since I skated, and it feels better than it did five days ago.

"I knew when I started this season what my chances were, but I wanted to give it one more try. I've done that now, and I think the best thing I can do now is quit for good and try to help the Blackhawks in any way I can other than playing. Hockey has given my family and me everything we have, and I hope now I can just give something back to it even though I will never play again. This is my final decision. I said when I started skating again during training camp that this would be my last comeback and it is."

With that, Orr announced his retirement as a player. He would remain an assistant coach for Bob Pulford with the Hawks.

And so it was over. He was only thirty years old, in the prime of his career. He was incomparable. Leigh Montville of the *Boston Globe* said it best. "How better was he? He simply was better. He was one level above anyone else. He was the sole prospect for the next highest league. He was playing in the highest league there is, and yet he still was better."

January 9, 1979, Boston, Massachusetts

Before an emotionally charged crowd, the Bruins retired Bobby Orr's number 4 and raised his banner to the rafters at the Boston Garden. The event preceded an exhibition game between the Bruins and the Soviet Wings. VIPs that were present on the ice for the ceremony included the Master of Ceremonies Tom Fitzgerald of the *Boston Globe*, the radio voice of the Bruins Bob Wilson, Orr's wife Peggy, Alan Eagleson, former NHL President Clarence Campbell, current President John Zeigler, the governor of Massachusetts Edward King, the treasurer of the Commonwealth of Massachusetts Bob Crane, the head of the Gallery Gods and representing the fans, Roger Naples, the president of the Bruins Paul Mooney, and Bruins' legend Milt Schmidt. As Orr walked onto the carpet at center ice, Organist John Kiley serenaded him with the Bruins' theme song, "Paree."

When Orr finally stepped to the microphone, he said, "Thank you, ladies and gentlemen. We're going to see a great hockey game here tonight, and I think that I just got orders from Tom Fitzgerald that we have to get the program underway. I love you. Thank you, and I'll be back in a second."

Johnny Bucyk presented Orr with his sweater and checks that were donated to the Boston Children's Hospital, Muscular Dystrophy Society, the Cystic Fibrosis Foundation, and the Doreen Grace Brain Research Foundation. A check was also presented to Bobby by teammate Wayne Cashman. A note concerning the sweater: although it looked the part, the striping on the arms and waistband was inconsistent to the game sweaters worn during the Orr era.

Orr continued with his speech. "Thank you very much, ladies and gentlemen. I've been thinking a week trying to figure out what to say to you." At this point, Orr donned the Bruins' sweater, much to the delight of the crowd and went on. "I came out here and was going to be kind of formal, I'm finding it kind of difficult. I know one thing, when I get back to Chicago and the Blackhawks see [boos from the crowd]… I would like to acknowledge Mr. Billy Wirtz and Mr. Tommy Ivan of the Blackhawks. Billy and Tommy, thank you. Ladies and gentlemen, the players, I don't know what to say, I love you all so much. I spent ten years here in Boston, and they're the best ten years of my life. If you were to talk to most athletes that have been around the league, they would say Boston is the place to play. My wife, Peggy, and I have had a ball today. I shouldn't have looked at you, Peg. We have had a ball. She loves Boston. My mother and father are not here tonight, but they're sitting at home tonight, watching television. I'd like to say hi to them. Cheesie, Cash, Doakie, guys that are still here, this is a heck of a place, I love you and thank you very much."

January 9, 1979. *Top photo:* Al Secord, Terry O'Reilly, and Peter McNab greet Orr at jersey retiring ceremony. *Bottom photo:* Orr watches as his number is raised to the rafters at the Boston Garden.

June 13, 1979, Montreal, Quebec

Bobby Orr became the youngest (thirty-one) and fastest after retirement (seven months) to be voted into the Hockey Hall of Fame. The Hall of Fame election committee waived the three-year waiting period and elected him immediately. Other players elected with him at that time were longtime New York Ranger Harry Howell and Montreal Canadien great Henri Richard. The induction ceremony would take place in September.

September 1979, Toronto, Ontario

Before nearly one thousand onlookers at the Royal York Hotel, Orr, Howell, and Richard were inducted into the Hockey Hall of Fame. Orr was presented at the ceremony by Mrs. Weston Adams, the wife of the late owner of the team. Mrs. Adams was "extremely touched… and Orr felt totally inadequate," when asked by Orr to introduce him at the ceremony.

October 1988, Boston, Massachusetts

The New England Sports Museum chose Armand LaMontagne of Scituate, Rhode Island, to sculpt a life-size wooden likeness of former Bruins' superstar Bobby Orr. LaMontagne had previously done Larry Bird of the Boston Celtics. The artists' creations of Ted Williams and Babe Ruth are on display at the Baseball Hall of Fame in Cooperstown, New York. In addition to sports figures, he has done sculptured busts of General George Patton, President Gerald Ford, and Eleanor Roosevelt.

March 15, 1989, Boston, Massachusetts

The Orr sculpture was unveiled at a dinner in Boston. The current location for the masterpiece has been the New England Sports Museum located in the TD Garden.

June–July, 1996, Somewhere in Outer Space

Canadian astronaut Robert Thirsk flying in the Space Shuttle Columbia on Mission STS-78 carried Bobby Orr's 1970 Stanley Cup ring and a Bruins' jersey into space. A photo of Thirsk emulating Orr's 1970 Stanley Cup winning goal while wearing Orr's jersey and ring gained worldwide attention.

1998

Elected to the Canada Walk of Fame (Toronto, Ontario).

May-November, 2009, Somewhere in Outer Space

Thirsk's second shuttle flight, this time on the Russian Soyuz, was highlighted by his wearing Orr's 1972 Stanley Cup ring.

May 10, 2010, Boston, Massachusetts

On the fortieth anniversary of the Goal, an eight-hundred-pound bronze statue of Bobby Orr was unveiled at the west entrance to the TD Garden. The statue was sculpted by Harry Weber, a native of St. Louis. Ironically, the Bruins defeated the St. Louis Blues for the Stanley Cup on that fateful day back in 1970.

The ceremony was witnessed by Boston mayor Tom Menino and Orr's team-mates Johnny Bucyk, Derek Sanderson, Ken Hodge, Johnny McKenzie, Don Marcotte, and Gary Doak. Thousands of fans gathered around the statue for the unveiling. Kathy Bailey, the late Ace Bailey's wife, was also in attendance. Bailey was killed in the attacks of September 11, 2001. Former Bruins' General Manager Harry Sinden and team owner Jeremy Jacobs also attended the event. The statue was donated by the Boston Bruins as a gift to the city of Boston and the fans of the Boston Bruins.

April 2016, Boston, Massachusetts

The Bobby Orr statue, located near the west end of the TD Garden, was moved to Portal Park at the east end of the building. The statue now has the backdrop of the Zakim-Bunker Hill Bridge. While construction in the front of the building is undertaken, the statue will remain there although the small park appears to be a perfect spot for a permanent location of the iconic attraction.

Orr statue at Portal Park

Armand LaMontagne's sculpture located inside the New England Sports Museum at TD Garden

APPENDICES

1966–1967: The Rookie Season

Owner: Boston Professional Hockey Association
President and Governor: Weston Adams
General Manager: Hap Emms
Coach: Harry Sinden
Publicity Director: Les Stout
Trainer: Dan Canney, John Forristall
Chief Scout: Harold "Baldy" Cotton
Team colors: Black & gold
Home: Boston Garden
Training camp: London, Ontario
Radio: WHDH (850)
Announcers: Jim Laing
Attendance: 444,715 (12,706 per game)

Team hotels:	Chicago	LaSalle
	Detroit	Sheraton Cadillac
	Montreal	Sheraton Mount Royal
	New York	Manhattan
	Toronto	Royal York

Minor officials:	Scorers	Nick Del Ninno, Bill Quackenbush

Game timer	Carroll Getchell
Penalty timer	Tony Notagiacomo
Goal judges	Sonny Hunter, Benny Bertini, Bernie Bailey, Tom Moon
Statisticians	John Carleton, John Kane

Trophy winners:

Calder (Bobby Orr)
Dufresne (Bobby Orr)
Lester Patrick (Charles Adams)

All-stars:

Bobby Orr (second team)

1966 amateur draft

Player	Drafted from
Barry Gibbs	Estevan
Rick Smith	Hamilton
Garnet Bailey	Edmonton
Tom Webster	Niagara Falls

1966–67 roster

	GP	G	A	PTS	PIM
Awrey, Don	4	1	0	1	6
Beverley, Nick	2	0	0	0	0
Buchanan, Ron	3	0	0	0	0
Bucyk, Johnny	59	18	30	48	12
Connelly, Wayne	64	13	17	30	12
(Acquired from San Francisco for cash, 6/14/1966)					
Dillabough, Bob	60	6	12	18	14
Doak, Gary	20	0	1	1	20
Goldsworthy, Bill	18	3	5	8	21
Green, Ted	47	6	10	16	67
Hodgson, Ted	4	0	0	0	0
Krake, Skip	15	6	2	8	4
Lonsberry, Ross	8	0	0	0	2
Marotte, Gilles	67	7	8	15	65

Martin, Pit	70	20	22	42	40
McKenzie, John	69	17	19	36	98
Murphy, Ron	39	11	16	27	6
Oliver, Murray	65	9	26	35	16
Orr, Bobby	61	13	28	41	102
Parise, Jean Paul	18	2	2	4	10
Rivers, Wayne	8	2	1	3	59
Sanderson, Derek	2	0	0	0	0
Sather, Glen	5	0	0	0	0
Schock, Ron	66	10	20	30	8
Smith, Dallas	33	0	1	1	24
Stewart, Ron	56	14	10	24	31
Watson, Joe	69	2	13	15	38
Westfall, Eddie	70	12	24	36	26
Wilkins, Barry	1	0	0	0	0
Williams, Tommy	29	8	13	21	2
Woytowich, Bob	64	2	7	9	43

	GP	W	L	T	GA	GAA	SO
Cheevers, Gerry	22	5	11	6	72	3.33	1
12 PIM							
Johnston, Eddie	34	9	21	2	116	3.70	0
Parent, Bernie	18	3	11	2	62	3.64	0
2 PIM							

Orr 1966–1967	Games played	Goals	Assists	Points
October	5	1	1	2
November	11	5	5	10
December	7	1	3	4
January	12	0	6	6
February	13	3	5	8
March	12	3	8	11
April	1	0	0	0
Total	61	13	28	41

Goals

First-period goals	4
Second-period goals	3
Third-period goals	6

Even strength	9
Power Play	3
Shorthanded	1
Game winners	0

Home	6	Road	7
Vs.		Vs.	
Chicago	1	Chicago	0
Detroit	3	Detroit	3
Montreal	1	Montreal	0
New York	1	New York	2
Toronto	0	Toronto	2

Goaltender victims

Hank Bassen (Detroit)	1
Johnny Bower (Toronto)	1
Roger Crozier (Detroit)	3
George Gardner (Detroit)	1
Eddie Giacomin (New York)	4
Glenn Hall (Chicago)	1
Terry Sawchuck	1
Gump Worsley (Montreal)	1

But He Can't Play Goal

When Orr wasn't making checks or scoring goals, he was blocking them, even moving into the crease when their goaltender was pulled. Once during a game against St. Catharines, Orr's team, the Generals, pulled their goaltender for an extra attacker. The Hawks managed to score a goal on Orr, who was guarding the net. The Hawks Steve Latinovich swung a one-hand bounce shot over Orr's stick.

Hawks manager Ken Campbell opined, "At least we've found that Orr has a weakness. He's not too good in goal."

Remembering Bobby Orr by Craig MacInnis

To Bobby Orr

"To Bobby Orr, who came as close to perfection on ice as any NHL player I've ever seen" (Brian McFarlane's *Original Six* - The Bruins).

Practice Makes Perfect

This from Coach Harry Sinden: "I used to have to kick him [Orr] out of practice. He'd ruin them because he always had the puck. I had to send him off early so we could get a proper practice" (From *Number Four, Bobby Orr* by Michael Farber, *Sports Illustrated*).

Maclean's Magazine, 1965

The February 20, 1965, issue of Maclean's, Canada's national magazine features Bobby Orr on the cover. The Hamilton Red Wing player wearing number 20 is future NHL'er Peter Mahovlich, the brother of NHL star Frank Mahovlich. Orr was described as follows: "Bobby Orr is a swift, powerful skater with instant acceleration, instinctive anticipation, a quick accurate shot, remarkable composure, an unrelenting ambition, a solemn dedication, humility, modesty, and a fondness for his parents and his brothers and sisters that often turns his eyes moist."

The International Boat Show—Boston

Manuel Sherman, the President of the International Boat Show, had enticed sports stars to appear at the Boston Boat Show. Over the years, he's had Ted Williams, Joe Namath, Sandy Koufax, Ken Harrelson, and George Blanda as featured attractions.

On Bobby Orr

"Well, a few years ago, around 1967, we were trying to promote our boat show, and our advertising guy got the idea that what is a boat show without an Orr? I got in touch with Alan Eagleson, and oh, what a nightmare. Okay, finally through Eagleson we've got Bobby Orr, but we really paid through the nose. But nothing to do with Bobby Orr.

"In walks this cherub, pink-cheeked, like a little boy. I ask myself, this is Bobby Orr! You're imagining someone big. We'll, we were opening on a Saturday at 1:00 p.m., and I ask Orr to come in at 11:00 a.m. to talk to the press and so forth. And there were about fourteen thousand people out front already. And for two solid hours, Bobby stood there and greeted everybody, shook everybody's hand, had a pleasant word to say. I would say that drawing the number of people to our Boston show, he was our biggest attraction ever. I legitimately made money on Bobby Orr."

No Underwear, No Shorts, No Problem

After Orr's career was done, he appeared on Don Cherry's *Grapevine* television show. After Cherry told the audience that Orr didn't wear any underwear or socks when he played, Orr explained:

"I wore cut-off underwear. In junior hockey, we only had one pair of socks. In the pros, you have all kind of socks. One trip I forgot my socks, and I started going without socks, and I just got used to it."

News from 1967

- Israel and Arab forces battled in the Six-Day War.
- Racial violence erupted over the United States with riots in Detroit, Rochester, New York, Spanish Harlem in New York City, Birmingham, Alabama and New Britain, Connecticut.
- Thurgood Marshall became the first black justice of the US Supreme Court.
- Astronauts Virgil Grissom, Edward White, and Roger Chaffee were killed in a fire during a test launch on January 27.
- US population was 198,712,056 with unemployment at 3.8 percent.
- Congress created the Public Broadcasting System (PBS).
- *Rolling Stone* and *New York Magazine* made their debut.
- *A Man for All Seasons* won the Academy Award for best movie. Other movies debuting included *The Graduate, Bonnie and Clyde, Guess Who's Coming to Dinner?, In the Heat of the Night,* and *Cool Hand Luke.*
- Record of the year was Frank Sinatra's "Strangers in the Night" while song of the year was "Michelle" by the Beatles.
- *Sgt. Pepper's Lonely Hearts Club Band* was released to rave reviews.
- The world's first successful heart transplant was performed by a team of surgeons led by Dr. Christiaan Barnard in South Africa. The patient died eighteen days later.
- Spencer Tracy, Woodie Guthrie, and Che Guevara passed away.
- Dow Jones average on 12/31/1967: $906.84.
- Top television shows: *Bonanza, The Red Skelton Show, The Andy Griffith Show, The Lucy Show, The Jackie Gleason Show.*

1967–1968: A New Beginning

Owner:	Boston Professional Hockey Association
President and Governor:	Weston Adams
General Manager:	Milt Schmidt
Coach:	Harry Sinden
Publicity Director:	Les Stout, Herb Ralby
Trainer:	Dan Canney
Chief scout:	Garry Young
Club colors:	Black and gold
Home:	Boston Garden
Training camp:	London, Ontario
Radio:	WHDH (850)
Announcers:	Bob Wilson
Television:	WSBK (TV 38)
Announcers:	Don Earle
Attendance:	511,812 (13,832 average)
Team hotels:	Chicago: LaSalle
	Detroit: Sheraton Cadillac
	Los Angeles: Hacienda
	Montreal: Sheraton Mt. Royal
	Minnesota: Leamington

New York: Sheraton-Atlantic
Oakland: Edgewater Inn
Philadelphia: Sheraton
Pittsburgh: Penn Sheraton
St. Louis: Chase Park Plaza
Toronto: Royal York

Minor officials:		
	Scorers	Woody Dumart, Nick Del Ninno
	Game timer	Carroll Getchell
	Penalty timer	Tony Notagiacomo
	Goal judges	Benny Bertini, Sonny Hunter, Tom Moon, Bernard Bailey
	Statistician	John Carlton

Trophy winners:

Calder (Derek Sanderson)
Norris (Bobby Orr)
Dufresne (Phil Esposito)
Lester Patrick (Walter Brown)

All-stars:

Bobby Orr (first team)
Phil Esposito (second team)
Johnny Bucyk (second team)

1967 amateur draft

Player	Drafted from
Meehan Bonner	St. Thomas Jr. B

1967–68 roster

	GP	G	A	PTS	PIM
Arbour, John	4	0	1	1	11
Awrey, Don	74	3	12	15	150
Bucyk, John	72	30	39	69	8
Cashman, Wayne	12	0	4	4	2
Doak, Gary	59	2	9	11	100
Esposito, Phil	74	35	49	84	21

(Acquired with Ken Hodge and Fred Stanfield from Chicago for Pit Martin, Gilles Marotte, and Jack Norris, 5/15/1967)

Gibbs, Barry	16	0	0	0	2
Green, Ted	72	7	36	43	133
Hodge, Ken	74	25	31	56	31

(Acquired with Phil Esposito and Fred Stanfield from Chicago for Pit Martin, Gilles Marotte, and Jack Norris, 5/15/1967)

Krake, Skip	68	5	7	12	13
Lonsberry, Ross	19	2	2	4	12
McKenzie, John	74	28	38	66	107
Murphy, Ron	12	0	1	1	4
Orr, Bobby	46	11	20	31	63
Sanderson, Derek	71	24	25	49	98
Sather, Glen	65	8	12	20	34
Shack, Eddie	70	23	19	42	107

(Acquired Eddie Shack from Toronto for Murray Oliver, 5/15/1967)

Smith, Dallas	74	4	23	27	65
Stanfield, Fred	73	20	44	64	10

(Acquired with Ken Hodge and Phil Esposito from Chicago for Pit Martin, Gilles Marotte, and Jack Norris, 5/15/1967)

Westfall, Eddie	73	14	22	36	38
Williams, Tommy	68	18	32	50	14

	GP	W	L	T	GA	GAA	SO
Cheevers, Gerry	47	23	17	5	125	2.83	3
Gill, Andre	5	3	2	0	13	2.89	1
Johnston, Eddie	28	11	8	5	73	2.87	0

Orr 1967–1968	Games Played	Goals	Assists	Points
October	7	2	4	6
November	12	3	5	8
December	8	2	6	8
January	10	2	4	6

February	5	2	1	3
March	4	0	0	0
April	4	0	0	0
Total	46	11	20	31

Goals

First-period goals	4
Second-period goals	3
Third-period goals	4

Even strength	7
Power Play	3
Shorthanded	1
Game winners	1

Home	6	Road	5
Vs.		Vs.	
Detroit	2	Chicago	2
Minnesota	1	Montreal	1
Montreal	1	New York	1
New York	1	Toronto	1
Toronto	1		

Goaltender victims

Gary Bauman: Minnesota	1
Johnny Bower: Toronto	2
Roger Crozier: Detroit	1
Denis DeJordy: Chicago	2
Dave Dryden: Chicago	1
George Gardner: Detroit	1
Eddie Giacomin: New York	2
Rogatien Vachon: Montreal	1

1967–68 playoff roster

	GP	G	A	PTS	PIM
Awrey, Don	4	0	1	1	4
Bucyk, John	3	0	2	2	0
Cashman, Wayne	1	0	0	0	0
Doak, Gary	4	0	0	0	4
Esposito, Phil	4	0	3	3	0
Green, Ted	4	1	1	2	11
Hodge, Ken	4	3	0	3	2
Krake, Skip	4	0	0	0	2
McKenzie, John	4	1	1	2	8
Murphy, Ron	4	0	0	0	0
Orr, Bobby	4	0	2	2	2
Sanderson, Derek	4	0	2	2	9
Sather, Glen	3	0	0	0	0
Shack, Eddie	4	0	1	1	6
Smith, Dallas	4	0	2	2	0
Stanfield, Fred	4	0	1	1	0
Westfall, Eddie	4	2	0	2	2
Williams, Tommy	4	1	0	1	2

	GP	W	L	T	GA	GAA	SO
Cheevers, Gerry	4	0	4	0	15	3.75	0

Orr 1968 PLAYOFFS	Games played	Goals	Assists	Points
April	4	0	2	2

Sometimes, It Pays to *Not* Have AAA

This vignette appeared in Ken McKenzie's "Passing the Puck" column in the *Hockey News*. Substitute schoolteacher Tom Capucci of nearby Waltham, Massachusetts, had attended a recent Bruins' game on a snowy night in Boston. After the game, he became stuck in the snow. A fellow came over to him and for twenty minutes, helped him dig out of the snow, and slush. "At first, I didn't recognize him. I even offered him something for his troubles. Finally, I realized it was Bobby Orr of the Bruins."

I Gotta Get Out of This Place

When an unidentified college professor exited through the wrong door and ended up on the Garden's fire escape, he might have had to spend the whole night there. However, his incessant pounding on the door was heard by none other than Orr, who opened the door to the relief of the professor.

Can It Get Any Better Than This?

"You watch him every game, and you say, 'There's the best play he ever made.' Then you look again, and he's doing something even better" (Milt Schmidt).

"Orr's appeal is that he's what they (the small fry) dream of becoming, a kid starring in the major leagues. Carl Yastrzemski of the Boston Red Sox is like a businessman. He's been around awhile. He's had his ups and downs, and now he's made it. But this kid, Bobby Orr, is a kid" (Will McDonough of the *Boston Globe*).

It's Better in the Bahamas

Reports are that Orr and Eagleson were already partners in a carwash near Toronto and part ownership in a golf course. "I match Bobby dollar for dollar in all these investments," crowed Eagleson. To guard Orr's financial future, a Toronto business expert claims that Orr is registered as a Bahamian corporation, which includes tax advantages. Orr's outside income is estimated at about $50,000.

Highlights for February 20, 1968, on Boston Television

- 8:00 p.m. *The Jerry Lewis Show* with guest Tony Randall (channel 4).
- 10:00 p.m. *CBS Reports*: Viet Cong, the most faceless enemy that the US has ever fought with Marvin Kalb (channel 5)
- 10:30 p.m. *Firing Line* with William Buckley: actor Robert Vaughan joins Buckley in a discussion on the war in Vietnam (channel 2)
- 11:00 p.m. *The Professionals* with Bobby Orr and the Boston Bruins (channel 38)
- 11:30 p.m. *The Tonight Show* with Steve Allen. Guests include Jack Webb, Alice Faye, and Shecky Greene (channel 4)

He's worth more…

Says Orr: "A lot of people think hockey players and players in all sports are different, but just because I play hockey doesn't make me different from a guy who is a lawyer or a student in school. I eat the same food, do the same things. Yet some people are scared to come and talk to me. I'd like to talk to them."

"I don't know what they're paying him, but whatever it is, he's worth it. In fact, he's worth more." (Jod Watson, former teammate of the *Philadelphia Flyers*)

Former roommate and current Philadelphia Flyer Joe Watson

News from 1968

- On January 23, North Korea seized the US Navy ship *Pueblo*.
- North Vietnam launched the Tet Offense, a turning point in the Vietnam War.
- American soldiers massacred 347 civilians at My Lai.
- President Johnson announced he will not seek reelection on March 31.
- Martin Luther King was slain in Memphis on April 4. James Earl Ray was later sentenced to ninety-nine years in prison for the murder.
- Senator Robert Kennedy was assassinated in a Los Angeles hotel and died on June 6.
- US population topped 200 million for the first time. Unemployment was 3.8 percent.
- A first-class stamp rose from 0.05 to 0.06 cents on January 7.
- *60 Minutes* debuts on the CBS network.
- *In the Heat of the Night* won the Academy Award for best movie. Other significant movies to debut are *2001: A Space Odyssey*, *Romeo and Juliet*, *Funny Girl*, *The Lion in Winter*, and *Oliver*.
- The motion picture rating system started with the ratings of G, PG, R, and X.
- Record and song of the year was the Fifth Dimension's "Up, Up and Away."
- Album of the year was *Sgt. Pepper's Lonely Hearts Club Band*.
- The *Apollo 8* made the first successful flight to orbit the moon. The astronauts on the flight were Frank Borman, James Lovell, and William Anders.
- In addition to Martin Luther King and Robert Kennedy's deaths, 1968 also saw the passing of Helen Keller, Upton Sinclair, and John Steinbeck.
- Dow Jones average on 12/31/1968: $947.73.
- Top television shows: *The Andy Griffith Show*, *The Lucy Show*, *Gomer Pyle, USMC*, *Gunsmoke*, *Family Affair*.

1968–1969: The Final Stumbling Block

Owner:	Boston Professional Hockey Association
President and Governor:	Weston Adams
General Manager:	Milt Schmidt
Coach:	Harry Sinden
Club colors:	Black and gold
Publicity Director:	Les Stout, Herb Ralby
Chief Scout:	Garry Young
Home:	Boston Garden
Training camp:	London, Ontario
Radio:	WHDH (850)
Announcers:	Bob Wilson
Television:	WSBK (TV 38)
Announcers:	Don Earle
Attendance:	563,654 (14,833 average)

Minor officials:	Scorers	Woody Dumart, John Carlton
	Game timer	Carroll Getchell
	Penalty timer	Tony Notagiacomo
	Goal judges	Benny Bertini, Sonny Hunter, Tom Moon, Bernard Bailey
	Statistician	Jim Lombard
	Supervisor	Sumner Wolley

Team hotels:	Chicago: LaSalle
	Detroit: Sheraton-Cadillac
	Los Angeles: Holiday Inn
	Montreal: Sheraton Mount Royal
	Minnesota: Leamington
	New York: Park Sheraton
	Oakland: Edgewater Inn
	Philadelphia: Sheraton
	Pittsburgh: Penn Hilton
	St. Louis: Chase Park Plaza
	Toronto: Royal York

Trophy winners:

Hart: Phil Esposito
Ross: Phil Esposito
Norris: Bobby Orr
Dufresne: Phil Esposito
7th Player: Eddie Westfall

All-stars:

Bobby Orr (first team)
Phil Esposito (first team)
Ted Green (second team)

1968 amateur draft

Player	Drafted from
Danny Schock	Estevan
Fraser Rice	Halifax Jr.
Brian St. John	U. of Toronto

1968–69 roster

	GP	G	A	PTS	PIM
Atkinson, Steve	1	0	0	0	0
Awrey, Don	73	0	13	13	149
Bailey, Garnet	8	3	3	6	10
Bucyk, John	70	24	42	66	18
Cashman, Wayne	51	8	23	31	49

Doak, Gary	22	3	3	6	37
Erickson, Grant	2	1	0	1	0
Esposito, Phil	74	49	77	126	79
Gauthier, Jean	11	0	2	2	8
Gibbs, Barry	8	0	0	0	2
Green, Ted	65	8	38	46	99
Harrison Jim	16	1	2	3	21
Hodge, Ken	75	45	45	90	75
Hurley, Paul	1	0	1	1	0
Leiter, Bobby	1	0	0	0	0
Lesuk, Bill	5	0	1	1	0
Lonsberry, Ross	6	0	0	0	2
Lorentz, Jim	11	1	3	4	6
Marcotte, Don	7	1	0	1	2
McKenzie, John	60	29	27	56	99
Murphy, Ron	60	16	38	54	26
Orr, Bobby	67	21	43	64	133
Sanderson, Derek	63	26	22	48	146
Sather, Glen	76	4	11	15	67
Shack, Eddie	50	11	11	22	74
Smith, Dallas	75	4	24	28	74
Smith, Rick	47	0	5	5	29
Stanfield, Fred	71	25	29	54	22
Webster, Tom	9	0	3	3	9
Westfall, Eddie	70	18	24	42	22
Wilkins, Barry	1	1	0	1	0
Williams, Tom	26	4	7	11	19

	GP	W	L	T	GA	GAA	SO
Cheevers, Gerry	52	28	12	12	145	2.80	3
14 PIM							
Johnston, Eddie	24	14	6	4	74	3.08	2
1 assist							
Junkin, Joe	1	0	0	0	0	0.00	
Played 8 minutes							

Orr 1968–1969	Games played	Goals	Assists	Points
October	10	3	4	7
November	11	2	7	9
December	13	5	10	15
January	14	3	11	14
February	3	1	3	4
March	16	7	8	15
Total	67	21	43	64

Goals

First-period goals	8
Second-period goals	8
Third-period goals	5

Even strength	17
Power Play	4
Shorthanded	0
Game winners	2

Home 12

Vs.

Chicago	5
Los Angeles	1
Montreal	1
New York	2
Oakland	1
St. Louis	1
Toronto	1

Road 9

Vs.

Chicago	1
Detroit	2
Minnesota	1
Montreal	1
New York	1
Oakland	1
Pittsburgh	2

Goaltender victims

Les Binkley (Pittsburgh)	1
Roger Crozier (Detroit)	1
Joe Daley (Pittsburgh)	1

Denis DeJordy (Chicago)   1
Gerry Desjardins (Los Angeles)   1
Dave Dryden (Chicago)   5
Roy Edwards (Detroit)   1
Tony Esposito (Montreal)   1
Bruce Gamble (Toronto)   1
Eddie Giacomin (New York)   2
Glenn Hall (St. Louis)   1
Fern Rivard (Minnesota)   1
Don Simmons (New York)   1
Rogatien Vachon (Montreal)   1
Chris Worthy (Oakland)   2

Orr 1969 PLAYOFFS	Games played	Goals	Assists	Points
April	10	1	7	8

First-period goals   0
Second-period goals   0
Third-period goals   1

Even strength   1
Power Play   0
Shorthanded   0
Game winners   0

Home   1   Road   0
Vs.   Vs.
Montreal   1
Goaltender victims
Rogatien Vachon   1
(Montreal)

News From 1969

- Richard Nixon was inaugurated as the thirty-seventh president of the United States.
- *Apollo 11* astronauts Neil Armstrong and Edwin Aldrin took the first walk on the moon on July 20.
- Senator Edward Kennedy of Massachusetts pleaded guilty to leaving the scene of an accident at Chappaquiddick in which Mary Jo Kopechne drowned. Kennedy received a two-month suspended sentence.
- US population was 202,676,946 with unemployment at 3.6 percent.
- The FCC banned all cigarette advertising on television and radio.
- The use of DDT was banned in residential areas.
- ARPA (Advanced Research Projects Agency) goes online in December, connecting four major universities. It was the background on which the internet was eventually built.
- Woodstock Festival drew one-half million people to hear performers such as Jimi Hendrix, Janis Joplin, Crosby, Stills, Nash and Young, Jefferson Airplane, Sly and the Family Stone, and Joan Baez.
- A Rolling Stones fan was killed by the Hell's Angels at the Altamont, California, concert.
- *Sesame Street* debuts on the Children's Television Workshop.
- *Oliver* won the Academy Award for best movie of the year. Other notable movies included *Midnight Cowboy*, *Butch Cassidy and the Sundance Kid*, and *Easy Rider*.
- Record of the year was "Mrs. Robinson" by Simon and Garfunkel while "Little Green Apples" won song of the year. Album of the year was *By the Time I Get to Phoenix* by Glen Campbell.
- Mario Puzo's *The Godfather* and Kurt Vonnegut's *Slaughterhouse Five* were published.
- 1969 deaths include former president Dwight Eisenhower, Ambassador Joseph Kennedy, and novelist Jack Kerouac.
- Dow Jones average on 12/31/1969: $809.20.
- Top television shows: *Rowan and Martin's Laugh-In, Gomer Pyle, USMC, Bonanza, Mayberry RFD, Family Affair*.

1969–1970: Mission Accomplished

Owner:	Boston Professional Hockey Association
Governor:	Weston Adams Jr.
Coach:	Harry Sinden
Trainers:	Dan Canney and John Forristall
Publicity Director:	Herb Ralby
Club colors:	Black and gold
Home:	Boston Garden
Training camp:	London, Ontario
Radio:	WBZ (1030)
Announcer:	Fred Cusick
Television:	WSBK (TV 38)
Announcer:	Don Earle
Attendance:	563,654 (14,833 per game)

Minor officials:	Scorer	Woody Dumart
	Game timer	Tony Notagiacomo
	Penalty timer	Sonny Hunter
	Goal judges	Bennie Bertini, Tom Moon, Bernard Bailey
	Statistician	John Carlton
	Spare official	Ed Sandford
	Supervisor	Sumner Wolley

Team hotels:	Chicago: LaSalle
	Detroit: Sheraton Cadillac
	Los Angeles: Sheraton Inn
	Montreal: Sheraton Mount Royal
	Minnesota: Leamington
	New York: Statler Hilton
	Oakland: Edgewater Inn
	Philadelphia: Sheraton
	Pittsburgh: Pitt Hilton
	St. Louis: Chase Park Plaza
	Toronto: Royal York
Trophy winners:	Stanley Cup: Boston Bruins
	Hart: Bobby Orr
	Ross: Bobby Orr
	Norris: Bobby Orr
	Conn Smythe: Bobby Orr
	Lester Patrick: Eddie Shore
	Dufresne: Bobby Orr
	7th Player: John McKenzie
All-stars:	Bobby Orr (first team)
	Phil Esposito (first team)
	John McKenzie (second team)

	Player	Drafted from
1969 amateur draft	Don Tannahill	Niagara Falls
	Frank Spring	Edmonton
	Ivan Boldirev	Oshawa
	Art Quoquochi	Montreal
	Nels Jacobson	Winnipeg
	Ron Fairbrother	Saskatoon
	Jeremy Wright	Calgary
	Jim Jones	Peterborough

1969–70 roster

	GP	G	A	PTS	PIM
Awrey, Don	73	3	10	13	120
Bailey, Garnet	58	11	11	22	82
Beverley, Nick	2	0	0	0	2
Bucyk, John	76	31	38	69	13
Carleton, Wayne	42	6	19	25	23

(Acquired from Toronto for Jim Harrison, 12/10/1969)

	GP	G	A	PTS	PIM
Cashman, Wayne	70	9	26	35	79
Doak, Gary	44	1	7	8	63
Esposito, Phil	76	43	56	99	50
Harrison, Jim	23	3	1	4	16

(Traded to Toronto for Wayne Carleton, 12/10/1969)

	GP	G	A	PTS	PIM
Hodge, Ken	72	25	29	54	87
Lesuk, Bill	3	0	0	0	0
Lorentz, Jim	68	7	16	23	30
Marcotte, Don	35	9	3	12	14
McKenzie, John	72	29	41	70	114
Murphy, Ron	20	2	5	7	8
Orr, Bobby	76	33	87	120	125
Sanderson, Derek	50	18	23	41	118
Smith, Dallas	75	7	17	24	119
Smith, Rick	69	2	8	10	65
Speer, Bill	27	1	3	4	4
Spring, Frank	1	0	0	0	0
Stanfield, Fred	73	23	35	58	14
Webster, Tom	2	0	1	1	2
Westfall, Eddie	72	14	22	36	28
Wilkins, Barry	6	0	0	0	2

	GP	W	L	T	GA	GAA	SO
Cheevers, Gerry		41	24	8	8	108	2.72	4

4 PIM

	GP	W	L	T	GA	GAA	SO
Johnston, Eddie		37	16	9	11	108	2.98	3

2 assists

2 PIM

Orr 1969–1970	Games played	Goals	Assists	Points
October	8	2	12	14
November	14	5	16	21
December	13	4	14	18
January	12	5	17	18
February	13	8	11	19
March	13	7	14	21
April	3	2	4	6
Total	76	33	88	121

Goals

First-period goals	13
Second-period goals	12
Third-period goals	8

Even strength	18
Power Play	11
Shorthanded	4
Game winners	3

Home	8	Road	15
Vs.		Vs.	
Detroit	4	Los Angeles	1
Los Angeles	1	Minnesota	4
Minnesota	3	Montreal	2
Montreal	2	New York	1
New York	2	Philadelphia	3
Philadelphia	2	Pittsburgh	1
Pittsburgh	2	Toronto	3
St. Louis	1		
Toronto	1		

Goaltender victims

Roger Crozier (Detroit)	3
Joe Daley (Pittsburgh)	2
Gerry Desjardins (Los Angeles)	1
Roy Edwards (Detroit)	1
Marv Edwards (Toronto)	1
Doug Favell (Philadelphia)	2
Bruce Gamble (Toronto)	3
Eddie Giacomin (New York)	3
Cesare Maniago (Minnesota)	7
Bernie Parent (Philadelphia)	3
Wayne Rutledge (Los Angeles)	1
Al Smith (Pittsburgh)	1
Rogatien Vachon (Montreal)	4
Ernie Wakely (St. Louis)	1

1969–70 playoff roster

	GP	G	A	PTS	PIM
Awrey, Don	14	0	5	5	32
Bucyk, John	14	11	8	19	2
Carleton, Wayne	14	2	4	6	14
Cashman, Wayne	14	5	4	9	50
Doak, Gary	8	0	0	0	9
Esposito, Phil	14	13	14	27	16
Hodge, Ken	14	3	10	13	17
Lesuk, Bill	2	0	0	0	0
Lorentz, Jim	11	1	0	1	4
Marcotte, Don	14	2	0	2	11
McKenzie, John	14	5	12	17	35
Orr, Bobby	14	9	11	20	14
Sanderson, Derek	14	5	4	9	72
Schock, Dan	1	0	0	0	0
Smith, Dallas	14	0	3	3	19
Smith, Rick	14	1	3	4	17

Speer, Bill	8	1	0	1	4
Stanfield, Fred	14	4	12	16	6
Westfall, Eddie	14	3	5	8	4

	GP	W	L	T	GA	GAA	SO
Cheevers, Gerry	13	12	1	0	29	2.23	0
1 assist							
2 pim							
Johnston, Eddie	1	0	1	0	4	4.00	0
2 pim							

Orr 1970 PLAYOFFS	Games played	Goals	Assists	Points
April–May	14	9	11	20

Goals

First-period goals	2
Second-period goals	3
Third-period goals	3
Overtime goals	1
Even strength	4
Power play	3
Shorthanded	2
Game winners	1

Home	4	Road	
Vs.		Vs.	
New York	3	New York	4
St. Louis	1	Chicago	1

Goaltender victims

Tony Esposito (Chicago)	1
Eddie Giacomin (New York)	7
Glenn Hall (St. Louis)	1

Peace on the earth, goodwill toward men… and a Gordie Howe hat trick

It was Christmas night in Boston, and the Bruins
were hosting the Los Angeles Kings.

'Twas Christmas night
In front of a full house
All the fans were cheering
Even a mouse (probably, really a rat)
The patrons were snuggled all in their seats
With visions of goals and other scoring feats
When down on the ice, the players were flying
The gold-suited Kings, are they really crying
It's EJ, Dallas, Ricky, and Cheesie
Doak, Donnie, Bobby, and Bailey
Don't forget Espo, Hodge, Swoop, and Westfall
If they keep scoring, it could be the Kings' downfall
So Pie, Chief, Turk, Jim, and Freddy, let's score
Even strength, power play, and shortie, we want more
The only thing missing on this night of goodwill
Is a Gordie How hat trick, not another penalty kill

The Authors

Orr had a shorthanded goal at 4:13 of the second stanza. At 7:55, he received a fighting major along with Bill "Cowboy" Flett of Los Angeles. After serving his penalty, he assisted on Johnny Bucyk's seventeenth goal at 16:44 of the second period thus completing the "Gordie Howe" hat trick.

Mr. Superbruin… a few thoughts by Marian Christy of the *Boston Globe*

- Orr has a book coming out soon called *Orr on Ice* written by Dick Grace of Acton, Massachusetts.
- Orr bought a double-breasted brown muskrat coat from Ken Nanfield of Lakeville.
- Orr purchased two neon suits from Truc, a boutique in Harvard Square.
- Orr loves westerns, especially *Old Yeller*.
- Orr, a Baptist, goes to midnight Mass every Christmas Eve.
- Orr is the godfather of Patti Boyle of Lynn, Massachusetts.
- Orr can make a pretty good roast beef without the aid of a cookbook.
- Orr is anti–Vietnam War although he disagrees with the on campus demonstrations.
- Orr is building a new home for his parents back in Parry Sound.
- Orr drives a red GTO.
- Orr is a spokesman for General Motors, Canada.

Jacques is nimble, Jacques is quick with the quote… about Orr

"You are watching the strongest, fastest skater this league has ever seen" (Jacques Plante, St. Louis Blues goaltender on Orr).

But Can He Do Hertz Commercials?

"'Bobby's like O. J. Simpson on skates,' declared Gary Bergman of the Detroit Red Wings" (*Sports Illustrated*, January 12, 1970).

Are You Kidding Me?

In a *Hockey Pictorial* poll of thirty-one of the top NHL forwards evaluating defensemen, Orr was rated ninth behind Tim Horton (Toronto), Terry Harper (Montreal), Al Arbour (St. Louis), Leo Boivin (Minnesota), Bobby Baun (Detroit), Carl Brewer (Detroit), Brad Park (New York), and Ted Green of the Bruins, who has been on the disabled list since the beginning of the season.

From Shore to Orr

On March 10, 1970, Eddie Shore received the Lester Patrick Award on for his contributions to hockey at a dinner in New York City. Shore commented: "I haven't had that much chance to see Orr play. When I first saw him as junior, I said he would be outstanding. He's obviously a fine skater, but I think the best thing about him is his ability to adjust his own speed and to anticipate the speed of the player to whom he is giving a pass."

Woody on Bobby

How to you stop Orr? "I don't think putting someone on him is going to work. I know I wouldn't want the job. With the moves he has, it would be awfully tough. It might also be disruptive to the team trying to do it. Putting someone on Orr would keep a man out of the play. Orr lying back at center ice would take a man out of the defense and even then he would be tough to cover. Covering a forward is easier than covering a defenseman. Get a couple of steps in front of your man, as Eddie Westfall does with Bobby Hull, then how is he going to get past you? He's got to go in. Orr doesn't have to go in.

Former Bruin Woody Dumart on Bobby Orr

Wish You Were Here

Concord-Carlisle High School (Massachusetts) held a birthday party for Bobby Orr in the school cafeteria. Orr was twenty-two on March 20. Orr wasn't in attendance, but the students enjoyed the cakes anyway, baked by the school's home economics class.

Superstitious Superstitions

Orr claimed he has never been caught up in superstition. "I get to the games very early. I like to be in to think about it and to chew my nails. But you notice right above my seat on the bench in our dressing room I have a religious medal hanging there. A young girl sent it to me, and I hung it up. The rest of the guys come by and touch it before a game. I've been doing it myself. But it's not superstitious."

News from 1970

- US troops invaded Cambodia on May 1.
- Four students at Kent State University in Ohio were killed by National Guardsman on May 4. The students were protesting the US invasion into Cambodia.
- Earthquake in Peru killed 50,000.
- US population was 205,052,174 with unemployment at 3.5 percent.
- The Beatles break up.
- *Midnight Cowboy* won the Academy Award for best movie. It was the first and only time an X-rated movie won an Oscar.
- Other movie releases included *M*A*S*H*, *Airport*, *Love Story*, and *Patton*.
- Record of the year was "Aquarius / Let the Sun Shine In" by the Fifth Dimension while "Games People Play" was song of the year. Album of the year is "Blood, Sweat, and Tears."
- IBM introduced the floppy disk.
- Deaths in 1970 included Jimi Hendrix, Janis Joplin, and Sonny Liston.
- Dow Jones average on 12/31/1970: $838.92.
- Top television shows: *Rowan and Martin's Laugh-In*, *Gunsmoke*, *Bonanza*, *Mayberry RFD*, *Family Affair*.

1970–1971: The "Dynasty" Ends

Owner:	Boston Professional Hockey Association
Governor:	Weston Adams Jr.
General Manager:	Milt Schmidt
Coach:	Tom Johnson
Trainers:	Dan Canney and John Forristall
Publicity Director	Herb Ralby
Club colors:	Black and gold
Home:	Boston Garden
Training camp:	London, Ontario
Radio:	WBZ (1030)
Announcer:	Fred Cusick
Television:	WSBK (TV 38)
Announcers:	Don Earle and Johnny Peirson
Attendance:	584,748 (14,993 average)

Minor officials:	Scorer	Woody Dumart
	Game timer	Tony Notagiacomo
	Penalty timer	Sonny Hunter
	Goal judges	Bennie Bertini, Tom Moon, Bernard Bailey
	Statistician	John Carlton

Spare official	Ed Sanford
Supervisor	Sumner Wolley

Team hotels:

Buffalo: Statler Hilton
Chicago: LaSalle
Detroit: Pontchartrain
Los Angeles: Sheraton Inn
Montreal: Sheraton Mount Royal
Minnesota: Leamington
New York: Statler Hilton
Oakland: Edgewater Inn
Philadelphia: Sheraton
Pittsburgh: Pitt Hilton
St. Louis: Chase Park Plaza
Toronto: Royal York
Vancouver: Vancouver

Trophy winners:

Prince of Wales: Boston Bruins
Hart: Bobby Orr
Ross: Phil Esposito
Norris: Bobby Orr
Lady Byng: Johnny Bucyk
Dufresne: Phil Esposito
7th Player: Fred Stanfield

All-stars:

Bobby Orr (first team)
Phil Esposito (first team)
Ken Hodge (first team)
Johnny Bucyk (first team)

1970 amateur draft

Player	Drafted from
Reggie Leach	Flin Flon
Rick MacLeish	Peterborough
Ron Plumb	Peterborough
Bob Stewart	Oshawa

Dan Bouchard	London
Ray Brownlee	U. of Brandon
Gordon Davies	Toronto
Robert Roselle	Sorel
Murray Wing	North Dakota
Glen Siddall	Kitchener

1970–71 roster

	GP	G	A	PTS	PIMS
Awrey, Don	74	4	21	25	141
Bailey, Garnet	36	0	6	6	44
Boldirev, Ivan	2	0	0	0	0
Bucyk, Johnny	78	51	65	116	8
Carleton, Wayne	69	22	24	46	44
Cashman, Wayne	77	21	58	79	100
Esposito, Phil	78	76	76	152	71
Green, Ted	78	5	37	42	60
Hodge, Ken	78	43	62	105	113
Leach, Reggie	23	2	4	6	0
Marcotte, Don	75	15	13	28	30
McKenzie, John	65	31	46	77	120
Orr, Bobby	78	37	102	139	91
Sanderson, Derek	71	29	34	63	130
Schock, Dan	2	0	0	0	0

(Traded with Rick MacLeish to Philadelphia for Mike Walton, 2/1/1971)

	GP	G	A	PTS	PIMS
Smith, Dallas	73	7	38	45	68
Smith, Rick	67	4	19	23	44
Speer, Billy	1	0	0	0	4

(Sold to Providence, 2/1971)

	GP	G	A	PTS	PIMS
Stanfield, Fred	75	24	52	76	12
Walton, Mike	22	3	5	8	10

(Acquired from Philadelphia via Toronto for Rick MacLeish & Danny Schock, 2/1/1971)

	GP	G	A	PTS	PIMS
Westfall, Eddie	78	25	34	59	48

	GP	W	L	T	GA	GAA	SO
Cheevers, Gerry	40	27	8	5	109	2.73	3

4 PIM

	GP	W	L	T	GA	GAA	SO
Johnston, Eddie	38	30	6	2	96	2.53	4

1 assist

6 PIM

Orr 1970–1971	Games played	Goals	Assists	Points
October	8	3	7	10
November	14	6	16	22
December	14	5	21	26
January	13	8	16	24
February	12	7	14	21
March	15	8	23	31
April	2	0	5	5
Total	78	37	102	139

Goals

First-period goals	11
Second-period goals	11
Third-period goals	15

Even strength	29
Power play	5
Shorthanded	3
Game winners	5

Home	22	Road	15
Vs.		Vs.	
Buffalo	2	Buffalo	2
California	2	California	5
Chicago	2	Los Angeles	1
Detroit	1	Minnesota	1

Los Angeles	2	Montreal	1
Montreal	1	New York	1
New York	3	Philadelphia	1
Philadelphia	1	Pittsburgh	2
Pittsburgh	1	Vancouver	1
St. Louis	3		
Toronto	2		
Vancouver	2		

Goaltender victims

Roger Crozier (Buffalo	2
Joe Daley (Buffalo	2
Denis DeJordy (Los Angeles)	1
Gerry Desjardins (Chicago)	1
Tony Esposito (Chicago)	1
Doug Favell (Philadelphia)	1
Bruce Gamble (Toronto)	3 (2 with Toronto, 1 with Philadelphia)
Eddie Giacomin (New York)	2
Glenn Hall (St. Louis)	2
Charlie Hodge (Vancouver)	1
Cesare Maniago (Minnesota)	1
Don McLeod (Detroit)	1
Phil Myre (Montreal)	1
Jack Norris (Los Angeles)	2
Al Smith (Pittsburgh)	3
Gary Smith (California)	5
Rogatien Vachon (Montreal)	1
Gilles Villemure (New York)	3
Ernie Wakely (St. Louis)	1
Dunc Wilson (Vancouver)	1
Chris Worthy (California)	2

1970–71 playoff roster

	GP	G	A	PTS	PIM
Awrey, Don	7	0	0	0	12
Bailey, Garnet	1	0	0	0	10
Bucyk, Johnny	7	2	5	7	0
Carleton, Wayne	4	0	0	0	0
Cashman, Wayne	7	3	2	5	15
Esposito, Phil	7	3	7	10	6
Green, Ted	7	1	0	1	25
Hodge, Ken	7	2	5	7	6
Leach, Reggie	3	0	0	0	0
Marcotte, Don	4	0	0	0	0
McKenzie, John	7	2	3	5	22
Orr, Bobby	7	5	7	12	25
Sanderson, Derek	7	2	1	3	13
Smith, Dallas	7	0	3	3	26
Smith, Rick	6	0	0	0	0
Stanfield, Fred	7	3	4	7	0
Walton, Mike	5	2	0	2	19
Westfall, Eddie	7	1	2	3	2

	GP	W	L	T	GA	GAA	SO
Cheevers, Gerry	6	3	3	0	21	3.50	0
4 PIM							
Johnston, Eddie	1	0	1	0	7	7.00	0

Orr 1971 Playoffs	Games played	Goals	Assists	Points
April	7	5	7	12

Goals
First-period goals 1
Second-period goals 2
Third-period goals 2

Even strength	3
Power play	1
Shorthanded	1
Game winners	0

Home	2		Road	3
Vs.			Vs.	
Montreal	2		Montreal	3

Goaltender victims
Ken Dryden (Montreal)   5

Frosty on His Roommate

Orr's roommate and confidante Frosty Forristall had this observation: "He's the key to everything… to the Boston Bruins, to the National Hockey League, to the whole game of hockey. And he skates like he's afraid he'll be sent back to the minors.

Orr on His Own Mistakes

"Let 'em say all the nice things, but I know I make mistakes, and I make plenty of them. They say practice makes perfect, and they're wrong. Practice'll make you better, but nothing will make you perfect. At least I'll never be. I do dumb things. Once I was rushing against the Rangers, and I crossed the blue line, and I heard a voice say, 'Drop it, drop it!' So I made this drop pass, and I skated in to screen the goalie, and by the time I turned around, Vic Hadfield was on a breakaway for New York, and he scored. He was the one saying, 'Drop it!'" (*Sports Illustrated*, December 21, 1970)

Derek Sanderson on Bobby Orr as Team Organizer

"In the old days, we'd usually play on Wednesday, Thursday, Saturday, and Sunday. On Monday, Bobby would get a bunch of us, and we would go and play different high schools. We'd show up with nothing but our skates, gloves, and sweat suits. The high school team would be in full gear, and we'd have a scrimmage. The town in which we were playing would come and jam the arena. After the scrimmage, Bobby would organize a big table and the players that came would sign autographs and greet the fans. We'd charge a dollar or two, and the town would make a few thousand dollars that would go to help the team."

Crime Does Not Pay

Marlboro, Massachusetts, police arrested Edward MacPherson of Framingham for passing around pictures of Bobby Orr at a local pub. The problem was that the picture of Orr appeared in the middle of a $10 bill. MacPherson was charged with larceny and passing counterfeit bills.

How Much Beer Will That Mug Hold?

Orr became the second Boston-based player, Carl Yastrzemski of the Red Sox being the first, to win the *Sports Illustrated*'s Man of the Year. The Grecian urn, as opposed to the Roman urn, has a capacity of 10.3 gallons. The Roman urn has a capacity of 6.7 gallons.

Down Goes Frazier, Down Goes Frazier

The boxing world had an impending "large bout" featuring Mohammed Ali versus Joe Frazier to be held at Madison Square Garden. Each fighter will receive $2.5 million dollars. The fight will be shown in theaters and closed-circuit television. Among the distributors will be United Artists theaters, and the Loew's theater group. Hollywood entertainers Andy Williams and Sergio Mendes are distributing throughout the south and midwest while Bobby Orr would be part of the group distributing in Canada.

The Philadelphia Story

The Philadelphia Sportswriters Association honored Bobby Orr as the professional athlete of the year. Notre Dame quarterback Joe Theismann was honored as the amateur athlete of the year.

Jim Krulicki, New York Rangers

Jim Krulicki played twenty-seven games for the New York Rangers during the 1970–71 season.

"When I was playing junior hockey against Orr, I came into the OHL as a seventeen-year-old. Orr was a seventeen-year-old at the time, and we were only a few days apart in age. He was entering his third year in the league, and I was entering my first year in the league, so his reputation was pretty large then. He used to dominate players in junior hockey, but he dominated at the NHL level even more so than at the junior level. I remember going out against the Bruins and thinking this guy is even better than before."

News from 1971

- US population was 207,660,677 with unemployment at 4.9 percent.
- US Supreme Court ruled that busing of students may be ordered to achieve racial desegregation.
- Pentagon Papers were published on June 13.
- Twenty-Sixth Amendment to the US Constitution was passed, lowering the voting age to eighteen.
- Twelve thousand were arrested in Washington, DC, as militants attempted to disrupt government business.
- Cost of a first-class stamp was raised from .06 to .08 cents on May 16.
- *All in the Family* debuts on CBS television network.
- *Patton* won the Academy Award for best movie.
- Other movies released during 1971 include *A Clockwork Orange, The French Connection, Fiddler on the Roof,* and *The Last Picture Show.*
- "Bridge over Troubled Water" won record of the year, song of the year, and Album of the Year.
- Jim Morrison of the *Doors* and Duane Allman of the Allman Brothers, along with J. C. Penney of merchandising fame, passed away.
- Dow Jones average on 12/31/1971: $890.20.
- Top television shows: *Marcus Welby, MD, The Flip Wilson Show, Here's Lucy, Ironside, Gunsmoke.*

1971–1972: Redemption

Owner:	Boston Professional Hockey Association
Governor:	Weston Adams Jr.
General Manager:	Milt Schmidt
Coach:	Tom Johnson
Trainers:	Dan Canney and John Forristall
Publicity Director;	Herb Ralby
Club colors:	Black and gold
Home:	Boston Garden
Training camp:	London, Ontario
Radio:	WBZ (1030)
Announcer:	Bob Wilson and Ron Cantera
Television:	WSBK (TV 38)
Announcers:	Fred Cusick and Johnny Peirson
Attendance:	574,805 (14,995 average)

Minor officials:		
	Scorer	Woody Dumart
	Game timer	Tony Notagiacomo
	Penalty time	Sonny Hunter
	Goal judges	Benny Bertini, Ed Sandford, Bernie Bailey
	Statistician	John Carlton

Team hotels:	Buffalo (Statler Hilton)
	Chicago (Marriott)
	Detroit (Pontchartain)
	Los Angeles (Sheraton Inn)
	Montreal (Sheraton Mount Royal)
	Minnesota (Marriott)
	New York (Statler Hilton)
	Oakland (Edgewater Inn)
	Philadelphia (Marriott)
	Pittsburgh (Pitt Hilton)
	St. Louis (Chase Park Plaza)
	Toronto (Royal York)
	Vancouver (Vancouver)

Trophy winners:	Stanley Cup: Boston Bruins
	Prince of Wales: Boston Bruins
	Hart: Bobby Orr
	Ross: Phil Esposito
	Norris: Bobby Orr
	Conn Smythe: Bobby Orr
	Lester Patrick: Cooney Weiland
	Dufresne: Bobby Orr
	7th Player: Derek Sanderson
All-stars:	Bobby Orr: first team
	Phil Esposito: first team

1971 amateur draft	Player	Drafted from
	Ron Jones	Edmonton
	Terry O'Reilly	Oshawa
	Curt Ridley	Portage la Prairi Jr.
	Dave Bonter	Estevan
	Dave Hynes	Harvard
	Bert Scott	Edmonton
	Bob McMahon	St. Catherines

1971–72 roster

	GP	G	A	PTS	PIM
Awrey, Don	34	1	8	9	52
Bailey, Garnet	73	9	13	22	64
Beverley, Nick	1	0	0	0	0
Boldirev, Ivan	11	0	2	2	6

(Traded to California for Richie Leduc and Chris Oddleifson, 11/17/1971)

	GP	G	A	PTS	PIM
Bucyk, Johnny	78	32	51	83	4
Cashman, Wayne	74	23	29	52	103
Esposito, Phil	76	66	67	133	76
Green, Ted	54	1	16	17	21
Hodge, Ken	60	16	40	56	81
Jones, Ron	1	0	0	0	0
Leach, Reggie	6	7	13	20	12

(Traded with Rick Smith and Bob Stewart to California for Carol Vadnais and Don O'Donoghue, 2/23/1972)

	GP	G	A	PTS	PIM
Marcotte, Don	47	6	4	10	12
McKenzie, John	77	22	47	69	126
O'Reilly, Terry	1	1	0	1	0
Orr, Bobby	76	37	80	117	106
Peters, Garry	1	0	0	0	0
Ravlich, Matt	25	0	1	1	2
Roberts, Doug	3	1	0	1	0

(Acquired from California for cash, 9/4/1971)

	GP	G	A	PTS	PIM
Sanderson, Derek	78	25	33	58	108
Smith, Dallas	78	8	22	30	132
Smith, Rick	61	2	12	14	46

(Traded with Reggie Leach and Bob Stewart to California for Carol Vadnais and Don O'Donoghue, 2/23/1972)

	GP	G	A	PTS	PIM
Stanfield, Fred	78	23	56	79	12
Stewart, Bob	8	0	0	0	15
Vadnais, Carol	16	4	6	10	37

(Acquired with Don O'Donoghue from California for Reggie Leach, Bob Stewart & Rick Smith, 2/23/1972)

Walton, Mike	76	28	28	56	45
Westfall, Eddie	78	18	26	44	19

	GP	W	L	T	GA	GAA	SO
Cheevers, Gerry	41	27	5	8	101	2.50	2
2 points							
25 PIM							
Johnston, Eddie	38	27	8	3	102	2.71	2
4 assists							

Orr 1971–1972	Games played	Goals	Assists	Points
October	10	4	13	17
November	12	7	15	22
December	13	5	10	15
January	14	5	12	17
February	14	8	20	28
March	13	8	10	18
April	0	0	0	0
Total	76	37	80	117

Goals

First-period goals	10
Second-period goals	17
Third-period goals	10

Even strength	22
Power play	11
Shorthanded	4
Game winners	4

Home	22	Road	15
Vs.		Vs.	
Buffalo	2	Buffalo	1

Chicago	2	California	1
Detroit	2	Detroit	1
Los Angeles	3	Los Angeles	2
Minnesota	2	Minnesota	1
New York	2	Montreal	1
Philadelphia	2	New York	2
Pittsburgh	2	Philadelphia	1
St. Louis	1	Pittsburgh	1
Vancouver	4	St. Louis	1
Toronto	1		
Vancouver	2		

Goaltender victims

Les Binkley (Pittsburgh)	3
Andy Brown (Detroit)	1
Roger Crozier (Buffalo)	3
Joe Daley (Detroit)	1
Ken Dryden (Montreal)	2
Gary Edwards (Los Angeles)	5
Tony Esposito (Chicago)	1
Doug Favell (Philadelphia)	3
George Gardner (Vancouver)	1
Eddie Giacomin (New York)	3
Cesare Maniago (Minnesota)	1
Jim McLeod (St. Louis)	1
Gilles Meloche (California)	1
Jacques Plante (Toronto)	1
Al Smith (Detroit)	1
Gary Smith (Chicago)	1
Wayne Stephenson (St. Louis)	1
Gilles Villemure (New York)	1
Dunc Wilson (Vancouver)	4
Gump Worsley (Minnesota)	2

1971–72 playoff roster

	GP	G	A	PTS	PIM
Awrey, Don	15	0	4	4	45
Bailey, Garnet	13	2	4	6	16
Bucyk, Johnny	15	9	11	20	6
Cashman, Wayne	15	4	7	11	42
Esposito, Phil	15	9	15	24	24
Green, Ted	10	0	0	0	0
Hayes, Chris	1	0	0	0	0
Hodge, Ken	15	9	8	17	62
Marcotte, Don	14	3	0	3	6
McKenzie, John	15	5	12	17	37
Orr, Bobby	15	5	19	24	19
Peters, Garry	1	0	0	0	0
Sanderson, Derek	11	1	1	2	44
Smith, Dallas	15	0	4	4	22
Stanfield, Fred	15	7	9	16	0
Vadnais, Carol	15	0	2	2	43
Walton, Mike	15	6	6	12	13
Westfall, Eddie	15	4	3	7	10

	GP	W	L	T	GA	GAA	SO
Cheevers, Gerry	8	6	2	0	21	2.61	2
Johnston, Eddie	7	6	1	0	13	1.86	1

1972 Playoffs	Games played	Goals	Assists	Points
April–May	15	5	19	24

Goals

First-period goals	3
Second-period goals	1
Third-period goals	1

Even strength	1
Power play	4
Shorthanded	0
Game winners	1

Home	0	Road	5
		Vs.	
		New York	4
		Toronto	1

Goaltender victims

Eddie Giacomin (New York)	3
Bernie Parent (Toronto)	1
Gilles Villemure (New York)	1

But Can He Make the 7–10 Split?

On September 24, Bobby Orr filed a $100,000 suit against a Watertown sports company for using his name and image on clothing and pillowcases without his permission. Judge Reuben Lurie of Middlesex Superior Court issued the restraining order against Lubin's Rink and Bowling Supply Company. The company had asked permission to use Orr's name and picture but had never been granted the rights.

The suit was finally settled prior to the opening of the season. Max Lubin, the owner of the Lubin's Rink and Bowling Supply Company was to sell the remaining inventory of goods. Orr will receive a 5 percent royalty on the remaining sales. A royalty payment of $2,500 was made to Orr.

How to Be in the Wrong Place at the Wrong Time

How's this for being in the wrong place at the wrong time. Veteran Ron Stewart, a Bruin forward from a few seasons back, was sitting on the bench when a Vancouver clearing pass was deflected by Orr right into Stewart's jaw. Stewart was taken to Massachusetts General Hospital, where he was treated for a broken jaw.

Go to the Head of the Class

"Orr was the best player I ever saw. He's also the classiest. He was a classy guy, but so were guys like Gilbert and Ratelle. Orr, Ratelle, and Gilbert carried themselves on and off the ice like you wish you would have" (Jack Egers, forward, New York Rangers).

News From 1972

- President Nixon made an eight-day visit to Communist China on February 17.
- Nixon ordered Christmas bombing of North Vietnam.
- Britain took over direct rule of Northern Ireland.
- Eleven Israeli athletes were killed by Arab terrorists at the Summer Olympic Games held in Munich, Germany. Five of the terrorists and one policeman were also killed.
- US Supreme Court ruled the death penalty unconstitutional.
- Governor George Wallace of Alabama was shot and paralyzed by Arthur Bremer at Laurel, Maryland. Wallace was running for the Democratic nomination for president of the United States.
- The Watergate Scandal erupted when five men were arrested by police for attempting to bug the Democratic National Committee headquarters at the Watergate Complex in Washington, DC.
- US population was 209,896,021 with unemployment at 5.9 percent.
- The first pay cable network, HBO, was launched by Time Inc.
- *The French Connection* won the Academy Award for best movie.

- Other movies released in 1972 included *The Godfather*, *Deliverance*, *Cabaret*, and *Sleuth*.
- Carole King swept the Grammy's with "It's Too Late" as record of the year, "You've Got a Friend" as song of the year, and *Tapestry* as Album of the Year.
- CAT scanning was developed in England.
- The compact disc was developed by RCA.
- Electronic mail was introduced.
- The last manned moon landing, *Apollo XVII*, returned to Earth.
- Former President Harry Truman, FBI Director J. Edgar Hoover, and baseball great Gill Hodges all passed away.
- Dow Jones average on 12/31/1972: $1,031.68. The Dow industrial average climbed over the 1,000 mark for the first time on November 14.
- Top television shows: *All in the Family*, *The Flip Wilson Show*, *Marcus Welby, MD*, *Gunsmoke*, *ABC Movie of the Week*.

1972–1973: The Long Drought Commences

Owner:	Boston Professional Hockey Association
	Storer Broadcasting (December 7)
Governor:	Weston Adams Jr.
General Manager:	Harry Sinden
Coaches:	Tom Johnson and Bep Guidolin
Trainer:	Dan Canney, John "Frosty" Forristall
Publicity Director	Les Stout, Herb Ralby
Club colors:	Black and gold
Home:	Boston Garden
Training camp:	London, Ontario
Radio:	WBZ (1030)
Announcers:	Bob Wilson and Ron Cantera
Television:	WSBK (TV 38)
Announcers:	Fred Cusick and Johnny Peirson
Attendance:	585,117 (15,003 average)

Minor officials:	Scorer	Benny Bertini
	Game timer	Tony Notagiacomo
	Penalty timer	Sonny Hunter
	Goal judges	Bernie Bailey, Art Johnson, Ed Sandford

Statistician	Robert Rand
Spare official	John Carlton

Team hotels:

Atlanta: Marriott
Buffalo: Statler Hilton
Chicago: Marriott
Detroit: Pontchatrain
Los Angeles: Sheraton Inn
Montreal: Chateau Champlain
Minnesota: Marriott
New York Islanders: Holiday Inn, Hempstead
New York Rangers: Statler Hilton
Oakland: Edgewater Inn
Philadelphia: Sheraton
Pittsburgh: Pitt Hilton
St. Louis: Chase Park Plaza
Toronto: Royal York
Vancouver: Vancouver

Trophy winners:

Ross: Phil Esposito
Norris: Bobby Orr
Dufresne: Phil Esposito
7th Player: Dallas Smith
Phil Esposito wins the Lou Marsh Trophy as Canada's outstanding athlete for 1972.

All-stars:

Bobby Orr (first team)
Phil Esposito (first team)

1972 amateur draft

Player	Drafted from
Mike Bloom	St. Catherines
Wayne Elder	London
Michel Boudreau	Laval
Les Jackson	New Westminster
Brian Coates	Brandon
Peter Gaw	Ottawa

Gordie Clark   New Hampshire
Roy Carmichael   New Westminster

1972–73 roster

	GP	G	A	PTS	PIM
Awrey, Don	78	2	17	19	90
Bailey, Garnet	57	8	13	21	89
Beverley, Nick	76	1	10	11	26
Bucyk, John	78	40	53	93	12
Cashman, Wayne	76	29	39	68	100
Doak, Gary	5	0	0	0	2

(Acquired from Detroit for Ace Bailey and future considerations, Murray Wing, 6/4/1974, 3/1/1973)

	GP	G	A	PTS	PIM
Esposito, Phil	78	55	75	130	87
Hodge, Ken	73	37	44	81	58
Jones, Ron	7	0	0	0	2
Leduc, Richie	5	1	1	2	2
Marcotte, Don	78	24	31	55	49
O'Donnell, Fred	72	10	4	14	55
O'Reilly, Terry	72	5	22	27	109
Oddleifson, Chris	6	0	0	0	0
Orr, Bobby	63	29	72	101	99
Ravlich, Matt	5	0	1	1	0
Roberts, Doug	45	4	7	11	26
Sanderson, Derek	25	5	10	15	38
Sheppard, Greg	64	24	26	50	18
Smith, Dallas	78	4	27	31	72
Stanfield, Fred	78	20	58	78	10
Vadnais, Carol	78	7	24	31	72
Walton, Mike	56	25	22	47	37

	GP	W	L	T	GA	GAA	SO
Adams, John	14	9	3	1	39	3.00	1
Brooks, Ross	16	11	1	3	40	2.64	1
1 assist							
Johnston, Ed	45	24	17	1	137	3.27	5
1 assist							
2 PIM							
Plante, Jacques	8	7	1	0	16	2.00	2

(Acquired with third-round draft pick in 1973 from Toronto for 1973 first-round draft pick and future considerations (Ed Johnston, 5/22/1973)

2 assists

2 PIM

Orr 1972–1973	Games played	Goals	Assists	Points
October	3	1	2	3
November	7	7	6	13
December	12	2	13	15
January	13	2	21	23
February	13	6	16	22
March	14	11	13	24
April	1	0	1	1
Total	63	29	72	101

Goals

First-period goals	15
Second-period goals	6
Third-period goals	8

Even strength	21
Power play	7
Shorthanded	1
Game winners	3

Home	15	Road	14
Vs.	Vs.		
Atlanta	1	Atlanta	2
Buffalo	4	Buffalo	3
California	2	Chicago	1
Los Angeles	1	Minnesota	1
Minnesota	1	Islanders	1
Rangers	1	Philadelphia	1
Philadelphia	1	St. Louis	1
Pittsburgh	1	Toronto	3
St. Louis	1	Vancouver	1
Toronto	1		
Vancouver	14		

Goaltender victims

Dan Bouchard (Atlanta)	1
Jacques Caron (St Louis)	1
Roger Crozier (Buffalo)	6
Gerry Desjardins (Islanders)	1
Dave Dryden (Buffalo)	1
Ed Dyck (Vancouver)	1
Gary Edwards (Los Angeles)	1
Tony Esposito (Chicago)	1
Doug Favell (Philadelphia)	2
Eddie Giacomin (New York)	1
Gilles Gilbert (Minnesota)	1
Cesare Maniago (Minnesota)	1
Gord McRae (Toronto)	3
Gilles Meloche (California)	2
Phil Myre (Atlanta)	2
Cam Newton (Pittsburgh)	1
Jacques Plante (Toronto)	1
Wayne Stephenson (St. Louis)	1
Dunc Wilson (Vancouver)	1

1972–73 playoff roster

	GP	G	A	PTS	PIM
Awrey, Don	4	0	0	0	6
Beverley, Nick	4	0	0	0	0
Bucyk, John	5	0	3	3	0
Cashman, Wayne	5	1	1	2	4
Doak, Gary	2	0	0	0	2
Esposito, Phil	2	0	1	1	2
Hodge, Ken	5	1	0	1	7
Marcotte, Don	5	1	1	2	0
O'Donnell, Fred	5	0	1	1	5
O'Reilly, Terry	5	0	0	0	2
Orr, Bobby	5	1	1	2	7
Roberts, Doug	5	2	0	2	6
Sanderson, Derek	5	1	2	3	13
Sheppard, Greg	5	2	1	3	0
Smith, Dallas	5	0	2	2	2
Stanfield, Fred	5	1	1	2	0
Vadnais, Carol		0	0	0	8
Walton, Mike	5	1	1	2	2

	GP	W	L	T	GA	GAA	SO
Brooks, Ross	1	0	0	0	3	9.00	0
Johnston, Ed	3	1	2	0	9	3.38	0
Plante, Jacques	2	0	2	0	10	5.00	0

Orr 1973 Playoffs	Games played	Goals	Assists	Points
April	5	1	1	2

Goals

First-period goals	1
Second-period goals	0
Third-period goals	0

Even strength	1
Power play	0
Shorthanded	0
Game winners	0

Home	1	Road	0
Vs.			
Rangers	1		

Goaltender victims
Eddie Giacomin (New York)   1

Orr in Critical Condition

In a brief note written by Bob Kinsley in the *Boston Globe*, a reference was made to comments by Arva Orr, mother of Bobby. Keep in mind that an oxygen tent saved Bobby's life. The situation was quite critical in the first few days of Bobby's life. Orr was born at St. Francis Hospital in Parry Sound, Ontario.

Coping with Tension

A feature from Neil Singelais of the *Boston Globe* spoke of "how athletes cope with tension." According to Bruins' trainer Dan Canney, "Bobby comes in very early the night of a game—around four o'clock. He works on his sticks and maybe watches the end of a movie on TV. He's generally very quiet.

Eddie Johnston on the 1973 Playoff Loss to New York

The Rangers did a little different strategy against Orr. His knee was a little bad that year too, but they would double team him when he was bringing the puck out, and then he would have to pass off and then the Rangers would try to intercept the pass.

"We knew what the Rangers were doing. They were dumping the puck in his corner so they knew where the puck was and they would send two guys on him right away, make him get rid of the puck. They didn't want him carrying the puck because he would make the plays and do everything else. So they wanted him to get rid of the puck."

News from 1973

- US population was 211,908,788 while unemployment rate is 4.9 percent.
- A cease-fire was signed ending involvement of American groud troops in the Vietnam War.
- OPEC raised price of crude oil to punish the west for its involvement in the Yom Kippur War.
- President Nixon accepted responsibility for Watergate but not blame as he accepted the resignations of H. R. Haldeman and John Ehrlichman and fires John Dean.
- Spiro Agnew resigned as vice president and pleaded no contest to charges of evasion of income taxes while governor of Maryland.
- President Nixon fired special Watergate prosecutor Archibald Cox and Deputy Attorney William Ruckelshaus while Attorney General Elliot Richardson resigned in what came to be known as the Saturday Night Massacre.
- US Supreme Court ruled in *Roe v. Wade* the legalization of abortion in the first trimester of pregnancy.
- *The Godfather* won the Academy Award for best picture of the year. Sacheen Littlefeather stands in for Marlon Brando, who refused to accept his best actor Oscar, protesting the US government's treatment of Native Americans.
- Other movies that made their debut include *American Grafitti*, *The Exorcist*, and *The Sting*. Record of the year and song of the year. "The First Time

Ever I Saw Your Face" belonged to Roberta Flack while "The Concert for Bengladesh" won Album of the Year.

- Skylab, the first American space station, was launched.
- Transmission Control Protocol/Internet Protocol (TCP/IP) was designed and would become the standard for communicating between computers.
- Former President Lyndon Johnson, author Pearl Buck, actress Betty Grable and, painter Pablo Picasso were among the celebrity deaths in 1973.
- Dow Jones average on 12/31/1973: $866.32.
- Top television shows: *All in the Family, Sanford and Son, Hawaii Five-0, Maude, Bridget Loves Bernie.*

1973–1974: One Last Crack at the Cup

Owner:	Storer Broadcasting Company
Governor:	Weston Adams Jr.
General Manager:	Harry Sinden
Coach:	Bep Guidolin
Trainers:	Dan Canney, John "Frosty" Forristall
Publicity Director:	Herb Ralby
Chief Scout:	Gary Darling
Club colors:	Black and gold
Home:	Boston Garden
Training camp:	Fitchburg, Massachusetts
Radio:	WBZ (1030)
Announcers:	Bob Wilson and Ron Cantera
Television:	WSBK (TV 38)
Announcers:	Fred Cusick and John Peirson
Attendance:	578,874 (14,842 average)

Minor officials:	Scorer	Ben Bertini
	Game timer	Tony Notagiacomo
	Penalty timer	Sonny Hunter
	Goal judges	Bernie Bailey, Art Johnson, Ed Sandford

Statistician	Robert Rand
Spare official	John Carlton

Team hotels:

Atlanta: Marriott
Buffalo: Statler Hilton
Chicago: Marriott
Detroit: Pontchartrain
Los Angeles: Sheraton Inn
Montreal: Chateau Champlain
Minnesota: Marriott
New York Islanders: Island Inn
New York Rangers: Statler Hilton
Oakland: Edgewater Inn
Philadelphia: Sheraton
Pittsburgh: Pitt Hilton
St. Louis: Chase Park Plaza
Toronto: Sutton Place
Vancouver: Vancouver

Trophy winners:

Prince of Wales: Boston Bruins
Hart: Phil Esposito
Ross: Phil Esposito
Norris: Bobby Orr
Lady Byng: Johnny Bucyk
Lester Patrick: Weston Adams Sr.
Dufresne: Phil Esposito and Bobby Orr
7th Player: Carol Vadnais and Don Marcotte
Three-Star: Bobby Orr

All-stars:

Bobby Orr (first team)
Phil Esposito (first team)
Ken Hodge (first team)
Wayne Cashman (second team)

1973 amateur draft

Player	Drafted from
Andre Savard	Quebec

Jimmy Jones	Peterborough
Doug Gibson	Peterborough
Al Sims	Cornwall
Steve Langdon	London
Peter Crosbie	London
Jean Pierre Bougouyne	Shawinigan
Walter Johnson	Oshawa
Virgil Gates	Swift Current
Jim Pettie	St. Catherines
Yvan Boullion	Cornwall

1973–74 roster

	GP	G	A	PTS	PIM
Beverley, Nick	1	0	0	0	0
Bucyk, Johnny	76	31	44	75	8
Cashman, Wayne	78	30	59	89	111
Doak, Gary	69	0	4	4	44
Edestrand, Darryl	52	3	8	11	20
(Acquired from Pittsburgh for Nick Beverley, 10/25/1973)					
Esposito, Phil	78	68	77	145	58
Forbes, Dave	63	10	16	26	41
Gibson, Doug	2	0	0	0	0
Gryp, Bob	1	0	0	0	0
Hodge, Ken	76	50	55	105	43
Hynes, Dave	3	0	0	0	0
Leduc, Richie	28	3	3	6	12
Marcotte, Don	78	24	26	50	18
O'Donnell, Fred	43	5	7	12	43
(Traded with Chris Oddleifson and Mike Walton for Bobby Schmautz, 2/7/1974)					
O'Reilly, Terry	76	11	24	35	94
Oddleifson, Chris	49	10	11	21	25
(Traded with Fred O'Donnell and Mike Walton for Bobby Schmautz, 2/7/1974)					
Orr, Bobby	74	32	90	122	82
Roberts, Doug	7	0	1	1	2

(Acquired from Detroit for cash, 11/22/1973)

Sanderson, Derek	29	8	12	20	48
Savard, Andre	72	16	14	30	39
Schmautz, Bobby	27	7	13	20	31

(Acquired from Vancouver for Chris Oddleifson, Fred O'Donnell, and Mike Walton, 2/7/1974)

Sheppard, Greg	5	16	31	47	21	
Simmons, Al	3	0	0	0	0	
Sims, Al		77	3	9	12	22
Smith, Dallas	77	6	21	27	64	
Vadnais, Carol	78	16	43	59	123	

	GP	W	L	T	GA	GAA	SO
Broderick, Ken	5	2	2	1	16	3.20	0

1 assist

Acquired from San Diego (WHL) for cash, 3/10/1973

	GP	W	L	T	GA	GAA	SO
Brooks, Ross	21	16	3	0	46	2.36	3

2 PIM

	GP	W	L	T	GA	GAA	SO
Gilbert, Gilles	54	34	12	8	158	2.95	6

1 assist

9 PIM

Acquired from Minnesota for Fred Stanfield, 5/22/1973

Orr 1973–1974	Games played	Goals	Assists	Points
October	10	5	13	18
November	12	7	13	20
December	11	5	12	17
January	13	6	16	22
February	9	2	13	15
March	16	5	17	22
April	3	2	4	6
Total	74	32	88	120

Goals

First-period goals	6
Second-period goals	12
Third-period goals	14

Even strength	21
Power play	11
Shorthanded	0
Game winners	4

Home	19	Road	13	
Vs.		Vs.		
Buffalo	2	Buffalo		1
California	1	Los Angeles	1	
Los Angeles	2	Minnesota	2	
Islanders	1	Islanders	1	
Rangers	3	Rangers	3	
Pittsburgh	2	Philadelphia	3	
St. Louis	3	Pittsburgh	1	
Toronto	2	St. Louis	1	
Vancouver	3			

Goaltender victims

Andy Brown (Pittsburgh)	2
John Davidson (St. Louis)	1
Gerry Desjardins (Islanders)	1
Dave Dryden (Buffalo)	3
Ed Dyck (Vancouver)	2
Gary Edwards (Los Angeles)	2
Tony Esposito (Chicago)	1
Eddie Giacomin (Rangers)	4
Gary Inness (Pittsburgh)	1
Cesare Maniago (Minnesota)	2
Peter McDuffe (Rangers)	2
Bernie Parent (Philadelphia)	1

Gary Smith (Vancouver)   2
Wayne Stephenson (St. Louis)   2
Bobby Taylor (Philadelphia)   2
Rogatien Vachon (Los Angeles)   1
Jim Watt (St. Louis)   1
Dunc Wilson (Toronto)   2

1973–74 playoff roster

	GP	G	A	PTS	PIM
Bucyk, Johnny	16	8	10	18	4
Cashman, Wayne	16	5	9	14	46
Edestrand, Darryl	16	1	2	3	15
Esposito, Phil	6	9	5	14	25
Forbes, Dave	16	0	2	2	6
Gibson, Doug	1	0	0	0	0
Hodge, Ken	16	6	10	16	16
Leduc, Richie	5	0	0	0	9
Marcotte, Don	16	4	2	6	8
O'Reilly, Terry	16	2	5	7	38
Orr, Bobby	16	4	14	18	28
Savard, Andre	16	3	2	5	24
Schmautz, Bobby	16	3	6	9	44
Sheppard, Greg	16	11	8	19	4
Simmons, Al	1	0	0	0	0
Sims, Al	16	0	0	0	2
Smith, Dallas	16	1	7	8	20
Vadnais, Carol	16	1	12	13	42

	GP	W	L	T	GA	GAA	SO
Gilbert, Gilles	16	10	6	0	43	2.64	1

3 assists
8 PIM

Orr 1974 PLAYOFFS	Games played	Goals	Assists	Points
April/ May	16	4	14	18

Goals

First-period goals	0
Second-period goals	2
Third-period goals	2

Even strength	3
Power play	1
Shorthanded	0
Game winners	2

Home	3	Road	1
Vs.		Vs.	
Philadelphia	3	Toronto	1

Goaltender victims

Doug Favell (Toronto)	1
Bernie Parent (Philadelphia)	3

Gene Carr of the New York Rangers

Gene Carr played parts of three seasons with the Rangers. He was known for his road runner speed and quickness. "Well, I can tell you that there was nobody quicker than me. Probably one guy that was quicker than anybody on the planet was Bobby Orr. I think Orr was faster than me, but I was probably in the top three or four in the league.

The Trophy Case Is Full

Orr's winning of the Norris Trophy gave him thirteen NHL awards in his eight-year career, more than any player in history. The old record of twelve was held by Gordie Howe of the Detroit Red Wings.

News from 1974

- House Judiciary Committee adopted three articles of impeachment against President Richard Nixon, charging him with obstruction of justice, failure to uphold laws, and refusal to produce material subpoenaed by the committee. President Nixon resigned as president of the United States on August 9.
- Vice President Gerald Ford succeeded Nixon and became the thirty-eighth president of the United States. Ford granted Nixon a full and absolute pardon on September 8.
- Patricia Hearst, nineteen-year-old daughter of publisher Randolph Hearst, was kidnapped by the Symbionese Liberation Army on February 5.
- US population stood at 213,853,928 with unemployment at 5.6 percent.
- The cost of a first-class stamp rose from 0.08 to 0.10 as of March 2.
- OPEC lifted the oil embargo begun in 1973 during the Yom Kippur War.
- *People Magazine*, with Mia Farrow on the cover, made its debut.
- *The Sting* won the Oscar for best movie while *Chinatown*, *Blazing Saddles*, *The Godfather II*, and *The Towering Inferno* made their debuts.
- For the second year in a row, Roberta Flack won record of the year and song of the year. This time, the hit tune was "Killing Me Softly with His Song." Album of the Year was *Innervisions* by Stevie Wonder.
- The first punk rock single, "Hey Joe," is released by Patti Smith.
- Celebrities passing away in 1974 include comedian Bud Abbott, baseball great Dizzy Dean, musician Duke Ellington, Aviator Charles Lindbergh, and television personality Ed Sullivan.
- Dow Jones average on 12/31/1974: $632.04.
- Top television shows: *All in the Family*, *The Waltons*, *Sanford and Son*, *M*A*S*H*, *Hawaii Five-0*.

1974–1975: The Bleeding Accelerates

Owner:	Storer Broadcasting Company
Governor:	Weston Adams Jr.
General Manager:	Harry Sinden
Coach:	Don Cherry
Trainer:	Dan Canney, Frosty Forristall
Publicity Director:	Nate Greenberg
Chief Scout:	Gary Darling
Club colors:	Black and gold
Home:	Boston Garden
Training camp:	Fitchburg, Massachusetts
Radio:	WBZ (1030)
Announcers:	Bob Wilson
Television:	WSBK (TV 38)
Announcers:	Fred Cusick and John Peirson
Attendance:	585,514 (14,637 average)

Minor officials:		
	Scorers	Benny Bertini, Ed Sandford
	Game timer	Tony Notagiacomo
	Penalty timer	Sonny Hunter
	Goal judges	Bernie Bailey, Art Johnson, Larry Stafford
	Statistician	Robert Rand

Team hotels:

Atlanta: Marriott Motor Hotel
Buffalo: Holiday Inn Airport
California: Edgewater Hyatt House
Chicago: Chicago Marriott
Detroit: Pontchatrain
Kansas City: Plaza Inn
Los Angeles: Sheraton Inn Airport
Minnesota: Bloomington Marriott Inn
Montreal: Le Chateau Champlain
New York Islanders: Island Inn Motor Hotel
New York Rangers: Statler Hilton Hotel
Philadelphia: Hilton Inn
Pittsburgh: Pitt Hilton
St. Louis: Chase Park Plaza
Toronto: Sutton Place Hotel
Vancouver: Hotel Vancouver
Washington: Sheraton Inn Washington NE

Trophy winners:

Ross: Bobby Orr
Norris: Bobby Orr
Dufresne: Bobby Orr
7th Player: Terry O'Reilly
Three Star: Phil Esposito

All-stars:

Bobby Orr (first team)
Phil Esposito (second team)

1974 amateur draft

Player	Drafted from
Don Larway	Swift Current
Mark Howe	Toronto
Peter Sturgeon	Kitchener
Tom Edur	Toronto
Bill Reed	Sault Ste. Marie
Jim Bateman	Quebec
Bill Best	Sudbury

Ray Maluta	Flin Flon
Darryl Drader	North Dakota
Peter Roberts	St. Cloud Jr.
Peter Waselovich	North Dakota

1974–75 roster

	GP	G	A	PTS	PIM
Anderson, Earl	19	2	4	6	4
(Acquired with Hank Nowak from Detroit for Walt McKechnie, 2/18/1975)					
Bucyk, Johnny	78	29	52	81	10
Cashman, Wayne	42	11	22	33	24
Clark, Gordie	1	0	0	0	0
Doak, Gary	40	0	0	0	30
Edestrand, Darryl	68	1	9	10	56
Esposito, Phil	79	61	66	127	62
Forbes, Dave	69	18	12	30	80
Graham, Rod	14	2	1	3	7
Hodge, Ken	72	23	43	66	90
Hynes, Dave	19	4	0	4	2
Langdon, Steve	1	0	1	1	0
Marcotte, Don	80	31	33	64	76
McKechnie, Walt	53	3	3	6	8
(Acquired from New York Rangers for Derek Sanderson, 6/12/1974)					
(Traded to Detroit for Earl Anderson and Hank Nowak, 2/18/1975)					
Nowak, Hank	21	4	7	11	26
Acquired with Earl Anderson from Detroit for Walt McKechnie, 2/18/1975					
O'Reilly, Terry	68	15	20	35	146
Orr, Bobby	80	46	89	135	101
Rathwell, Jake	1	0	0	0	0
Sarner, Craig	7	0	0	0	0
Savard, Andre	77	19	25	44	45
Schmautz, Bobby	56	21	30	51	63
Sheppard, Greg	76	30	48	78	19
Sims, Al	65	4	8	12	73

Smith, Dallas	79	3	20	23	84
Vadnais, Carol	79	18	56	74	129

	GP	W	L	T	GA	GAA	SO
Broderick, Ken	15	7	6	0	32	2.39	1
2 pim							
Brooks, Ross	17	10	3	3	48	2.98	0
Gilbert, Gilles	53	23	17	11	158	3.13	3
1 assist							
10 pim							

Orr 1974–1975	Games played	Goals	Assists	Points
October	9	4	11	15
November	14	11	15	26
December	13	8	19	27
January	13	7	10	17
February	14	6	16	22
March	14	8	14	22
April	3	2	2	4
Total	80	46	87	133

Goals

First-period goals	17
Second-period goals	18
Third-period goals	11

Even strength	28
Power play	16
Shorthanded	2
Game winners	4

Home	33	Road	13
Vs.		Vs.	

Atlanta	3	Atlanta	2
Buffalo	2	California	1
California	3	Detroit	2
Chicago	1	Montreal	1
Detroit	2	Rangers	1
Kansas City	1	Pittsburgh	4
Los Angeles	1	St. Louis	1
Minnesota	1	Vancouver	1
Montreal	2		
Islanders	2		
Rangers	1		
Philadelphia	1		
Pittsburgh	1		
St. Louis	2		
Toronto	2		
Washington	8		

Goaltender victims

Michel Belhumeur (Washington)	1
Dan Boushard (Atlanta)	2
Gary Bromley (Buffalo)	2
John Davidson (St. Louis)	3
Ken Dryden (Montreal)	3
Gary Edwards (Los Angeles)	1
Eddie Giacomin (Rangers)	1
Gary Inness (Pittsburgh)	4
Ron Low (Washington)	7
Cesare Maniago (Minnesota)	1
Bill McKenzie (Detroit)	1
Gord McRae (Toronto)	3
Gilles Meloche (California)	3
Phil Myre (Atlanta)	3
Bernie Parent (Philadelphia)	1
Michel Plasse (Pittsburgh)	1
Curt Ridley (Rangers)	1

Jim Rutherford (Detroit)   3

Gary Simmons (California)   1

Billy Smith (Islanders)   2

Gary Smith (Vancouver)   1

Mike Veisor (Chicago)   1

1973–74 playoff roster

	GP	G	A	PTS	PIM
Bucyk, Johnny	16	8	10	18	4
Cashman, Wayne	16	5	9	14	46
Edestrand, Darryl	16	1	2	3	15
Esposito, Phil	16	9	5	14	25
Forbes, Dave	16	0	2	2	6
Gibson, Doug	1	0	0	0	0
Hodge, Ken	16	6	10	16	16
Leduc, Richie	5	0	0	0	9
Marcotte, Don	16	4	2	6	8
O'Reilly, Terry	16	2	5	7	38
Orr, Bobby	16	4	14	18	28
Savard, Andre	16	3	2	5	24
Schmautz, Bobby	16	3	6	9	44
Sheppard, Greg	16	11	8	19	4
Simmons, Al	1	0	0	0	0
Sims, Al	16	0	0	0	2
Smith, Dallas	16	1	7	8	20
Vadnais, Carol	16	1	12	13	42

	GP	W	L	T	GA	GAA	SO
Gilbert, Gilles	16	10	6	0	43	2.64	1

3 assists

8 PIM

1975 Playoffs	Games played	Goals	Assists	Points

April	3	1	5	6

Goals

First-period goals	0				
Second-period goals	0				
Third-period goals	1				

Even strength	0	
Power play	0	
Shorthanded	1	
Game winners	0	

Home	1		Road	0
Vs.				
Chicago	1			

Goaltender victims

Tony Esposito (Chicago)   1

Gillette Cavalcade of Sports Champions Award

Bobby Orr of the Bruins and John Havlicek of the Boston Celtics were nominated for the third annual Gillette Cavalcade of Champions Award.

I Play No Favorites

Bobby Orr was the only player to score against every NHL team during the 1974–75 season.

News from 1975

- President Ford escaped assassination attempts by Lynette "Squeaky" Fromme in Sacramento, California, on September 5, and on September 22, by Sara Jane Moore in San Francisco, California.
- April 30 marked the end of the Vietnam War as Saigon surrendered and the remaining Americans were evacuated.
- American merchant ship *Mayaguez* was seized by Cambodian forces. The US Navy and Marines rescued the vessel.
- US population was pegged at 215,973,199 while unemployment spikes to 8.5 percent.
- The cost of first-class postage rose from 0.10 to 0.13 on December 31.
- George Carlin hosted the first "Saturday Night Live" on NBC on October 11.
- ABC, CBS, and NBC agreed to create a "family hour," an early evening time slot devoid of violence and sex.
- *The Godfather II* won the Academy Award for best picture. *One Flew over the Cuckoo's Nest, Jaws, Nashville*, and *Dog Day Afternoon* made their debuts.
- Record of the year was Olivia Newton-John's "I Honestly Love You" while Song of the Year was "The Way We Were" by Barbara Streisand. "Fulfillingness First Finale" by Stevie Wonder won Album of the ear.
- The Betamax by Sony and the *VHS* by Matsushita were developed in Japan leading the way for the home videotaping systems.
- Baseball legend Casey Stengel and shipping magnate Aristotle Onassis passed away.
- Dow Jones average on 12/31/1975: $852.41.
- Top television shows: *All in the Family, Sanford and Son, Chico and the Man, The Jeffersons, M*A*S*H*.

1975–1976: Over So Fast

Owner:	Sportsystems of Buffalo
President and Governor:	Paul Mooney
General Manager:	Harry Sinden
Coach:	Don Cherry
Trainers:	Dan Canney, Frosty Forristall
Publicity Director:	Nate Greenberg
Director of Scouting:	Gary Darling
Club colors:	Black and gold
Home:	Boston Garden
Training camp:	Fitchburg, Massachusetts
Radio:	WBZ (1030)
Announcers:	Bob Wilson
Television:	WSBK (TV 38)
Announcers:	Fred Cusick and John Peirson
Attendance:	570,287 (14,257 average)

Minor officials:		
	Scorers	Ben Bertini, Ed Sandford
	Timekeeper	Tony Notagiacomo
	Penalty Timekeeper	Sonny Hunter
	Goal Judges	Bernie Bailey, Larry Stafford
	Statistician	Robert Rand

Team hotels:

Atlanta: Fairmont Colony Square
Buffalo: Sheraton Inn East
California: Edgewater Hyatt House
Chicago: Chicago Marriott
Detroit: Pontchatrain
Kansas City: Marriott
Los Angeles: Marriott
Minnesota: Bloomington Marriott Inn
Montreal: Le Chateau Champlain
New York Islanders: Island Inn Motor Hotel
New York Rangers: Statler Hilton Hotel
Philadelphia: Hilton Inn
Pittsburgh: Pitt Hilton
St. Louis: Quality Inn / Forest Park
Toronto: Sutton Place Hotel
Vancouver: Bayshore Inn
Washington: Sheraton Inn Washington NE

Trophy winners:

Lady Byng: Jean Ratelle
Adams: Don Cherry
Dufresne: Greg Sheppard
7th Player: Greg Sheppard
Three-Star: Jean Ratelle

All-stars:

Brad Park (first team)

1975 amateur draft

Player	Drafted from
Doug Halward	Peterborough
Barry Smith	New Westminster
RickAdduono	St. Catherines
Denis Daigle	Montreal
Stan Jonathan	Peterborough
Matti Hagman	HIFK Helsinki, Finland
Gary Carr	Toronto
Bo Berglund	Djurgarden, Stockholm, Sweden

| Joe Rando | New Hampshire |
| Kevin Nugent | University of Notre Dame |

1975–76 roster

	GP	G	A	OTS	PIM
Adduono, Rick	1	0	0	0	0
Anderson, Earl	5	0	1	1	2
Bucyk, Johnny	77	36	47	83	20
Cashman, Wayne	80	28	43	71	87
Clark, Gordie	7	0	1	1	0
Doak, Gary	58	1	6	7	60
Edestrand, Darryl	77	4	17	21	103
Esposito, Phil	12	6	10	16	8

(Traded with Carol Vadnais to New York Rangers for Brad Park, Jean Ratelle, and Joe Zanussi, 11/7/1975)

	GP	G	A	OTS	PIM
Forbes, Dave	79	16	13	29	52
Gibson, Doug	50	7	18	25	0
Halward, Doug	22	1	5	6	6
Hodge, Ken	72	25	36	61	42
Jonathan, Stan	1	0	0	0	0
Langdon, Steve	4	0	0	0	2
Maluta, Ray	2	0	0	0	2
Marcotte, Don	58	16	20	36	24
Milbury, Mike	3	0	0	0	9
Nowak, Hank	66	7	3	10	41
O'Neil, Paul	1	0	0	0	0
O'Reilly, Terry	80	23	27	50	150
Orr, Bobby	10	5	13	18	22
Park, Brad	43	16	37	53	95

(Acquired with Jean Ratelle and Joe Zanussi from New York Rangers for Phil Esposito and Carol Vadnais, 11/7/1975)

	GP	G	A	OTS	PIM
Ratelle, Jean	67	31	59	90	16

(Acquired with Brad Park & Joe Zanussi from New York Rangers for Phil Esposito & Carol Vadnais, 11/7/1975)

	GP	G	A	OTS	PIM
Ruhnke, Kent	2	0	1	1	0

Savard, Andre	79	17	23	40	60
Schmautz, Bobby	75	28	34	62	116
Sheppard, Greg	70	31	43	74	28
Simmons, Al	7	0	1	1	21

(Sold to New York Rangers, 11/14/1975)

Sims, Al	48	4	3	7	43
Smith, Barry	19	1	0	1	2
Smith, Dallas	77	7	25	32	103
Vadnais, Carol	12	2	5	7	17

(Traded with Phil Esposito to New York Rangers for Brad Park, Jean Ratelle, and Joe Zanussi, 11/7/1975)

Zanussi, Joe	60	1	7	8	30

(Acquired with Jean Ratelle & Brad Park from New York Rangers for Phil Esposito & Carol Vadnais, 11/7/1975)

	GP	W	L	T	GA	GAA	SO
Cheevers, Gerry	15	8	2	5	41	2.73	1
2 PIM							
Gilbert, Gilles	55	33	8	10	151	2.90	3
18 PIM							
Reece, Dave	14	7	5	2	43	3.32	2

Orr 1975–1976	Games played	Goals	Assists	Points
November	10	5	13	18

Goals

First-period goals	0
Second-period goals	2
Third-period goals	3
Even strength	1
Power play	3
Shorthanded	1
Game winners	0

Home	2	Road	3
Vs.		Vs.	
Minnesota	1	Atlanta	1
Toronto	1	Detroit	1
Rangers	1		

Goaltender victims

Pete LoPresti (Minnesota)	1
Phil Myre (Atlanta)	1
Ed Giacomin (Detroit)	1
Wayne Thomas (Toronto)	1
John Davidson (Rangers)	1

Orr's Contract Negotiations

The *Toronto Globe and Mail*, through Orr's attorney Alan Eagleson, reported that Orr's contract would not be affected by Canada's newly adopted wage and price controls. The law only applied to corporations with more than five hundred employees.

Quote from Wayne Cashman

"If that cut on my foot had been over another inch, if my Achilles' heel had been severed, if it ended my career, I would have given my knees to Bobby Orr for 10 percent of his salary."

Fred Cusick: Voice of the Boston Bruins

Fred Cusick broadcast Bruins' games on television and radio beginning in 1952 and continued for forty-four years. As the Bruins' broadcaster, he called more games involving Bobby Orr than any other announcer. Cusick states that "while moving around New England, the fans approach me saying that they appreciate the Orr years and my commentary on the broadcasts. They call those years the happiest years of their lives. Just unbelievable, heck, I was just the messenger."

"All the lies they told about Bobby Orr were true"
(Bruins' defenseman Ted Green).

News from 1976

- The United States celebrated its bicentennial on July 4.
- Mysterious disease struck the American Legion convention in Philadelphia killing twenty-nine.
- James Earl Carter was elected president of the United States on November 2, defeating Gerald Ford.
- US Supreme Court ruled that the death penalty is constitutional.
- US population reached 218,035,164 with unemployment at 7.7 percent.
- *One Flew over the Cuckoo's Nest* won the Academy Award for the best picture. Other releases in 1976 included *Rocky*, *Taxi Driver*, *Network*, and *All the President's Men*.
- Captain and Tennille scored the record of the year with "Love Will Keep Us Together" while "Send in the Clowns" won song of the year. Album of the year was Paul Simon's "Still Crazy after All These Years."
- Alex Haley's *Roots* was published.
- NBC broadcasted *Gone with the Wind* to record-breaking numbers.
- Dow Jones average on 12/31/1976: $1,004.65.
- Top television shows: *All in the Family*, *Rich Man, Poor Man*, *Laverne and Shirley*, *Maude*, *The Bionic Woman*.

More Orr Contract Talk

While on an Atlanta radio sports talk show, Orr responded to a question by saying he did not think he would sign a new contract until sometime next year.

4 Orr Square is located near Shirley Avenue in Revere, Massachusetts.

Jim Piwinski of Somerville, Massachusetts carries Orr on his back.

A Final Look Back

Bobby Orr (Born March 20, 1948) at Parry Sound, Ontario

Regular Season

	Team	GP	Goals	Even	PP	Short	Assists	Points	PIMs	GWG
1966–67	Boston	61	13	9	3	1	28	41	102	0
1967–68	Boston	46	11	8	3	0	20	31	63	1
1968–69	Boston	67	21	17	4	0	43	64	133	0
1969–70	Boston	76	33	18	11	4	87	120	125	3
1970–71	Boston	78	37	29	5	3	102	139	91	5
1971–72	Boston	76	37	22	11	4	80	117	106	4
1972–73	Boston	63	29	21	7	1	72	101	99	3
1973–74	Boston	74	32	21	11	0	90	122	82	4
1974–75	Boston	80	46	28	16	2	89	135	101	4
1975–76	Boston	10	5	1	3	1	13	18	22	0
1976–77	Chicago	20	4	2	2	0	19	23	25	0
1977–78	Chicago	Did not play								
1978–79	Chicago	6	2	2	0	0	2	4	4	0
Total		657	270	178	76	16	645	915	954	24

NHL Second All-Star Team	1967
NHL First All-Star Team	1968, 1969, 1970, 1971, 1972, 1973, 1974, 1975
Calder Memorial Trophy	1967
James Norris Trophy	1968, 1969, 1970, 1971, 1972, 1973, 1974, 1975
Art Ross Trophy	1970, 1975
Hart Trophy	1970, 1971, 1972
Conn Smythe Trophy	1970, 1972
NHL plus/minus leader	1969, 1970, 1971, 1972, 1974, 1975
Lester Pearson Award	1975
Lester Patrick Trophy	1979

(Signed as a free agent by the Chicago Blackhawks, June 24, 1976)

Orr scored more goals against (24) Eddie Giacomin
than any other goaltender in the league.

Next up was Roger Crozier who surrendered nineteen goals (19) to Orr.

Goaltending victims: 270 total goals (regular season)

Ed Giacomin: New York Rangers (23), Detroit (1)	24
Roger Crozier: Buffalo (11), Detroit (8)	19
Cesare Maniago: Minnesota	12
Dave Dryden: Chicago (6), Buffalo (4)	10
Gary Edwards: Los Angeles (9), Minnesota (1)	10
Doug Favell: Philadelphia	9
Rogatien Vachon: Montreal (7), Los Angeles (1), Detroit (1)	9

Phil Myre: Atlanta (7), Montreal (1)   8

Gary Smith: California (5), Vancouver (2), Chicago (1)   8

Dunc Wilson: Vancouver (6), Toronto (2)   8

Bruce Gamble: Toronto (6), Philadelphia (1)   7

Ron Low: Washington   7

Joe Daley: Pittsburgh (3), Buffalo (2), Detroit (1)   6

Gord McRae: Toronto   6

Gilles Meloche: California   6

John Davidson: St. Louis (4), New York Rangers (1)   5

Gerry Desjardins: New York Islanders (2), Los Angeles (2), Chicago (1)   5

Ken Dryden: Montreal   5

Tony Esposito: Chicago (4), Montreal (1)   5

Gary Inness: Pittsburgh   5

Bernie Parent: Philadelphia   5

Al Smith: Pittsburgh (4), Detroit (1)   5

Les Binkley: Pittsburgh   4

Denis DeJordy: Chicago (3), Los Angeles (1)   4

Glenn Hall: St. Louis (3), Chicago (1)   4

Chris Worthy: California   4

Billy Smith: New York Islanders   4

Dan Bouchard: Atlanta   3

Johnny Bower: Toronto   3

Andy Brown: Pittsburgh (2), Detroit (1)   3

Ed Dyck: Vancouver   3

George Gardner: Detroit (2), Vancouver (1)   3

Jim Rutherford: Detroit   3

Wayne Stephenson: St. Louis   3

Gilles Villemure: New York Rangers   3

Gump Worsley: Minnesota (2), Montreal (1)   3

Gary Bromley: Buffalo   2

Roy Edwards: Detroit   2

Eddie Johnston: St. Louis   2

Peter McDuffe: New York Rangers   2

Jack Norris: Los Angeles   2

Jacques Plante: Toronto   2

Bobby Taylor: Philadelphia	2
Ernie Wakely: St. Louis	2
Hank Bassen: Detroit	1
Gary Bauman: Minnesota	1
Michel Belhumer: Washington	1
Jacques Caron: St. Louis	1
Marv Edwards: Toronto	1
Gilles Gilbert: Minnesota	1
Charlie Hodge: Vancouver	1
Pete LoPresti: Minnesota	1
Bill McKenzie: Detroit	1
Don McLeod: Detroit	1
Jim McLeod: St. Louis	1
Cam Newton: Pittsburgh	1
Michel Plasse: Pittsburgh	1
Curt Ridley: New York Rangers	1
Fern Riverd: Minnesota	1
Wayne Rutledge: Los Angeles	1
Terry Sawchuck: Toronto	1
Don Simmons: New York Rangers	1
Gary Simmons: California	1
Ed Staniowski: St. Louis	1
Wayne Thomas: Toronto	1
Mike Veisor: Chicago	1
Jim Watt: St. Louis	1

Goals against goaltenders with same names

Dryden (15)	Dave (10), Ken (5)
Edwards (13)	Gary (10), Roy (2), Marv (1)
McLeod (2)	Don (1), Jim (1)
Simmons (2)	Gary (1), Don (1)
Smith (17)	Gary (8), Al (5), Billy (4)

Total goals (270) by period:	First	90
	Second	96
	Third	84

Venue of regular season goals

At Home	155		Away	115
Atlanta	4		Atlanta	5
Buffalo	12		Buffalo	7
California/Oakland	8		California/Oakland	8
Chicago	12		Chicago	8
Detroit	14		Detroit	10
Kansas City	1		Los Angeles	5
Los Angeles	11		Minnesota	10
Minnesota	9		Montreal	7
Montreal	8		New York Islanders	2
New York Islanders	3		New York Rangers	13
New York Rangers	16		Philadelphia	9
Philadelphia	7		Pittsburgh	11
Pittsburgh	9		St. Louis	5
St. Louis	12		Toronto	10
Toronto	11		Vancouver	5
Vancouver	10			
Washington	8			

Venue of playoff goals

At Boston			At Chicago	1
Vs. Chicago	1		At Chicago	1
Vs. Montreal	3		At Montreal	3
Vs. New York Rangers	4		At New York Rangers	7
Vs. Philadelphia	3		At St. Louis	1
Vs. St. Louis	1		At Toronto	2
Total	12		Total	14

Goaltending victims—twenty-six total goals (playoffs)

Ed Giacomin: New York Rangers	11
Ken Dryden: Montreal	5
Bernie Parent: Philadelphia (3) Toronto (1)	4
Tony Esposito: Chicago	2
Rogatien Vachon: Montreal	1
Glenn Hall: St. Louis	1
Gilles Villemure: New York Rangers	1
Doug Favell: Toronto	1

Miscellaneous Notes

Boston Bruins (regular season)

First home game (at Boston)	10/19/1966	Boston (6), Detroit (2)
First road game (at Montreal)	10/22/1966	Montreal (3), Boston (1)
First point: Detroit (at Boston)	10/19/1966	Assist on goal by Wayne Connelly at 5:44 of second period
First goal: Montreal (at Boston)	10/23/1966	Unassisted at 4:13 of third period—Gump Worsley in goal for Montreal
First minor penalty (at Montreal)	10/22/1966	7:43 of second period
First major penalty (at New York)	10/19/1966	2:22 of second period—matching major penalties with Vic Hadfield of the New York Rangers
First misconduct penalty	1/22/1967	2:28 of third period vs. Toronto at Boston
Last regular season game	11/26/1975	at New York—Boston (6), New York Rangers (4)
Last regular season goal	11/26/1975	at New York—0:34 of the second period (assisted by Ratelle) against John Davidson in goal for Rangers
Last regular season assist	11/26/1975	Assisted (along with Ken Hodge) on goal by Jean Ratelle at 5:48 of the first period

Boston Bruins playoffs

First home game (at Boston)	4/9/1968	Montreal (5), Boston (2)
First road game (at Montreal)	4/4/1968	Montreal (2), Boston (1)
First goal	4/20/1969	18:43 of the third period against Rogatien Vachon on Montreal
First assist	4/6/1968	Assisted (along with John Bucyk) on goal by Ted Green at 13:06 of the second period
First minor penalty	4/11/1968	8:48 of the first period at Boston
First major penalty	4/15/1971	5:23 of the third-period matching majors with Pete Mahovlich of the Montreal Canadiens
First misconduct penalty	4/7/1971	9:05 of the third period vs. Montreal
Last playoff game	4/11/1975	At Chicago
Last playoff goal	4/10/1975	1:31 of the third period (assisted by Bobby Schmautz and Gregg Sheppard) against Tony Esposito of Chicago
Last playoff assist	4/11/1975	Assisted (along with Bobby Schmautz) on a goal by Gregg Sheppard at 18:58 of the second period

Chicago Blackhawks (regular season)

First home game (at Chicago)	10/10/1976	Chicago (5), Vancouver (1)
First road game (at St. Louis)	10/7/1966	Chicago (6), St. Louis (4)
First assist	10/7/1976	Assist on goal by Pit Martin at 1:32 of the first period
First goal	10/7/1976	1:27 of the second period (assisted by Cliff Koroll and Dick Redmond)— Ed Staniowski in goal for St. Louis
First minor penalty	10/10/1976	13:54 of the third period
First major penalty	10/15/1976	17:37 of the third period, matching fighting major with Roger Lemelini of the Colorado Rockies

First misconduct penalty	none	
Last regular-season game	10/29/1978	At Chicago vs. Montreal
Last regular-season goal	10/28/1978	At Detroit—goal at 14:42 of the third period (assisted by Ivan Boldirev and Alain Daigle—Rogie Vachoon in goal for Detroit)
Last regular-season assist	10/19/1978	At Chicago vs. Minnesota (assisted along with Doug Hicks) on goal by John Marks at 4:13 of the first period

Orr had thirty-eight multiple goal games in his career. He had nine (9) three-goal and twenty-nine (29) two-goal games during his career.

March 20

Bobby Orr shares his March 20 birthday with some interesting company:

- Fred Rogers (1928–2003) of the children's program *Mr. Rogers*
- Spike Lee, move director
- Ozzie Nelson (1906–1975) of the *Ozzie and Harriet* television show
- Hal Linden of television's *Barney Miller*
- Former Canadian Prime Minister Brian Mulroney
- Carl Reiner, television writer and comedian

Records still owned or shared by Orr:

Regular Season

Most assists by a defenseman, one season: 102 (1970–71 season, 78-game schedule)

Most assists by a defenseman, one game: 6 (January 1, 1973, Boston [8] and Vancouver [2])

Record is shared with the following:

Babe Pratt (Toronto)

Pat Stapleton (Chicago)

Ron Stackhouse (Pittsburgh)

Paul Coffey (Edmonton)

Gary Suter (Calgary)

Most points by a defenseman, one season: 139 (1970–71 season, 78-game schedule)

Best plus/minus, one season: 124 (1970–71)

Orr has a career plus/minus of 597 in 657 games. This is the second best total in league history. Larry Robinson (Montreal Canadiens–Los Angeles Kings) has the best total in league's history with a plus/minus of 730 in 1384 games)

Playoffs

Most goals by a defenseman, one game: 3 (April 11, 1971—Boston [5] at Montreal [2])

Record is shared with the following:

- Dick Redmond (Chicago)
- Denis Potvin (New York Islanders)
- Paul Reinhart (Calgary, twice)
- Doug Halward (Vancouver)
- Al Iafrate (Washington)
- Eric Desjardins (Montreal)
- Gary Suter (Chicago)
- Brian Leetch (New York Rangers)
- Andy Delmore (Philadelphia)

Not Exactly the Cover of the *Rolling Stone*

Although Orr never appeared on the cover of the *Rolling Stone*, he did appear on the cover of *Sports Illustrated*. In fact, Orr was featured on the face of the weekly magazine five times. Orr's first appearance was on December 11, 1967 in a story titled "Hockey's Wildest Season." Orr's next appearance was on February 3, 1969, in the story "Boston on Top with Bobby Orr." In the magazine dated May 4, 1970, six days before Orr's flying Stanley Cup winner, Orr made his third cover, "Boston's Mighty Orr."

Number 4's fourth cover: "Sportsman of the Year—BOBBY ORR of the Boston Bruins.

On May 8, 1972, Orr makes his last showing, this time with fellow Bruin Phil Esposito. "Boston's Big Guns: The Stanley Cup Finals" is the featured story dated three days before Boston captures their fifth Stanley Cup Championship. This Stanley Cup win would be the Bruins' last for thirty-nine years.

Orr worked as a spokesman for BayBanks in the 1990s.

Bibliography

Books

Babineau, Steve, and Rob Simpson. *Black and Gold: Four Decades of the Boston Bruins in Photographs.* John Wiley and Sons Canada Ltd., 2008.

Booth, Clark. *Boston Bruins: Celebrating 75 years.* Tehabi Books. 1998.

Brunt, Stephen. *Searching for Bobby Orr.* Triumph Books, 2007.

Bucyk, Johnny. *Hockey in My Blood.* Charles Scribner's Sons, 1972.

Cheevers, Gerry, and Trent Frayne. *Goaltender.* Dodd, Mead and Company, 1972.

Cusick, Fred. *Fred Cusick, Voice of the Bruins.* Sports Publishing LLC, 2006.

Devaney, John. *We Love You Bruins.* Sport Magazine Press, 1972.

Esposito, Phil, and Gerald Eskanazi. *Hockey Is My Life.* Dodd, Mead and Company, 1972.

Fischler, Stan. *Bobby Orr and the Big, Bad Bruins.* Dodd, Mead and Company, 1969.

———. *Boston Bruins: Greatest Moments and Players.* Sports Publishing Inc., 1999.

———. *Hockey Stars of 1969.* Pyramid Books, 1969.

———. *Hockey Stars of 1971.* Pyramid Books, 1971.

———. *Hockey Stars of 1973.* Pyramid Books, 1973.

———. *The Burly Bruins: Hockey's Tempestuous Team.* Prentice Hall, Inc., 1971.

Hiam, C. Michael. *Eddie Shore and That Old Time Hockey.* McClelland and Stewart, 2010.

Johnson, Richard, and Brian Codagnone. *The Bruins in Black and White 1924–1966.* Arcadia Press, 2003.

———. *The Bruins in Black and White 1966 to the Twenty-First Century.* Arcadia Press, 2004.

Kalman, Matt. *100 Things Bruins Fans Should Know and Do before They Die.* Triumph Books, 2010.

Keene, Kerry. *Tales from the Boston Bruins.* Sports Publishing LLC, 2003.

MacInnis, Craig. *Remembering Bobby Orr.* Stoddart Publishing Company Limited, 1999.

McFarlane, Brian. *The Bruins. Brian McFarlane's Original Six.* Stoddart Publishing Company Limited, 1999.

Moran, Jay. *The Rangers, the Bruins, and the End of an Era: A Tribute to a Great Rivalry.* Author House, Bloomington, Indiana. 2009.

Number Four: Bobby Orr. The complete Sports Illustrated Collection. Time Inc., 2013.

Orr, Bobby, and Mark Mulvoy. *Bobby Orr: My Game.* Little, Brown and Company, 1974.

Podnieks, Andrew. *The Goal: Bobby Orr and the Most Famous Goal in NHL Stanley Cup History.* Triumph Books, 2003.

Sanderson, Derek, and Kevin Shea. *Derek Sanderson: Crossing the Line.* Triumph Books, 2012.

Sinden, Harry, and Dick Grace. *The Picture History of the Boston Bruins.* The Bobbs-Merrill Company Inc., 1976.

Game Programs

Boston Bruins game programs (1966 to 1975)
New York Rangers Hockey Magazine

Magazines

Boston Sports Review: More than a Dream '67. Seaman's Publishing, July 2007.
Hockey Illustrated
Hockey Pictorial
Hockey World
Life Magazine, February 27, 1970.
Sport Magazine
Sports Illustrated
The Hockey News
The Sporting News

Media Guides

Boston Bruins media guides (1966–1967 to 1975–76).

Newspapers

The Boston Globe
The Boston Herald-Traveler
The Boston Record American
The Hockey News

Ted Williams, Larry Bird, Bobby Orr, and Tom Brady—Boston icons.
Mural from the 621 Restaurant in Malden, Massachusetts.

Photo Credits

Cover: Jerry Buckley, S & B archives
Page 3: *Hockey Illustrated*, April/May 1966
Page 11: Hockey Pictorial, November 1966
Page 12: Boston Garden program
Page 37: Boston Bruins 1966–67 press and radio guide
Page 46: Boston Garden program, January 14, 1968
Page 78: *Sport Magazine*, December 1969
Page 80: *Canadiens Sports Magazine*
Page 104: Courtesy of Jamie Kelly
Page 220: Kevin Vautour photo
Page 278: Kevin Vautour photos
Page 284: *Sports Illustrated* photos
Page 285: Kevin Vautour collection
Page 287: Kevin Vautour photo
Page 347: Kerry Keene collection
All other photos: Kevin Vautour collection

About the Authors

KEVIN VAUTOUR IS THE AUTHOR of *The Bruins Book* and a member of the Society for International Hockey Research (SIHR) and the Rhode Island Reds Heritage Society. He resides in Melrose, Massachusetts, with his wife, Chris.

Kerry Keene is a freelance writer and lifelong follower of Boston sports who resides in Raynham, Massachusetts. He is the author of several sports books, including *Tales from the Boston Bruins Locker Room*.

CPSIA information can be obtained
at www.ICGtesting.com
Printed in the USA
BVHW050806220222
629763BV00016B/320

9 781644 245972